Windows® Small Business Server 2008

Administrator's Pocket Consultant

Craig Zacker

PUBLISHED BY
Microsoft Press
A Division of Microsoft Corporation
One Microsoft Way
Redmond, Washington 98052-6399

Library of Congress Control Number: 2009920803

Printed and bound in the United States of America.

1 2 3 4 5 6 7 8 9   QWE   4 3 2 1 0 9

Distributed in Canada by H.B. Fenn and Company Ltd.

A CIP catalogue record for this book is available from the British Library.

Microsoft Press books are available through booksellers and distributors worldwide. For further information about international editions, contact your local Microsoft Corporation office or contact Microsoft Press International directly at fax (425) 936-7329. Visit our Web site at www.microsoft.com/mspress. Send comments to input@microsoft.com.

Acquisitions Editor: Martin DelRe
Developmental Editor: Karen Szall
Project Editor: Kathleen Atkins
Editorial Production: Macmillan Publishing Solutions
Technical Reviewer: Bob Hogan, Technical Review services provided by Content Master, a member of CM Group, Ltd.
Cover: Tom Draper Design

Body Part No. X14-95038

Contents at a Glance

Contents

What do you think of this book? We want to hear from you!

Microsoft is interested in hearing your feedback so we can continually improve our
books and learning resources for you. To participate in a brief online survey, please visit:

microsoft.com/learning/booksurvey

What do you think of this book? We want to hear from you!

Microsoft is interested in hearing your feedback so we can continually improve our books and learning resources for you. To participate in a brief online survey, please visit:

microsoft.com/learning/booksurvey

Introduction

When local area networks first appeared in the business world, their primary function was to share files and printers. This is still a critical application for most business networks, but networks can provide many other functions as well. Virtually all business owners want to provide their users with access to the Internet and e-mail, but they must be able to do so securely. Many businesses also want to host their own Web sites and run specialized applications. Microsoft Windows Server 2008 provides many of these functions, and other Microsoft products provide other capabilities. For example, Microsoft Exchange Server 2007 provides comprehensive e-mail services and Microsoft SQL Server 2008 provides a robust database management environment.

Installing and configuring these products usually requires a certain amount of experience and expertise. Companies with the appropriate resources purchase the products they need and hire IT personnel to install and maintain their networks. However, many small businesses cannot afford to keep full-time IT people on staff, or even to purchase some of the more expensive networking software products. Microsoft developed Microsoft Windows Small Business Server (SBS) 2008 for this reason.

Windows SBS 2008 includes Windows Server 2008, Exchange Server 2007, several other components, and (optionally) SQL Server 2008, all for an attractive price. Even more attractive to the small business owner, however, is the fact that the product includes a setup program that installs and configures all the software components at once, using a standardized configuration that requires almost no user interaction.

In addition to the setup program, Windows SBS 2008 includes Windows SBS Console, a management program that provides simplified access to the most commonly used administrative controls. The result is a sophisticated network environment that can support up to 75 users and that small businesses can afford to purchase, deploy, and maintain without full-time IT staff.

How to Use This Book

Windows Small Business Server 2008 Administrator's Pocket Consultant is designed to help new and relatively inexperienced network administrators deploy and maintain a Windows SBS 2008 network. However, experienced administrators who are new to Windows SBS 2008 can also benefit. The book takes you through the process of planning a small business network, evaluating and purchasing the required hardware, installing Windows SBS 2008, and performing the required post-installation tasks.

For first-time network administrators, Chapter 2, "A Networking Primer," and the "An Active Directory Primer" section in Chapter 5, "Working with Users, Computers, and Groups," provide background information on basic networking and directory service concepts. More experienced administrators can skip these elements or refer back to them as needed.

Once you have planned, assembled, installed, and configured your network, *Windows Small Business Server 2008 Administrator's Pocket Consultant* takes you through the process of administering the various network applications, using the tools provided with Windows SBS 2008. Windows Server 2008, Exchange Server 2007, and SQL Server 2008 are all large and complex products, each of which can support a book of its own. In fact, separate *Administrator's Pocket Consultants* for all these products are available from Microsoft Press.

Because it would not be possible to provide comprehensive coverage of all the Windows SBS 2008 components in one book of this size, *Windows Small Business Server 2008 Administrator's Pocket Consultant* concentrates primarily on the basic administrative tasks you are likely to perform frequently, using the Windows SBS Console and other tools that are exclusive to Windows SBS 2008. For example, the book covers only the process of creating user and computer objects in Active Directory Domain Services using the Windows SBS console, but you can also create them using the Active Directory Users And Computers console.

Conventions Used in This Book

This book uses a number of elements to help keep the text clear and easy to follow. You'll find code listings in monospace type, and text that you must type when performing a task appears in **boldface** type. New technical terms appear in *italics*, and are followed by a definition.

Support

Every effort has been made to ensure the accuracy of this book. Microsoft Press provides corrections for books through the World Wide Web at the following address:

http:/www.microsoft.com/mspress/support

If you have comments, questions, or ideas about this book, please send them to Microsoft Press using either of the following methods:

Postal Mail:

Microsoft Press

Attn: *Windows Small Business Server 2008 Administrator's Pocket Consultant* Editor

One Microsoft Way

Redmond, WA 98052-6399

E-mail:

MSPINPUT@MICROSOFT.COM

Please note that product support isn't offered through the mail addresses. For support information, visit Microsoft's Web site at *http://support.microsoft.com/.*

CHAPTER 1

Introducing Microsoft Windows Small Business Server 2008

- What's Included with Windows SBS 2008? **2**
- Standard or Premium Edition? **8**
- Why Use Windows SBS 2008? **8**
- What Can't Windows SBS 2008 Do? **12**
- What's New in Windows SBS 2008? **13**

Simply put, a *server* is a software application that provides services or furnishes resources to other computers. Although many organizations have computers that are dedicated to server tasks, virtually any computer can function as a server. If you use your Microsoft Windows workstation to share files or a printer with other users, your computer is acting as a server. Medium-size and large businesses typically have multiple computers running various server applications. Separate computers might function as file servers, mail servers, database servers, and so on. In addition to its Windows Server products, Microsoft has a full line of server applications that can provide virtually any service a business might need.

Purchasing these servers and licensing these server applications can be an expensive proposition, as can learning to install and maintain them. For small businesses, it is often not economically feasible to purchase the hardware, the software, and the expertise needed to implement a full set of business server applications. This is where Microsoft Windows Small Business Server (SBS) 2008 enters the picture. Windows SBS is a single product that bundles a comprehensive set of server applications with the Windows Server 2008 operating system and also provides a simplified administration interface that enables a reasonably proficient Windows user to manage all the server functions.

1

What's Included with Windows SBS 2008?

Windows SBS includes a number of Microsoft server applications, some of which are retail products and others that are available as free downloads. Even in the case of a free product, however, you benefit by obtaining it with Windows SBS in several ways, including ease of installation and automated configuration.

Windows SBS 2008 is available in two editions, Standard Edition and Premium Edition, as shown in Figure 1-1. Windows SBS Standard Edition is designed for use on a network that consists of one server and up to 75 workstations, while Windows SBS Premium Edition adds the ability to install a second server and run line-of-business applications. In both products, one primary server performs all the infrastructure services required for the operation of the network.

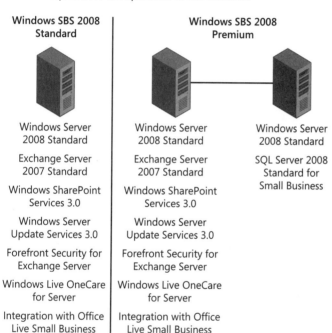

Windows SBS 2008 Standard	Windows SBS 2008 Premium	
Windows Server 2008 Standard	Windows Server 2008 Standard	Windows Server 2008 Standard
Exchange Server 2007 Standard	Exchange Server 2007 Standard	SQL Server 2008 Standard for Small Business
Windows SharePoint Services 3.0	Windows SharePoint Services 3.0	
Windows Server Update Services 3.0	Windows Server Update Services 3.0	
Forefront Security for Exchange Server	Forefront Security for Exchange Server	
Windows Live OneCare for Server	Windows Live OneCare for Server	
Integration with Office Live Small Business	Integration with Office Live Small Business	

FIGURE 1-1 Windows SBS 2008 editions

The following sections examine each of the components included in the Windows SBS products.

Windows Server 2008 Standard

The Windows Server 2008 operating system is a fundamental component of the Windows SBS package; it provides the environment in which all the other components run. Both editions of Windows SBS include Windows Server 2008 Standard, with all the components found in the retail and original equipment manufacturer (OEM) operating system products.

Windows Server 2008 includes a large collection of applications and services, many of which Windows SBS relies on to provide the infrastructure that your network needs to run. The biggest difference between Windows Server 2008 and a stand-alone version of the operating system is that SBS automatically installs and configures many of these applications and services for you, while with a stand-alone Windows Server 2008 product, you must add the roles that define the functions you want the server to perform yourself.

For example, to configure the server to function as a domain controller, you must install the Active Directory Domain Services role and then run a wizard to promote the server. When you install Windows SBS, the setup program adds the Active Directory Domain Services role for you, along with many of the other available roles, and configures them as needed. In a large business environment, this automatic configuration would not be practical because there are likely to be multiple servers on the network, with each one dedicated to a few specific roles. On a small business network with only one infrastructure server, however, SBS installs all the roles, services, and applications required for a typical network. You can, of course, disable elements that you do not need after the installation, or install additional roles as needed (with some limitations).

MORE INFO For more information on exactly what components Windows SBS installs and configures during the setup process, see Chapter 3, "Installing Microsoft Windows Small Business Server (SBS) 2008."

Another big difference between the Windows SBS version of Windows Server 2008 and the stand-alone versions is the inclusion of the Windows SBS Console tool, shown in Figure 1-2. This console, not included in the stand-alone versions of Windows Server 2008, provides a central administration tool for all the applications and services installed with Windows SBS. This console also insulates the relatively inexperienced administrator from many of the more advanced, yet infrequently used, configuration settings provided by the standard Windows Server tools. As you gain experience with Windows SBS, or if you are already an experienced Windows administrator, you still have access to all the familiar tools included with Windows Server 2008.

The version of Windows Server 2008 in Windows SBS 2008 includes a five-pack of the SBS 2008 Client Access License (CAL) Suite. This enables up to five users or devices to connect to the server and access its services. To support more than five users, you must purchase additional CALs. Unlike the CALs supplied with, and sold for, Windows Server 2008, which only provide clients with access to the server, the Windows SBS CALs provide clients with access to all the applications included with the product. With Windows SBS, you do not need to purchase separate licenses for Microsoft Exchange Server or Microsoft SQL Server clients; for example, the SBS 2008 CAL Suite provides client access to Exchange Server 2007 as well as Windows

Server 2008. For Windows SBS Premium, the SBS 2008 CAL Suite for Premium includes client access to the second server and to SQL Server applications.

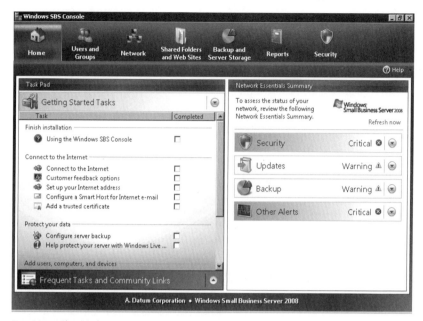

FIGURE 1-2 The Windows SBS Console

Exchange Server 2007 Standard

E-mail has become a staple of business communications, and Exchange Server 2007 is Microsoft's flagship e-mail messaging product. Exchange Server provides an organization with internal e-mail messaging, plus incoming and outgoing Internet e-mail access. The mail is stored on the server so that users can access their messages from different computers, and with a variety of client interfaces, including Microsoft Office Outlook on the desktop; Outlook Web Access (OWA), a Web-based interface that provides access from any computer, inside or outside the enterprise; and even mobile devices, such as smart phones. In addition to e-mail, Exchange Server also provides storage for calendar data, contacts, journals, and to-do lists, all of which users can share over the network, creating a variety of collaborative business solutions.

Exchange Server is a complex product, with many features and settings. However, in Windows SBS, the critical configuration settings for the Exchange Server application and access to parameters for individual users are integrated into

Windows SBS Console, simplifying the administration process considerably. As with Windows Server 2008, though, more experienced administrators can use the standard tools supplied with Exchange Server, such as the Exchange Management Console.

MORE INFO For more information on Exchange Server 2007, see Chapter 9, "Administering E-Mail."

Windows SharePoint Services 3.0

As part of its default setup procedure, Windows SBS 2008 installs Internet Informa-tion Services (IIS), the Web server application included with Windows Server 2008, on the primary server. Windows SBS uses IIS to host a number of Web sites for various administration purposes, such as client deployment and update distribution. Windows SBS also creates a default company Web site, as shown in Figure 1-3, using Microsoft Windows SharePoint Services 3.0 and the Internal Database feature of SQL Server 2005. Windows SharePoint Services is a free, Web-based collaboration environment that enables users to share files, schedule calendar appointments, create task lists, and participate in forum-style group discussions.

FIGURE 1-3 A default company Web site created using Windows SharePoint Services 3.0

Windows SharePoint Services 3.0 requires a SQL Server database to store user files, messages, and other information. Windows Server 2008 includes a feature called Windows Internal Database, essentially a special-purpose implementation of

SQL Server, which Windows SharePoint Services uses by default. Do not confuse the SQL Server implementation in the Windows Internal Database with the full-featured one supplied with Windows SBS Premium Edition. Both the Standard and Premium editions of Windows SBS 2008 include Windows SharePoint Services 3.0 and install it on the primary server using Windows Internal Database. However, if you are running the Premium Edition, it is possible to configure SharePoint Services to use the full SQL Server 2008 Standard product on your secondary server to host the database.

Windows Server Update Services 3.0

Regular operating system updates are a fact of life for all Windows users and administrators. Microsoft releases security updates, bug fixes, and feature enhancements on a regular basis, and Windows SBS uses Windows Server Update Services (WSUS) 3.0 to automate the process of downloading new updates and distributing them to the computers on the network.

By using a central distribution point, you can conserve bandwidth on your Internet connection by downloading updates once instead of letting each computer download its own copy. WSUS also enables administrators to evaluate and test the updates and then decide whether to deploy them to the rest of the network.

> **MORE INFO**   For more information on WSUS 3.0, see Chapter 6, "Deploying Updates."

Forefront Security for Exchange Server

Windows SBS includes a four-month trial subscription to Forefront Security for Exchange Server, a product that screens e-mail messages for viruses, worms, spam, and other potentially damaging content. Forefront Security uses multiple scanning engines to provide a multivector approach to malware detection and also enables administrators to filter out objectionable language and content from e-mail messages.

Windows Live OneCare

The initial release of Windows SBS 2008 includes a four-month trial subscription to Windows Live OneCare, a security product that provides protection against viruses and other malware, as well as other network security and performance optimization services. However, Microsoft has announced that, as of June 30, 2009, the Windows Live OneCare product will be discontinued, and that the Service Pack 1 release of Windows SBS 2008 will remove it.

Integration with Office Live Small Business

Office Live Small Business is a Microsoft service that enables small business owners to establish a presence on the Internet easily by registering a domain name, creating a Web site, and employing various marketing and management tools. You can create and manage Office Live Small Business Web sites using controls integrated into the Windows SBS Console interface.

SQL Server 2008 Standard for Small Business

SQL Server 2008 is a relational database manager application that you can use to deploy line-of-business applications designed to run within the environment that it provides. SQL Server 2008 Standard for Small Business is included only with Windows SBS 2008 Premium Edition, along with a second copy of Windows Server 2008, to install on a second server.

NOTE Windows SBS 2008 Premium Edition includes Windows Server 2008 and SQL Server 2008 Standard in both 32- and 64-bit versions. Therefore, while the primary server must run on a computer with a 64-bit processor, the secondary server can be 32- or 64-bit.

The primary server in a Windows SBS 2008 deployment performs a large number of functions, including domain controller, Exchange Server, and Web server. Adding SQL Server to the mix would be too much, so Windows SBS Premium Edition requires a second computer running Windows Server 2008, which runs SQL Server 2008 and any applications that require its database services.

SQL Server is a database manager, which means that it provides the services that applications need to store data and supply it to clients. *Structured Query Language (SQL)* is a language that applications use to send instructions to the database manager. The instructions enable the database manager to add information to a database stored on the server or retrieve specific information and supply it to another application.

A typical SQL Server implementation in a Windows SBS environment might consist of a Web application running on the primary server along with a Web site that is accessible from the Internet. Users accessing the Web site supply information via a form, and the Web server stores the information in a SQL Server database on the secondary server. Later, internal users access the information in the database, using an intranet Web interface or a dedicated client, as shown in Figure 1-4.

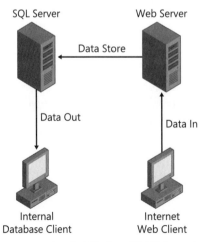

FIGURE 1-4 A typical Windows SBS SQL Server deployment

For clients on the Windows SBS network to access the SQL Server applications, they must have a special license called the CAL Suite for Premium Users/Devices. This license is more expensive than the standard CAL Suite, but only the clients that access the database require it. If, for example, some users need access to the SQL Server databases and some do not, you can purchase CAL Suite Premium only for those who need it and use the less expensive, standard CAL Suite for those that do not.

MORE INFO   For more information on SQL Server 2008 Standard, see Chapter 14, "Adding a Second Server."

Standard or Premium Edition?

The question of whether to purchase the Standard Edition or the Premium Edition of Windows SBS 2008 should be based solely on your need for a second server to run line-of-business applications. The functionality of the primary server is identical in both editions, so if you do not have any applications that require SQL Server and you don't plan on adding any in the near future, then you are better off with Windows SBS 2008 Standard Edition.

The price difference between the two editions can be substantial, as discussed later in this chapter, and as yet, there is no upgrade path from Windows SBS 2008 Standard Edition to Windows SBS 2008 Premium Edition or from Standard Edition CALs to Premium Edition CALs. However, it is possible to install additional servers on a Windows SBS 2008 network that you have licensed separately.

Therefore, a purchaser of Windows SBS 2008 Standard Edition could install a second server and purchase Windows Server 2008 and SQL Server with the appropriate licenses as stand-alone products. The overall cost will likely be more than Windows SBS Premium Edition, but it is important to know that purchasing Standard Edition does not lock you into a single-server network configuration for the rest of the product's lifetime.

Why Use Windows SBS 2008?

When it comes to networking their computers, small businesses can suffer from a variety of shortcomings. The chief problem, not surprisingly, is a limited budget. Business owners accustomed to purchasing workstation software products for a few hundred dollars might be shocked at the four-figure prices of server software plus the additional cost of licensing the client users.

Another big problem for the small business owner is information technology (IT) staffing. Many small businesses cannot justify the expense of a full-time IT employee, which leaves them two alternatives: train someone in the organization to manage the network part-time or hire a freelance consultant as needed.

Windows SBS 2008 addresses both of these problems in various ways, as explained in the following sections.

Pricing

One of the biggest benefits of Windows SBS 2008, as compared to the Microsoft stand-alone server products that it replaces, is its cost. Purchasing server operating systems and server applications can be a complicated business. You must consider the hardware requirements, operating system requirements, software interoperability, and other factors for each component. Without careful evaluation, you can end up purchasing products that do not work together or paying too much for more software than you need.

Windows SBS 2008 eliminates many of these worries by bundling together most, if not all, of the server products that a small business needs into a single package, with one set of hardware requirements and one price. Table 1-1 lists the suggested retail prices for the various SBS editions and CAL packs, as of Fall 2008.

TABLE 1-1 Windows Small Business Server 2008 Retail Pricing

PRODUCT	RETAIL PRICE*
Windows SBS 2008 Standard (including a 5-pack of SBS 2008 CAL suite)	$1,089
Windows SBS 2008 Premium (including a 5-pack of SBS 2008 CAL suite)	$1,899
Windows SBS 2008 CAL Suite 1-pack	$77
Windows SBS 2008 CAL Suite 5-pack	$385
Windows SBS 2008 CAL Suite 20-pack	$1,540
Windows SBS 2008 CAL Suite for Premium Users/Devices 1-pack	$189
Windows SBS 2008 CAL Suite for Premium Users/Devices 5-pack	$945
Windows SBS 2008 CAL Suite for Premium Users/Devices 20-pack	$3,780

* All prices are in U.S. dollars.

Using these prices, the total product cost for a sample network consisting of one Windows SBS 2008 server and 25 client workstations would be $2,629 (that is, $1,089 for the Windows SBS 2008 Standard product plus $1,540 for 20 additional CALs). If you were to purchase the server software products separately, the total cost, based on the current retail prices, would add up as shown in Table 1-2.

TABLE 1-2 *Cost of Products Equivalent to Windows SBS Purchased Separately*

PRODUCT	RETAIL PRICE
Windows Server 2008 Standard with 5 CALs	$999
Windows Server 2008 CAL 20-pack	$799
Exchange Server 2007 Standard	$699
(25) Exchange Server 2007 CALs	$1,675
Total	**$4,172**

NOTE Windows SharePoint Services 3.0 and Windows Server Update Services 3.0 are free products, while Forefront Security for Exchange Server and Windows Live OneCare for Server are supplied in trial versions in Windows SBS. Therefore, these products add no cost to the equation. Because this is an example of a network using Windows SBS 2008 Standard, SQL Server 2008 is also not part of the calculations.

Of course, additional costs are involved in setting up a small-business network, including the client operating systems, the hardware, and various networking expenses. However, a savings of $1,543 on the server software and client licenses is remarkable, especially when you consider that you are receiving the benefits of the unified installation and administration tools as a bonus.

System Requirements

The literature for every software product on the market includes a list of the system hardware that you need to run the software. Before you purchase a software product, you must make sure that your computer has a processor of the appropriate type and speed, sufficient memory and hard disk space, and the proper peripherals, as specified by the software manufacturer. However, for a single server running a variety of applications and services, determining exactly what hardware you need can be problematic.

In its system requirements for Windows Server 2008, Microsoft specifies minimum and recommended processor speeds, amounts of memory, and hard disk sizes. However, the actual requirements of a server can vary greatly. For example, a computer running Windows Server 2008 that functions only as a file server requires far less memory and disk space than one that is configured to be a domain controller. And when you install additional roles on the server, even more memory is required. Without actual testing, it would be difficult for a small-business purchaser to estimate exactly what hardware is required for a complex Windows Server 2008 configuration like the one created by Windows SBS 2008.

Complicating the matter even further are the hardware requirements for all the additional applications that you might want to install on a server. Products such as Windows SharePoint Services 3.0 and Windows SUS 3.0 have their own requirements, which you must consider cumulatively, along with the hardware needed for the operating system. Exchange Server 2007 is even more of a problem, because the hardware resources that it requires depend on the role that the individual server plays in an enterprise Exchange Server deployment.

With Windows SBS 2008, the system requirements for the product account for all the components, including Exchange Server 2007, as installed in the default configuration. You don't have to consider the roles that will be installed on the server or the additional components included with the product.

> **MORE INFO**   The system requirements for Windows SBS 2008 are discussed in detail in Chapter 3.

Installation

The actual process of installing the software for a server is where the question of who will administer the small-business network becomes significant. Assuming a business small enough that it cannot justify a full-time IT staffer, the process of installing the Microsoft server components individually can be puzzling to an inexperienced administrator.

The Windows SBS 2008 setup itself is relatively straightforward. Microsoft has streamlined the operating system installation process so much that virtually any user familiar with the Windows interface can do it. However, once the operating system installation is completed, the administrator must add more than a dozen roles and features and, in some cases, configure them as well. Following that is the installation of Exchange Server 2007 and the other server components, some of which you must download from Microsoft's Web site and some of which have software prerequisites that you must install first. Overall, the server installation process is complicated when you use the individual software components; it requires a good working knowledge of the Windows Server 2008 tools and components and some background in networking.

With Windows SBS 2008, the installation process for all the server components is performed by a single setup program. The beginning of the process is no different from a standard Windows Server 2008 installation, but once the operating system is installed, the setup program prompts the user for some basic business information and then proceeds to install and configure all the necessary roles and features, as well as the additional server applications included with the product. This integrated setup routine makes it possible for virtually anyone to install Windows SBS 2008.

> **NOTE**   The comprehensive, integrated setup routine in Windows SBS 2008 is possible only because the designers of the product have made a great many installation and configuration decisions for the user, to create a well-integrated, multifunction server platform. One of the big advantages of Windows Server 2008 is the flexibility provided by the roles and features that administrators can install as needed. On a medium-size or large enterprise network, administrators typically use multiple servers to perform different roles. It is therefore not possible to anticipate the roles and features each server needs.

Administration

Once the installation of Windows SBS 2008 is complete, the server restarts and the user—after logging on—sees the Windows SBS Console. The Home page of this console contains a list of tasks the administrator should perform to get started, and the various other pages contain the most frequently used controls for the product's various components.

By integrating the most important controls into a single interface, and eliminating the more advanced, less frequently used ones, Windows SBS 2008 makes it far easier for the beginning administrator to manage a small-business network.

What Can't Windows SBS 2008 Do?

There are, inevitably, some limitations to what Windows SBS 2008 can do compared with the stand-alone products that compose it. As mentioned previously, one of the main advantages of Windows SBS is its integrated installation and administration tools, and these tools exist only because the product's developers have made many important installation and configuration decisions for you. The Windows SBS server environment is carefully designed to provide most, if not all, of the services a small business needs.

Because this configuration is so carefully wrought, Windows SBS 2008 has some limitations that Windows Server 2008 does not, such as the following:

- **75 users**   Windows SBS 2008 is limited to a maximum of 75 client users, while Windows Server 2008 can support many more. For networks of more than 75 users, Microsoft has a similar bundled product called Windows Essential Business Server (EBS) 2008, which supports up to 500 clients.

- **64-bit processors**   The Windows SBS 2008 primary server can run only on a computer with a 64-bit processor. Although there is a 32-bit version of Windows Server 2008, Exchange Server 2007 is 64-bit only, as are many of Microsoft's latest server products.

- **One network interface**   A Windows SBS primary server can have only one network interface, which means that you cannot configure the computer to function as a router as you can with Windows Server 2008, using the Routing and Remote Access Service (RRAS).

- **No Terminal Services**   The primary server in a Windows SBS 2008 installation cannot function as a terminal server for any purpose other than the Remote Desktop for Administration interface. While you can install the Terminal Services role on the computer, attempts to change the licensing mode to any setting other than Remote Desktop for Administration results in errors. You can, however, configure the secondary server in a Windows SBS 2008 Premium Edition installation to function as a terminal server.

- **No upgrade from Windows SBS 2003 R2** If you are running an earlier version of Windows SBS, you can migrate your data to a new Windows SBS 2008 server but you cannot perform an in-place upgrade. The primary reason for this is the product's changeover to the 64-bit processor platform.

What's New in Windows SBS 2008?

The success of Windows SBS in its prior editions has led Microsoft to expand on the concept. Windows SBS is now part of a product family called Windows Essential Server Solutions, which includes two new products: Windows Home Server and Windows Essential Business Server (EBS) 2008. All these products share the management interface found in Windows SBS Console.

The most obvious difference between Windows SBS 2008 and the previous version, Windows SBS 2003 R2, is the latest versions of the software components. Table 1-3 lists the versions of the software components included in the two products.

TABLE 1-3 Software Components Upgraded in Windows SBS 2008

WINDOWS SBS 2003 R2	WINDOWS SBS 2008
Windows Server 2003 R2	Windows Server 2008
Exchange Server 2003 SP2	Exchange Server 2007 Standard
SQL Server 2005 Workgroup Edition (Premium only)	SQL Server 2008 Standard Edition (Premium only)
Windows SharePoint Services 2.0	Windows SharePoint Services 3.0
Windows Server Update Services 2.0	Windows Server Update Services 3.0

The most notable upgrade in Windows SBS 2008 Premium Edition is the inclusion of SQL Server 2008 Standard Edition instead of the SQL Server 2008 Workgroup Edition provided with Windows SBS 2003 R2. SQL Server Workgroup Edition is designed to store data for branch applications, which communicate with a main database at another location. SQL Server Standard Edition, by contrast, is a complete product that provides comprehensive data management services.

Windows SBS 2003 R2 and Windows SBS 2008 also differ in some of their software elements. Table 1-4 lists the new components in Windows SBS 2008 and the components from Windows SBS 2003 R2 that have been omitted from Windows SBS 2008.

TABLE 1-4 Software Components Omitted and Added in Windows SBS 2008

WINDOWS SBS 2003 R2 COMPONENTS OMITTED FROM WINDOWS SBS 2008	WINDOWS SBS 2008 COMPONENTS NOT INCLUDED IN WINDOWS SBS 2003 R2
Microsoft Internet and Security Acceleration (ISA) Server 2004	Forefront Security for Exchange Server
Microsoft Office FrontPage 2003	Windows Live OneCare for Server
	Integration with Office Live Small Business

The Microsoft Internet and Security Acceleration (ISA) Server product included in Windows SBS 2003 R2 has been retooled, and is now known as Forefront Threat Management Gateway (TMG). Forefront TMG is not included in Windows Server 2008, as security is handled by the Forefront Security for Exchange Server and Windows Live OneCare for Server components, but it is included as part of Windows Essential Business Server 2008.

NOTE Microsoft has discontinued the FrontPage product line, of which Microsoft Office FrontPage 2003 was the final version. FrontPage has been replaced by the Microsoft SharePoint Designer and Microsoft Expression Web products, neither of which is included in Windows SBS 2008.

Pricing Changes

The pricing model for Windows SBS has changed significantly in Windows SBS 2008, causing a good deal of consternation in some customers, who believe that prices have risen substantially. However, this is not actually the case. Table 1-5 compares the prices of Windows SBS 2003 R2 with those of Windows SBS 2008, as of Fall 2008.

TABLE 1-5 Prices of Windows SBS 2003 R2 and Windows SBS 2008 Editions

	WINDOWS SBS 2003 R2 STANDARD	WINDOWS SBS 2003 R2 PREMIUM	WINDOWS SBS 2008 STANDARD	WINDOWS SBS 2008 PREMIUM
SBS with 5 CALs	$599	$1,299	$1,089	$1,899
CAL Suite 1-pack	Not available	Not available	$77	Not applicable
CAL Suite 5-pack	$489	$489	$385	Not applicable
CAL Suite 20-pack	$1,929	$1,929	$1,540	Not applicable

TABLE 1-5 Prices of Windows SBS 2003 R2 and Windows SBS 2008 Editions

	WINDOWS SBS 2003 R2 STANDARD	WINDOWS SBS 2003 R2 PREMIUM	WINDOWS SBS 2008 STANDARD	WINDOWS SBS 2008 PREMIUM
CAL Suite Premium 1-pack	Not available	Not available	Not applicable	$189
CAL Suite Premium 5-pack	Not available	Not available	Not applicable	$945
CAL Suite Premium 20-pack	Not available	Not available	Not applicable	$3,780

While the price of the core Windows SBS Standard Edition product has risen from $599 to $1,089, you must factor in the prices of the CALs to get the true picture. Windows SBS 2003 R2 has only one CAL type for both editions of the product, so Standard Edition customers are essentially subsidizing the Premium Edition licensees while getting none of the benefits. Windows SBS 2008 has two CAL types designed for Standard Edition and Premium Edition users. The Standard Edition CAL for Windows SBS 2008 costs $77, as opposed to approximately $97 for a Windows SBS 2003 R2 CAL. Therefore, the cost for a 25-user installation has risen from $2,528 for Windows SBS 2003 R2 to $2,629 for Windows SBS 2008 Standard, a difference of only $101. For networks with fewer users, the cost increase is greater ($1,088 to $1,474 for 10 users, for example), but once you reach 30 users, Windows SBS Standard is actually slightly cheaper than Windows SBS 2003 R2 ($3,017 versus $3,014).

For Premium Edition users, there is a more substantial cost increase. A 25-user installation is $3,228 for Windows SBS 2003 R2 and $5,679 for Windows SBS 2008. However, Windows SBS 2008 provides two distinct licensing advantages for Premium Edition users. The first is the ability to mix Standard Edition and Premium Edition CALs on a Premium Edition network. This means that you have to purchase only the more expensive Premium Edition CALs for the clients that require access to the applications on the computer running SQL Server. Clients with Standard Edition CALs can still access all the services provided by the primary server.

The second advantage is that you can now purchase single-user CALs for Windows SBS 2008. With Windows SBS 2003 R2, you can purchase CALs only in packs of 5 or 20, so many customers end up having to buy licenses that they do not need. Single-user CALs enable you to purchase exactly the number of licenses you need now and expand your network later if necessary.

New System Requirements

As mentioned repeatedly in this chapter, Windows SBS 2008 requires a computer with a 64-bit processor, running at 2 gigahertz (GHz) or faster. Microsoft has also increased the minimum memory requirement to 4 gigabytes (GB), up from 512 megabytes (MB) for Windows SBS 2003 R2 Standard Edition. This is a surprisingly realistic requirement. For Windows SBS 2003 R2, 512 MB is barely enough to run the operating system adequately, never mind adding Exchange Server and the other product components.

Windows SBS 2008 runs with 2 GB of memory; it's extremely sluggish, but it runs. The product runs quite well with the minimum recommended 4 GB of memory, although as always, more is better. Incidentally, this memory requirement explains, in part, the need for a 64-bit processor, as the 32-bit version of Windows Server 2008 is limited to 4 GB of physical memory. Microsoft has also increased the disk space requirement. Windows SBS 2008 does not install on a disk with less than 40 GB of free space, up from 16 GB in Windows SBS 2003 R2.

A Networking Primer

B efore you begin installing Microsoft Windows Small Business Server (SBS) 2008, or even purchasing the hardware you need, you should spend some time planning your network and, if necessary, learning more about how a network functions. In the planning phase, you think about what you expect to accomplish with your network and take the time to determine what you must do to achieve those goals.

For Windows SBS 2008 purchasers and administrators who have little or no computer networking experience, this section provides a basic outline of the networking concepts that apply most often when managing a Windows environment. Windows Server 2008 is quite good at keeping its networking complexities hidden, but understanding what goes on under the surface is often a good thing.

Keep in mind that computer networking is an extraordinarily complex subject. Many engineers spend their entire careers working with one small aspect of the networking process in great detail. A brief overview such as this cannot begin to provide a comprehensive study, nor do you need one to manage a Windows SBS 2008 network. If you already have network training or experience, you might want to skip this section now and refer back to it as needed.

What Is a Computer Network?

You probably know this already, but simply stated, a *network* is a group of computers that are connected in such a way that any one computer can communicate with any other computer. To build a Windows SBS 2008 network, you must purchase computers and connect them using some type of network medium. When you send an e-mail message to a friend, you know that the message somehow leaves your computer and travels to the recipient's computer, as specified by the destination address you used. However, the process by which the message gets from your computer to your friend's computer is far more complicated than you might think.

Clients and Servers

A *client* is a computer that requests access to a service or resource provided by another computer on the network, which is called a *server*. Although many people use the terms *client* and *server* to refer to entire computers, both of these elements are actually software components running on a computer.

All Microsoft Windows computers can function as both clients and servers. When connecting to Web sites using a browser, retrieving e-mail, or accessing a shared folder on another system, a computer is functioning as a client. By sharing its own printers or folders, or hosting a Web site using Internet Information Services, a computer is functioning as a server. If you have a few computers in your home or office, you might connect them to a hub or switch to create a network, so that they can share each other's files and printers. This is called a *peer-to-peer network*, because all the computers are performing roughly the same roles.

When you install a Windows SBS 2008 network, you are creating a *client/server network*, because you are installing a computer that is dedicated to server functions. All the other computers, the clients, rely on the server for its resources and services. This does not mean that the clients are incapable of performing server functions, however. The clients can still share their files or attached printers, and by doing so, they perform server roles. But your primary Windows SBS 2008 server provides many more server functions and does not have a user sitting at it running productivity applications, such as word processors and spreadsheets.

Protocols and the OSI Model

For teaching purposes, the networking process is often broken down into seven layers, as depicted in the *Open Systems Interconnection (OSI) reference model*, shown in Figure 2-1. At the bottom of the model is the physical layer, which includes the cables and other components that physically connect the computers. At the top is the application layer, which is represented by the programs that you use to initiate network communications, such as the application in which you compose and send your e-mail. In between are various layers containing protocols that move the data from one location to another.

A *protocol* is, in essence, a language that computers use to communicate with one another. When you write a ZIP code on an envelope and drop it in a mailbox, you know that postal workers all over the country know what area that ZIP code represents. Computers prepare data for transmission over a network in the same way, using protocols that they know other computers understand. Collectively, the functions at the layers of the OSI model form what is known as a *protocol stack*. So long as two computers are running the same protocols at each layer of the stack, they can communicate.

| Application |
| Presentation |
| Session |
| Transport |
| Network |
| Data-link |
| Physical |

FIGURE 2-1 The OSI reference model

Every networked computer has a combination of hardware and software components that form a protocol stack, based roughly on the OSI model. When you send an e-mail to your friend, the message originates in the application layer in your computer and travels down through the stack to the physical layer, which transmits it over the network. When the message reaches the destination computer, it arrives at the physical layer and works its way up through the protocol stack to a program at the application layer, which your friend uses to read the message. The process is illustrated in Figure 2-2.

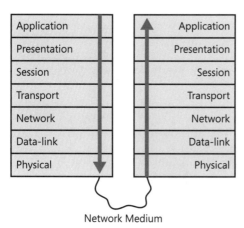

Application		Application
Presentation		Presentation
Session		Session
Transport		Transport
Network		Network
Data-link		Data-link
Physical		Physical

Network Medium

FIGURE 2-2 The network communications process

What goes on in the various layers of the OSI model is covered in the following sections.

Networking Hardware

The physical layer defines the hardware that connects the computers on the network. Traditionally, this term refers to network cables that carry signals using copper conductors or fiber optic threads, but today, wireless networking is an equally viable medium for the small-business network. The following sections examine the various physical components that you must consider when planning your Windows SBS 2008 deployment.

Network Interface Adapters

Every computer that connects to the network must have a network interface adapter. The *network interface adapter* is the component that transmits and receives signals, using either a cable or radio frequencies. Virtually all the personal computers sold today have at least one network interface adapter built into them. Desktop computers typically have an IEEE 802.3ab adapter incorporated into the motherboard. IEEE 802.3ab, also known as 1000Base-T or *Gigabit Ethernet*, is the current industry standard for cabled local area networking.

> **NOTE** The Institute of Electrical and Electronics Engineers (IEEE) is an international body responsible for the development, publication, and maintenance of industry standards for the electronics field. Industry standards are an essential element of computer networking, because they define the protocols that products made by various manufacturers use to communicate with each other.

Laptop computers usually have the same type of adapter, and often include an IEEE 802.11g (or WiFi) wireless network interface as well. If you have computers without network interface adapters that you want to connect to the network, you must purchase adapters for them, either in the form of a network interface card (NIC), as shown in Figure 2-3, or a universal serial bus (USB) device.

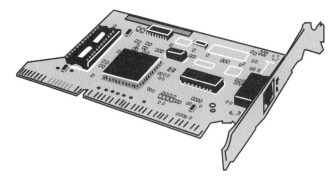

FIGURE 2-3 A network interface card

NOTE Most network interface adapters are compatible with previous standards, which run at slower speeds. For example, IEEE 802.3ab adapters nearly always support IEEE 802.3u (100Base-TX or Fast Ethernet) and IEEE 802.3i (10BaseT or standard Ethernet). In the same way, IEEE 802.11g wireless adapters usually support IEEE 802.11b and IEEE 802.11a.

When you are evaluating the network interface adapters built into computers or purchasing adapters to install into your computers, your primary concern should be that all the adapters on your network support the same standards and the same type of cable. In most cases, this is not a big problem. The majority of the network interface adapters for cabled networks that are manufactured today support IEEE 802.3ab, using copper cable. The exceptions are those that use fiber optic cable, which are easily recognized and far more expensive.

Network interface adapters can be quite inexpensive. Low-end products are available for as little as $10, although as with most things, spending a little more buys better quality. Higher-end adapters typically include support for more advanced features, such as network management, which are unsupported and unnecessary on a Windows SBS 2008 network.

Network Cables

Most of the cabled networks used today use a type of cable called *unshielded twisted pair (UTP)*. A UTP cable consists of four pairs of wires, with each pair twisted separately, inside a plastic or Teflon sheath, as shown in Figure 2-4.

FIGURE 2-4 A UTP cable

At each end of the cable is a male connector called an *8P8C* (often referred to, incorrectly, as an RJ-45), which uses the same modular design as a telephone connector, as shown in Figure 2-5, but with eight copper connectors instead of four. A network interface adapter has a female 8P8C connector, to receive the cable, as do other networking components, such as switches and routers.

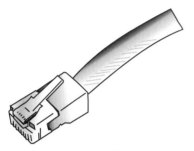

FIGURE 2-5 A UTP cable with an 8P8C connector

When building a UTP network from scratch, you have two choices: use prefabricated cables or use a bulk cable installation. Prefabricated cables have the connectors already attached and are available in varying lengths and colors. For a network with computers all in the same general area, prefabricated cables are relatively inexpensive and easy to install yourself. You can also roll them up and take them with you if you move. Depending on how concerned you are with appearance, you can run the cables loose along the floor or secure them to walls or baseboards with staples, as shown in Figure 2-6. If you match the color of the cables to your decor, you can achieve a reasonably professional-looking installation. Your main concern must be that the cables are protected from damage; do not run them under rugs or carpets, and make sure to protect them from foot or wheeled traffic.

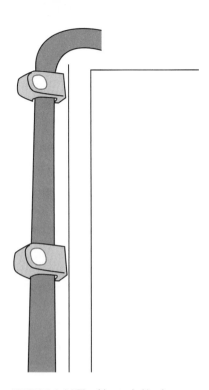

FIGURE 2-6 A UTP cable, stapled in place

A bulk cable installation usually requires a professional contractor because specialized tools and skills are involved. The installers arrive with a large spool of cabling that they pull through hollow walls and ceilings, cut to fit, and attach to connectors mounted in wall plates (like those shown in Figure 2-7) or patch panels. You then connect the computers to the wall plates using short, prefabricated patch cables. This is the most professional-looking type of installation because most of the cable is hidden inside the walls and ceilings, but it can also be substantially more expensive. If you are having telephone cables installed, however, the process for installing network cables is essentially the same, and you might be able to save money by having both installed at the same time.

FIGURE 2-7 Wall plates used in a bulk cable installation

The current industry standard for the installation of a data network using UTP cable is TIA/EIA-568-B, published by the Telecommunications Industry Association (TIA) and the Electronic Industries Alliance (EIA). Among other things, this standard defines several levels of performance characteristics for the UTP cabling itself, referred to as categories. IEEE 802.3ab networks require at least Category 5 UTP cabling, although there is also an enhanced version called Category 5e, which can provide greater reliability in certain circumstances. When you purchase prefabricated cables or contract for a cable installation, make sure that the cabling is Category 5 or 5e. You should also make that your installation complies with the maximum cable length specifications for your network (which is 100 meters for IEEE 802.3ab) and with all building codes in your area.

IMPORTANT Installations that run cable through building air shafts, called *plenums*, are sometimes required to use a special type of cable that does not emit toxic gases when it burns. Whether you are installing cables yourself or contracting the job out, you alone are responsible for the network's compliance with safety codes, and you alone suffer the consequences if you use the wrong type of cable.

Hubs and Switches

One end of a network cable connects to a computer. The other end connects to a device that joins all the separate cables into a single network. This device, called an *Ethernet hub* or *switch,* enables any computer on the network to communicate with any other computer. The hubs and switches for small-business networks are typically stand-alone boxes with a series of female 8P8C ports, as shown in Figure 2-8, and one or more light emitting diodes (LEDs) for each port.

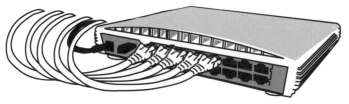

FIGURE 2-8 An Ethernet switch

Once you connect all your computers to the hub or switch, as shown in Figure 2-9, the effect is the same as if you connected them all with a single cable. The hub or switch can forward signals arriving through any one of its ports out through one of or all the other ports, so that a signal transmitted by one computer can reach any of the other computers on the network.

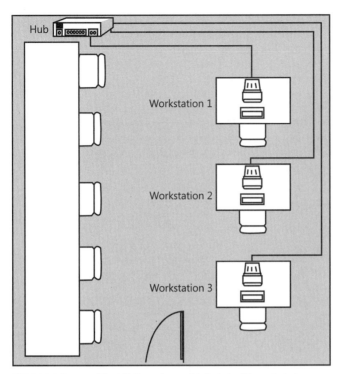

FIGURE 2-9 A network installation using prefabricated cables and a hub

The difference between a hub and a switch is one of intelligence. A hub is a relatively simple electrical device. When a signal arrives through any one of its ports, the hub forwards that signal out through all its other ports. The hub has no intelligence, in other words. A switch is different in that when a signal arrives through one of its ports, the switch interprets the signal to ascertain its intended destination and forwards it via the port connected to only the destination computer. Because it can read the signals that it receives, a switch is said to be intelligent.

The advantage of using a switch over a hub is that it reduces the amount of traffic passing over the network. When you connect your computers to a hub, the hub always forwards transmissions destined for a single computer to all the computers on the network. This means that all the computers except one end up processing the incoming transmissions and discarding them. With a switch, transmissions destined for a single computer go only to that computer, as shown in Figure 2-10.

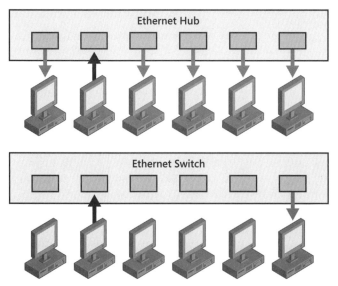

FIGURE 2-10 Network communications using Ethernet hubs and switches

Because they are more complicated devices, switches were at one time substantially more expensive than hubs, but today, switches have all but replaced hubs, particularly in the small-business-networking market. As with cables and network interface adapters, you must make sure that the hubs or switches that you purchase support the same networking standards. IEEE 802.3ab network interface adapters can run at full speed only if they are connected to a hub or switch that also supports IEEE 802.3ab.

If you are building a network using prefabricated cables, you must purchase cables that are long enough to run all the way from each computer to the hub or switch. For a bulk cable installation, the installer typically cables the wall plates at the computer locations to a patch panel in a central location. A patch panel is simply a cabling terminus, that is, a box or wall-mounted framework containing a sufficient number of female connectors for all the cable runs, like the panel in Figure 2-11.

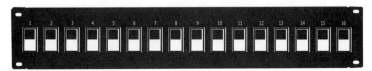

FIGURE 2-11 A patch panel used in bulk cable installations

Just as you connect each computer to a wall plate with a patch cord, you use another patch cord to connect each corresponding port in the patch panel to the hub or switch.

Routers

An *internetwork* is a network or networks, that is, a number of networks connected. The Internet is the ultimate example of an internetwork, consisting of thousands of networks all over the globe. When you connect your computers to a hub or switch, you are creating a network. When you connect your network to the Internet, you are adding it to the global internetwork.

The devices that connect networks, forming internetworks, are called routers. A *router* is a device with two network interfaces that relays traffic from one network to the other. Large enterprise installations often have multiple internal networks connected by routers. However, for the purposes of your Windows SBS 2008 installation, the only router you need is a small device that enables you to connect your network to the Internet. An Internet access router is a small box with one network interface that connects to your internal network, and a second interface that connects to your Internet service provider's (ISP's) network.

If you plan to use a dial-up Internet connection, you need a router containing a modem, which connects directly to a telephone line. Most small-business networks use a broadband connection, however, in which case the router has a second Ethernet adapter that you connect to the modem-like device supplied by your ISP.

Many of the routers intended for the home and small-business markets actually combine several different devices into one unit. Internet access routers often have multiple switched ports, enabling you to plug all your computers directly into the router, and might also include a wireless access point, providing connectivity for WiFi devices as well.

Wireless Networking

For many small-business owners, wireless networking is an attractive alternative to cables, which can be unsightly and expensive to install. The IEEE 802.11g standard enables wireless computers to communicate with each other from any location in a typical office.

When deciding whether to build a cabled or a wireless network, you should consider the following factors:

- **Cost** Wireless network interface adapters are more expensive than copper cable adapters, and desktop computers do not have them as standard equipment (although most laptops do). However, wireless networking can sometimes be cheaper in the long run because there is no need to purchase and install cables.

- **Security** Wireless networks are inherently less secure than cabled networks, because anyone with a wireless-equipped computer can conceivably connect to them, even from outside the premises. Therefore, you must use one of the available security protocols to encrypt your wireless network traffic, such as WiFi Protected Access (WPA). Make sure that all the wireless network interface adapters that you use on your network support the security protocol you plan to use.

- **Speed** IEEE 802.11g wireless networks run at a maximum speed of 54 Mb/sec (megabits per second), which is sufficient for Internet access and general network use, and can usually support high-bandwidth applications, such as streaming audio and video. However, this is still relatively slow compared to the 1,000 Mb/sec speed of a cabled IEEE 802.3ab network

- **Interference** Wireless network connections are susceptible to interference from a variety of sources, including machinery, electronics, architectural obstructions, and environmental conditions. It is a good idea to perform some tests at your network site with two or three wireless computers, under working conditions, before you make a large investment in wireless technology.

- **Peripherals** To connect printers or other devices to a wireless network, these devices must have wireless network adapters as well. There are wireless printers on the market, as well as network interface adapters made specifically for printers, but the more common solution is to create a hybrid wired/wireless network and connect standard peripheral devices using wires.

In the simplest type of wireless network, you install a wireless network adapter into each of your computers, and the systems communicate directly with each other. This is called an *ad hoc network*, as shown in Figure 2-12

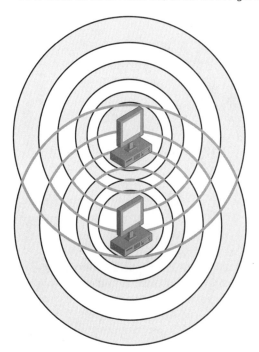

FIGURE 2-12 An IEEE 802.11g wireless network using the ad hoc topology

The more common arrangement for wireless networks in a business environment is called an *infrastructure network*, in which all the wireless-equipped computers communicate with a central transceiver unit called a *wireless access point*, as shown in Figure 2-13. The access point functions as a hub that enables each computer to communicate with any other computer.

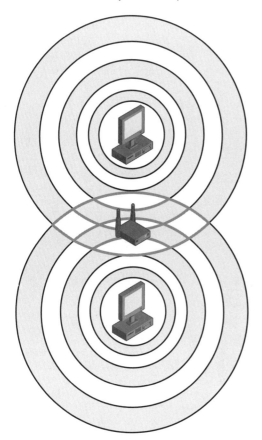

FIGURE 2-13 An IEEE 802.11g wireless network using the infrastructure topology

The advantage of the infrastructure topology is that the access point provides wireless users with access to cabled network resources, such as printers and Internet connections. In its simplest form, an access point is a small box with one or more antennas for its transceivers and a female 8P8C port for a cabled network connection. You connect the access point to a hub or switch, to which you can also connect computers or other devices. This enables any device on the network, wired or wireless, to communicate with any other device.

This type of simple access point is actually relatively rare in today's market. Most of the wireless access points available today are integrated into combination units that include routing and switching, among other capabilities. These units, which manufacturers typically market as wireless broadband routers, typically contain any of or all the following:

- **Broadband router**   Connects to the modem-like device supplied by your broadband ISP and routes traffic between your internal network and your ISP's network

- **Wireless access point**   Enables wireless devices on your network to communicate with each other, with the Internet, and with cabled devices

- **Ethernet switch**   Enables cabled devices on your network to communicate with each other, with the Internet, and with wireless devices

- **Web server**   Hosts a self-contained Web-based interface that you use to configure and manage the device

- **DHCP (Dynamic Host Configuration Protocol) server**   Provides computers and other devices on your network with Internet Protocol (IP) address and other configuration settings

- **Firewall**   Protects computers on the internal network from potential intruders on the Internet

This sort of device is often ideal for the typical small-business network because it enables you to create a hybrid network that uses both wired and wireless technologies, as shown in Figure 2-14. For example, you might consider installing a wireless broadband router in a closet or other central location where you plan to locate your Windows SBS 2008 server. You can connect the server, and perhaps a printer, to the switched ports using cables, use wireless connections for your clients, and provide Internet access to all, using the broadband connection.

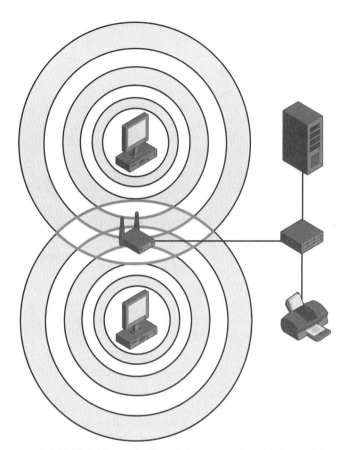

FIGURE 2-14 A hybrid network with a wireless access point cabled to a switch

Diagramming the Network

As part of the network planning process, you should take special care in document-ing everything you plan to do, especially if you will be using contractors for some of or all the installation. Create or obtain a floor plan of your site and use it to diagram the locations of all your equipment and the cable runs that connect them. This is particularly important if you are installing cables or other equipment in relatively inaccessible places, such as closets, walls, and ceilings.

Keep a record of every hardware device on your network, including the manu-facturers' names, model numbers, serial numbers, and firmware revisions. This way, if you have to call for support later, you will not need to crawl through closets and under desks to find this information.

If you use contractors for cable installation or network support, make sure that you get detailed documentation of everything they do. Don't count on the contractor to maintain this documentation. The firm might go out of business, or you might decide to use someone else later.

Ethernet/IEEE 802.3

The second layer of the OSI reference model, the data-link layer, is represented by the IEEE 802.3 protocol, commonly known as *Ethernet*. The Ethernet protocol is responsible for the basic communication between computers on the same network. In a typical local area network (LAN), the Ethernet implementation takes the form of the network interface adapters in the computers and the device drivers that enable the computers to use the adapters.

Ethernet is a *packet-switching network*, meaning that the computers divide the data that they want to transmit into small pieces, called *packets*, and transmit them individually over the network. When the packets reach their destination, the receiving computer reassembles them back into their original form. The packet switching concept makes it possible for a computer to run multiple network applications simultaneously and for multiple computers to share a single network cable.

NOTE The alternative to a packet-switching network is a *circuit-switching network*, in which one device establishes a physical connection through the network to another device. The connection, or circuit, remains open all the time that the two devices are communicating until one or the other device terminates it. The public telephone network is an example of a circuit-switching network.

The Ethernet protocol prepares packets for transmission by encapsulating them within a *frame*, which consists of a header and footer, as shown in Figure 2-15. The function of the frame to an Ethernet network is equivalent to that of an envelope in a postal system. The frame contains the address of the computer sending the packet, as well as the destination computer.

Header	Message	Footer

FIGURE 2-15 An Ethernet frame

The addresses that Ethernet networks use to identify computers and other devices are called *Media Access Control (MAC) addresses*. A MAC address is a six-byte hexadecimal address that network interface adapter manufacturers code into their hardware devices. The first three bytes identify the manufacturer of the adapter and the last three bytes are a unique identifier for the individual unit. You can display the MAC address of any Windows computer using the System Information utility, as shown in Figure 2-16.

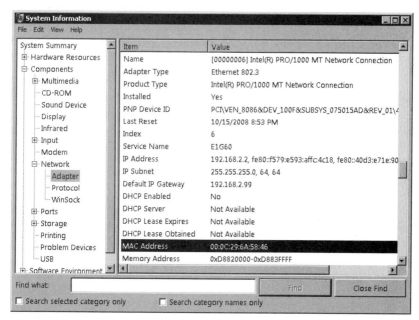

FIGURE 2-16 A MAC address displayed in the System Information application

Ethernet is a complicated protocol that merits further study, but the only other issue pertinent to a Windows SBS 2008 administrator is likely to be the complicated terminology used to refer to Ethernet technologies. *DIX Ethernet* is the name for a particular type of packet-switching, local area network technology, standardized in the 1970s by Digital Equipment Corporation, Intel, and Xerox. To create a non-proprietary standard, the IEEE published its first 802.3 document in 1983. The technology used today is based on the IEEE 802.3 standards, but the term *Ethernet,* along with variants, such as *Fast Ethernet* and *Gigabit Ethernet,* are still in common use.

Both the DIX Ethernet and the IEEE 802.3 standards have been modified over the years to support different network media and ever-increasing transmission speeds. Another common shorthand identifier for Ethernet/IEEE 802.3 networks uses the network speed, *BASE,* to indicate that the network uses baseband transmissions, and a third term that indicates something about the type of network medium. The first of these identifiers was 10BASE5, referring to a 10 Mb/sec baseband network with a maximum segment length of 500 meters.

Table 2-1 list the designations for the most common types of UTP Ethernet networks in use today.

TABLE 2-1 Ethernet UTP Designations

IEEE STANDARD	COMMON NAME	SHORTHAND IDENTIFIER	TRANSMISSION SPEED
802.3i	Ethernet	10BASE-T	10 Mb/sec
802.3u	Fast Ethernet	100BASE-TX	100 Mb/sec
802.3ab	Gigabit Ethernet	1000BASE-T	1,000 Mb/sec

NOTE Table 2-1 does not include the many types of Ethernet/IEEE 802.3 technologies designed to run on coaxial, fiber optic, and other cable types, nor does it include standards for networking technologies that have never been successfully introduced to market.

TCP/IP Basics

The third layer of the OSI reference model, the network layer, is where you first encounter the most commonly-known networking protocols: *Transmission Control Protocol/Internet Protocol (TCP/IP)*. Sometimes known as the Internet protocol suite, TCP/IP is a collection of protocols that encompass six of the seven layers of the OSI model. The protocol that runs at the network layer, the *Internet Protocol (IP)*, is the most important one in the suite because it carries the messages generated by most of the other protocols.

Ethernet is a LAN protocol, meaning that it is concerned only with transmitting data to other computers on the local network segment. In terms of a Windows SBS 2008 network, the computers connected to your switch, or to your wireless access point, form your LAN. IP, by contrast, is an end-to-end protocol, meaning that it is concerned with the ultimate destination of the message, not just the first, local network hop.

In the same way that Ethernet uses MAC addresses to identify the recipients of its packets, IP uses its own type of address, called an *IP address*. And in the same way that Ethernet encapsulates information using a frame, IP performs its own encapsulation, creating what is called a *datagram*. An IP datagram is essentially another envelope, with its own source and destination addresses, that will end up inside the frame envelope created by the Ethernet implementation, as shown in Figure 2-17. However, while the destination address of an Ethernet frame is always the MAC address of another device on the LAN, the destination IP address on the datagram in that same packet always identifies the final recipient of the message, whether it is a computer on the LAN or an Internet server thousands of miles away.

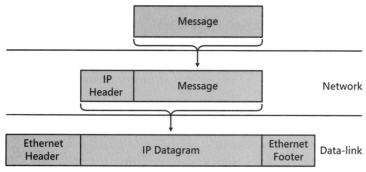

FIGURE 2-17 A message encapsulated in an IP datagram, which is in turn encapsulated in an Ethernet frame

For example, when one of your clients attempts to access a file on your Windows SBS server, the Ethernet frame specifies the server's MAC address and the IP header contains the server's IP address. In other words, the two are different addresses referring to the same computer. On the other hand, when the client uses a browser to connect to a server on the Internet, the datagram contains the IP address of the Internet server, which is the packet's final destination, but the Ethernet frame contains the MAC address of the router that provides the LAN with access to the Internet. The two addresses point to different devices.

The IP address, because it is an end-to-end protocol, can refer to any computer, on any network, anywhere. The MAC address, however, must point to a device on the local network. Therefore, when the computer recognizes that the destination IP address refers to a computer on another network, it sends the packet to a router that provides access to other networks. The packet is then passed along, from router to router, until it reaches the network hosting the destination computer.

IPv4 Addresses

As currently standardized in Internet Protocol version 4 (IPv4), IP addresses are 32 bits long and are notated as four eight-bit decimal numbers, separated by periods. Because each of the four decimal numbers (sometimes referred to as an *octet* or a *quad*) is eight bits long, it can have 256 (that is 2^8) possible values, ranging from 0 to 255.

A TCP/IP network consists of devices, called *hosts*, each of which must have a unique IP address. In a personal computer, the network interface adapter is the host, so a computer can conceivably have two hosts, and therefore two different IP addresses.

An IP address consists of two parts: a *network identifier* and a *host identifier*. When IP routers forward datagrams to distant locations, they use the network identifier to locate the correct network, and then use the host identifier to locate the correct computer. Unlike MAC addresses, however, IP addresses are not split neatly down the middle. The size of the network and host identifiers can vary. For example, the IP standard originally used a system called *classful addressing,* which specifies three address classes with different size identifiers, as shown in Table 2-2.

TABLE 2-2 IP Address Classes

CLASS	CLASS A	CLASS B	CLASS C
Subnet mask	255.0.0.0	255.255.0.0	255.255.255.0
Number of network identifier bits	8	16	24
Number of possible networks	256	65,536	16,777,216
Number of host identifier bits	24	16	8
Number of possible hosts per network	16,777,214	65,534	254

> **NOTE** Classes D and E exist, but are reserved only for multicast and experimental use.

To determine where the split between the network identifier and the host identifier is located, the classful addressing system uses a value called a *subnet mask.* The subnet mask is another 32-bit number, which, in its binary form, uses 1s to represent network bits and 0s to represent host bits. For example, the subnet mask for a Class A IP address is 255.0.0.0, which in binary form, is 11111111.00000000.00000000. 00000000. The eight 1s indicate that the first eight bits of the accompanying IP address are the network identifier bits, and the 24 0s indicate that the last 24 bits of the address are the host identifier bits.

> **NOTE** An IP network address (that is, an address that includes zeroes for all its host bits) identifies the network itself, rather than a specific host on that network.

Unfortunately, the IP addressing system is further complicated by the fact that the split between the network and host identifier bits need not fall on one of the eight-bit boundaries. To provide greater flexibility in IP address assignments, a system called *Classless Inter Domain Routing (CIDR)* uses a process called *variable-length subnet masking,* which enables an administrator to subdivide an IP network into smaller units, thus allocating additional bytes to the network identifier. For example, an IP network can have 12 network identifier bits, resulting in a subnet mask value of 255.240.0.0 (or 11111111.11110000.00000000.00000000, in binary form).

What is fortunate, however, is that for the purposes of administering a small Windows SBS 2008 network, you don't have to be concerned with these complexities. The only element of CIDR that you might encounter is its alternative form of notation, which consists of a network address, followed by a slash and the length of the network identifier. For example, CIDR notation would use an address like 10.0.0.0/12 to refer to an address using the same 12 network identifier bits.

Using Private IP Addresses

To be accessible from the Internet, a computer must have a *registered IP address*, that is, an address that some authority has assigned to that computer. This is necessary because every computer on the Internet must have an IP address that is unique. The ultimate authority for IP address assignments is the Internet Corporation for Assigned Names and Numbers (ICANN). However, users do not usually deal with ICANN directly; instead, they obtain addresses from their ISPs or Web hosting services.

The assignment of registered IP addresses occurs on two levels, and this is the primary reason why IP addresses have a network identifier and a host identifier. ICANN, or one of its proxies, assigns a network address to a particular registrant, and then the administrator of the network address assigns the host addresses to the individual computers on the network.

Be sure to understand that this discussion of registered addresses refers only to computers that must be accessible to clients on the Internet, such as public Web servers. You do not need registered addresses for clients that access servers on the Internet. For most, if not all, of the computers on your Windows SBS 2008 network, you use private IP addresses, which are addresses reserved for use on unregistered networks. Table 2-3 lists the ranges of IP addresses that are free for use on private networks.

TABLE 2-3 Private IP Addresses

CLASS	CLASS A	CLASS B	CLASS C
IP address range	10.0.0.0 to 10.255.255.255	172.16.0.0 to 172.31.255.255	192.168.0.0 to 192.168.255.255
Subnet mask	255.0.0.0	255.255.0.0	255.255.255.0
Number of addresses	16,777,216	1,048,576	65,536

The primary reason for using private IP addresses is to prevent the depletion of the IPv4 address space. If every computer connected to the Internet had a registered IP address, the supply of addresses might run out. To enable computers with private IP addresses to access Internet services, routers that connect private networks to the Internet typically use a technique called *Network Address Translation (NAT)*. The NAT router processes all the packets sent to the Internet by computers on the private network and replaces their private IP addresses with a single registered address. For packets arriving from the Internet, the NAT router performs the same process in reverse. As a result, all the computers on the private network can share a single registered address, with the NAT router taking the responsibility for sending the packets to the correct destinations.

NOTE The use of private IP addresses also enhances the security of a network. Computers on the Internet cannot address traffic to private networks directly; they must go through a NAT router. Therefore, the only way for an attacker on the Internet to access a computer on a private network is if the private network computer initiates the communication. Unfortunately, these attackers have developed clever schemes that dupe unsuspecting users into running programs that initiate contact with attack servers on the Internet.

IPv6

While IPv4 is still predominant on the Internet, a relatively new version of the protocol, Internet Protocol version 6 (IPv6) is gradually being introduced. The tremendous growth of the Internet during the past decade and the increasing use of TCP/IP for devices other than desktop computers, such as smart phones and handheld computers, has caused experts to fear a depletion of the existing 32-bit IP address space. IPv6 expands the address space to 128 bits, which is more than sufficiently large to provide every device on the planet with a registered address. This eliminates the need for private IP addresses or technologies designed to preserve the current address space, such as NAT.

NOTE To calculate the number of possible addresses provided by a given address space, one raises 2 to the power of n (that is, 2^n), where n equals the number of bits in the space. Thus, the IPv4 address space consists of 2^{32}, or 4,294,967,296, possible addresses. By contrast, the IPv6 address space consists of 2^{128}, or 340,282,366,920,938, 463,463,374,607,431,770,000,000 possible addresses. This number is sufficiently large to allocate 52,351,133,372,452,071,302,057,631,913 addresses to each of the approximately 6.5 billion people living today.

Unlike IPv4 addresses, which use decimal notation, IPv6 addresses use hexadecimals. An IPv6 address consists of eight 16-bit (that is, two-byte) values, separated by colons, as in the following arrangement:

XX:XX:XX:XX:XX:XX:XX:XX

In this arrangement, each *X* is an eight-bit (or one-byte) hexadecimal value, for a total of 128 bits, or 16 bytes. An example of an IPv6 address would appear as follows:

FDC0:0:0:02BD:FF:BECB:FEF4:961D

NOTE In hexadecimal notation, also known as Base 16, each digit can have 16 possible values. The traditional means of representing this mathematically is to use the numerals 0 to 9 and the letters A to F to represent those 16 values. Remember, an eight-bit (one-byte) binary number can have 2^8, or 256, possible values. If each hexadecimal digit can have 16 values, then two characters are needed to express the 256 possible values for each byte of the address ($16^2 = 256$). This is why some of the two-byte XX values in the sample IPv6 address require four digits in hexadecimal notation.

To simplify an IPv6 address, you can omit the zero blocks and replace them with a double colon, as in the following example:

```
FDC0::02BD:FF:BECB:FEF4:961D
```

At this time, although Windows Server 2008 fully supports IPv6, Internet communications are still based on IPv4, as are Microsoft Exchange Server e-mail communications.

TCP/IP Configuration Settings

Windows computers obtain their IP addresses in one of three ways: a network administrator can assign them manually; an automated service, such as DHCP, can assign them; or the computers can self-assign them. Generally speaking, manual address assignment is difficult on a network scale. You must keep track of the addresses you have assigned to ensure that there are no duplicates on the network. However, there are situations in which you might have to configure a Windows computer manually, and even if you never do, it is worthwhile knowing the functions of the various configuration parameters for the Windows TCP/IP client.

When you open the Internet Protocol Version 4 (TCP/IPv4) Properties sheet on a Windows Server 2008 computer, as shown in Figure 2-18, you see the following parameters:

- **IP address**   Uniquely identifies the computer on the network
- **Subnet mask**   Specifies which bits of the IP address form the network identifier and which bits form the host identifier
- **Default gateway**   Specifies the IP address of a router that the computer can use to access other networks
- **Preferred DNS server**   Specifies the IP address of a Domain Name System (DNS) server that the computer can use to resolve host and domain names into IP addresses
- **Alternate DNS server**   Specifies the IP address of a second DNS server that the computer can use, should the preferred DNS server be unavailable

The Internet Protocol Version 6 (TCP/IPv6) Properties sheet contains the same parameters, but with larger fields to accept the longer IPv6 addresses. As with IPv4, Windows computers can obtain IPv6 addresses from a DHCP server or through manual configuration. IPv6 also supports stateless address autoconfiguration, in which the computer uses router discovery messages to obtain network configuration information from routers on the network.

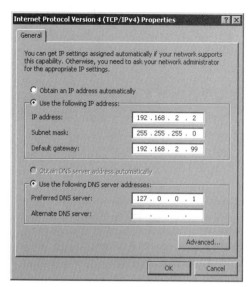

FIGURE 2-18 The Internet Protocol Version 4 (TCP/IPv4) Properties sheet

Static vs. Dynamic Address Configuration

When you manually configure the IP address and other TCP/IP configuration parameters on a Windows computer, the values you assign are permanent; they remain in place until someone manually changes them. This is called a *static IP address*. When a computer obtains an IP address from a DHCP server, it is possible for the address to change at some future time. This is called a *dynamic IP address*.

> **NOTE** A DHCP server has a pool of IP addresses, called a *scope*, which it leases to clients on the network for a specific length of time, usually a matter of days. Each client must renew its lease periodically to continue using that address. If a client's lease expires because the system has been turned off for an extended period of time, the computer must obtain a new address the next time it starts. If the old address is no longer available, the DHCP server assigns the computer a different one.

Client computers are better off with dynamic addresses for several reasons. DHCP eliminates the possibility of address duplication and enables you to add, move, and remove computers without having to configure their TCP/IP parameters manually. However, servers should have static IP addresses in most cases, so that clients can always locate them. By default, your primary Windows SBS 2008 server configures itself with a static IP address on the same network as your router if it detects one during installation. Even if you decide to use DHCP to configure your clients, you should use a static address for your server.

Transport Layer Protocols

TCP, the other half of TCP/IP, is a protocol that runs at the fourth, or transport, layer of the OSI reference model. Two primary protocols actually operate at the transport layer: TCP and User Datagram Protocol (UDP).

TCP is a connection-oriented protocol designed for the transmission of relatively large amounts of data. A *connection-oriented protocol* is one in which the two computers involved in a transaction exchange messages that establish a connection before they transmit any application data. TCP also provides guaranteed delivery, meaning that the receiving computer sends acknowledgements for all the data packets it receives. The result is a highly reliable transport service, at the cost of some additional network overhead.

When you use a Web browser, such as Windows Internet Explorer, to connect to a Web server, the two computers establish a TCP connection before the browser sends its Web request and the server responds with a reply. The connection establishment process confirms that the two computers are ready to send and receive data and also enables them to perform other tasks, such as flow control, which regulates transmission speed. Once they have finished sending their data, the computers exchange messages that terminate the TCP connection.

UDP, by contrast, is a *connectionless protocol*, which means that the computers do not exchange connection establishment messages. UDP is intended primarily for brief transactions that consist of a single request message and a single reply, such as DHCP and DNS transactions. When a computer sends a message to its DNS server to resolve a server name into an IP address, for example, the computer transmits a single packet containing that message, using UDP, and waits for a reply. The sending computer receives no acknowledgment; if a reply is not forthcoming, the computer simply resends the message. From a network traffic standpoint, this is far more efficient that transmitting connection establishment and packet acknowledgment messages that add up to more data than the original message.

NOTE Network applications also use UDP for the transmission of large data files that are not bit-sensitive, such as streaming audio and video. A video stream can survive the loss of a few packets; there might be a brief interruption in the video display, but the loss is tolerable. For this reason, a nonguaranteed service is acceptable. When a computer is transmitting an application or a document file, however, the loss of a single bit can render the file unusable, so a guaranteed service such as TCP is preferable.

Both TCP and UDP perform their own data encapsulations, just as IP and Ethernet do at the lower layers of the OSI model. When an application generates a message to be transmitted over the network, it passes it down to the appropriate transport layer protocol, which adds its own header. A message with a TCP header is called a *segment*, and as in IP, a message with a UDP header is called a *datagram*. Figure 2-19 illustrates the entire encapsulation process a packet undergoes before transmission.

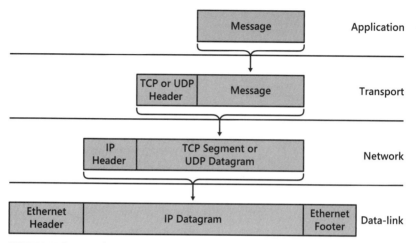

FIGURE 2-19 Transport layer encapsulation

The transport layer protocol is not involved in getting the message to the correct destination computer; that is the job of IP and Ethernet. Instead, the transport layer protocol header contains values called port numbers, which identify the application that generated the message and the application that will receive it. Therefore, while IP is responsible for getting data packets to the correct destination computers, TCP and UDP are responsible for getting the messages in those packets to the correct applications running on those destination computers.

> **NOTE** There are two additional OSI model layers between the transport and the application layers: the session and presentation layers. No dedicated protocols operate at these layers; the transport and application layer protocols include the session and presentation layer functions.

Application Layer Protocols

At the top layer of the OSI model, the application layer, are the protocols that provide network communication services to applications running on a computer. For example, a Web browser uses the Hypertext Transfer Protocol (HTTP) to generate messages containing requests for a specific document on a Web server. The messages travel down through the layers of the protocol stack, out across the network, and into the Web server, where they travel up the server's stack to the HTTP implementation there.

Among the protocols operating at the application layer are the following:

- **Hypertext Transfer Protocol (HTTP)** A protocol that Web browsers and Web servers use to exchange request and reply messages
- **Dynamic Host Configuration Protocol (DHCP)** A protocol and service that automatically assigns IP addresses and other configuration settings to network clients

- **Domain Name System (DNS)** A protocol and service that computers use to resolve domain and host names into IP addresses
- **Simple Mail Transfer Protocol (SMTP)** A protocol that e-mail clients and servers use to transmit messages
- **Post Office Protocol (POP)** A protocol and service that maintains mailboxes for e-mail clients and enables them to download their messages
- **Internet Message Access Protocol (IMAP)** A protocol and service that maintains mailboxes for e-mail clients and enables them to store their messages on a server
- **File Transfer Protocol (FTP)** A protocol that enables clients to transfer files to and from servers, and to perform basic file management tasks
- **Telnet** A protocol that enables clients to log on to a server and execute programs from the command prompt

Understanding Domains

As noted earlier in this chapter, TCP/IP communication is based on IP addressing. Every packet transmitted over the network must have IP addresses identifying its source and its intended destination. Using numerical addresses, as TCP/IP does, is great for computers but not as good for humans. How would you like it if, whenever you wanted to access your favorite Web site, you had to remember a Uniform Resource Locator (URL) like *http://192.168.43.181*?

To make them easier for people to remember, TCP/IP networks use friendly names to refer to specific computers. Therefore, when you type a URL like *http://www.adatum.com* into your Web browser, the computer first converts the name to its equivalent IP address, and then sends an HTTP request to the Web server using that address.

The names for specific computers on a TCP/IP network, like their equivalent addresses, must be unique, and this presents a problem. How do you assign unique names to the millions of computers on the Internet without having to use long, complex strings that are just as hard to remember as IP addresses? The answer is the same as that for IP addresses: you divide the name into administrative units, and let individual network administrators assign names to computers within each unit.

> **NOTE** The distribution of administrative tasks is one of the key architectural principles of TCP/IP and the Internet that you see again and again. Instead of creating a centralized point of administration that is responsible for all IP addresses or all domain names, the system is designed to distribute the administrative tasks among networks all over the Internet.

On the Internet, the administrative unit is called a *domain*. An organization registers a domain name with ICANN or one of its many registrars, and then has the right to create host names within that domain. For example, in the *www.adatum.com* name mentioned earlier, *adatum.com* is the name of the domain, and *www* is the name that the domain administrator assigned to a host in that domain. Together, the host name and the domain name are called a *fully qualified domain name (FQDN)*.

The Domain Namespace

Domain names are hierarchical constructions consisting of two or more words, separated by periods, reading from the bottom to the top of the hierarchy as you go from right to left. The rightmost word, *com* in this example, is a top-level domain name. The *com* domain is one of three generic top-level domains created early in the history of the domain namespace. The others are *net* and *org*. In addition to these, there are two-letter country-code top-level domain names that represent most of the countries in the world, such as *fr* for France and *jp* for Japan. Some additional generic top-level domains were created later, such as *biz* and *info*.

> **NOTE** In addition to the generic top-level domains mentioned, there are a number of sponsored top-level domains, such as edu, gov, mil, and int, for which potential registrants must prove eligibility before they can register a name.

The generic top-level domain names are administered by ICANN, which is also responsible for designating an appropriate trustee for each of the country-code top-level domains. Network administrators can obtain a name in any of the generic top-level domains, and many of the country-code top-level domains, by contacting an appropriate registrar and paying a fee. The registrant then receives all rights to a second-level domain beneath that top-level domain, including the right to create hosts and subdomains within that second-level domain.

For example, the organization that owns *adatum.com* registered that name and, so long as they continue to pay their fees, own the rights to it. They can therefore assign the host name *www* to their Web server, creating the FQDN *www.adatum. com*. If they want to, they can also create additional domain name levels, such as *sales.adatum.com*.

The Domain Name System

In the early days of the Internet, when it was an experimental network consisting of only a few dozen computers, every system had a *hosts* file, which contained a simple list of all the computers on the net, with their host names and equivalent IP addresses. Eventually, the *hosts* list became too large and changed too often to be manageable, so a new solution of equating host names and IP addresses was needed.

The main reason for the hierarchical design of the domain namespace is to facilitate the creation of that new solution, which is called the *Domain Name System (DNS)*. The fundamental design principle of the DNS is that instead of storing and managing information about the entire domain namespace in one location, the administrators of each domain are responsible for maintaining information about their own computers.

A *DNS server* is essentially a specialized type of database application, designed to store name and address information about computers in a domain. When you register a second-level domain name for your organization, you must specify the addresses of two DNS servers that will become the authoritative servers for your domain. Then, for each computer on your network, you must create a *resource record* on your DNS server, which specifies the computer's host name and its equivalent IP address.

> **NOTE** Administrators can create DNS resource records manually, but computers also can create them automatically. For example, if you use the DHCP Server role on your Windows SBS 2008 server to assign IP addresses to your clients, the system automatically creates DNS resource records for each DHCP client.

DNS Name Resolution

DNS servers are also responsible for converting host names into IP addresses, at the request of clients on the network. This process is known as *name resolution*. In the name resolution process, DNS servers all over the Internet communicate with each other to locate the authoritative information for specific computers. This process occurs as follows:

1. When you type the URL *http://www.adatum.com* into your Web browser, the first thing your browser does is use your computer's DNS client, called a *resolver*, to send a name resolution request to your DNS server, as shown here. The name of the DNS server is specified in the computer's TCP/IP configuration. This request contains the *www.adatum.com* FQDN, and is asking for its equivalent IP address in return. Unless your computer's DNS server happens to be the authoritative source for the *adatum.com* domain, it must pass the request on to other servers to get the information it needs.

Your computer   Your DNS server

2. The DNS server starts at the top of the domain hierarchy and forwards your request to an authoritative server for the *com* domain, as shown here. The *com* domain is hosted by one of the root name servers whose addresses are coded into every DNS server. Because the root name server is the authoritative source for the *com* domain, it contains resource records for all the

second-level domains beneath *com,* including *adatum.com.* Registrars create these resource records using the information supplied by people registering second-level domains. The *com* server responds to the request by sending the resource record for the *adatum.com* domain back to your DNS server.

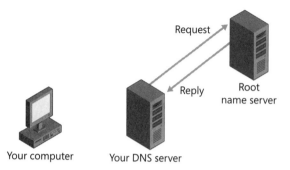

Request
Reply
Root
name server
Your computer   Your DNS server

3. Your DNS server now knows where to go to get information about the *adatum.com* domain, so it forwards the original name resolution request to the *adatum.com* server it learned about from the *com* server, as shown here. The *adatum.com* server replies by sending the resource record for the *www* host back to your DNS server. This resource record, which the administrator of the *adatum.com* domain created, contains the IP address of the *www* host in that domain.

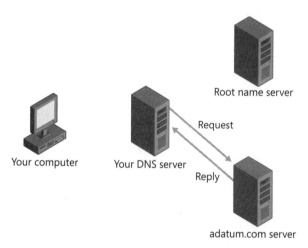

Root name server

Request
Your computer   Your DNS server
Reply

adatum.com server

4. Your DNS server now knows the IP address of the *www.adatum.com* computer, so it replies to your resolver's original request by forwarding the *www.adatum.com* resource record to your computer, as shown here.

Root name server

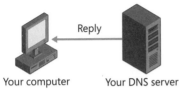

Reply

Your computer   Your DNS server

adatum.com server

5. Your computer now has the IP address for *www.adatum.com*, so it sends the HTTP message the Web browser created to the Web server, using that address.

Despite its complexity, the DNS name resolution process occurs very quickly, and it may be more or less complicated, depending on the name being resolved and current conditions on the network. For example, resolving a name beneath one of the country-code top-level domains requires an additional step because the root domain servers do not host these domains. On the other hand, the name resolution process might be abbreviated due to the caching capabilities of DNS servers.

DNS servers are designed to cache the resource records they receive from other DNS servers, for a specified length of time. For example, if you use your browser to access the *www.adatum.com* Web server and, a few minutes later, someone else on your network tries to connect to the same Web site, your DNS server still has the *www.adatum.com* resource record in its cache, so it does not have to perform the entire name resolution process again.

NOTE The DNS resource records that specify IP address equivalents for host names are called Host (A) records. However, by supporting other types of resource records, DNS servers can perform other functions in addition to name resolution. For example, Mail Exchanger (MX) records enable computers to locate the address of the mail server for a specific domain.

Active Directory Domains

When you install Windows SBS 2008 on your primary server, the setup program asks you to supply a name for your domain. It is not an Internet domain name the program is referring to, however; it is an Active Directory Domain Services (AD DS) domain name. As part of the installation process, the setup program installs the AD

DS role and creates a domain using the name you specify, plus the top-level domain name *local.*

AD DS also uses domains to create administrative divisions within a Windows network. In the case of a Windows SBS 2008 installation, you need only one domain, but large enterprise networks can have many domains, grouped into larger divisions called *trees* and *forests.* AD DS uses DNS for name resolution also, as well as for other internal functions, but the AD DS domain on your server is not accessible from the Internet because *local* is not an official top-level domain. This protects your internal domain from Internet intrusion.

> **NOTE**   It is theoretically possible to use the same domain name for your organization's Internet presence and for its internal AD DS domain, but this can put your AD DS domain at risk. It is also possible to use a second-level domain name, such as adatum.com, on the Internet and create a third-level domain, such as int.adatum.com, for internal use. However, using a local domain name internally and a completely separate second-level domain name on the Internet is the most secure arrangement; this is why Windows SBS 2008 uses this method.

CHAPTER 3

Installing Microsoft Windows Small Business Server (SBS) 2008

Although the Microsoft Windows Small Business Server (SBS) 2008 setup program makes many installation and configuration decisions for you, there is still a good deal of work to do before you actually start the installation process. This chapter discusses the tasks you should perform before you begin installing your server, as well as covering the various types of installations supported by Windows SBS 2008.

Planning a Windows SBS 2008 Deployment

Planning is a crucial part of any network deployment process. The following sections guide you through the predeployment decisions you should make, including what hardware to purchase and what information you must have ready when you begin the installation.

Selecting Server Hardware

Obviously, you must have at least one server before you can install Windows SBS 2008. Table 3-1 lists the official system requirements for servers running Windows SBS 2008.

TABLE 3-1 System Requirements for Windows SBS 2008 Servers

	PRIMARY SERVER	SECONDARY SERVER (PREMIUM ONLY)
Processor	x64 processor, 2 gigahertz (GHz) or faster	x86 or x64 processor, 2 GHz or faster
Memory	4 Giga Bytes minimum, 32 GB maximum	2 GB recommended, 4 GB maximum (x86), 32 GB maximum (x64)
Available disk space	60 GB minimum	10 GB minimum, 40 GB recommended
Optical drive	DVD-ROM drive	DVD-ROM drive
Network interface	Ethernet	Ethernet
Graphic display	Super VGA (800 x 600) or higher resolution	Super VGA (800 x 600) or higher resolution

The main requirement to consider is that the primary server running Windows SBS 2008 must have a 64-bit processor, which means that you have to purchase a new computer unless you have a suitable one that you bought relatively recently. In its default configuration, Windows SBS 2008 can run reasonably well on a computer with the minimum recommended hardware.

The actual hardware resources that a server running Windows SBS 2008 needs are based on a multiplicity of factors, including the following:

- **Number of users** The more users who access the server, the more likely it is that you need additional hardware resources to support them.

- **Pattern of use** Resource utilization increases when multiple users are working simultaneously. Therefore, an organization running a single shift of 30 clients will require more server resources than an organization running three shifts of 10 users each. Resource utilization also spikes if many users perform the same task at the same time, such as if 30 users log on to the domain at the same time each morning.

- **Request types** Different types of client requests can require different server resources. For example, file services can benefit from increased storage subsystem performance, while Microsoft Exchange Server can benefit from both storage performance and memory upgrades.

- **Storage requirements** The amount of storage that your applications and users require depends on their number and their activities. Users who work with video files require more storage than users working with still images, and both require much more storage than users who work primarily with text documents.

- **Additional applications**   If you plan to install additional applications on your servers running Windows SBS, you must account for their hardware requirements in addition to those for the default server functions.

Processors

When selecting a processor for a server running Windows SBS 2008, you certainly do not want to skimp, but you should also be conscious of the fact that the performance boost you realize from a faster processor might not be worth the expense. This is particularly true at the high end of the market; the latest and fastest processors are often a great deal more expensive than those a few steps down from the top of the line. For example, the difference in performance between a 2.33 GHz and a 2.66 GHz processor might be worth $100 but is probably not worth $300. In addition, for a server running Windows SBS, it probably makes more economic sense to purchase a server with a single processor that has dual or quad cores, rather than one with multiple processors.

Memory

In a server configuration, it is more important to consider the amount of memory in the computer and the maximum amount it can hold than compare memory types or speeds. Memory is usually the most inexpensive way to increase the performance of a server, or indeed any computer. For a primary server running Windows SBS 2008, 4 GB of memory is adequate, but 6 or 8 GB would be better. You should also make sure that your server supports at least twice as much memory as you have installed initially.

> **TIP**   When evaluating servers, you should consider the configuration of the memory modules as well. If the computer has eight memory slots and you plan to install 8 GB initially, do not use eight 1 GB modules, as you have to replace some of them when you upgrade.

Storage

Hard disk storage, like memory, is relatively inexpensive, and it is always a good idea to have more disk space than you think you need. However, for a server, you must consider not only the amount of storage space, but also the configuration of the storage subsystem. Once you have decided how much storage space you need in your server, you must consider the nature of the data and its value to your organization.

Depending on the sensitivity of the data you plan to store on your server, and how critical the continued availability of that data is to your business, you might want to invest in a disk array that uses *redundant array of independent disks (RAID)* or some other high-availability technology. RAID is a system that uses two or more hard disk drives to store your data, along with duplicate or parity information that enables the server to survive a drive failure without data loss. Many servers are available with drive arrays that include RAID controllers, as well as other fault-tolerance features, such as hot-pluggable drives (that is, drives that you can remove from the server and replace without having to shut the server down).

There are many different types of RAID, which are defined in numbered levels. Table 3-2 lists the RAID levels most commonly found in today's servers and storage products. There are many other RAID implementations, some of which have rarely, if ever, appeared in the market, and others that are proprietary technologies of a specific manufacturer.

TABLE 3-2 RAID Levels Commonly Found in Server and Storage Products

RAID LEVEL	RAID FUNCTIONALITY	MINIMUM REQUIRED NUMBER OF DISKS	FAULT-TOLER-ANT?	DESCRIPTION
RAID 0	Stripe set without parity	2	No	The system writes data one stripe at a time to each successive disk. No fault tolerance, but enhances performance.
RAID 1	Mirror set without parity	2	Yes	Also called *disk mirroring,* the system writes the same data to identical volumes on two different disks Provides increased read performance, as well as fault tolerance.
RAID 5	Stripe set with distributed parity	3	Yes	The system stripes data and parity blocks across all the disks, without ever storing a block and its parity information on the same disk. Parity calculations add to system overhead, but provide more usable storage space than a mirror set.
RAID 6	Stripe set with dual distributed parity	4	Yes	Same as RAID 5, except that the system stripes two copies of the parity information, along with the data, enabling the array to survive the failure of two drives.
RAID 0+1	Mirrored stripe sets	4	Yes	The system creates a stripe set and then mirrors it. Provides fault tolerance and improved performance. If a drive fails, its entire mirror set goes offline.

TABLE 3-2 RAID Levels Commonly Found in Server and Storage Products

RAID LEVEL	RAID FUNCTIONALITY	MINIMUM REQUIRED NUMBER OF DISKS	FAULT-TOLER-ANT?	DESCRIPTION
RAID 10 (or 1+0)	Striped mirror sets	4	Yes	The system stripes data across two or more mirror sets. Provides fault tolerance and improved performance. If a drive fails, all the remaining drives continue to function.
RAID 50 (or 5+0)	Striped RAID 5 sets	6	Yes	The system stripes data across two or more identical RAID 5 sets.

So long as you have the appropriate number of disk drives in the computer, Windows Server 2008 is capable of creating volumes using RAID levels 0, 1, and 5. This is an inexpensive solution, but software-based RAID implementations can impose a penalty in system overhead. When you create a RAID 5 volume, for example, the same processor that performs all the other roles on your server must also calculate parity information for each block the system writes to the RAID array.

NOTE In Windows Server 2008, RAID level 0 is referred to as a striped volume and RAID level 1 as a mirrored volume. Only RAID level-5 volumes use the RAID designation in Microsoft Windows.

Hardware-based RAID takes the form of a dedicated host adapter, either integrated into the computer's motherboard or implemented as an expansion card. The host adapter performs all the necessary functions, including parity calculations, so there is no additional burden on the system processor.

High-availability hardware products, such as RAID arrays, can add significantly to the cost of a server, and it is important to understand that this technology does not eliminate the need for regular system backups. Manufacturers design high-availability products for organizations that cannot tolerate server downtime. For example, if you run an order-entry application on your server, a hard disk failure can mean lost business and lost income, so the additional expense of a RAID array might be worthwhile. However, if a server outage due to a disk failure would be no more than a minor inconvenience to your organization, then standard hard disk drives might be a more reasonable and economical solution.

Other Server Components

In their basic components, servers are different from workstations only in matters of degree; they tend to have faster processors, more memory, and larger amounts of storage space, for example. However, as you can see in the case of the RAID storage solutions, server technologies are available that greatly enhance the performance and fault-tolerance capabilities of the computer. You can also purchase servers with redundant power supplies and fans, multiple processors, and many other elaborate and expensive components. In the case of a small-business server, however, most of these components are usually not necessary, and avoiding them can save you some money.

OEM or DVD?

You have two ways to purchase Windows SBS 2008: as a retail product, in which case you receive the product on DVDs, or as an original equipment manufacturer (OEM) purchase, in which case the product comes preinstalled on a computer. The OEM option is one solution to the problem of purchasing a suitable server to run Windows SBS 2008, but it does not save you a great deal of work. The Windows SBS installation process is quite simple, so if you can conceivably save money by purchasing the computer hardware and the Windows SBS 2008 product separately, then you should do so.

Selecting Clients

The clients on a Windows SBS 2008 network must be running one of the following operating systems:

- Windows Vista Business
- Windows Vista Enterprise
- Windows Vista Ultimate
- Windows XP Professional with SP2 or later
- Windows Mobile 5.0 or later

Table 3-3 lists the published system requirements for the Windows Vista and Windows XP operating systems.

TABLE 3-3 System Requirements for Windows SBS 2008 Clients

	WINDOWS VISTA BUSINESS, ENTERPRISE, AND ULTIMATE	WINDOWS XP PROFESSIONAL
Processor	X86 or x64 processor, 1 GHz or faster	x86 processor, 300 megahertz (MHz) or faster
Memory	1 GB minimum	128 megabytes (MB) recommended
Hard disk space	40 GB, with 15 GB available	1.5 GB available

TABLE 3-3 System Requirements for Windows SBS 2008 Clients

	WINDOWS VISTA BUSINESS, ENTERPRISE, AND ULTIMATE	WINDOWS XP PROFESSIONAL
Optical drive	DVD-ROM drive	CD-ROM or DVD-ROM drive
Network interface	Ethernet or IEEE 802.11a/b/g wireless	Ethernet or IEEE 802.11a/b/g wireless

Selecting Network Components

The first decision that you must make before purchasing the networking hardware you need for your Windows SBS 2008 installation is whether you intend to build a cabled network, a wireless network, or a hybrid network that supports both. For a cabled network, you need Ethernet network interface adapters for all your computers, the cables themselves, and an Ethernet switch to connect the computers. For a wireless network, you need wireless network interface adapters for your computers, and a wireless access point. Finally, if you plan to connect your network to the Internet, you need a router.

> **MORE INFO**   For the purposes of this chapter, and throughout the rest of this book, network discussions will mainly use the term Ethernet to refer to the packet-switching network defined in the 802.3 standards published by the Institute of Electrical and Electronics Engineers (IEEE). For a discussion of Ethernet terminology, see the section "Ethernet/IEEE 802.3" in Chapter 2, "A Networking Primer."

Selecting an Internet Service Provider

Virtually all businesses want to connect their networks to the Internet, even if it is only for e-mail access. Your network planning process should include a consideration of how much bandwidth your network needs and what Internet service provider (ISP) you will use to supply it. The ISP is the only networking component you need that takes the form of a service rather than a hardware product. The service provided by the ISP is also one of the regular network expenses that you must add to your budget.

The Internet bandwidth you need for your network is primarily for client connections. The primary server running Windows SBS 2008 is not designed to function as an Internet router or Internet Web server, although the underlying Windows Server 2008 operating system is capable of doing so. This is because the primary server is performing critical functions for your internal network, such as being an Active Directory Domain Services (AD DS) domain controller, and making it accessible from the Internet is a serious breach of accepted security practices.

> **SECURITY**   To protect their internal networks from intrusion, small businesses that want to run Web sites on the Internet typically use commercial Web hosting services instead of running the site from one of their internal servers.

The typical uses for the Internet connection on a small-business network are e-mail transfers and Web browsing, neither of which requires massive amounts of bandwidth. Therefore, you can roughly calculate the bandwidth you need by allocating 50 Kbps (kilobits per second) of downstream bandwidth for each simultaneous Web/e-mail user. If you plan to support remote network access using virtual private network (VPN) connections, you should allocate another 50 Kbps of upstream bandwidth per user.

BEST PRACTICES Many types of Internet connections are asymmetrical, meaning that they have different upload and download speeds. Most broadband connections, for example, provide much more downstream bandwidth than upstream. When evaluating Internet connection services, be sure to consider your upstream as well as downstream bandwidth needs.

Using these calculations, you can assume that a Windows SBS 2008 network with 25 internal users needs approximately 1,250 Kbps (1.25 megabits per second, or Mbps). A standard broadband connection from a cable or digital subscriber line (DSL) provider can usually meet these needs. Networks with more users might require a higher-speed connection.

TIP Do not confuse network bandwidth speeds, which are measured in kilobits (Kb), megabits (Mb), or gigabits (Gb) per second, with the download speeds displayed by your computers, which are measured in kilobytes (KB) or megabytes (MB) per second. One byte equals eight bits, so one kilobyte equals eight kilobits.

While calculations such as these can give you a rough idea of how much bandwidth your network needs, the most practical method of approaching the problem is to begin by determining what types of Internet connections are available at your location. Small businesses typically use standard consumer ISPs; they generally do not have the bandwidth needs or the budget for elaborate connection technologies such as T-1 lines. In most areas, you should be able to select from the following types of providers:

- **Dial-up** Available anywhere there is a telephone line, dial-up connections are inexpensive but slow, with a maximum bandwidth of 56 Kbps that line quality can reduce even further.
- **DSL** A DSL connection is supplied by a telephone provider using the available bandwidth on a standard telephone line. Consumer DSL connections are asymmetrical and are often available in multiple speeds, for varying prices. DSL availability and reliability depends on the distance from your location to the provider's nearest central office.
- **Cable** Delivered using the same private fiber optic network used for cable television services, cable-based Internet connections are asymmetrical and similar to DSL in their bandwidth capabilities, often providing two or more tiers of service.

- **Satellite**   Similar in speed, but generally more expensive than cable or DSL, satellite Internet providers typically target customers in remote locations that have no access to other high-speed Internet services.

When contacting the ISPs that service your area, you should find out what connection speeds they provide and, of course, the prices. When discussing the price of a connection, be sure to consider the following points:

- **Contracts**   Some ISPs discount the monthly connection fee if you sign a contract for a year of service or more. You might want to evaluate the service for a month or two before you commit, but the savings can be significant. Bear in mind, however, that there are penalties for early termination of the contract.

- **Hardware leasing**   Broadband connections require a hardware device that, for simplicity's sake, is referred to as a *modem*. In many cases, you must choose between leasing a modem from the ISP, for an additional monthly fee, and purchasing one outright. The modems are usually not expensive, and purchasing the device can often begin to save you money within one or two years.

- **Networking**   Some ISPs have different tiers of service, and different prices, for business customers or customers who connect the service to a network rather than a single computer.

In most cases, small-business administrators decide on one of the broadband solutions available in their area. Depending on the ISP and the conditions of your site, you might have to schedule an installation, but in many cases, you can obtain a self-installation kit and connect the modem to the ISP's network yourself.

Selecting a Router

In many ways, the key component for your network is the router because you will probably purchase a unit that combines the broadband routing function with other important networking components. The components in the router that you select often dictate what features you have to look for in your other networking equipment.

For a small-business network, a consumer-grade router that also includes firewall and network connectivity functions is usually sufficient. Business-grade products are more expensive and usually separate the routing capabilities from the other functions, forcing you to purchase individual router, switch, and wireless access point products. If you choose to purchase separate components, you must be sure that all the products you select are compatible in the networking standards and protocols that they support.

> **TIP**   A consumer-grade broadband router typically includes an Ethernet switch, a wireless access point, or both. In most cases, the difference in price between a unit with wireless capabilities and one without is minimal, so you might consider purchasing a broadband router with both wireless and cabled Ethernet switching capabilities, even if you do not plan to use one or the other right away.

The consumer-grade router that you choose for your network should have all or most of the following capabilities:

- **Broadband connectivity**   The device has an Ethernet wide area network (WAN) port, which connects to your broadband modem using a standard Ethernet patch cable. A broadband client built into the unit enables you to specify the user name and password for your ISP account, as well as configure account parameters.

- **Switched Ethernet ports**   Virtually all broadband routers have at least one switched Ethernet port, but few have more than four or five. If you intend to have more than a few cabled devices on your network, you need a separate Ethernet switch that provides a larger number of ports. The switched ports on most routers support standard 10 Mbps Ethernet and 100 Mbps Fast Ethernet. If you have 1,000 Mbps Gigabit Ethernet devices on your network, they automatically negotiate down to Fast Ethernet when you connect them to the switch.

  TIP   If you are running a Gigabit Ethernet network with a separate switch, plugging the router into the switch establishes a connection at 100 Mbps. There is no need to search for a broadband router with Gigabit Ethernet ports because the connection between the switch and the router only carries traffic to and from the Internet, and Internet connections run at far slower speeds than local area network (LAN) connections.

- **Wireless access point**   Routers with wireless networking capabilities have antennas, a transceiver, and an access point that enables wireless devices to connect to the network. Most of the wireless routers on the market today support the 54 Mbps IEEE 802.11g standard, but they can also support devices using the slower IEEE 802.11b and IEEE 802.11a standards.

- **Wireless security protocols**   While older wireless devices can usually connect to an IEEE 802.11g transceiver, they might not support the latest wireless security protocols. Most of the current wireless router products support the WiFi Protected Access (WPA and WPA2) security protocols, while older devices might support only *Wired Equivalent Privacy (WEP)*, which has critical weaknesses. Routers can typically use only one wireless security protocol at a time, so all your wireless devices must support the protocol that you elect to use.

- **Web-based administration**   Broadband routers typically have an internal Web server that you access to configure the device's properties. You therefore must connect a computer to the router before you can use it to connect to your ISP's network.

- **Dynamic Host Configuration Protocol (DHCP) server**   Most routers include DHCP server capability, which enables them to assign Internet Protocol (IP) addresses and other Transmission Control Protocol/Internet Protocol (TCP/IP) configuration settings to clients on the network. Windows SBS

Server also includes a DHCP server. You must decide whether you want to use DHCP to configure your client workstations, and if so, which DHCP server implementation you want to use.

- **Universal Plug and Play (UPnP)** UPnP is a set of protocols that enable devices on the same network to communicate and automatically configure their networking settings. Windows SBS 2008 can communicate with a UPnP router to determine what IP address it should use and open the appropriate firewall ports for the services running on the computer.

- **Network Address Translation (NAT)** NAT is the router technology that enables the computers on your internal network to use private IP addresses and still access the Internet. NAT also protects your network from Internet intrusion.

  MORE INFO For more information on NAT, see the section "Using Private IP Addresses," in Chapter 2, and the section entitled "Understanding Network Address Translation" in Chapter 12, "Optimizing Network Security."

- **Virtual private networking (VPN)** A VPN connection is when an authenticated user at a remote location connects to the Internet and accesses your private network through your router. This enables users who are traveling or working at home to access their files, Exchange Server e-mail, and other network resources. To enable VPN connections, the router must be able to open the appropriate port for the VPN protocol the client uses to connect to the network server.

- **Access restrictions** Many broadband routers enable you to specify which of the computers on your network are allowed to access the Internet, or restrict Internet access to certain days and times. These features can prevent casual intruders from accessing the Internet through your router, but they are relatively ineffective against determined and knowledgeable attackers.

- **Content filtering** Many broadband routers enable you to block client access to specific network services on the Internet, specific Web site addresses, or Web sites containing specific keywords. Knowledgeable users can often find ways to bypass these features, but they are reasonably effective on casual users.

- **Firewall** Broadband routers usually have a variety of firewall features that are designed to protect your network from various types of attacks. Features such as packet filtering and *stateful packet inspection (SPI)* analyze incoming traffic to limit the network's susceptibility to specific types of attacks from the Internet.

Selecting Cables, Adapters, and Switches

If you decide to install a cabled network, you must have an Ethernet network interface adapter in each of your computers, a switch that functions as the central connection point, and, of course, the cables themselves. As mentioned in Chapter 2, the main concern when selecting Ethernet equipment is that all the components support the same standards.

CABLES

Choosing cables is a relatively simple matter. If you plan to use prefabricated cables throughout the network, purchase Category 5 or 5e cables of appropriate lengths. The maximum length for the cable connecting an Ethernet device to the switch is 100 meters. Category 5e cable is more expensive than Category 5, and the standards do not require it, but if you are planning to run Gigabit Ethernet throughout your network, Category 5e cable is usually worth the additional expense. If you are having bulk cable installed at your site, make sure that the contract calls for all cables and connectors to be Category 5 or 5e. You also must purchase prefabricated patch cables to connect your computers to the wall plates and your patch panel ports to the switch.

> **MORE INFO** For more information about purchasing and installing cables, see the section "Network Cables," in Chapter 2.

NETWORK ADAPTERS

Most of the desktop computers sold today have an Ethernet adapter integrated into the motherboard. Higher-end workstations and virtually all servers have 1,000 Mbps Gigabit Ethernet adapters, while some budget workstations have 100 Mbps Fast Ethernet. No matter what the maximum speed, however, virtually all Ethernet adapters and switches can negotiate down to accommodate slower speeds. For example, if you plug a computer with a Gigabit Ethernet adapter into a Fast Ethernet switch, the two devices negotiate the fastest speed they have in common, which is 100 Mbps. Switches perform separate negotiations on each port, so it is possible to mix Ethernet devices running at different speeds on the same network.

> **NOTE** For most network applications, 100 Mbps Fast Ethernet is more than sufficient. However, if many of the computers that you intend to purchase have integrated Gigabit Ethernet adapters, a Gigabit Ethernet switch is not that much more expensive than a Fast Ethernet one.

If you have computers with no Ethernet adapter, or if you want to upgrade a computer to a faster Ethernet standard, you can purchase network interface cards (NICs) that plug into an expansion slot. Before you select NICs, be sure that each computer has a free slot and check what type of slot it is. For computers without free slots, there are external network interface adapters available, which plug into a universal serial bus (USB) port.

SWITCHES

Apart from the Ethernet standards they support, the other main issue when purchasing a switch is the number of ports. Switches are available in a variety of sizes, with as many as 48 ports, often clustered in multiples of eight. As with computer memory or hard disk space, buying more switches than you think you need is usually a good idea. Having a switch with extra ports enables you to expand your network later simply by plugging additional computers or other devices into the switch.

When evaluating switches, you will notice that prices range from under $100 to well up in the tens of thousands of dollars. For a small business, you are again more likely to be looking at lower-end consumer-grade switches rather than high-end, enterprise network products. Some of the other features that you might encounter when shopping for a switch are as follows:

- **Form factor** Most small-business networks want external switches and routers, that is, freestanding devices with their own cases. Networking devices are also available in rack-mounted form factors, which are efficient and convenient if you have a formal data center but are beyond the means of most small businesses.

- **Uplink negotiation** A twisted pair cable contains some wires that are dedicated to transmitting data and some that are dedicated to receiving it. For communication between two devices to occur, the transmit pins on one have to be crossed over to the receive pins on the other. Ordinarily, the switch performs this crossover. However, when you expand a network by connecting a second switch to your first one, the two crossovers cancel each other out. Older Ethernet hubs and switches have a designated *uplink* port, which lacks the crossover circuit, for a connection to another hub or switch. Modern switches have an *uplink negotiation* feature that enables all the ports to detect automatically whether they are connected to a computer or another switch and adjust the crossover circuit accordingly. This is a feature worth having, which adds little cost to the device.

- **Management** A managed switch, like a managed router or other network component, is a device with one or more interfaces that administrators can use to control its operation. This is a high-end, enterprise networking feature that most small-business networks do not need and cannot afford. Unmanaged switches are preferable for virtually all Windows SBS 2008 networks.

Diagramming the Network

As you decide what computers and components to purchase, you should create a diagram showing the layout of the network. Figure 3-1 shows a typical hybrid network for a small business with one server running Windows SBS 2008, eight workstations, and a broadband router that also contains a wireless access point. All the computers and the router are connected to an Ethernet switch.

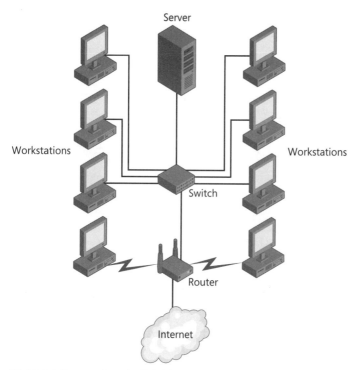

FIGURE 3-1 Diagram of a typical hybrid network

This type of diagram is useful as a guide for building your network, and as a reference, especially if you must familiarize employees or consultants with the network layout. However, this type of diagram shows only the relationships between the components; it is not a true map of your site showing the actual equipment locations. If you are opening a new office or renovating an existing one, and you have a floor plan available, you might want to create a second diagram that shows not only the placement of each component, but also the cable runs connecting them.

> **REAL WORLD**   If you are having a bulk cable installation performed by a contractor, you should insist on a diagram showing the locations of all the cable runs. This way, if you ever need to service or upgrade the cabling, you do not have to search for them inside walls or ceilings.

Preparing for the Installation

Once you have selected and purchased all the hardware and software that you need to build your network, you can begin assembling the pieces and collecting the information you need to perform the Windows SBS 2008 installation.

Physical Security

Selecting a secure location for your network components is an important first step in the deployment process. You must choose a location that protects your servers, routers, and switches from theft, damage (accidental or otherwise), excessive heat and moisture, electromagnetic interference, airborne dust and fumes, and other extreme environmental conditions. You should also have a clean source of power for your equipment, which, in the case of your server, means an *uninterruptible power supply (UPS)* that both conditions the power and provides battery backup in case of a power outage.

> **BEST PRACTICES** UPS devices are available in three types: offline, line interactive, and online. Both offline and line interactive devices perform a brief transition when a power failure occurs, while online UPSs do not because they always supply the computer with power from the continuously replenishing battery. Therefore, an online UPS is preferable for your servers.

When it comes to physical security, wireless access points are a special case for several reasons. First, while the wireless radio signals can penetrate walls and other barriers, they are susceptible to *attenuation*, meaning that the signals weaken when they have to pass through too many barriers or barriers that are too dense. If the signal between a computer and the access point becomes sufficiently weak, the system might have to drop down to a slower transmission speed or even lose the connection entirely. Second, there is the danger of outside intrusion occurring when you place the access point too close to an outside wall. Choosing a central location within your building can help prevent unauthorized users in the parking lot from connecting to your network.

Connecting Your Router

If you are using a shared broadband Internet connection for your network, you should consider setting up the connection and your router before you install your server running Windows SBS 2008. It is not absolutely necessary, but there are multiple benefits to doing so. During the installation, the Windows SBS 2008 setup program attempts to detect a UPnP router on the network by transmitting a variety of discovery messages and listening for replies. If the server locates a router and is able to access the Internet through that router, it proceeds as follows:

- The server configures its own TCP/IP client with a static IP address on the same subnet as the router and with the router's IP address as its Default Gateway address.
- With the installer's permission, the server downloads the latest operating system updates from Microsoft's Web site and installs them during the installation process.

After the Windows SBS 2008 installation, when you run the Connect To The Internet Wizard, if the server detects an operational DHCP server on the router, the server configures its own DHCP server to distribute IP addresses on the same subnet as the router and then disables the router's DHCP server.

If the server fails to detect a router on the network during the Windows SBS 2008 installation, it configures its own TCP/IP client with the static IP address 192.168.0.2 and no default gateway address. The server still installs the DHCP Server role during the installation, but it does not configure or activate the DHCP Server service. After the installation is completed, you must configure the DHCP Server on the router or the server manually if you want to dynamically allocate IP addresses to your network clients.

> **MORE INFO** For more information on configuring DHCP, see Chapter 16, "Managing Infrastructure Services."

The procedures for installing your broadband Internet connection and your router vary depending on your ISP and router manufacturer. However, in most cases, you must perform the following basic steps:

1. Connect the broadband modem to a power source, and to the jack providing access to the ISP's network, using the appropriate cable.

2. Connect the router to a power source and then to the modem using an Ethernet cable. In most cases, the router automatically obtains an IP address and other settings from a DHCP server on the ISP's network.

3. If you are using a separate switch, connect it to a power source and then connect both the router and a computer running Windows to the switch using Ethernet cables. If your router has switched ports or an integrated wireless access point, you can also connect the computer directly to the router.

4. Start your Web browser and connect to the router's administrative interface, using the default IP address supplied by the router manufacturer.

5. Configure the router to access the Internet by applying the settings supplied by your ISP. These settings typically consist of a user name and password and might include other parameters as well.

Once the computer is able to access the Internet through the router, you can connect your server to a power source and to your new network. At this point, the hardware is ready for the Windows SBS 2008 installation.

Provisioning Disk Space

Early in the Windows SBS 2008 installation process, you must specify the hard disk on which you want to install the Windows Server 2008 operating system and other software products. Using the interface from the Windows SBS 2008 setup program shown in Figure 3-2, you can select an entire unallocated disk on the computer or create a new volume using part of the unallocated space on a disk. Before you actually perform this task, you should consider how you are going to use the disk space on your server so that you can create the appropriate volumes.

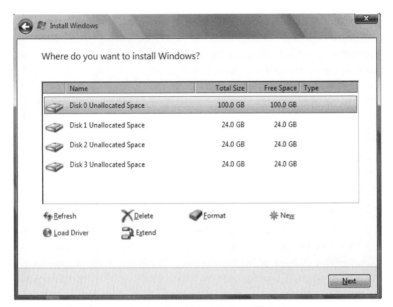

FIGURE 3-2 The volume creation interface in the Windows SBS 2008 setup program

During the Windows SBS 2008 installation, you can create only simple volumes on your server disks; you cannot create striped, spanned, or RAID-5 volumes. Therefore, if you are planning to use these volume types for your user data or other purposes, you must create them using the Disk Management snap-in for the Microsoft Management Console (MMC), after the installation is completed.

For the purposes of the installation, you must decide which hard disk you want to use for the *system volume* (that is, the volume on which the operating system is installed), and how much disk space you want to use to create that volume. As noted earlier in this chapter, the Windows SBS 2008 system requirements call for a minimum of 60 GB, but you might want to allocate more disk space. A level of 100 GB is good; much more than that could be wasteful. As a general rule, you should avoid storing documents and other user data on the system volume. You can create a separate volume for data either during or after the installation.

In addition to the Windows Server 2008 operating system itself, Windows SBS 2008 creates the Exchange Server e-mail stores on the system volume and stores its library of Windows Server Update Services (WSUS) updates there. Depending on how many users you have on your network and how they use e-mail, the Exchange Server stores might grow to consume a great deal of disk space, especially if the users do not delete their old e-mails. The WSUS library also gets larger over time. Fortunately, however, Windows SBS 2008 includes tools that enable you to move the Exchange Server store and WSUS library to another volume easily. Therefore, you do not have to account for these in the size you select for your system volume, so long as you have another volume where you can store them.

Selecting Names

During the installation process, the Windows SBS 2008 setup program prompts you to supply names for your server, for your internal domain, and for an administrative user. The program suggests server and domain names based on the company name you supplied earlier, but you might want to change them. Computer names and domain names cannot be more than 15 characters long and can consist only of letters, numbers, and the underscore and hyphen characters. These names are not case-sensitive.

CAUTION Consider the server and domain names that you choose carefully because you cannot change them once the installation is complete.

COMPUTER NAMING

The best practice, when selecting a name for your server, and for all your network computers, is to choose consistent, logical names that make sense to all the network's users. Remember, there will be many times in the future when people need to know the names of specific computers, and unless you want to receive a phone call every time that happens, you want to avoid using whimsical or nonsensical names. You should avoid using people's names for computers as well because it only causes confusion when employees change jobs or leave the organization.

On a small-business network that has only a few servers, simple names such as SERVERA or SERVER1 is appropriate, as are names reflecting each server's primary role, such as SVR-DC for your domain controller and SVR-FILE for your file server. For workstations, generic names such as WKSTN-01 and WKSTN-02 are suitable, but you might also consider names that reflect the locations of the computers, such as WK-RECEP for the system on the receptionist's desk and WK-BKPG1 and WK-BKPG2 for the computers in the bookkeepers' office. Whatever convention that you elect to use, create a naming rule and use it consistently for all your computers.

DOMAIN NAMING

The domain name that you supply is the name that the setup program assigns to your AD DS domain, appended with the suffix *local*. You do not have to register the name that you choose for use on the Internet. Indeed, this domain cannot be Internet-accessible because *local* is not an official top-level domain. However, if you have a registered Internet domain name, such as *adatum.com*, you can elect to use the same second-level name on your internal domain, as in *adatum.local*, if you want.

MORE INFO For more information on domains, both on the Internet and in AD DS, see the section "Understanding Domains," in Chapter 2.

It is possible to use a suffix other than *local* for your internal domain name, but to do so, you must install Windows SBS 2008 using an answer file. In fact, if you are connecting Apple Macintosh computers running OS X version 10.3 or higher to your network, you must use a different suffix because OS X uses the *local* suffix for its Rendezvous service. An *answer file* is an Extensible Markup Language (XML) file you create that automates the installation process by supplying responses to the setup program's user prompts. The file also enables you to configure additional installation parameters that do not appear during an interactive installation or trigger a server migration.

> **MORE INFO** For more information on using answer files, see the section "Creating an Answer File," later in this chapter.

If you intend to use an internal domain name with a suffix other than *local*, you should be careful not to use a domain name that someone else has already registered for Internet use. Your internal use of the domain name does not affect the legal registrant's rights, but it does prevent users on your internal network from accessing that name on the Internet.

Internal domain names typically use some permutation of the organization's name. For example, the A. Datum Corporation might use *adatum.local* for its internal domain. Once you decide on a name for your internal domain, you might want to consider registering that name on the Internet, in the .com, .net, or .org top-level domain. Even if you do not need an Internet domain name right now, registering it prevents anyone else from taking it.

USER NAMING

After you supply your server and internal domain names, the setup program prompts you to create a network administrator account. For security reasons, the setup program disables the operating system's built-in Administrator account at the end of the installation, so you must create an account to use in its place. Before you do this, you might want to consider a user naming convention for your network as well. A common convention for smaller networks is to create account names from the user's first name and last initial, as in MarkL. For larger networks, where there is more likely to be a name conflict, you might want to use the first initial and surname, as in MLee.

Instituting a user naming convention for your network is not essential. It is certainly less necessary than a computer naming convention, but letting users select their own account names only increases the burden on the network administrator. When an administrator knows what a user's account name should be without having to ask, the account maintenance process runs more smoothly for everyone involved.

Installing Windows SBS 2008

Once your hardware is in place and you have made all the necessary decisions, you are ready to perform the Windows SBS 2008 installation. Considering all that the setup process accomplishes, the installation process for Windows SBS 2008 is remarkably easy. A clean installation (that is, an installation performed on a blank hard disk) requires only a small amount of interaction; the setup program does nearly everything itself. Migrations from earlier versions of Windows SBS are a bit more problematic, however.

Performing a Clean Windows SBS 2008 Installation

To perform a clean installation of Windows SBS 2008 on a new computer, or on a computer with a hard disk that you can wipe clean, use the following procedure:

1. Turn on the computer and insert Disk 1 from the Windows SBS 2008 package into the DVD-ROM drive.

2. Press a key to boot from the DVD if the system prompts you to do so. The computer reads from the DVD and displays the first page of the Install Windows Wizard, shown here.

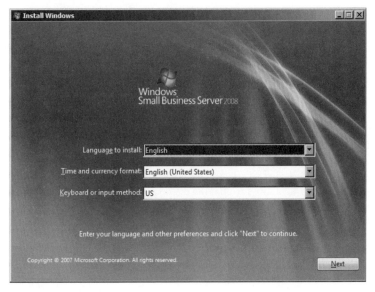

3. If you plan to use language, time, and currency format, or keyboard settings other than the defaults, select your preferences from the three drop-down lists. Then click Next. The Install Now page appears, as shown here.

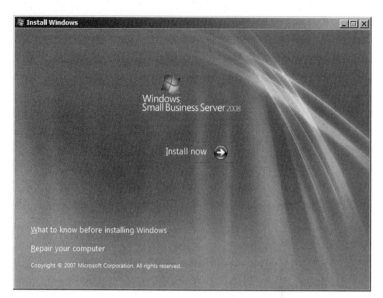

4. Click Install Now. The Type Your Product Key For Activation page appears, as shown here.

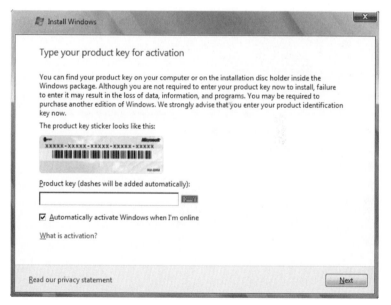

5. In the Product Key text box, type the 25-character product key supplied with your Windows SBS 2008 product. Leave the Automatically Activate Windows When I'm Online check box selected and click Next. The Please Read The License Terms page appears, as shown here.

IMPORTANT Windows SBS 2008 Standard retail packages are supplied with two product keys, one for a physical installation of Windows SBS 2008 and one for an installation on a virtual machine in a Windows Hyper-V or other virtual operating system environment. The Windows SBS Premium package comes with additional physical and virtual product keys for the second server, as well as a key for Microsoft SQL Server 2008 Standard Edition for Small Business. This procedure, and all the procedures in this book, assume that you are performing a physical Windows SBS 2008 installation.

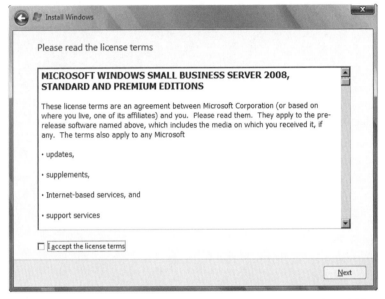

6. Select the I Accept The License Terms check box and click Next. The Which Type Of Installation Do You Want? page appears, as shown here.

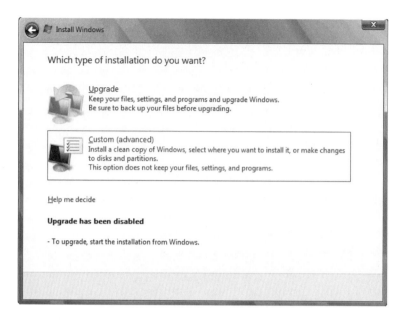

IMPORTANT The Upgrade option on this page is disabled because there is no upgrade path for the Windows SBS 2008 product. If you have an existing Windows SBS installation, you can migrate it to another server, but you cannot upgrade it. For more information, see the section "Performing a Windows SBS 2008 Migration Installation," later in this chapter.

7. Click Custom (Advanced). The Where Do You Want To Install Windows? page appears, as shown here.

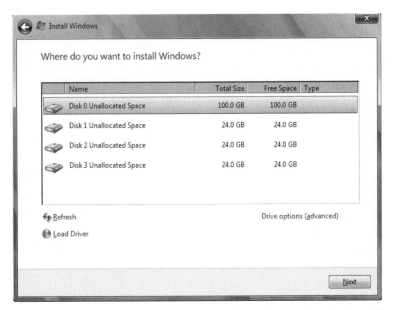

8. To create a partition on a disk, click Drive Options (advanced) to display additional controls.

9. Select the disk on which you want to create the partition and click New. In the Size box that appears, specify a size greater than 60,000 MB (60 GB) for the partition and click Apply. The new partition appears in the list, as shown here.

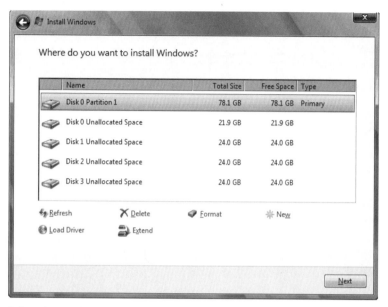

10. Select the partition on which you want to install Windows SBS 2008 and click Next. The Installing Windows page appears, as shown here, and the setup program proceeds through the various stages of the Windows Server 2008 operating system installation.

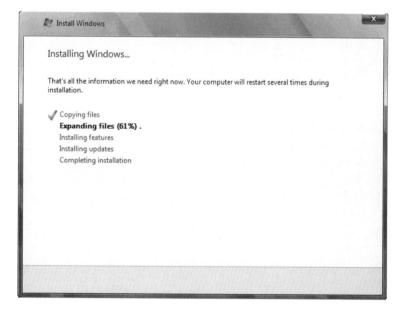

11. When this phase of the installation process is completed, the computer restarts, and the Continue Installation page appears, as shown here.

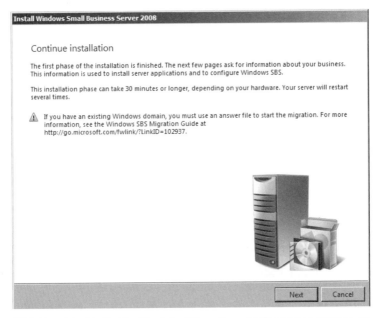

12. Click Next. The Verify The Clock And Time Zone Settings page appears, as shown here.

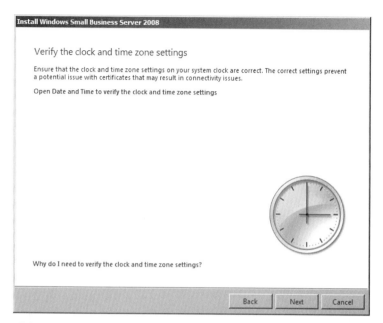

Install Windows Small Business Server 2008

Verify the clock and time zone settings

Ensure that the clock and time zone settings on your system clock are correct. The correct settings prevent a potential issue with certificates that may result in connectivity issues.

Open Date and Time to verify the clock and time zone settings

Why do I need to verify the clock and time zone settings?

[Back] [Next] [Cancel]

13. Click Open Date And Time To Verify The Clock And Time Zone Settings. The Date And Time dialog box appears, as shown here.

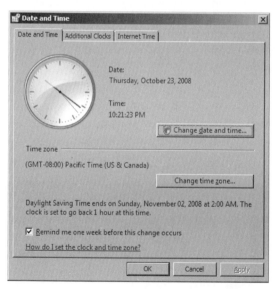

Date and Time

Date and Time | Additional Clocks | Internet Time |

Date:
Thursday, October 23, 2008

Time:
10:21:23 PM

[Change date and time...]

Time zone

(GMT-08:00) Pacific Time (US & Canada)

[Change time zone...]

Daylight Saving Time ends on Sunday, November 02, 2008 at 2:00 AM. The clock is set to go back 1 hour at this time.

☑ Remind me one week before this change occurs

How do I set the clock and time zone?

[OK] [Cancel] [Apply]

14. Verify that the Date, Time, and Time Zone settings are correct. If they are not, click Change Date And Time or Change Time Zone to correct them. Then click OK to close the Date And Time dialog box.

15. Click Next. The Get Important Updates page appears, as shown here.

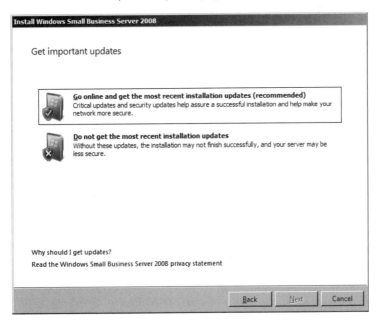

16. If you have already installed a router and an Internet connection on your network, click Go Online And Get The Most Recent Installation Updates. The Connecting Your Server page appears, displaying the progress of the setup program as it searches for the router, configures the server's TCP/IP client, and downloads updates from the Microsoft Web site.

17. When the process is complete, the Company Information page appears, as shown here.

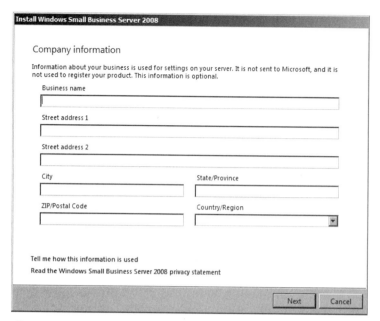

18. Fill out the text boxes with the name and address of your organization and click Next. The Personalize Your Server And Your Network page appears, as shown here.

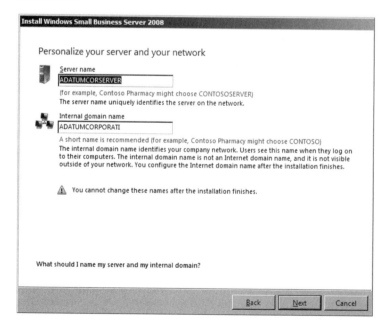

19. In the Server Name text box, type the name you selected for your server running Windows SBS 2008.

20. In the Internal Domain Name text box, type the name you selected for your AD DS domain, without the *local* suffix. Then click Next. The Add A Network Administrator Account page appears, as shown here.

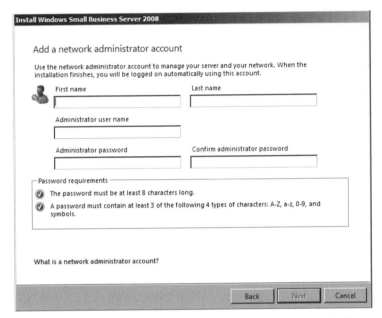

21. Fill out the first and last names of the network administrator and, in the Administrator User Name field, type an account name that conforms to your naming convention. Then type an appropriate password in the Administrator Password and Confirm Administrator Password text boxes and click Next. The Install Security Services page appears, as shown here.

NOTE The name that you specify in the Administrator User Name field can contain uppercase or lowercase letters, numbers, or the _#$%&'-^{}~! symbols. The password you specify must be at least eight characters long, and contain three of the following character types: uppercase letters, lowercase letters, numbers, and symbols.

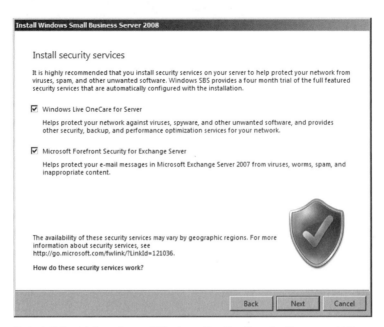

Install Windows Small Business Server 2008

Install security services

It is highly recommended that you install security services on your server to help protect your network from viruses, spam, and other unwanted software. Windows SBS provides a four month trial of the full featured security services that are automatically configured with the installation.

☑ Windows Live OneCare for Server

Helps protect your network against viruses, spyware, and other unwanted software, and provides other security, backup, and performance optimization services for your network.

☑ Microsoft Forefront Security for Exchange Server

Helps protect your e-mail messages in Microsoft Exchange Server 2007 from viruses, worms, spam, and inappropriate content.

The availability of these security services may vary by geographic regions. For more information about security services, see
http://go.microsoft.com/fwlink/?LinkId=121036.

How do these security services work?

Back   Next   Cancel

22. To install the trial versions of Windows Live OneCare for Server and Microsoft Forefront Security for Exchange Server, leave their respective check boxes selected and click Next. The That Is All The Information Needed page appears, as shown here, containing the values that you supplied on the previous pages.

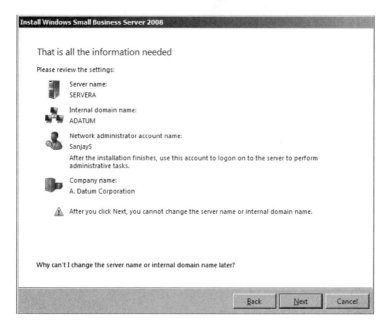

Install Windows Small Business Server 2008

That is all the information needed

Please review the settings:

> Server name:
> SERVERA

> Internal domain name:
> ADATUM

> Network administrator account name:
> SanjayS
>
> After the installation finishes, use this account to logon on to the server to perform administrative tasks.

> Company name:
> A. Datum Corporation

⚠ After you click Next, you cannot change the server name or internal domain name.

Why can't I change the server name or internal domain name later?

[Back] [Next] [Cancel]

23. Click Next. The Expanding And Installing Files page appears, tracking the program's progress as it completes the installation.

24. The system restarts twice during this phase of the installation process, returning to the Expanding And Installing Files page each time. When the process is complete, the computer restarts one final time and the Successful Installation page appears, as shown here.

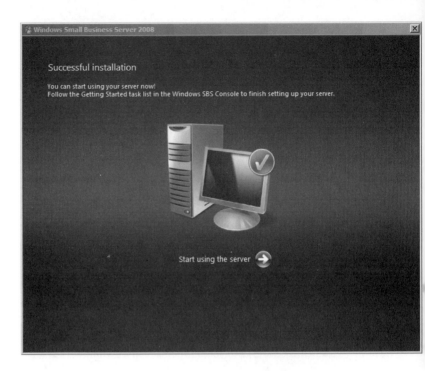

Performing an OEM Windows SBS 2008 Installation

If you purchase a server with the OEM version of Windows SBS 2008 preinstalled, the software is already on the computer's hard disk, but you must perform an abbreviated version of the setup procedure. The OEM setup procedure omits the generic operating system installation tasks, which the computer manufacturer has already performed at the factory, leaving only the tasks that require company-specific input to proceed.

When you turn on the computer for the first time, the Install Windows Wizard displays the same first four pages as a DVD installation (shown in steps 1 to 6 of the procedure in the previous section). These pages enable you to change the language, time, and currency format, and keyboard settings (if necessary), enter your product key, and accept the license terms. In an OEM package, the manufacturer usually supplies the Windows SBS 2008 product keys on a Certificate of Authenticity sticker attached to the computer. You might also find that you do not have to enter the product key yourself because the manufacturer has entered it as part of the factory setup.

NOTE If you purchase Windows SBS 2008 Standard, the Certificate of Authenticity sticker on your server should contain both the physical and virtual product keys. If you purchase Windows SBS 2008 Premium, the sticker contains only the physical product keys. Microsoft supplies the virtual keys and the key for SQL Server 2008 on a separate card.

After you have completed the four initial pages, the setup procedure skips to the Continue Installation page and resumes from there (starting at step 12). The installation is identical to the DVD-based procedure from this point.

REAL WORLD One additional thing to remember is that when you purchase Windows SBS 2008 in a bundle with a computer, you might not receive installation DVDs. If this is the case, the media are on the computer's hard disk. One of the first things you should do once you have completed the setup procedure is create a set of installation DVDs in case you ever have to reinstall the computer.

Understanding the Installation Process

When you install the stand-alone Windows Server 2008 product, you are left with what is essentially a clean slate. The operating system includes a large collection of services, packaged in groups called *roles,* but the setup program does not install any of them by default. You must add and configure them yourself. With Windows SBS 2008, the situation is extremely different. The setup program not only installs the operating system, it also adds and configures many of the supplied roles to create a default server environment that requires very little additional configuration.

Most of the configuration tasks that the setup program performs are invisible to the user during the installation process. However, it is a good idea for administrators to know what the setup program has done so that they can work with the various server components later. The following sections list the various roles the setup program installs and describe how the program configures them.

Active Directory Certificate Services

A *digital certificate* is an electronic document, issued by a trusted source called a *certification authority (CA),* that verifies the identity of a user or computer. When you connect to a secured Web site on the Internet, for example, your browser downloads a certificate from a third-party CA that verifies that you really are connecting to the correct site. The setup program for Windows SBS 2008 installs the Active Directory Certificate Services role, which enables your server to function as a CA for your internal network.

In addition to installing the role, the setup program uses the new CA to issue two certificates to your server: a Domain Controller certificate and a Web Server certificate. These two certificates, self-signed by your server, enable clients on the network to establish secured connections to the Web sites hosted by your server and to the authentication services provided by the AD DS role.

AD DS

One of the most important roles of your primary server running Windows SBS 2008 is that of an AD DS domain controller. Among many other functions, the domain controller maintains a central database of your user and computer accounts, which is accessible to all the computers on the network. Without an AD DS domain, you would have to create and maintain separate user accounts on each of the network's computers. With AD DS, your users log on to the domain, not individual computers. The domain controller is responsible for authenticating the users and granting them access to network resources.

During the Windows SBS 2008 installation process, the setup program adds the AD DS role on your server and, using the internal domain name you specified on the Personalize Your Server And Your Network page, promotes the server into a domain controller. These are both tasks that you must perform manually on a stand-alone computer running Windows Server 2008. When the installation is finished, you can begin creating AD DS user and computer accounts immediately.

> **MORE INFO** For more information on AD DS, see "An Active Directory Primer" in Chapter 5, "Working with Users, Computers, and Groups."

DHCP Server

As mentioned earlier in this chapter and in Chapter 2, the DHCP Server role enables your server to issue IP addresses and other TCP/IP configuration settings to other computers on your network automatically. The Windows SBS 2008 setup program always installs the DHCP Server role, but it configures and activates the DHCP server only if it can obtain the information that it needs from a router on the network.

If the server does not detect a router during the installation, it leaves the DHCP server unconfigured and does not start the DHCP Server service. You must start the service manually and configure it using the DHCP console.

DNS Server

As discussed in Chapter 2, the Domain Name System (DNS) stores information about domains and computers, most particularly their names and IP addresses. The computers on your network use the DNS server to resolve domain and host names into the IP addresses they need to initiate TCP/IP communications with other computers, locally and on the Internet.

In addition to this basic connectivity function, DNS also plays a vital role in AD DS. As the setup program promotes the server into a domain controller, it installs the DNS Server role and creates a zone representing your internal domain. In this zone, the program creates a variety of resource records that enable clients on the network to locate not only the server, but also specific Web sites and AD DS services on that computer, as shown in Figure 3-3.

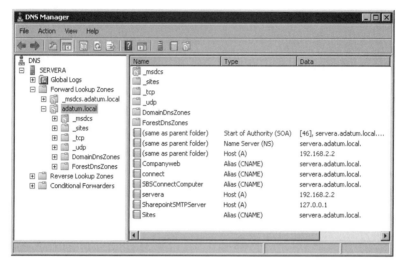

FIGURE 3-3 Resource records in a DNS zone

For example, the zone for your domain contains a Host (A) resource record for the server name you specified during the installation, with the IP address that the program configured the server to use. The program also created an Alias (CNAME) record for the name Companyweb, which points to the server's Host (A) record. When a client uses a Web browser to connect to the *http://companyweb.yourdomain. local* address, the client uses the DNS server to resolve the Companyweb alias and receives the server name in return. The client then resolves the server name and receives the server's IP address in return. The client can now send a message to the specific Web site on the server.

> **NOTE** In this example, using your Windows SBS 2008 server configuration, the need for two-name resolution processes to establish a connection to a Web server that is running on the same computer as the DNS service might seem strange, but the Web server could just as easily be running on another computer.

File Services

The Windows SBS 2008 setup program installs the File Services role but does not add all the available role services. In addition to the File Services role, which enables the computer to share its files and of which all computers running Windows Server 2008 run by default, the program installs the File Server Resource Manager role service. This role service, using the File Server Resource Manager console shown in Figure 3-4, enables you to establish storage quotas for your users, which limit how much server disk space they can consume; define file screening policies, which limit the types of files that users can store on the server; and generate reports on storage consumption.

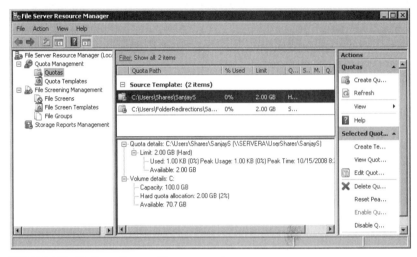

FIGURE 3-4 The File Server Resource Manager console

Network Policy and Access Services

When the setup program installs the Network Policy and Access Services role, it selects only the Network Policy Server and Routing and Remote Access role services. Network Policy Server enables you to specify conditions that clients must satisfy before the server allows them to establish a connection.

Windows SBS 2008 uses network policies to control server access through VPN connections and the Terminal Services Gateway. For the server to grant them access, users must be members of the correct security groups and connect with a specific authentication protocol.

The setup program installs the Routing and Remote Access role service, but only with its Remote Access Service capabilities. The Routing option, which the program does not install, is intended to enable a computer running Windows Server 2008 to function as a router, connecting two networks and forwarding traffic between them. Windows SBS 2008 is designed to support only one network interface on its primary server, so the server configuration omits the Router module.

The Remote Access Service option enables you to configure your server to host incoming VPN connections, which enables users at remote locations to connect to the server through the Internet. Although the setup program installs the role service required for this function, it does not configure it. You must do this manually using the Routing And Remote Access console, shown in Figure 3-5.

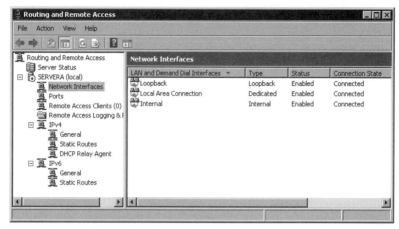

FIGURE 3-5 The Routing And Remote Access console

MORE INFO For more information on configuring Routing and Remote Access, see Chapter 15.

Terminal Services

Windows SBS 2008 cannot function as a terminal server. The setup program does install the Terminal Services role, but it selects only the TS Gateway role service. TS Gateway enables users at remote locations to connect to the server running Windows SBS using the Remote Desktop Connection client only for administrative purposes. Windows SBS 2008, like all the Windows Server 2008 products, includes Remote Desktop for Administration, which is essentially a two-user Terminal Services license. Administrators can access the server desktop, but they cannot use other Terminal Services functions, such as RemoteApp.

As part of the TS Gateway installation, the setup program creates one connection authorization policy (CAP), which specifies the users allowed to access the gateway, and two resource authorization policies (RAPs), which identify the servers that the users are allowed to access. The CAP limits access to members of the Domain Users group, and the RAPs provide access to systems in the Domain Computers and Domain Controllers groups. You can modify the configuration of the TS Gateway or create additional CAPs and RAPs using the TS Gateway Manager console, as shown in Figure 3-6.

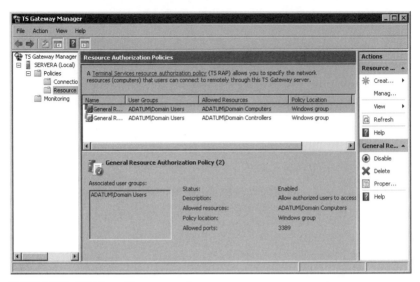

FIGURE 3-6 The TS Gateway Manager console

Web Server (IIS)

Windows SBS 2008 uses Web interfaces for a variety of its applications and services, so the Web Server (IIS) role is a critical part of the product installation. The setup program installs the role with all its dozens of role services, and also creates a large number of Web sites and applications, as shown in Figure 3-7. These Web sites include the default Microsoft SharePoint Services site, the SharePoint Central Administration site, the WSUS administration site, and the Outlook Web Access site for Exchange Server.

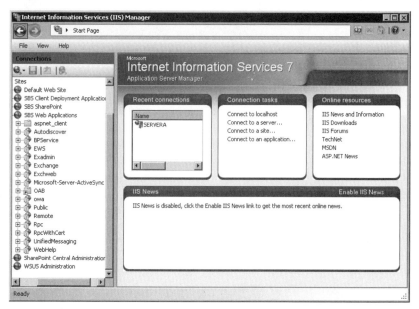

FIGURE 3-7 The Internet Information Services (IIS) Manager console

Performing a Windows SBS 2008 Migration Installation

For users of previous versions of Windows SBS, Windows SBS 2008 is not a simple upgrade. Microsoft does not provide an in-place upgrade path from Windows SBS 2003 R2 to Windows SBS 2008 for several reasons, including the following:

- **Hardware requirements** Windows SBS 2003 R2 runs on a computer with a 32-bit processor and a maximum of 4 GB of memory. Windows SBS 2008 requires a 64-bit processor and a minimum of 4 GB of memory. Exchange Server 2007 is also a 64-bit application, while Exchange Server 2003 SP2 is 32-bit, which complicates the process of porting existing e-mail to the new platform.

- **Network configuration** Windows SBS 2003 R2 is designed to function as a router between the private small-business network and the Internet. The Premium Edition includes the Internet and Security Acceleration (ISA) Server 2004 product to help secure this configuration. However, in Windows SBS 2008, Microsoft recognizes that connecting a domain controller to the Internet is an inherently insecure practice, and in response, it redesigned the default configuration to use a single network interface on the server and a separate router device connecting the network to the Internet.

- **Application compatibility** Windows SBS 2008 adds new applications to the product package, such as a new administrative interface, Windows Live OneCare for Server, and Forefront Security for Exchange Server, and omits the ISA Server 2004 and Microsoft Office FrontPage 2003 products from Windows SBS 2003 R2. All the applications common to both products receive upgrades.

- **Edition configurations** The Premium editions of Windows SBS 2003 R2 and Windows SBS 2008 both add SQL Server to the package, but the 2003 product incorporates it into its single-server environment. Windows SBS 2008 Premium Edition calls for a second computer, on which you install SQL Server.

To upgrade from Windows SBS 2003 R2 to Windows SBS 2008, you must install a new server computer, migrate your domain, configuration settings, and data from the old system to the new, and then demote or remove the old computer. If you purchase Windows SBS 2008 Premium, you can conceivably perform the migration to a new server, and then use the old computer as your secondary server, which can be either 32-bit or 64-bit.

NOTE Microsoft has not yet announced any upgrade pricing for Windows SBS 2008.

The process of migrating from Windows SBS 2003 R2 to Windows SBS 2008 consists of the following steps:

1. Prepare the existing Windows SBS 2003 R2 server for migration.
2. Create a migration answer file.
3. Install Windows SBS 2008 using the answer file.
4. Run the Migration Wizard to transfer settings and data.
5. Demote the Windows SBS 2003 R2 server.
6. Reconfigure Folder Redirection.

The following sections examine each of these steps in greater detail.

Preparing for Migration

For the migration process to complete successfully, it is critical that your existing server running Windows SBS be properly prepared. Be sure to complete all the tasks in the following sections before you begin your server migration.

BACK UP

The migration process makes significant changes to your existing server, so it is imperative that you perform a full backup, including the system state, before you proceed with the migration. You should also perform some test restores of individual files to make sure that you have a viable backup. If the migration fails, or you want to return to your old Windows SBS version for any reason, your only recourse might be to restore the server from this backup.

INSTALL UPDATES

Install the latest service packs on your Windows SBS 2003 R2 server, as well as all the latest critical updates. Retail editions of Windows SBS 2003 R2 already have Windows Server 2003 SP2 incorporated into them, as do most OEM editions. You must also install the latest service packs for Windows SBS 2003 itself, Exchange Server 2003, SharePoint Services, SQL Server Management Studio Express, and Microsoft Core XML Services (MSXML) 6.0. Finally, make sure that the computer has Microsoft .NET Framework 2.0 or later installed.

RECONFIGURE THE NETWORK

If your Windows SBS 2003 R2 server provides the shared Internet connection for your network, you must unplug the network adapter connected to the modem or other Internet access device. Then you must purchase and install a separate router device and configure it to connect to the Internet, as described in the sections "Selecting a Router" and "Connecting Your Router," earlier in this chapter.

PLAN APPLICATION MIGRATIONS

If you are running any third-party applications on your server, you should consult the product documentation or the software manufacturers for information on how to migrate them to your new server. In most cases, you must reinstall the application on your new server running Windows SBS 2008 and migrate your data from the old one.

SYNCHRONIZE COMPUTER CLOCKS

For the migration process to succeed, the server running Windows SBS 2003 R2 and the new server running Windows SBS 2008 must have the same date and time zone settings, and their clocks must be set to within five minutes of each other.

RUN THE BEST PRACTICES ANALYZER

Download the Microsoft Windows Small Business Server 2003 Best Practices Analyzer (BPA) from the Microsoft Download Center at *http://www.microsoft.com/ downloads*, and then install and run it on your Windows SBS 2003 R2 server. The BPA is capable of identifying a large number of problems related to Windows Server, Exchange Server, SQL Server, WSUS, and SharePoint Services. Not all these problems can affect the outcome of the migration, but you should attempt to correct as many of them as possible before you begin the migration process.

RAISE THE AD DS FUNCTIONAL LEVELS

To complete the migration successfully, you must configure your Windows SBS 2003 domain controller to use the Windows Server 2003 domain functional level and forest functional level. If you have additional domain controllers on your network running Microsoft Windows 2000 or Microsoft Windows NT 4.0, you must demote them.

To raise the domain functional level and forest functional level, use the following procedure:

1. Log on to the Windows SBS 2003 R2 server, using an account in the Domain Admins group.

2. Click Start, Administrative Tools, and then Active Directory Domains And Trusts. The Active Directory Domains And Trusts console appears, as shown here.

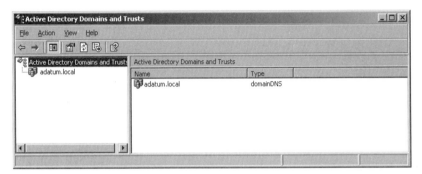

3. Right-click your domain and, on the context menu, select Raise Domain Functional Level. The Raise Domain Functional Level dialog box appears, as shown here.

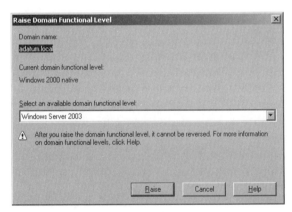

4. In the Select An Available Domain Functional Level drop-down list, select Windows Server 2003, and then click Raise.

5. Right-click the Active Directory Domains And Trusts node and, on the context menu, select Raise Forest Functional Level. The Raise Forest Functional Level dialog box appears, as shown here.

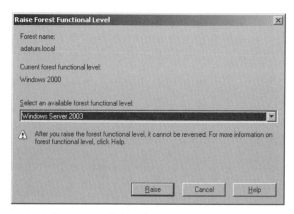

6. In the Select An Available Forest Functional Level drop-down list, select Windows Server 2003, and then click Raise.

7. Close the Active Directory Domains And Trusts console.

RUN THE MIGRATION PREPARATION TOOL

AD DS is based on a set of *schema*, which specify what kinds of objects can exist in the directory and what attributes are associated with each object type. The schema for Windows SBS 2003 R2 are different from those in Windows SBS 2008, so you must update your existing server by running the Migration Preparation Tool, found on Disk 1 in your Windows Server 2008 product package.

To run the tool, use the following procedure:

1. Log on to your Windows SBS 2003 R2 server, using an account that must be a member of the Domain Admins, Enterprise Admins, and Schema Admins groups.

2. Insert Windows SBS 2008 Disk 1 into the computer's DVD-ROM drive.

3. When the Windows Small Business Server 2008 screen appears, click Tools. A Windows Explorer window appears, displaying the contents of the Tools folder on the disk.

4. Double-click the SourceTool.exe file. The Source Server Migration Tool Wizard appears, displaying the Prepare Your Source Server For Migration page, as shown here.

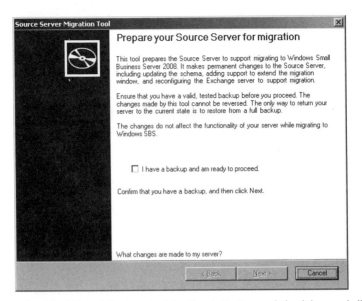

Source Server Migration Tool [X]

Prepare your Source Server for migration

This tool prepares the Source Server to support migrating to Windows Small Business Server 2008. It makes permanent changes to the Source Server, including updating the schema, adding support to extend the migration window, and reconfiguring the Exchange server to support migration.

Ensure that you have a valid, tested backup before you proceed. The changes made by this tool cannot be reversed. The only way to return your server to the current state is to restore from a full backup.

The changes do not affect the functionality of your server while migrating to Windows SBS.

☐ I have a backup and am ready to proceed.

Confirm that you have a backup, and then click Next.

What changes are made to my server?

[< Back] [Next >] [Cancel]

5. Select the I Have A Backup And Am Ready To Proceed check box and click Next. The Preparing Your Source Server To Support Migration page appears and displays the wizard's progress as it updates the schema on your existing server and modifies the permissions to enable the migration to Windows SBS 2008 to occur. The wizard also converts Exchange Server from mixed mode to native mode and sets a time limit during which the Windows SBS network can have two domain controllers. Once you have completed the migration, your original server can function as a domain controller for up to 21 days before you must demote it.

WARNING The changes made to the computer running Windows Server 2003 R2 by the Migration Preparation Tool at this time are permanent and irrevocable. The only way to return to your previous server configuration is to perform a full restore from a system backup.

6. When the Source Server Prepared Successfully page appears, as shown here, click Finish.

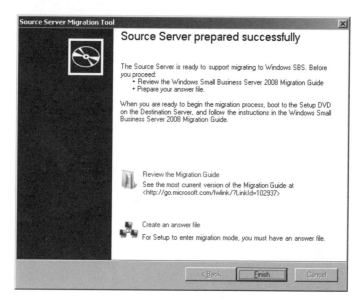

NOTE If desired, you can click Create An Answer File to run the Windows Small Business Server 2008 Answer File Tool at this time. However, you can also choose to create the answer file at a later time, using any other computer running Windows. See the next section for instructions on running the tool and creating an answer file.

7. A Source Server Migration Tool message box appears, prompting you to restart the system. Click Yes. The system restarts.

Creating an Answer File

Although the Source Server Migration Tool Wizard enables you to run the Windows Small Business Server 2008 Answer File Tool right on your existing server, you do not have to run it there, nor do you have to run it immediately after preparing the source server for migration. You can run the Answer File Tool from any computer running Windows at any time.

To create a migration answer file, use the following procedure:

1. Insert Windows SBS 2008 Disk 1 into the computer's DVD-ROM drive.

2. When the Windows Small Business Server 2008 screen appears, click Tools. A Windows Explorer window appears, displaying the contents of the Tools folder on the disk.

3. Double-click the SBSAfg.exe file. The Windows Small Business Server 2008 Answer File Tool appears.

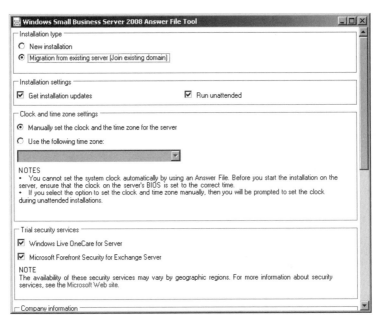

4. In the Installation Type box, select the Migration From Existing Server check box.

5. Fill out the fields in each of the following sections of the Answer File Tool:

   ■ **Installation settings** Specifies whether the new server should download the latest installation updates from the Microsoft Web site during the setup process, and whether the setup program should perform an unattended installation. In an unattended installation, the setup program does not display the options for which it finds settings in the answer file; if you leave this check box cleared, all the options appear during the installation, with the settings from the answer file preloaded for the installer's approval.

   ■ **Clock and time zone settings** Enables you to specify a time zone for the new server. You cannot modify the actual system clock time using an answer file, so if you select the Manually Set The Clock And The Time Zone For The Server option, you must set the clock in the system BIOS before beginning the new server installation.

   ■ **Trial security services** Specifies whether you want to install trial versions of the Windows Live OneCare for Server and Microsoft Forefront Security for Exchange Server products.

   ■ **Company information** Contains the same name and address fields as the Company Information page in the Install Windows Wizard, plus an additional Certificate Authority Name field, in which you can specify a nondefault name for the CA on the new server. The Certificate Authority Name value cannot be the same as your domain name.

- **Source (existing) server information**   Contains fields in which you specify information about your existing server running Windows SBS and domain, including the server and domain names, the computer's IP Address and Default Gateway settings, and the name and password for an administrative account.

- **Destination (new) server information**   Contains fields in which you specify the name and IP address values you want to assign to your new server running Windows SBS 2008. When performing a migration, the name that you specify for your new server must be unique on your network. You cannot use the same name for your servers running Windows SBS 2003 R2 and Windows SBS 2008.

6. Click Save As. The Save As combo box appears. Save the answer file to the root of a USB flash drive, using the file name SBSAnswerFile.xml, and click Save.

7. Close the Windows Small Business Server 2008 Answer File Tool.

NOTE   The previous procedure covers the information fields you must fill out when creating an answer file for a migration to Windows SBS 2008. When you select the New Installation option in the tool's Installation Type section, the program omits the migration-specific sections: Source (Existing) Server Information and Destination (New) Server Information, and adds the following three different sections instead:

- Server information   Enables you to specify Server Name and Internal Domain Name values for the new server installation. There is also a Full DNS Name text box, in which you can specify a name for your AD DS domain with a suffix other than *local*.

- Network administrator account   Contains the same fields as the Add A Network Administrator Account page, which the setup program uses to create an administrative account on the new server running Windows SBS 2008.

- Network settings for the server   Enables you to specify whether the setup program should detect a router on the network and configure the server's TCP/IP client using the router information automatically or use the IP Address and Default Gateway settings that you supply.

Apart from these field changes, the procedure for creating an answer file for the installation of a new server running Windows SBS 2008 is exactly the same.

Installing Windows SBS 2008 with an Answer File

Once you have created your answer file and saved it to a removable drive, you can begin the Windows SBS 2008 installation. To perform a migration installation, use the following procedure:

1. Turn on the computer and insert Disk 1 from the Windows SBS 2008 package into the DVD-ROM drive.

2. Press a key to boot from the DVD if the system prompts you to do so. The computer reads from the DVD and displays the first page of the Install Windows Wizard.

3. If you plan to use language, time, and currency format, or keyboard settings other than the defaults, select your preferences from the three drop-down lists. Then click Next. The Install Now page appears.

4. Insert the storage device containing the answer file in the appropriate drive or slot and click Install Now. The Type Your Product Key For Activation page appears.

5. In the Product Key text box, type the 25-character product key supplied with your Windows SBS 2008 product. Leave the Automatically Activate Windows When I'm Online check box selected and click Next. The Please Read The License Terms page appears.

6. Select the I Accept The License Terms check box and click Next. The Which Type Of Installation Do You Want? page appears.

7. Click Custom (Advanced). The Where Do You Want To Install Windows? page appears.

8. Select or create a partition on a disk, using the Drive Options (Advanced) controls, if necessary. Then click Next. The Installing Windows page appears, and the setup program proceeds through the various stages of the Windows Server 2008 operating system installation.

NOTE If, when communicating with your existing server running Windows SBS, the setup program detects any migration requirements that the server does not meet, it displays a Source Server Does Not Meet Minimum Requirements For Migration page that lists the issues that you must address before the migration can proceed.

When this phase of the setup process is completed, the computer restarts, locates the answer file, and proceeds with the rest of the installation. If you configured the answer file to perform an unattended installation, the setup process continues without displaying the various configuration pages, but it restarts several times and displays the various progress indicator pages, such as Expanding And Installing Files.

TROUBLESHOOTING If the screen saver appears and locks the desktop during the installation process, you can unlock it by pressing Ctrl+Alt+Del and entering the appropriate password. Depending on where in the installation process the lock occurs, you might have to unlock it using either the new server's local Administrator account, which has a blank password at this point, or the domain account for which you supplied a name and password in the answer file.

9. When the installation is complete (which can take a great deal longer than a new Windows SBS 2008 installation), the Installation Finished page appears, as shown here.

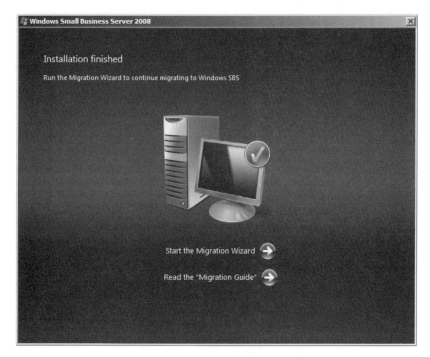

The Installation Finished page prompts you to proceed by running the Migration Wizard. However, clicking the Start The Migration Wizard link simply closes the page and starts the Windows SBS Console. When you perform a migration installation, the console contains an extra Migrate To Windows SBS entry in the Getting Started Tasks list, as shown in Figure 3-8.

FIGURE 3-8 The Windows SBS Console after a migration installation

The Migration Wizard displays a list of the various tasks that you must perform within 21 days of the installation to complete the process of transferring all your settings and data from the old server to the new one. These tasks, and the other tasks you must perform to complete your migration to Windows SBS 2008, are covered in the section "Completing Post-Migration Tasks" in Chapter 4, "Getting Started."

Getting Started

The Microsoft Windows Small Business Server (SBS) 2008 installation process performs a large number of configuration tasks that administrators have to perform manually in the case of a stand-alone Windows Server 2008 installation. This is not to say that a server running Windows SBS is ready for users when the installation is finished, however. You still must perform a variety of tasks to prepare your server for use, not the least of which is familiarizing yourself with the Windows SBS Console.

Using the Windows SBS Console

The Windows SBS Console is a new administrative tool that replaces the Server Management console from Windows SBS 2003. Unlike Server Management, Windows SBS Console is not a Microsoft Management Console (MMC) snap-in; it is a stand-alone application that groups together many of the basic server management and monitoring functions that require separate applications in Windows Server 2008.

> **TIP** Windows SBS Console does not replace the standard Windows Server 2008 tools; it merely supplements them. While Windows SBS Console includes many of the tools that administrators use most often, the various Windows Server 2008 utilities offer many more advanced functions.

Starting Windows SBS Console

When you log on to Windows SBS 2008 for the first time, after the installation finishes, the Windows SBS Console window opens by default and displays the interface shown in Figure 4-1. You can also start the program at any time by selecting Start, Administrative Tools, Windows SBS Console, and then clicking Continue in the User Account Control dialog box.

FIGURE 4-1 The Windows SBS Console

You might notice that the Administrative Tools group also contains a Windows SBS Console (Advanced Mode) shortcut. Selecting this shortcut opens a version of the Windows SBS Console that includes links to other Windows Server 2008 tools, such as the Active Directory Users and Computers, DHCP, and DNS Manager consoles.

> **TIP** In addition to running the Windows SBS Console application on the server itself, you can access it from remote locations. From another computer on the local network, you can use the Remote Desktop Connection client to access the server and start Windows SBS Console. You can also use the Remote Web Workplace (RWW) site to access the server from anywhere on the Internet. The address for your RWW site is *http://remote.domain_name.com*, where *domain_name.com* is the name of your Internet domain.

Using the Windows SBS Console Interface

The Windows SBS Console has seven main pages represented by seven buttons at the top of the window. Clicking Home displays a page, different in appearance from the other six, which consists of two task panes and a status area. Each of these two panes has an arrow button on the right. Clicking the down arrow on the open pane minimizes it and moves to the bottom, so that the other pane can open and take its place, as shown in Figure 4-2.

FIGURE 4-2 Swapping the task pane in the Home page of the Windows SBS Console

The other six pages in the console consist of tabbed lists of operating system elements on the left, as shown in Figure 4-3, and a context-sensitive task list on the right, which you can use to perform specific actions.

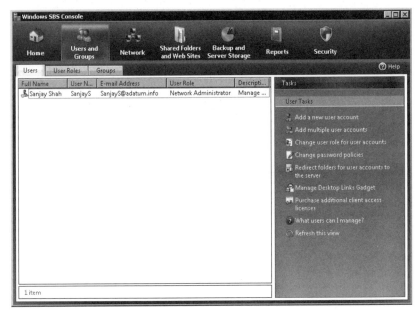

FIGURE 4-3 The tabbed interface of the Windows SBS Console

The functions found in the main pages of the Windows SBS Console are as follows:

- **Home**
  - Getting Started Tasks   Contains a list of post-installation tasks to perform on your server
  - Frequent Tasks and Community Links   Contains links to the console's most frequently-used functions, and to Windows SBS resources on the Internet
  - Network Essentials Summary   Contains status displays for the servers on your network, along with links to appropriate pages with more information
- **Users And Groups**
  - Users   Contains a list of the user accounts you have created in your domain and enables you to create new user accounts and manage existing ones
  - User Roles   Enables you to create and manage templates that simplify the process of creating user accounts
  - Groups   Contains a list of the Windows SBS security and distribution groups in your domain and enables you to create new groups and manage group memberships

- **Network**
  - Computers   Contains a list of the computers on your network, and enables you to add new computers and monitor existing ones
  - Devices   Contains a list of shared fax and print devices on the network, and enables you to manage existing devices and share additional ones
  - Connectivity   Contains a list of Windows SBS network and Internet resources, and enables you to manage their properties
- **Shared Folders And Web Sites**
  - Shared Folders   Contains a list of the shared folders on the network and enables you to create new shares and manage existing ones
  - Web Sites   Contains list of the intranet and Internet Web sites for the organization and enables you to manage their properties and permissions
- **Backup And Server Storage**
  - Backup   Contains a list of the scheduled backup jobs for the server and enables you to configure the jobs, check their status, and restore files from backups
  - Server Storage   Contains a list of the server's storage volumes and enables you to move specific data stores to other locations
- **Reports**   Contains a list of the Windows SBS reports that the system is configured to generate and enables you to view the reports and create new ones
- **Security**
  - Security   Contains a list of the security mechanisms on the server, and enables you to check their status and view their properties
  - Updates   Contains a list of the updates downloaded by Windows Server Update Services (WSUS), tracks their status, and enables you to deploy or decline them

Performing Post-Installation Tasks

As soon as possible after you install Windows SBS 2008 on your primary server, you should begin addressing the items in the Getting Started Tasks list on the Home page of the Windows SBS Console. Some of these tasks link to wizards that help you to configure various server functions, while others display help files that provide useful information about administering your server and your network.

The following sections describe the functions of the various tasks in the list. As you finish each task, select its Completed check box to keep track of your progress.

Using the Windows SBS Console

For administrators working with Windows SBS for the first time, it is a good idea to familiarize yourself with the management tools supplied with Windows SBS 2008, especially the Windows SBS Console. Clicking the Using The Windows SBS Console link on the Home page opens a help window that describes the basic capabilities of the Windows SBS and provides links to more detailed help pages on specific subjects.

Some of the other entries in the Getting Started Tasks list link to help files as well, including How Can Users Access Computers On The Network? and How Can I Add A Shared Printer To The Network? For more information on these subjects, see Chapter 5, "Working with Users, Groups, and Computers" and Chapter 8, "Sharing Printers."

MORE INFO If you migrated your server running Windows SBS 2008 from an earlier version of Windows SBS, an additional Migrate To Windows SBS task appears in the Getting Started Tasks list. For more information on completing the migration process, see the section entitled "Performing Post-Migration Tasks," later in this chapter.

Connecting to the Internet

The Connect To The Internet Wizard is an important part of the Windows SBS 2008 setup process; many of the other wizards in the Getting Started Tasks list do not run until you complete it. If you installed your server running Windows SBS 2008 before setting up an Internet access router on your network, this wizard detects the router and configures the server to use it for Internet access. The wizard also configures the DHCP Server service on the computer to supply Internet Protocol (IP) addresses and other Transmission Control Protocol/Internet Protocol (TCP/IP) configuration settings to the client workstations that you are connecting to the network.

TIP You should run the Connect To The Internet Wizard again if you ever install a new router on your network or reconfigure your router to use a different IP address. You can access the wizard from the Home page of the Windows SBS Console, or by switching to the Network page, selecting the Connectivity tab, and, in the Tasks pane, clicking Connect To The Internet.

To complete the Connect To The Internet Wizard, set up your router on the network and then use the following procedure:

1. Log on to your primary server running Windows SBS 2008 using an account with network Administrator privileges. The Windows SBS Console appears.

2. On the Home page of the Windows SBS Console, click Connect To The Internet. The Connect To The Internet Wizard appears, displaying the Before You Begin page, as shown here.

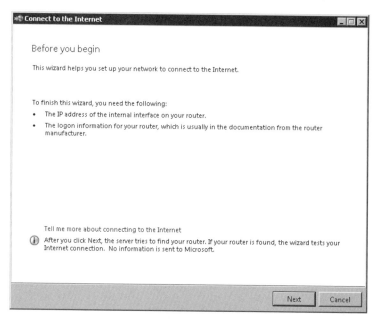

Before you begin

This wizard helps you set up your network to connect to the Internet.

To finish this wizard, you need the following:
- The IP address of the internal interface on your router.
- The logon information for your router, which is usually in the documentation from the router manufacturer.

Tell me more about connecting to the Internet

(i) After you click Next, the server tries to find your router. If your router is found, the wizard tests your Internet connection. No information is sent to Microsoft.

As noted on the Before You Begin page, you should locate the IP address of your router's internal interface before you proceed with the wizard. Stand-alone router devices usually have a Web-based administration interface and a factory-configured IP address that is specified in the product documentation. To access the administration interface, you type that IP address in a Web browser and log in using the access password, also specified in the product documentation.

MORE INFO TCP/IP routers, by definition, have two IP addresses because their function is to connect two networks. The internal interface is the one connected to your private network, for which the router uses an address in the designated private IP address ranges. The external network interface is the one connected to your Internet service provider's (ISP's) network, which typically has a Dynamic Host Configuration Protocol (DHCP) server that assigns an IP address to the router.

3. Click Next. The Detecting The Existing Network page appears.

The wizard attempts to detect a router on the network and access its settings. If the attempt is successful, the Detecting The Router And Configuring Your Network page appears, as shown here. This page specifies the IP address of the router's internal interface, which becomes the Default Gateway address for all your network computers, and the IP address that the wizard configures your server to use.

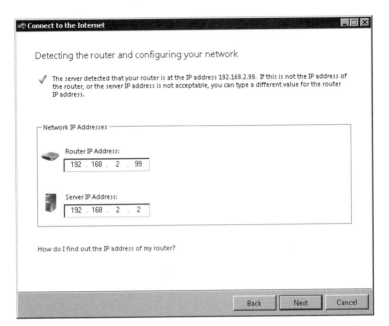

If there is a router on your network and the wizard fails to detect it, the wizard leaves the Router IP Address and Server IP Address text boxes blank. Click Cancel to exit the wizard, troubleshoot your router, and restart the wizard.

4. If the Router IP Address and Server IP Address values that appear on the page are correct, click Next. If the Router IP Address and Server IP Address fields are incorrect or blank, then troubleshoot your router (if necessary), supply the correct values, and click Next. The wizard configures your server, and the Your Network Is Now Connected To The Internet page appears.

5. Click Finish. The wizard closes.

MORE INFO The previous procedure assumes that you have a properly functioning router connected to your network and configured to access the Internet. For more information on choosing and setting up an Internet access router, see the sections entitled "Selecting a Router" and "Connecting Your Router," in Chapter 3, "Installing Microsoft Windows Small Business Server (SBS) 2008."

The basic function of the Connect To The Internet Wizard is to configure your server with an IP address on the same network as your router, and a Default Gateway address that is the same as the router's IP address. This enables the server to access the Internet through the router. In addition, the wizard configures the DHCP Server service on the computer running Windows SBS.

The Windows SBS 2008 setup program installs the DHCP Server role during the server installation whether a router is present on the network or not, leaving it unconfigured and the service stopped. The wizard configures the DHCP server by starting the service and creating a scope. In DHCP parlance, a *scope* is a range of IP addresses that the server can allocate dynamically to clients on the network as needed.

As you can see in the DHCP console, shown in Figure 4-4, the wizard has created a scope consisting of the IP addresses from *x.x.x.*1 to *x.x.x.*254 on the network it detected from the router. The wizard has also excluded two addresses from the scope: *x.x.x.*99, which is the address of the router, and *x.x.x.*2, which is the address of the server.

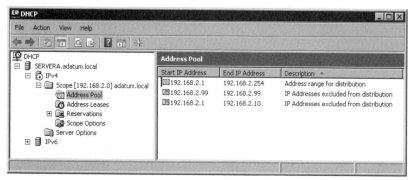

FIGURE 4-4 The DHCP console, showing the scope that the Connect To The Internet Wizard created

NOTE In Figure 4-4, the DHCP scope is using the 192.168.2.0 network address because this happens to be the private network address that the router uses. Your router might use a different address, and the wizard configures the DHCP scope accordingly.

In addition to the range of IP addresses, the wizard also configures the DHCP scope with scope options. *Scope options* are additional TCP/IP configuration settings that the DHCP server delivers to clients, along with an IP address. The scope options that the wizard configures are as follows:

- **003 Router**   Specifies the IP address of the router, which the client should use for its Default Gateway address
- **006 DNS Servers**   Specifies the IP address of the server running Windows SBS 2008, which the client should use for its Preferred DNS Server address
- **015 DNS Domain Name**   Specifies the name of the internal domain that you created during the Windows SBS 2008 installation

If the wizard fails to detect a router on the network, you can still specify values for the Router IP Address and Server IP Address fields. After you confirm that you want the server configuration process to continue, the wizard configures the TCP/IP and DHCP Server settings just as if a router were present and then displays pages that help you to configure your router for Internet access.

The Configure Your Router page, shown in Figure 4-5, enables you to connect to your router's administration console so that you can manually configure it and then test its Internet connectivity. This function assumes that the router uses Web-based configuration and the standard port number for its interface. If the router is configured to use a nonstandard port number for the administrative interface, you can connect to it with a Web browser using a uniform resource locator (URL) that specifies both an IP address and a port number, as in the following example: *http://192.168.2.99:4096*. If the router uses a different type of administrative interface, consult the router manufacturer's documentation to determine how to access it.

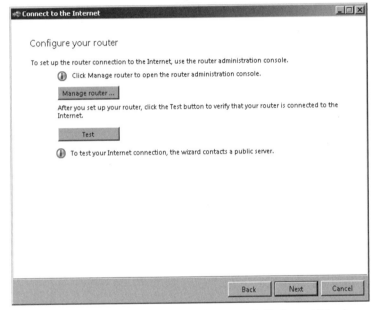

FIGURE 4-5 The Configure Your Router page of the Connect To The Internet Wizard

Before you proceed with the other wizards in the Getting Started Tasks list, you must complete the wizard successfully by connecting to the Internet through a router on your network. The Windows SBS Console does not permit the other wizards requiring Internet access to launch until the Connect To The Internet Wizard succeeds.

Customer Feedback Options

Selecting the Customer Feedback Options link causes a Customer Experience Improvement Program dialog box to appear, which asks if you want to allow Windows SBS to send information about your system hardware and usage trends anonymously to Microsoft for analysis.

Set Up Your Internet Address

For your users to send and receive Internet e-mail, or access your network services from a remote location, you must establish a presence on the Internet. This is different from simply accessing the Internet, which you configured the server to do when you ran the Connect To The Internet Wizard. Establishing a presence on the Internet enables users on the Internet to access your network's resources. To receive e-mail from users outside your organization, for example, their messages must be able to reach your server running Microsoft Exchange Server.

By default, Windows SBS 2008 configures your server to use a private IP address and a domain name with a *local* suffix (both of which are inaccessible from the Internet) by design. To establish an Internet presence, you must register a domain name with an Internet domain registrar and configure your router to admit Internet traffic addressed to your server. The domain name enables Internet users to locate your network, and the router configuration lets the packets coming from those users pass through your firewall. Both of these tasks can be relatively complicated, but fortunately, Windows SBS 2008 includes an Internet Address Management Wizard that helps you to complete them.

The Internet Address Management Wizard prompts you to select a domain name that is accessible from the Internet, as opposed to the local name you specified for your Active Directory Domain Services (AD DS) domain during the Windows SBS 2008 installation. The most common practice is to use the same second-level domain name, but with a different top-level domain. For example, if you use *adatum.local* for your internal domain, you might choose *adatum.com* for your Internet domain. You don't have to use the same second-level domain, however; you can use any domain name that is available for registration.

If the Internet domain name you select is available, the wizard enables you to register it with one of several commercial domain registrars. If you already have a registered domain name, the wizard lets you use that instead. Once you have a registered domain name, the wizard then configures your server, your router, and the Domain Name System records for the new domain.

Registering a New Domain

The Internet Address Management Wizard requires access to the Internet, so you must complete the Connect To The Internet Wizard first. Then, to run the wizard and register a new domain name, use the following procedure:

1. Log on to your Windows SBS 2008 primary server using an account with network Administrator privileges. The Windows SBS Console appears.

2. On the Home page of the Windows SBS Console, click Set Up Your Internet Address. The Internet Address Management Wizard appears, displaying the Before You Begin page, as shown here.

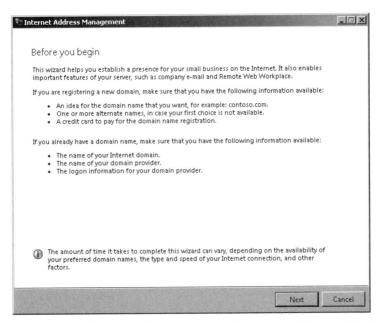

The Before You Begin page lists the resources that you need to complete the wizard, which vary, depending on whether you are registering a new domain name or using an existing one. To register a new name, you must have some idea what name you want to use and a credit card to pay the registration fee.

TIP Determining what domain name to use for your organization can often be the hardest part of this entire process. In fact, you might want to begin your search for a domain name before you install Windows SBS 2008 and create your internal domain. The most popular generic top-level domains (gTLDs) on the Internet: *com*, *net*, and *org*, have millions of names already registered, and you might find it difficult to find a satisfactory name that is available for use.

If your company name is already taken in the *com*, *net*, and *org* domains, you must either choose a variation on the company name, or select a different gTLD. For example, if you are the owner of an eponymously named company that manufactures kilts, and your surname is the same as that of a well-known fast food restaurant chain, you will probably not be able to register your company name in the *com* domain. Your alternatives are to either vary the name, such as by adding the word kilts to your surname, or register your surname in a less popular gTLD, such as *biz*.

To check on the availability of specific domain names before you run the Internet Address Management Wizard, you can use the WHOIS service provided by the Internet Corporation for Assigned Names and Numbers (ICANN), available at *http://www.internic.net/whois.html.*

3. Click Next. The Do You Want To Register A New Domain Name? page appears, as shown here.

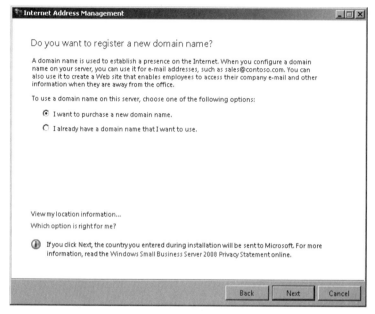

4. Select the I Want To Purchase A New Domain Name option and click Next. The Type The Domain Name You Want To Register page appears, as shown here.

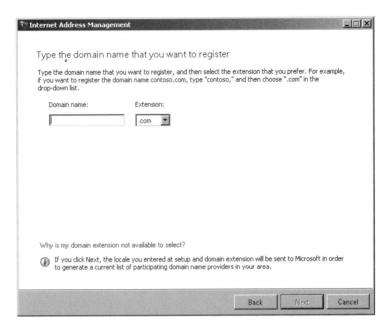

Type the domain name that you want to register

Type the domain name that you want to register, and then select the extension that you prefer. For example, if you want to register the domain name contoso.com, type "contoso," and then choose ".com" in the drop-down list.

Domain name: Extension:

[   ]   [.com ▼]

Why is my domain extension not available to select?

ⓘ If you click Next, the locale you entered at setup and domain extension will be sent to Microsoft in order to generate a current list of participating domain name providers in your area.

[Back]   [Next]   [Cancel]

5. In the Domain Name text box, type the second-level domain name that you want to register. Then, from the Extension drop-down list, select the top-level domain that you want to use and click Next. The Choose A Domain Name Provider page appears.

The wizard displays a list of domain name registrars, based on the domain name that you entered and the location that you specified during the Windows SBS 2008 installation.

IMPORTANT Although you can use any registrar to register your domain name, you must select one of the registrars suggested by the wizard for Windows SBS 2008 to manage your domain fully.

6. Select the domain registrar that you want to use and click Next. The wizard sends the name you specified to the selected registrar.

TIP You might want to examine each of the registrars' Web sites before you commit to one of them. Domain registration has become a highly competitive business in recent years, and prices can vary widely.

7. If the name you specified is not available for registration, the Choose A Different Domain Name page appears, as shown here, offering variations on the name that are available. Type an alternative name in the fields provided and click Search.

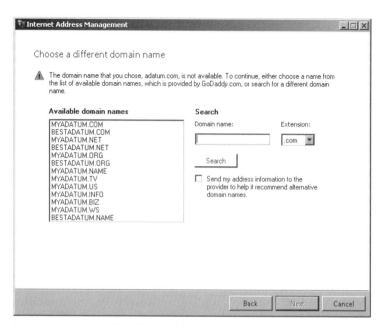

8. If the name you specified is available for registration, the Register And Purchase The Domain Name page appears, as shown here. Click Register Now to open Windows Internet Explorer and connect to the registrar's Web site.

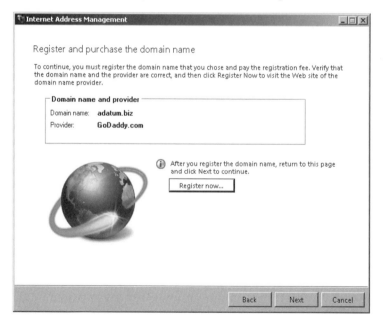

BEST PRACTICES Domain name registrars are commercial enterprises, and they may very likely try to sell you a variety of additional products and services before you complete the registration process. While you might want to consider some of their offers, you don't need anything other than a standard domain name registration to complete the wizard and finish configuring your server.

9. Use the form on the registrar's Web site to register your selected domain name. You have to supply, at minimum, your name, mailing address, telephone number, and credit card information to complete the registration process.

IMPORTANT The registrar adds the contact information that you supply to the WHOIS database, where it is available to anyone who searches for your domain name. Domain name registration listings must have an administration, a billing, and a technical contact. These can all be the same person, or you can specify a different individual for each one. Because this is public information, many organizations use a post office box or pay an additional fee for a private registration to prevent their contact information from being harvested by spammers.

10. Once you have completed the registration process on the Web site, return to the wizard and click Next. The Store Your Domain Name Information page appears, as shown here.

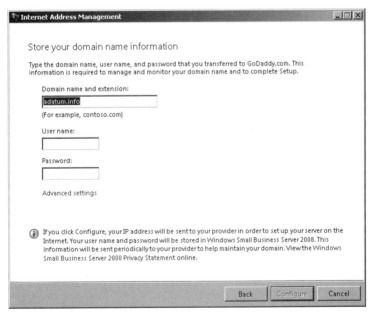

11. In the Domain Name And Extension text box, type your full domain name, with the suffix.

12. In the User Name and Password text boxes, type the credentials that provide access to your account on the registrar's Web site.

> **NOTE** Some registrars have you supply the user name and password that you want to use during the registration process, while others assign credentials to you.

By default, the wizard uses the name *remote* for the Windows SBS 2008 Remote Web Workplace site, so that the Internet URL for the domain *adatum. info* would be *http://remote.adatum.info*. If you want to use a different name, click Advanced Settings to display the Advanced Settings dialog box, shown here, in which you can specify an alternative.

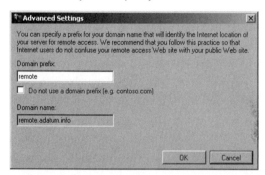

13. Click Configure. The Configuring Your Server page appears, as shown here, displaying the wizard's progress as it configures the server, the router, and the DNS resource records for the domain.

14. When the configuration process finishes, the Congratulations! page appears, summarizing the wizard's results and displaying any warnings that might have occurred.

15. Click Finish. The wizard closes.

Using an Existing Domain

If you already have a registered domain on the Internet, you can still use the Internet Address Management Wizard to configure your network to use it. When you select the I Already Have A Domain Name That I Want To Use option on the Do You Want To Register A New Domain Name? page and click Next, a How Do You Want To Manage Your Domain Name? page appears, providing you with the following two options:

- **I Want The Server To Manage The Domain Name For Me**   To use this option, your domain name must be registered with one of the registrars supported by the wizard. If you have registered your domain with another registrar, the wizard gives you the opportunity to transfer the domain to one of the supported registrars. Once you have completed the transfer, the wizard proceeds as with a newly registered domain.

- **I Want To Manage The Domain Name Myself**   If you decide to leave your domain name with another registrar, the wizard configures your server and your router, but it cannot create the new resource records your network needs on your registrar's DNS servers. In this case, you must create those resource records yourself, using the interface supplied by the registrar and the information in the next section.

Understanding the Wizard's Configurations

During the configuration phase, the Internet Address Management Wizard makes a variety of changes to the various components involved in your presence on the Internet. First, on your server running Windows SBS 2008, the wizard configures the following services:

- **Certification Authority (CA)**   The wizard has the CA on the server issue a certificate for the Remote Web Workplace Web site, as shown in Figure 4-6. This certificate enables users on the Internet to confirm that the RWW that they are connecting to is authentic.

FIGURE 4-6 The certificate for the Remote Web Workplace site, issued by the CA

- **Domain Name System (DNS)** On the server running Windows SBS 2008's DNS server, the wizard creates a zone for the *remote* third-level domain beneath the Internet domain that you registered, as shown in Figure 4-7. This makes the server the authoritative source for information about this third-level domain.

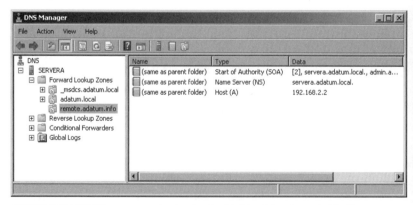

FIGURE 4-7 The DNS Manager console, showing the third-level domain created by the Internet Address Management Wizard

- **Internet Information Services (IIS)**   The wizard configures IIS on your server running Windows SBS 2008 to recognize incoming Web traffic addressed to the *remote* domain and forward it to the Remote Web Workplace site.
- **Simple Mail Transfer Protocol (SMTP)**   The wizard configures Exchange Server 2007 to process incoming SMTP traffic addressed to the domain you registered.

Next, the wizard uses the credentials you supplied to connect to your registrar's Web site and configure DNS records for your newly registered domain. What you are actually paying for when you register a domain is space on the registrar's DNS servers, where you can create resource records in that domain.

MORE INFO   For more information on domain names and the Domain Name System (DNS), see the section entitled "Understanding Domains" in Chapter 2, "A Networking Primer."

Using the interface provided by the registrar, the wizard automatically creates the resource records listed in Table 4-1.

TABLE 4-1 DNS Resource Records for Your Internet Domain

RECORD TYPE	NAME	RECORD SETTINGS	RECORD FUNCTION
Host (A)	Remote	IP address of your router's external interface	Maps the remote name in your domain to your router's Internet IP address
Mail Exchanger (MX)	*domain.com*	remote.domain.com	Directs SMTP mail traffic to your server running Windows SBS 2008
Text (TXT)	*domain.com*	v=spf1 a mx ~all	Prevents e-mail sent by your internal users from being flagged as spam
Service (SRV)	_autodiscover	Protocol = _tcp Priority = 0 Weight = 0 Port = 443 Target = remote.*domain.com*	Enables remote e-mail users to configure the Outlook Anywhere client automatically

NOTE In this table, replace *domain.com* with your full Internet domain name and suffix.

Finally, if your router conforms to the Universal Plug and Play (UPnP) standard, the wizard configures your router by opening ports 25, 80, 443, and 987, so that traffic arriving from the Internet using those ports can pass through the firewall to your server running Windows SBS 2008.

Add a Trusted Certificate

Digital certificates are electronic documents that verify the identity of a computer or a user. By default, a server running Windows SBS 2008 creates self-signed certificates for the intranet Web sites it hosts and for its domain controller functions. Self-signed certificates are sufficient for internal functions, because users on the network can trust the authority of their local server. When a client computer first uses one of these internal functions, it automatically applies for and receives a certificate from the server, a process called *autoenrollment*. The process is invisible to the users on the network, but they can open the Certificates snap-in on their computers and look at the certificates they have received.

However, Internet users are not logged on to the AD DS domain, so they cannot obtain certificates using autoenrollment. When a remote user on the Internet connects to a Windows SBS 2008 resource on your network, such as the Remote Web Workplace Web site, the browser displays an error message, as shown in Figure 4-8. This message appears because the Web server has generated its own certificate, and on the Internet, a computer that verifies its own identity is not trustworthy.

FIGURE 4-8 A certificate error in a Web browser

For users conscious of this situation, clicking the Continue To This Website (Not Recommended) link presents no danger, but to eliminate the error message, the server must have a certificate issued by a third party that both the clients and the server trust. The third party is typically a commercial CA that is in the business of confirming the identities of clients and issuing certificates attesting to that identity.

MORE INFO You can also eliminate the error message by deploying your server's self-signed certificate on the remote computer. For more information, see Chapter 12, "Optimizing Network Security."

The Getting Started Tasks page provides an Add A Trusted Certificate Wizard that simplifies the enrolling for and installing of a third-party certificate. To run the wizard, use the following procedure:

1. Log on to your Windows SBS 2008 primary server, using an account with network Administrator privileges. The Windows SBS Console window appears.

2. On the Home page of the Windows SBS Console, click Add A Trusted Certificate. The Add A Trusted Certificate Wizard appears, displaying the Before You Begin page, as shown here.

3. Click Next. The Get The Certificate page appears, as shown here.

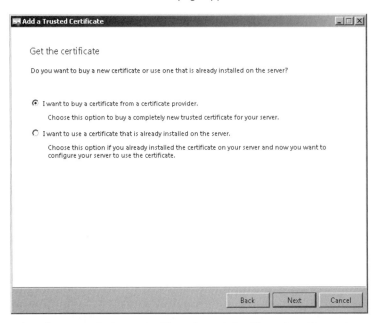

4. Select the I Want To Buy A Certificate From A Certificate Provider option and click Next. The Verify The Information For Your Trusted Certificate page appears, as shown here, containing the name of your *remote* site and the company and address information you supplied during the Windows SBS 2008 installation.

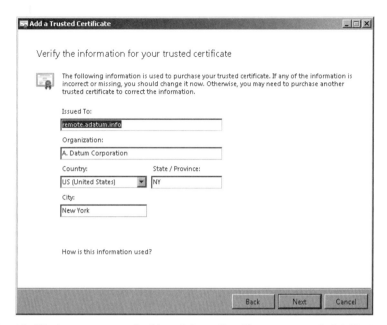

5. Modify the company and address information, if necessary, and click Next. The Generate A Certificate Request page appears, as shown here.

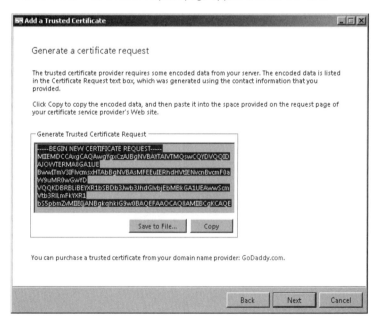

NOTE If your domain name registrar can also supply certificates, the wizard displays a link to its site. However, you can use any provider you want to obtain your certificate.

6. Click Copy to copy the certificate request to the clipboard or click Save To File to save the request as a file on your local drive.

7. Click Next. The A Request Is In Progress page appears, as shown here.

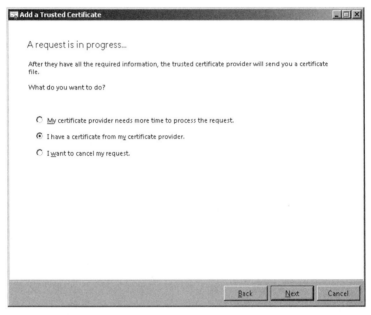

8. Open the Web site of the certificate provider that you want to use and submit your request by pasting the contents of the clipboard into the appropriate form or uploading the request file that you saved. After you pay a fee and supply the correct information, the provider issues a certificate, either as text you can copy to the Clipboard or as a file you can download.

9. Return to the Add A Trusted Certificate Wizard, make sure that the I Have A Certificate From My Certificate Provider option is selected, and click Next. The Import The Trusted Certificate page appears, as shown here.

Add a Trusted Certificate

Import the trusted certificate

If you receive encoded text from your certificate provider, paste the encoded text into the message box, and then click Next. If you receive a file from your certificate provider, click Browse to locate the file, and then click Next.

You may not use both methods to import your trusted certificate.

Trusted Certificate

Paste the encoded text from your certificate provider

Select the certificate file from your certificate provider

Browse...

Back   Next   Cancel

10. In the Trusted Certificate box, either paste the text that you copied from the certificate provider's site or click Browse to select the file that you downloaded, and then click Next. The The Trusted Certificate Is Imported Successfully page appears.

11. Click Finish. The wizard closes.

Configure Server Backup

The Getting Started Tasks list contains a link to the Configure Server Backup Wizard, which you can also access from the Backup And Server Storage page of the Windows SBS Console. For information on performing backups and restores on your server running Windows SBS 2008, see Chapter 13, "Backing Up and Restoring."

Adding Users and Computers

To connect workstations to your network, you must create user accounts and join the computers to your AD DS domain. The Add A New User Account Wizard in the Getting Started Tasks list is also accessible from the Users And Groups page in the Windows SBS Console. The Connect Computers To Your Network Wizard is also accessible from the Network page. For information on using these wizards, see Chapter 5.

Performing Post-Migration Tasks

When you perform a migration installation of Windows SBS 2008, your new server joins the existing AD DS domain and the setup program promotes it to a domain controller. Normally, Windows SBS does not permit more than one domain controller on the network, but for a 21-day period after the migration installation, your new server and your old one can coexist. During that time, you must complete the migration process by performing the tasks in the Migration Wizard. Once you have completed those tasks, the new server is ready to take over as the network's sole domain controller. You can then demote your old server and remove it from the network.

The following sections examine the various tasks involved in completing a migration from an earlier version of Windows SBS.

Reconfiguring Folder Redirection

Folder redirection is a Microsoft Windows feature that enables workstations in an AD DS environment to store the contents of certain folders, such as a user's Documents folder, on a server instead of the local disk. In a network environment, storing data files and other critical folders on server drives rather than local ones is generally preferable because it enables users to access their files from any computer and it enables administrators to back up the files more easily.

To use folder redirection, you configure Group Policy settings that specify where each workstation should store the contents of specific folders. These Group Policy settings are part of the AD DS database and are therefore copied to your new server as part of the Windows SBS migration process. However, while the migration installation process copies the settings themselves to the new server, it does not modify those settings; they still specify the old server's disk as the location for the redirected folders.

If you have been using folder redirection on your existing network running Windows SBS 2003, you must reconfigure it by performing the following steps:

1. Modify the migrated Group Policy settings to point to your new server instead of the old one.
2. Migrate the user and group accounts (using the Migration Wizard).
3. Enable folder redirection on your server running Windows SBS 2008 using the Windows SBS Console.

MORE INFO   For instructions on how to modify the migrated Group Policy settings and enable folder redirection in Windows SBS 2008, see Chapter 7, "Managing Storage."

These steps ensure that all the redirected data from your existing server running Windows SBS gets migrated to your new server running Windows SBS 2008, and that the required Group Policy settings are in place to ensure the future redirection of the desired folders.

Running the Migration Wizard

Performing a Windows SBS 2008 installation in migration mode, as described in Chapter 3, causes an extra Migrate To Windows SBS item to appears in the Getting Started Tasks list, as shown in Figure 4-9. Clicking this link starts the Migrate To Windows Small Business Server 2008 Wizard, which guides you through a series of tasks that completes the migration process.

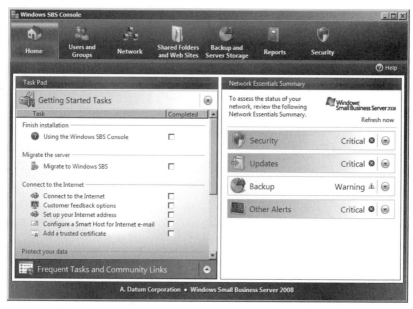

FIGURE 4-9 The Windows SBS Console, after a migration installation

When you click the Migrate To Windows SBS link, the Migration Wizard Home page appears, as shown in Figure 4-10. The Migrate To Windows Small Business Server 2008 Wizard is essentially a shell that provides access to information and links to other wizards and tracks your progress through the list of tasks. Some of the tasks are optional, and others are required. You must complete the tasks in the order given, although you do not have to perform them all in one session. As mentioned previously, you have 21 days to work your way through the list, skipping optional tasks, if desired, and completing the required ones.

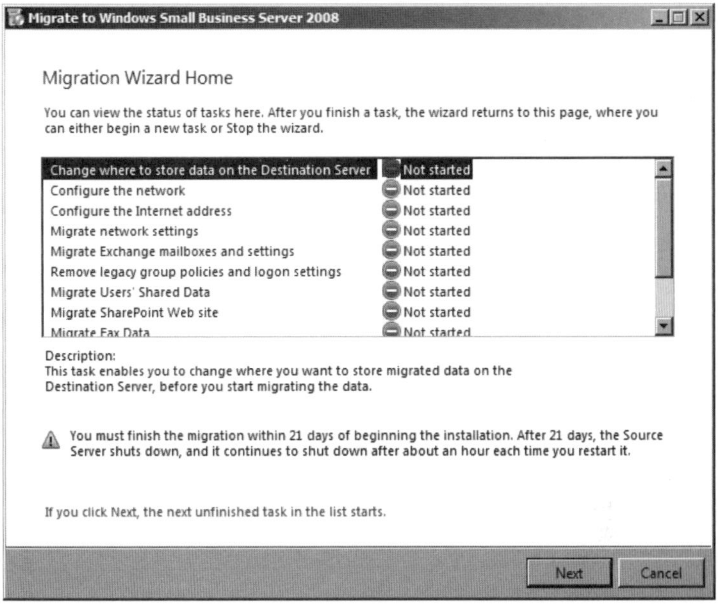
Migrate to Windows Small Business Server 2008
Migration Wizard Home
You can view the status of tasks here. After you finish a task, the wizard returns to this page, where you can either begin a new task or Stop the wizard.
Change where to store data on the Destination Server
Not started
Configure the network
Not started
Configure the Internet address
Not started
Migrate network settings
Not started
Migrate Exchange mailboxes and settings
Not started
Remove legacy group policies and logon settings
Not started
Migrate Users' Shared Data
Not started
Migrate SharePoint Web site
Not started
Migrate Fax Data
Not started
Description:
This task enables you to change where you want to store migrated data on the Destination Server, before you start migrating the data.
You must finish the migration within 21 days of beginning the installation. After 21 days, the Source Server shuts down, and it continues to shut down after about an hour each time you restart it.
If you click Next, the next unfinished task in the list starts.
Next
Cancel

FIGURE 4-10 The Migration Wizard Home page, in the Migrate To Windows Small Business Server 2008 Wizard

As you access each task in the list, an initial wizard page appears that explains what you must do and provides links to help pages, other wizards, or both. This page also contains option buttons that enable you to specify the current status of the task as Task In Progress, Task Complete, or Skip Task (for optional procedures). As you complete each task, you designate it as such, and the wizard allows you to proceed to the next one. You can cancel out of the wizard at any time, and your status indicators remain in place, so that the next time you start the wizard, you resume where you left off.

The following sections examine the various tasks in the Migrate To Windows Small Business Server 2008 Wizard.

Change Where To Store Data On The Destination Server Page

The optional Change Where To Store Data On The Destination Server Page task enables you to specify alternatives to the default data file locations on your server. By default, Windows SBS 2008 stores all its data files on the system drive because it is likely to be the only one available during the installation process. However, if you have other hard disks on the computer, you might want to store your data files on a different drive to distribute the input/output (I/O) load among the storage devices.

When you perform the Change Where To Store Data On The Destination Server task, a page appears containing links to individual wizards that enable you to specify locations for the various types of data files, as shown in Figure 4-11. By changing the locations before you migrate the data from your old server, you avoid having to allocate space for the data on the system drive and move it to another location later.

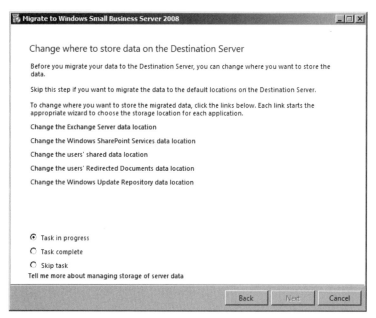

FIGURE 4-11 The Change Where To Store Data On The Destination Server page in the Migration Wizard

To store data files on a different volume, you must create the volume before you run the individual wizards. You might have created simple volumes on other disks during the Windows SBS 2008 installation process, but if you intend to use the other volume types that Windows SBS 2008 supports (such as striped, spanned, or RAID-5), or if you intend to use a third-party redundant array of independent disks (RAID) solution, you must create the volumes now, using the Disk Management snap-in for MMC or some other tool.

MORE INFO For more information on creating and working with disk volumes, see Chapter 7.

Set Up The Network

The Configure The Network task displays a page, shown in Figure 4-12, containing a link to the same Connect To The Internet Wizard that you can access from the Getting Started Tasks list. As in a new Windows SBS 2008 installation, you must run this wizard to configure your server's TCP/IP client and DHCP Server.

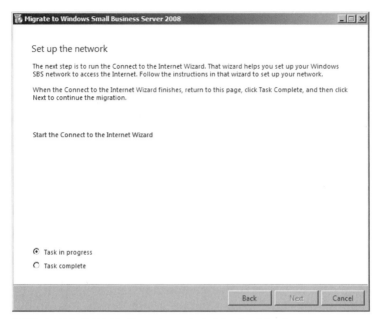

FIGURE 4-12 The Set Up The Network page in the Migration Wizard

> **MORE INFO** For information on running the Connect To The Internet Wizard, see the section entitled "Connecting to the Internet," earlier in this chapter.

Configure The Internet Address

Clicking Configure The Internet Address task displays a page that includes a link to the Internet Address Management Wizard that you ran earlier in this chapter. The page also has a link to a help page providing information on how to distribute the server's self-signed certificates to remote users.

> **MORE INFO** For information on running the Internet Address Management Wizard, see the section entitled "Set Up Your Internet Address," earlier in this chapter.

Migrate Network Settings

The Migrate Network Settings task displays a page, shown in Figure 4-13, from which you can migrate DNS forwarder settings and the Mobile Users group from your old server running Windows SBS to your new one. Both of these tasks are optional, depending on whether you have configured the DNS server on your existing network to use forwarders and whether you have mobile users on your network.

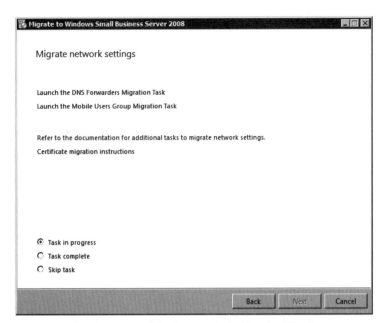

FIGURE 4-13 The Migrate Network Settings page in the Migration Wizard

A *forwarder* is a DNS server that receives name resolution requests from other DNS servers, usually on another network, and takes responsibility for completing the entire name resolution process before returning a response to the original server. For example, you might want to configure the DNS Server service on your server running Windows SBS to forward requests to your ISP's DNS server. This can reduce the amount of your network's Internet bandwidth consumed by DNS traffic. If you have configured your existing Windows SBS 2003 server to use DNS forwarders, clicking the Launch The DNS Forwarders Migration Task link transfers those settings to your new server running Windows SBS 2008.

Migrate Exchange Mailboxes And Settings

If you are running Exchange Server, the required Migrate Exchange Mailboxes And Settings task migrates all the Exchange Server mail stores and public folders from your server running Windows SBS 2003 to your new server running Windows SBS 2008. Depending on how many users that you have on your network and how much mail they have stored, this procedure can take a long time. Clicking the Migrate Exchange Server Mailboxes And Public Folders link on the Migrate Exchange Mailboxes and Settings page, shown in Figure 4-14, displays a help file containing instructions for migrating the various Exchange Server elements.

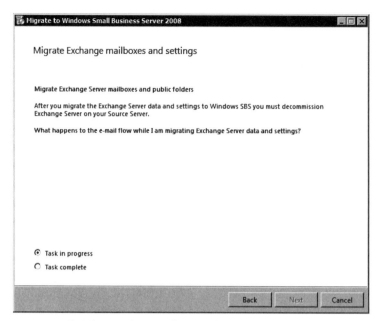

FIGURE 4-14 The Migrate Exchange Mailboxes And Settings page in the Migration Wizard

MORE INFO For more information on migrating Exchange Server elements, see Chapter 9, "Administering E-mail."

Remove Legacy Group Policies And Logon Settings

Windows SBS 2008 uses logon scripts and Group Policy objects (GPOs) that are different from those in Windows SBS 2003. However, the migration process has transferred your existing logon scripts and policy objects to your new server running Windows SBS 2008. Therefore, you must delete them. The Remove Legacy Group Policies And Logon Settings page, shown in Figure 4-15, contains links that display help files with instructions for deleting these elements.

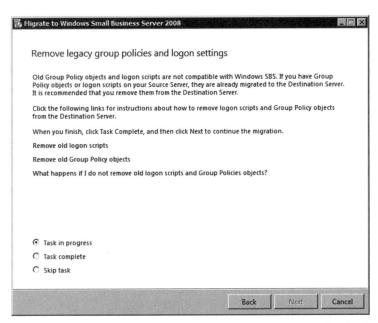

FIGURE 4-15 The Remove Legacy Group Policies And Logon Settings page in the Migration Wizard

REMOVING LEGACY LOGON SCRIPTS

To remove the migrated logon script file from your server running Windows SBS 2008, use the following procedure:

1. Log on to your server running Windows SBS 2008 using an account with network Administrator privileges. The Windows SBS Console window appears.

2. Click Start, and then click Run. The Run dialog box appears.

3. In the Open text box, type **\\localhost\sysvol*domain*.local\scripts**, where *domain* is the name of your domain, and click OK. A Windows Explorer window appears, displaying the contents of the Scripts folder.

4. Delete the SBS_LOGIN_SCRIPT batch file, as shown here.

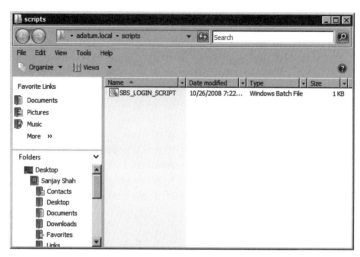

5. Close the Windows Explorer window.

REMOVING LEGACY GPOS

To remove the migrated Group Policy objects from your server running Windows SBS 2008, use the following procedure:

1. Log on to your Windows SBS 2003 server, using an account with network Administrator privileges. The Server Management console appears.

2. Browse to the Advanced Management\Group Policy Management\Forest: *domain*.local\Domains*domain*.local\Group Policy objects folder, where *domain* is the name of your domain.

3. Delete any of the following GPOs that appear in the folder:

- Small Business Server Auditing Policy
- Small Business Server Client Computer
- Small Business Server Domain Password Policy
- Small Business Server Internet Connection Firewall
- Small Business Server Lockout Policy
- Small Business Server Remote Assistance Policy
- Small Business Server Windows Firewall
- Small Business Server Windows Vista Policy
- Update Services Client Computers Policy
- Update Services Common Settings Policy
- Update Services Server Computers Policy

4. Browse to the Advanced Management\Group Policy Management\Forest: *domain*.local\Domains*domain*.local\WMI Filters folder, where *domain* is the name of your domain.

5. Delete the following WMI filters from the folder:
   - PreSP2
   - PostSP2

Migrate Users' Shared Data

Windows SBS 2008 provides no wizard or other automated mechanism for migrating the contents of users' shared folders from the old server to the new one. The Migrate Users' Shared Data page provides a link to a help screen describing the procedures by which you can complete the following basic steps manually:

1. On your new server running Windows SBS 2008, create and share folders corresponding to the shared folders on your old server.

2. Note the permissions on your old server's shared folders and duplicate them on the new shared folders that you created on your server running Windows SBS 2008.

3. Copy the files in the shared folders on your old server to the shared folders you created on your new server.

MORE INFO For more information on creating shares and managing permissions, see Chapter 7.

Migrate SharePoint Web Site

Migrating your existing Microsoft Office SharePoint Server Web site and its database is a complex procedure that is described on a help screen that appears when you click the link on the Migrate Your Internal Web Site page. For more information on this process, see Chapter 11.

Migrate Fax Data

If you have the Windows SBS Fax service installed and running on your Windows SBS 2003 server, the Migrate Fax Data page, shown in Figure 4-16, enables you to transfer the existing fax data from your old server to your new one. You can transfer the data to the default folders for the Fax service or to your SharePoint Server database.

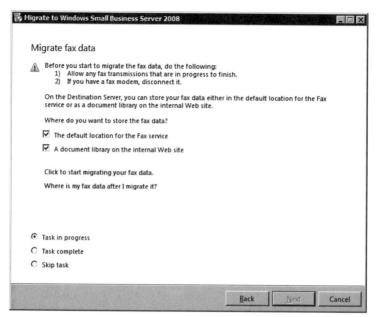

FIGURE 4-16 The Migrate Fax Data page in the Migration Wizard

To migrate your fax data, wait for any fax transmissions currently in progress to finish and unplug your fax modem or modems. Then select the Click To Start Migrating Your Fax Data link to begin the transfer.

Migrate Users And Groups

The Migrate Users And Groups task in the Migration Wizard is something of a misnomer because the users and groups that you created on your Windows SBS R2 server are actually AD DS objects, and the migration installation process has already copied those objects to your server running Windows SBS 2008. However, those users and groups do not appear on the Users And Groups page of the Windows SBS Console. The purpose of this task is to modify the users and groups so you can manage them with Windows SBS tools.

> **TIP** Although migrated users and groups do not appear in the Windows SBS Console by default, they do appear in the standard Windows Server 2008 tools, such as Active Directory Users And Computers.

MIGRATING GROUPS

The Migrate Groups page contains a link to a help screen that describes the procedure for modifying the group attributes. To modify your group objects, use the following procedure:

1. Log on to your server running Windows SBS 2008, using an account with network Administrator privileges.

2. Click Start. Then click Administrative Tools, ADSI Edit. Click Continue in the User Account Control dialog box, and the ADSI Edit console appears.

3. Right-click the ADSI Edit node and, from the context menu, select Connect To. The Connection Settings dialog box appears.

4. Click OK to accept the default settings. A Default Naming Context node for your server appears.

5. Expand the Default Naming Context node and browse to the *domain*\ MyBusiness\Security Groups folder, as shown here (where *domain* is the name of your domain).

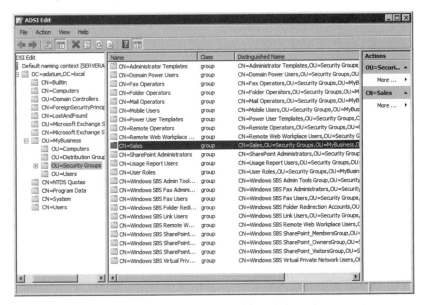

6. Right-click the first group that you want to modify and, from the context menu, select Properties. The Properties sheet for the group appears, as shown here.

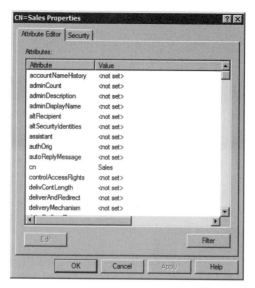

7. On the Attribute Editor tab, select the msSBSCreationState attribute and click Edit. The String Attribute Editor dialog box appears, as shown here.

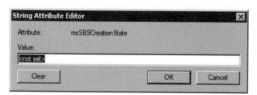

8. In the Value field, type *Created* and click OK.

9. Select the groupType attribute and click Edit. The Integer Attribute Editor dialog box appears, as shown here.

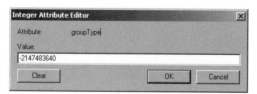

10. In the Value field, type **-2147483640** for a security group or **8** for a distribution group, and then click OK.

11. Click OK to close the Properties sheet.

12. Repeat steps 6 to 11 for each additional group you want to modify.

13. Close the ADSI Edit console.

MIGRATING USER ACCOUNTS

When you click Next on the Migrate Groups page, the Migrate User Accounts page appears. To modify your migrated user accounts, you must assign user roles to them. To do this, perform the following steps:

1. On the Migrate User Accounts page, click Run The Change User Role Wizard. The Change A User Role Wizard appears, displaying the Select A New User Role page, as shown here.

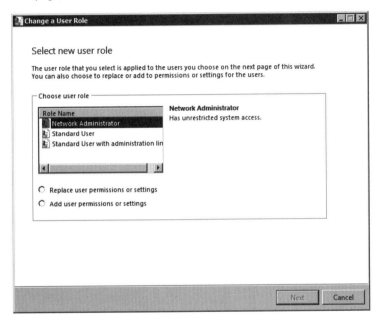

2. Select the role that you want to assign to your users.
3. Specify whether you want to replace or add the user permissions assigned to the role and click Next. The Select User Accounts page appears, as shown here.

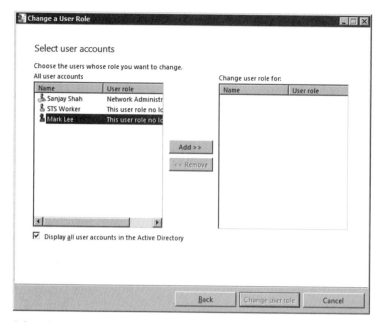

4. Select the user accounts that you want to modify and click Add. The users appear in the Change User Role For list.

5. Click Change User Role. The wizard changes the user roles, and the User Role Has Been Changed Successfully page appears.

6. Click Finish. The wizard closes.

> **TIP** Computer objects that you natively joined to the domain using your server running Windows SBS 2003 also do not appear in the Windows SBS Console. To manage these objects, you must use the Active Directory Users And Computers console to move them to the *domain*.local\MyBusiness\Computers\SBSComputers organizational unit.

Finish Migration

The final task in the Migration Wizard first gives you an opportunity to return to any of the previous tasks you have skipped, as shown in Figure 4-17. If you select the Finish The Migration option, or if all the previous tasks show a status of Completed, the Finish The Migration page appears, which leads you through the process of demoting your server running Windows SBS 2003, so that it no longer functions as an AD DS domain controller.

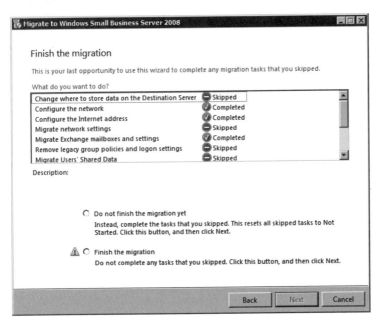

FIGURE 4-17 The Finish The Migration page in the Migration Wizard

IMPORTANT Before you demote the server running Windows SBS 2003, however, you must uninstall Exchange Server 2003 using Add Or Remove Programs in Control Panel, to remove all vestiges of it from the AD DS database.

To demote your computer running Windows SBS 2003, use the following procedure:

1. Log on to your server running Windows SBS 2003 using an account with network Administrator privileges.

2. Click Start, and then click Run. The Run dialog box appears.

3. In the Open text box, type **dcpromo** and click OK. The Active Directory Installation Wizard appears, displaying the Welcome page.

4. Click Next. An Active Directory Installation Wizard message box appears, warning about the server's Global Catalog status.

   NOTE Because your new server is functioning as a Global Catalog server, you can safely demote the server running Windows SBS 2003, despite this warning.

5. Click OK. The Remove Active Directory page appears, as shown here.

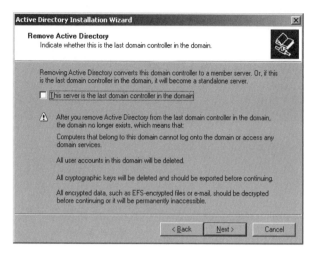

Active Directory Installation Wizard

Remove Active Directory
Indicate whether this is the last domain controller in the domain.

Removing Active Directory converts this domain controller to a member server. Or, if this is the last domain controller in the domain, it will become a standalone server.

☐ This server is the last domain controller in the domain

⚠ After you remove Active Directory from the last domain controller in the domain, the domain no longer exists, which means that:

Computers that belong to this domain cannot log onto the domain or access any domain services.

All user accounts in this domain will be deleted.

All cryptographic keys will be deleted and should be exported before continuing.

All encrypted data, such as EFS-encrypted files or e-mail, should be decrypted before continuing or it will be permanently inaccessible.

[< Back] [Next >] [Cancel]

6. Click Next to continue. (Do not select the This Server Is The Last Domain Controller In The Domain check box.) The Administrator Password page appears.

7. Type a strong password in the New Administrator Password and Confirm Password text boxes. Then click Next. The Summary page appears.

8. Click Next. The wizard demotes the server and the Completing The Active Directory Installation Wizard page appears.

9. Click Finish. An Active Directory Installation Wizard message box appears, prompting you to restart the computer.

10. Click Restart Now. The computer restarts.

MORE INFO Although you are removing the server running Windows SBS 2003 from your network, you cannot simply shut it down or reformat its drives. The AD DS database that you migrated to your new server running Windows SBS 2008 still contains references to the old server, and you must remove them by uninstalling Exchange Server and demoting the old server before you can physically remove it from the network.

The Windows SBS 2003 server is now no longer a domain controller; it is a member server in your domain. To remove the server from the domain completely, you must make it a member of a workgroup using the following procedure:

1. Log on to your server running Windows SBS 2003 using an account with network Administrator privileges.

2. Click Start. Then click Control Panel, System. The System Properties dialog box appears.

3. Select the Computer Name tab, and then click Change. The Computer Name Changes dialog box appears.

4. Select the Workgroup option, and then type a workgroup name in the text box and click OK.

5. A Computer Name Changes dialog box appears, prompting you for credentials to remove the computer from the domain.

6. In the User Name and Password text boxes, type the credentials for an administrative account in your domain. Then click OK.

7. A message box appears, welcoming you to the workgroup that you specified.

8. Click OK. A message box appears, informing you that you must restart the computer for the changes to take effect.

9. Click OK. Then click OK again to close the System Properties dialog box. A System Settings Change message box appears, prompting you to restart the computer.

10. Click Yes. The computer restarts.

Finally, you must remove the computer object from the AD DS database using the following procedure:

1. Log on to your server running Windows SBS 2008 using an account with network Administrator privileges.

2. Click Start. Then click Administrative Tools, Active Directory Users And Computers. The Active Directory Users And Computers console appears.

3. Browse to the *domain*.local\MyBusiness\Computers\SBSComputers container.

4. Delete the object representing your computer running Windows SBS 2003.

5. Close the Active Directory Users And Computers console.

Repurposing the Migrated Server

Once you have completed the migration process, you can use the server running Windows SBS 2003 for another purpose, such as a computer running Microsoft SQL Server, if you purchased Windows SBS 2008 Premium Edition, or as a file and print server. However, it is strongly recommended that you do not use the server in its post-migration state without reinstalling an operating system, as it might be left in an unstable condition.

CHAPTER 5

Working with Users, Computers, and Groups

W ith your Microsoft Windows Small Business Server (SBS) 2008 server installation and configuration all but complete, it is time to start thinking about the
other computers on your network, the workstations, and their users. To connect
workstations to your Windows SBS network, you must create accounts for your
users and then join the computers to your domain.

An Active Directory Primer

Active Directory Domain Services (AS DS) is a key element of the Windows SBS
2008 infrastructure, one that provides centralized authentication and authorization
services for the entire network. It is important for Windows SBS administrators
to understand the basic architecture of AD DS, although in most cases, it is not
necessary to delve into its vast complexities.

AD DS Functions

AD DS is, at its heart, a *directory service*, that is, a database that functions as a
repository for information about your network. When Windows SBS network users
sit down at their workstations and log on, they are logging on to the directory
service, not to the individual workstations themselves. Their user accounts and
passwords are stored in AD DS, and the directory service grants them access to the
network.

Two of the primary functions performed by AD DS are authentication and authorization. *Authentication* is the process by which a system verifies a user's identity. Computers can authenticate a user's identify by requiring that the user supply any or all of the following:

- Something the user knows, such as a password
- Something the user possesses, such as a smart card
- Something physical about the user, such as a fingerprint

Authentication protocols, such as *Kerberos*, enable these processes to occur without endangering passwords by transmitting them over the network. *Authorization* is the process by which a system grants a user access to specific resources. Once AD DS has authenticated a user, it can grant access to network resources by associating the user's verified identity with the access control system built into the resource. For example, every file on the NTFS disks in your Windows SBS 2008 servers and workstations has a list of the users who are permitted access to that file.

Without AD DS, users would require separate accounts and passwords on every computer they need to access. Imagine how arduous your role as an administrator would be if, each time a new employee joined the company, you had to create 10 or 20 separate user accounts for the same person, on 10 or 20 different computers. Imagine having to modify 10 or 20 separate accounts each time a user is required to change his or her password (which, for security reasons, should be pretty frequently). AD DS uses one user account and password for all network resources, greatly simplifying the administration process.

Domains and Domain Controllers

In AD DS, the fundamental administrative unit is the domain. An *AD DS domain* is a logical grouping of computers, users, and other network resources. By grouping elements into domains, administrators can create policies and assign them to all or part of a network at once.

AD DS is a highly flexible directory service that is sufficiently scalable to support networks of almost any size. A large enterprise network can consist of multiple domains, grouped in a hierarchical structure called a *domain tree*, and can even have multiple domain trees grouped in a structure called a *forest*. However, Windows SBS 2008 supports the use of only a single domain, which is more than sufficient to support the maximum of 75 workstations you can connect to the network.

One of the most complex parts of a large-scale AD DS deployment is designing the AD DS tree structure. Administrators of large networks must often devote a great deal of time and effort to creating a domain hierarchy that adequately represents their organizations. With Windows SBS 2008, however, there is no need for this effort. All you have to do is supply a name for your domain, and the Windows SBS setup program installs AD DS, creates the domain, and configures your server to support it.

A Microsoft Windows server with AD DS installed and configured is called a *domain controller*. The domain controller contains a copy of the AD DS database, as well as the various applications and services that enable AD DS to function. When a user logs on to the domain, it is the domain controller that authenticates the user's identity. When a user on a Windows SBS workstation accesses a server disk, the domain controller (which, in this case, is the same computer) authenticates the user's identity and authorizes access to the files that the user requests. Even when a user accesses resources on another workstation instead of a server, the domain controller is involved in the authentication and authorization processes. The computers on the network, therefore, require continual access to the domain controller.

Larger networks usually have multiple domain controllers for each domain, which replicate information back and forth to keep them all updated and in the same state. Windows SBS 2008, however, supports only one domain and one domain controller. This simplifies the network design and eliminates the need for complex replication systems, but it also makes the continued operation of the Windows SBS domain controller all the more critical. It is strongly recommended that you use fault-tolerance mechanisms, such as an uninterruptible power supply (UPS) and regular server backups, to prevent extended domain controller downtime.

Objects and Attributes

The AD DS database consists of *objects*, which represent specific network resources, both physical and logical. Every computer on your network has an AD DS object that represents it, as do users and groups. Each object consists of a set of *attributes*, which contain information about that object. For example, some of the attributes of a user object are designed to hold the individual's first and last names, address information, and password. When you open the Properties sheet for a user account, as shown in Figure 5-1, the properties that you can modify are actually attributes of the user object. Group objects contain, as an attribute, a list of the other objects that are members of the group.

FIGURE 5-1 The Properties sheet for a Windows SBS 2008 user object

The types of objects that you can create in the AD DS database, and the attributes of each object type, are specified in the *AD DS schema*. Applications can modify the schema to add object types to the AD DS implementation, or add attributes to existing object types. It is also possible for administrators to modify the schema manually, using tools provided with Windows Server 2008. However, the average Windows SBS 2008 administrator should not have reason to do this.

> **CAUTION** Modifying the AD DS schema is similar to modifying a Windows computers registry, in that a minor mistake can have a profound effect on the functionality of the system. Do not make any manual changes to the schema (or to the registry, for that matter), unless you know precisely what you are doing, and why.

In addition to objects that represent network resources, the AD DS has objects that represent logical divisions in the network, which you can use for organizational functions. The domain is such an object, as is a forest. Within a domain, you can also create objects called *organizational units (OUs)*, to subdivide the domain in various ways. Unlike domains, which you can create only by installing a new domain controller, you can create as many OUs as you want, at any time.

OUs are known as *container objects* because other objects can be subordinate to them. You can create user, group, and computer objects in an OU, or even other OUs. Objects that cannot contain other objects, such as user and computer objects, are known as *leaf objects*.

NOTE There are four container objects that appear in every domain by default, called Builtin, Computers, ForeignSecurityPrincipals, and Users. These are not OUs; the name of their object type is container. You cannot create new objects using the container type, but you can create objects, such as OUs, that are containers (in the generic sense).

The default domain for your Windows SBS 2008 network has a number of OUs, in addition to the Domain Controllers OU found in every AD DS domain. The MyBusiness OU has four OUs beneath it, called Computers, Distribution Groups, Security Groups, and Users, as shown in Figure 5-2. The Computers OU has two subordinate OUs of its own, called SBSComputers and SBSServers, and the Users OU has a subordinate OU called SBSUsers.

NOTE Group objects are a special case because while they have a list of other objects that are members of the group as an attribute, they do not contain those objects in the AD DS sense. Groups are therefore not considered container objects, as domains or OUs are.

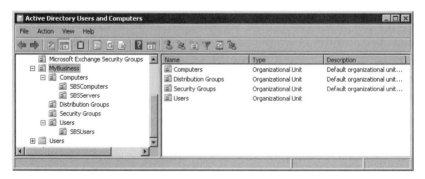

FIGURE 5-2 The default OU hierarchy in a Windows SBS 2008 domain

The function of these OUs is to separate the leaf objects that Windows SBS 2008 creates in your domain by their functions; users go in one OU, computers in another, and so forth. However, you can create OUs using any organizational paradigm you want. Some AD DS domains have OUs representing geographical locations, such as the locations of a company's branch offices, while others organize the domain using OUs named for the company's various departments.

Here again, Windows SBS 2008 has made the AD DS design decisions for you. It includes specialized tools that are based on this default design. To manage AD DS user, group, and computer objects using the Windows SBS Console, the objects must be located in the appropriate OUs. You can conceivably redesign the domain hierarchy by creating your own OUs and moving the objects into them, but you would then have to use the standard Windows Server 2008 tools to manage them instead of the Windows SBS Console. You would also have to reconfigure the default Windows SBS 2008 Group Policy objects (GPOs), which are designed around the default OU hierarchy.

CAUTION It is strongly recommended that you do not modify the default AD DS hierarchy, at least at first, until you fully understand the ramifications of your actions.

Group Policy

One of the most powerful tools in AD DS is Group Policy. *Group Policy* is a feature that enables you to deploy combinations of configuration settings (which are essentially registry settings) to large numbers of users or computers on an AD DS network at once.

To use Group Policy, you create a *Group Policy object (GPO)*, which is a collection of computer and/or user configuration settings packaged as a single unit. You then link the GPO to a domain, OU, or site object in AD DS. Once you do this, every leaf object in the domain, OU, or site to which you linked the GPO receives the configuration settings in it and applies them to the computer or the currently logged-in user.

NOTE You can link Group Policy objects only to domain, OU, or site objects. You cannot link them to individual leaf objects (including groups, strangely enough), nor can you link them to the predefined objects that use the container object type, such as the Computers and Users objects.

For example, you can use Windows Update on an individual computer to configure the Automatic Updates client so that it downloads and installs new operating system updates as they become available. Windows SBS 2008 includes Windows Server Update Services (WSUS), however, which enables your server to supply updates to the client workstations on the network. Rather than make you configure each individual workstation to download updates from the WSUS server, the Windows SBS 2008 setup program creates a GPO called Update Services Client Computers Policy, which contains Windows Update configuration settings, and links it to your domain, as shown in Figure 5-3. As a result, all the computers in the domain receive these settings and configure themselves to use WSUS for their updates.

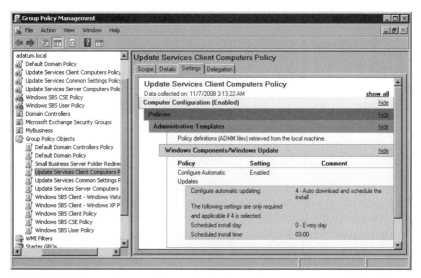

FIGURE 5-3 The Windows Update settings in the Update Services Client Computers Policy GPO

Because the Update Services Client Computers Policy GPO is linked to your domain object, all the computers on your network receive its settings. One of the main reasons for creating OUs, however, is to segregate objects that you want to receive different settings. For example, Windows SBS creates separate SBSComputers and SBSServers OUs in your domain so that it can assign different GPOs to the workstations and server.

Windows SBS 2008 includes a number of GPOs with different functions, which it links to appropriate objects in the default AD DS hierarchy. This is an excellent example of good Group Policy organization. GPOs have hundreds of possible settings, and keeping track of which ones you have deployed in what locations can be difficult. While you can conceivably create a single GPO that contains all the settings you want to deploy to certain users and computers, it is much more efficient, from an organizational standpoint, to create multiple GPOs for specific purposes.

Hierarchy and Inheritance

The use of terms like *tree* and *leaf* in AD DS terminology should give some idea of the directory service's hierarchical architecture. AD DS is based on domains, which you can group into trees and forests, but within each domain, you can build a rootlike structure using OUs. Just as in a file system, influence in a domain flows downwards through the container objects to the individual leaf objects. When you link a GPO to a domain object, the settings in that GPO flow down to all the OUs in the domain and all the leaf objects in the OUs. In the same way, linking a GPO to an OU causes all the leaf objects inside to receive the settings, even objects within subordinate OUs.

You can see one example of how the design of the AD hierarchy is useful to administrators in the default Windows SBS 2008 domain. As mentioned earlier, there is a Computers OU in your domain's MyBusiness OU, and in the Computers OU, there are two more OUs: SBSComputers and SBSServers. Why use three OU levels, though, when you could simply create the SBSComputers and SBSServers OUs directly beneath the MyBusiness OU?

One reason is that adding the level containing the Computers OU enables you to apply Group Policy settings in three different ways. By linking a GPO to the SBSComputers OU or the SBSServers OU, you can apply settings to all the client computers or all the servers in the domain. However, by linking a GPO to the Computers OU, you can apply settings to all the computer objects in the domain at once.

The downward flow of influence in an AD DS domain is not limited to Group Policy settings. AD DS has a system of permissions that define who can access particular objects and what they can do with the objects they access. The AD DS permissions system is completely independent from the other permission systems in Windows Server 2008, such as NTFS and registry permissions, but it works in very much the same way. If you assign permissions to a container object, such as a domain or an OU, then every object in that container inherits those permissions, including other container objects.

Using AD DS Tools

The Windows SBS Console enables you to perform many of the most common AD DS maintenance tasks, although it generally does not identify them as such. Windows SBS 2008 tries to insulate administrators from the complexities of AD DS, but when you create or manage a user or a group in the Windows SBS Console, you are actually creating an AD DS object and modifying its attributes.

Although you might want to stick to the Windows SBS Console when performing administrative tasks at first, you should also be aware of the AD DS tools included with the Windows Server 2008 operating system. These tools provide more comprehensive access to the AD DS and enable you to work with AD DS objects on any Windows Server computer.

> **NOTE** The procedures in this book use Windows SBS 2008 tools whenever possible. However, you can use the Windows Server 2008 tools to perform all the same tasks.

Using Active Directory Users And Computers

Active Directory Users And Computers is the most commonly used AD DS management tool. Like most Windows Server 2008 tools, it is a snap-in for the Microsoft Management Console (MMC) utility. Unlike Windows SBS Console, which displays only certain AD DS objects, Active Directory Users And Computers is based on a tree display of your entire domain, as shown in Figure 5-4.

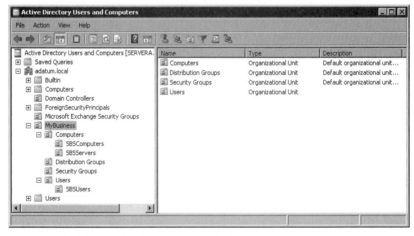

FIGURE 5-4 The Active Directory Users And Computers console

In the Active Directory Users And Computers console, the left pane (also called the *scope pane*) displays your domain and all the container and OU objects beneath it, using an expandable tree arrangement, just like the file system in Windows Explorer. Selecting a container or OU in the scope pane displays all the objects it contains in the right pane (also called the *detail pane*). Double-clicking a leaf object, such as user, computer, or group, opens the Properties sheet for the object, as shown in Figure 5-5.

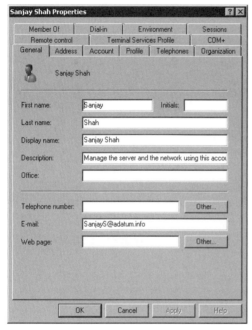

FIGURE 5-5 The Properties sheet for a user object in the Active Directory Users And Computers console

As you can see in Figure 5-5, a user object's Properties sheet in the Active Directory Users And Computers console contains much more information than its Windows SBS Console equivalent, and enables you to modify many more of the object's attributes. This is not the full extent of the console's capabilities, though.

To see even more information about your AD DS domain, you can select Advanced Features from the View menu to display additional objects, as shown in Figure 5-6. Few administrators require access to these advanced features on a regular basis, but it is good to know that they are available.

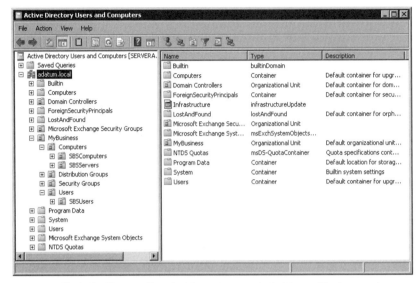

FIGURE 5-6 The Active Directory Users And Computers console, in Advanced Features mode.

The Advanced Features mode also displays additional attributes for each object. The Properties sheet for a user object, for example, has five additional tabs, as shown in Figure 5-7.

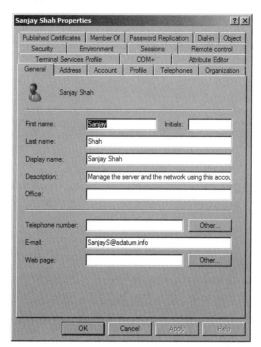

FIGURE 5-7 The Properties sheet for a user object in the Advanced Features mode of the Active Directory Users And Computers console

Using ADSI Edit

For even more complete access to object attributes, you can use the Active Directory Services Interface Editor (ADSI Edit) console, shown in Figure 5-8. This tool provides full access to all the attributes of every object in your AD DS domain, including a great many that the average administrator never has to use.

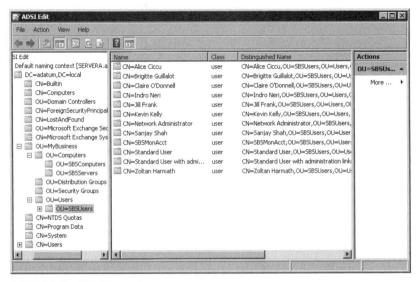

FIGURE 5-8 The ADSI Edit console

Opening the Properties sheet for an object in ADSI Edit displays an interface like that shown in Figure 5-9. Instead of the intuitive controls found in Active Directory Users And Computers, ADSI Edit provides direct access to the attributes and assumes that you are familiar with the correct syntax for the attributes that you intend to modify.

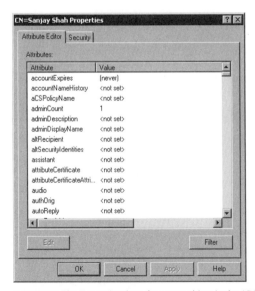

FIGURE 5-9 The Properties sheet for a user object in the ADSI Edit console

Using Group Policy Management

To manage Group Policy settings for your AD DS network, the primary tool is the Group Policy Management console, shown in Figure 5-10. Group Policy Management, like Active Directory Users And Computers, is an MMC snap-in that displays your GPOs, the settings they contain, and the domain, site, and OU objects to which you can link them.

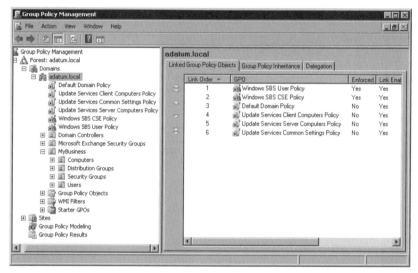

FIGURE 5-10 The Group Policy Management console

The basic functions of the Group Policy Management console are to display information about GPOs and manage the links between GPOs and AD DS objects. To edit the GPOs themselves, you use the Group Policy Management Editor console, shown in Figure 5-11. Each GPO has two main sections, one containing settings that apply to computers and one that applies to users. When a computer on the network starts, it downloads all the GPOs linked to it and applies the Computer Configuration settings. Then, when a user logs on to the domain, the system applies the User Configuration settings.

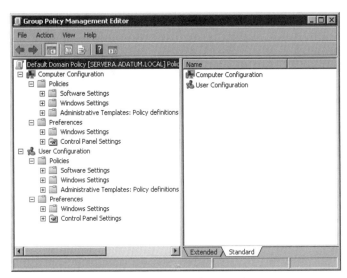

FIGURE 5-11 The Group Policy Management Editor console

Within each of the two sections is a hierarchy of nodes and folders containing hundreds of individual policy settings, as shown in Figure 5-12. You can enable as many or as few policy settings as you want in a particular GPO.

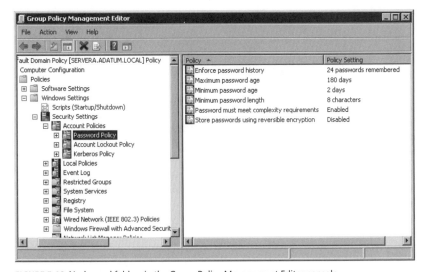

FIGURE 5-12 Nodes and folders in the Group Policy Management Editor console

When you select a Group Policy setting, a Properties sheet appears, as shown in Figure 5-13, containing controls that you use to configure the setting.

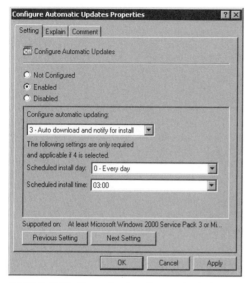

FIGURE 5-13 The Properties sheet for a setting in the Group Policy Management Editor console

NOTE Windows Server 2008 provides several other AD DS management tools, including the Active Directory Domain And Trusts console and the Active Directory Sites And Services console. These tools are intended for use on larger AD DS installations, with multiple domains and sites, and are not needed on Windows SBS 2008 networks.

Working with Users

Before you connect a workstation to the network, you should create user accounts for all the individuals that will be logging on using that workstation. The Windows SBS Console includes a link to the Add A New User Account Wizard in the Getting Started Tasks list, as well as on the Frequent Tasks And Community Links page and on the Users And Groups page. The Users tab on the Users And Groups page also provides controls you can use to manage existing user accounts.

Creating a User Account

To create a new user account in the Windows SBS Console, use the following procedure:

1. Log on to your Windows SBS 2008 primary server using an account with network Administrator privileges. The Windows SBS Console appears.

2. Click Users And Groups, and make sure the Users tab is selected, as shown here.

3. In the User Tasks list, click Add A New User Account. The Add A New User Account Wizard appears, displaying the Add A New User Account And Assign A User Role page, as shown here.

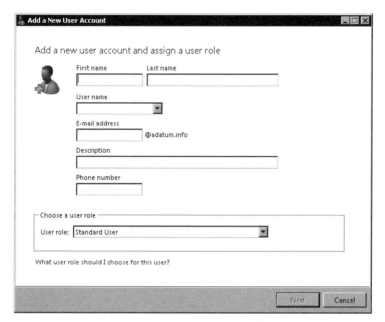

Add a New User Account

Add a new user account and assign a user role

First name   Last name

User name

E-mail address

@adatum.info

Description

Phone number

Choose a user role

User role: Standard User

What user role should I choose for this user?

Next   Cancel

4. In the First Name and Last Name text boxes, type the name of the user that you want to add.

5. In the User Name field, select one of the suggested names from the drop-down list or type a name of your own. The name that you specify appears in the E-mail Address text box.

> **TIP** If you select one of the suggested account names in the drop-down list, the wizard remembers your selection and uses the same naming convention when you create subsequent user accounts.

6. Add information to the Description and Phone Number text boxes, if desired.

7. In the User Role drop-down list, select the role that you want to apply to the account and click Next. The Create A Password For Accessing Your Network page appears, as shown here.

8. In the Password and Confirm Password text boxes, type a password that conforms to the requirements stated on the page.

> **MORE INFO** Windows SBS 2008 uses Group Policy settings to enforce the password length and complexity requirements for domain user accounts. You can modify these requirements by modifying the Password Policy settings in the Default Domain Policy GPO.

> **BEST PRACTICES** In many cases, administrators assign the same temporary password to all user accounts when they create them and then require the users to supply their own passwords after they log on for the first time. However, you can choose to assign a unique password to each user account when you create it and then supply the password to the user.

9. Click Add User Account. The wizard creates the user account and the User Account [User Name] Has Been Successfully Added To The Network page appears, as shown here.

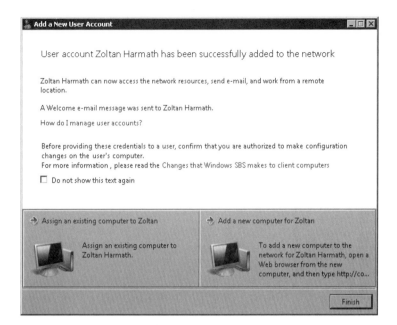

TIP Selecting the Do Not Show This Text Again check box streamlines the user creation process if you do not intend to add or assign a computer after creating each user account. This page also contains links that enable you to assign an existing computer to the user you just created or add a new computer by proceeding directly to the Connect Computers To Your Network Wizard.

10. Click Finish. The wizard closes and the user account appears on the Users And Groups page.

As mentioned earlier, the Add A New User Account Wizard creates a new user object in the AD DS database, but it also performs the following tasks:

- The wizard creates a folder, named for the user, in the C:\Users\Shares folder on the server. This folder appears on the network as *server*\UserShares, where *server* is the name of your server. Everyone has the Allow Full Control share permission for UserShares, and each user has the Full Control NTFS permission to his or her own folder. Users have no NTFS permissions for other users' folders, but the Administrators group has the Allow Full Control permission.

    MORE INFO For more information on share and NTFS permissions, see Chapter 12, "Optimizing Network Security."

- The wizard creates a Microsoft Exchange Server mailbox for the user, with a maximum mailbox size of 2 gigabytes (GB). Outlook Web Access is enabled, as are the Messaging Application Programming Interface (MAPI), Post Office

Protocol version 3 (POP3), and Internet Message Access Protocol (IMAP) client capabilities.

MORE INFO   For more information on Exchange Server and the messaging protocols it supports, see Chapter 9, "Administering E-Mail."

- The wizard sets two storage quotas for the user in the File Server Resource Manager console: a 2-GB soft quota, for the user's Folder Redirections folder, and a 2-GB hard quota for the user's shared folder.

MORE INFO   In File Server Resource Manager, soft quotas merely warn the users when they reach their storage limit, while hard quotas prevent users from exceeding their limits. For more information on using storage quotas, see Chapter 7, "Managing Storage."

- The wizard sends an e-mail to the user's mailbox, welcoming the user to the domain.
- The wizard adds the user account to several of the default groups created by the Windows SBS 2008 setup program. The group memberships are based on the user role you selected when creating the user. Table 5-1 lists the group memberships associated with each of the three default user roles.

TABLE 5-1 Group Memberships of the Windows SBS 2008 Default User Roles

	STANDARD USER	STANDARD USER WITH ADMINISTRATION LINKS	NETWORK ADMINISTRATOR
All Users	•	•	•
Windows SBS Admin Tools Group		•	•
Windows SBS Administrators		•	•
Windows SBS Fax Administrators			•
Windows SBS Fax Users	•	•	•
Windows SBS Link Users	•	•	•
Windows SBS Remote Web Workplace Users	•	•	•
Windows SBS SharePoint_MembersGroup	•	•	•
Windows SBS Virtual Private Network Users			•

Creating Multiple User Accounts

If you have to create a number of user accounts based on the same role, you can run the Add Multiple New User Accounts Wizard using the following procedure:

1. Log on to your Windows SBS 2008 primary server, using an account with network Administrator privileges. The Windows SBS Console appears.

2. Click the Users And Groups button, and make sure the Users tab is selected.

3. In the User Tasks list, click Add Multiple User Accounts. The Add Multiple New User Accounts Wizard appears, displaying the Choose A User Role And Add New User Accounts page, as shown here.

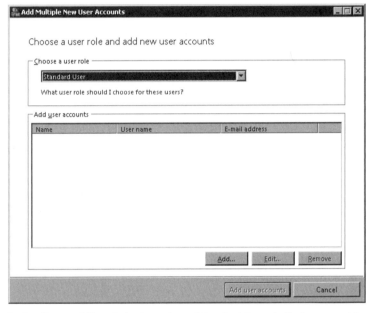

4. In the Choose A User Role drop-down list, select the role that you want to use to create the accounts.

5. In the Add User Accounts box, click Add. An Add Multiple New User Accounts dialog box appears, as shown here.

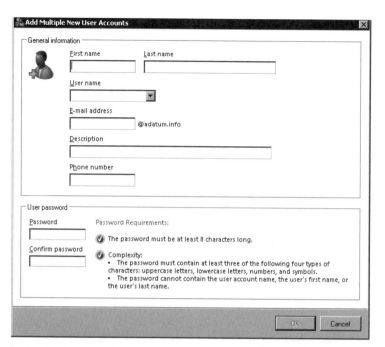

6. In the First Name and Last Name text boxes, type the name of the user that you want to add.

7. In the User Name field, select one of the suggested names from the drop-down list or type a name of your own. The name you specify appears in the E-mail Address text box.

8. Add information to the Description and Phone Number text boxes, if desired.

9. In the Password and Confirm Password text boxes, type a password that conforms to the requirements stated on the page.

10. Click OK. The user appears in the Add User Accounts list.

11. Repeat steps 5 to 10 to add more users to the list.

12. Click Add User Accounts. The wizard creates all the user accounts in the list, and the All New User Accounts Have Been Successfully Added To The Network page appears.

13. Click Finish.

Managing User Properties

Once you have created user accounts, they appear in the Windows SBS Console on the Users And Groups page, on the Users tab. On the right side of the page, the Tasks list is split into two sections: User Tasks, which contains links to general tools, such as the Add A New User Account Wizard, and a second section containing tasks that apply to the currently selected user. These tasks enable you to work with the attributes of the selected user object.

To modify the properties of a user account, use the following procedure.

1. Log on to your Windows SBS 2008 primary server, using an account with network Administrator privileges. The Windows SBS Console appears.

2. Click Users And Groups, and make sure the Users tab is selected.

3. Select one of the user accounts on the page and, in the Tasks list, click Edit User Account Properties. The Properties sheet for the user account appears.

4. Select one of the following pages in the dialog box and use the controls provided to modify the user's properties:

   • General   Contains the basic informational fields, such as name, e-mail address, and phone number, for which you supplied values when you created the user account, as shown here.

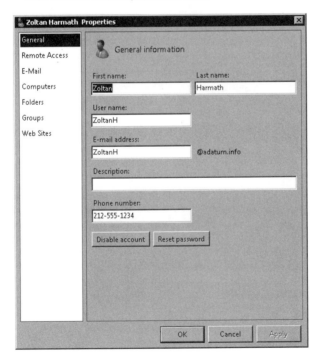

- **Remote Access** Specifies whether the user is permitted to access the network from remote locations using Remote Web Workplace (RWW) and virtual private networking (VPN) connections, as shown here.

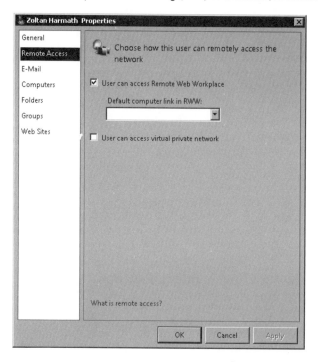

- E-Mail   Specifies whether the user's Exchange Server mailbox should be limited to a maximum size, and if so, specifies that size, as shown here.

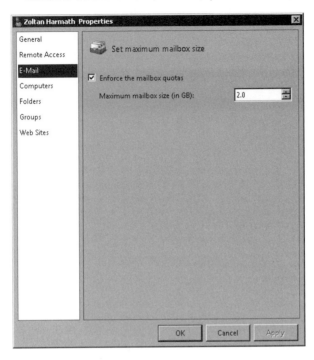

- Computers   Specifies which computers on the network the user is permitted to access, and what level of access the user is granted, as shown here.

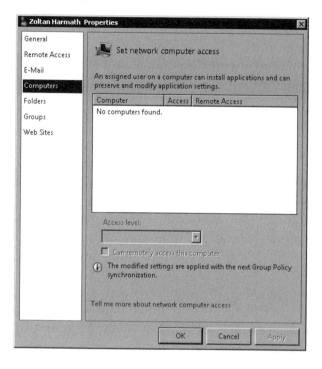

- Folders   Specifies whether the user's shared folder should have a storage quota, and if the user's data folders should be redirected to a server drive. You can also specify the size of the storage quotas for each, as shown here.

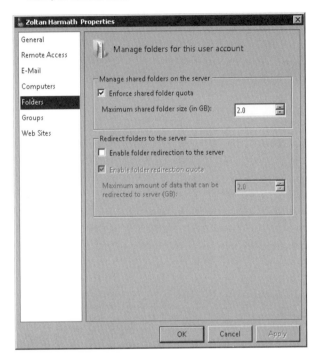

- **Groups** Specifies the groups of which the user is a member, as shown here.

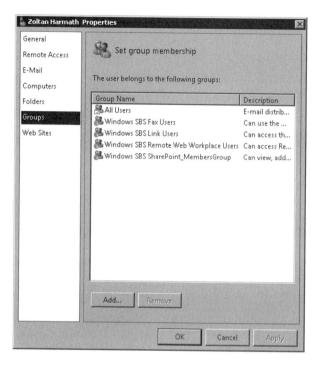

- Web Sites Specifies which of the default Windows SBS 2008 Web sites the user is permitted to access, as shown here.

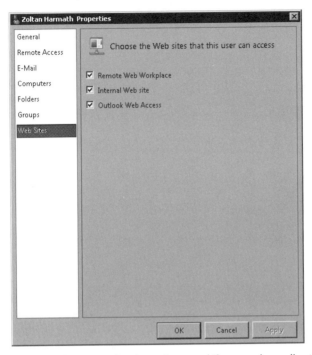

5. Click OK. The Properties sheet closes and the console applies the changes that you have made.

Printing Getting Started Pages

After creating a user account, the next step in deploying a workstation on a Windows SBS 2008 network is to connect the computer to the network. This is a procedure that users can perform themselves, and to simplify the process, Windows SBS 2008 enables you to print out a Getting Started page for each user, providing personalized instructions for logging on and connecting to the server, as shown in Figure 5-14.

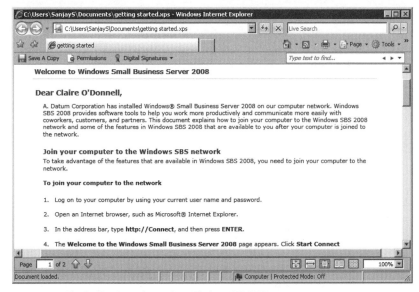

FIGURE 5-14 The Getting Started page for a Windows SBS 2008 user

To print the Getting Started page, select a user account on the Users And Groups page and click Print The Getting Started Page For This User Account. You can then print the document using any of the printers that the computer is configured to use.

Creating User Roles

In Windows SBS 2008, a user role is a set of account property values that function as a template for the creation of new user accounts. Without user roles, you would have to configure all the user properties for each account that you create individually, adding users to multiple groups and specifying which resources they can access, for example. When you run the Add A New User Account Wizard, you select one of the existing user roles as the basis for the new account. Once you actually create the account, you can modify its properties as needed.

Windows SBS 2008 includes three user roles by default, as follows:

- **Standard User**   Provides access to standard network resources, including network shares, printers and faxes, internal Web sites, RWW, and the Internet

- **Standard User with Administration Links**   Same as the Standard User role, with added access to the administration links in RWW and the desktop gadget links

- **Network Administrator**   Provides full access to all system resources

In addition to these three roles, you can create your own customized user roles with the procedures in the following sections.

Creating a New User Role

To create a new user role from scratch, use the following procedure:

1. Log on to your Windows SBS 2008 primary server, using an account with network Administrator privileges. The Windows SBS Console appears.

2. Click Users And Groups, and select the User Roles tab.

3. In the User Role Tasks list, click Add A New User Role. The Add A New User Role Wizard appears, displaying the Specify A Name And Description For The New User Role page, as shown here.

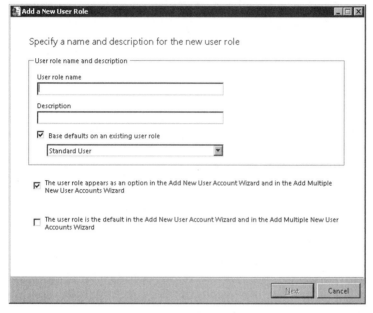

4. In the User Role Name text box, type the name that you want to assign to the role. In the Description text box, type a description of the role's capabilities, if desired.

5. If you want to base your new user role on one of the existing roles, select the Base Defaults On An Existing User Role check box and select the role that you want to use from the drop-down list.

6. Select the The User Role Appears As An Option In The Add New User Account Wizard And In The Add Multiple New User Accounts Wizard check box if you intend to create user accounts based on this role.

7. Select the The User Role Is The Default In The Add New User Account Wizard And In The Add Multiple New User Accounts Wizard check box if you intend to create most or all your user accounts with this role.

8. Click Next. The Choose User Role Permissions (Group Membership) page appears, as shown here.

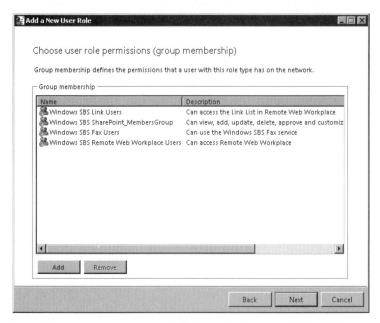

9. To modify the group memberships assigned to the role, click Add. The Choose Security Group Membership dialog box appears, as shown here.

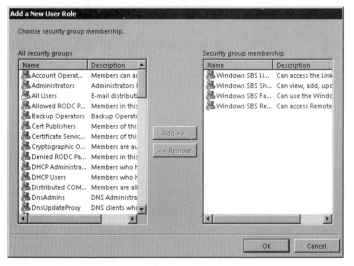

10. Select the groups that you want to assign to the role in the All Security Groups list and click Add. Select the groups that you want to delete from the role in the Security Group Membership list and click Remove. Then click OK.

11. Click Next. The Choose E-mail Settings page appears, as shown here.

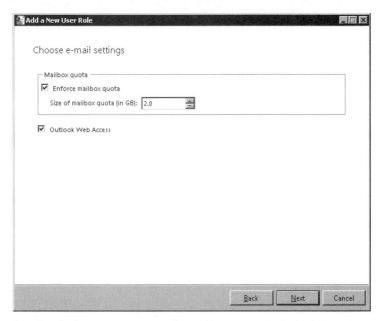

12. Specify whether you want to apply a mailbox quota and whether users should be able to access the Outlook Web Access Web site.

13. Click Next. The Choose Remote Access For This User Role page appears, as shown here.

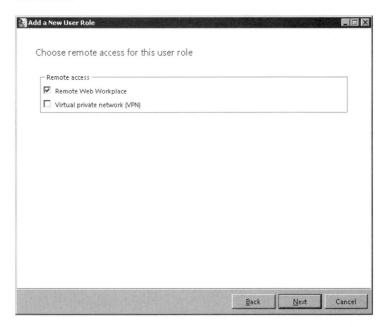

14. Specify whether users should be permitted to access the network using RWW and VPN connections.

15. Click Next. The Choose Shared Folder Access For This User Role page appears, as shown here.

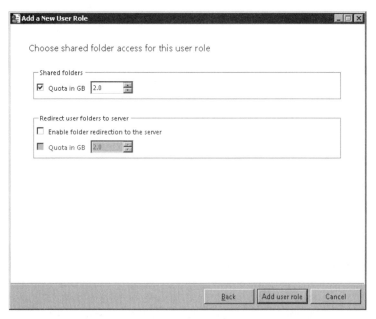

16. Specify whether the user's shared folder should have a storage quota, and if the user's data folders should be redirected to a server drive. You can also specify the size of the storage quotas for each.

17. Click Add User Role. The New User Role Was Added Successfully To The Network page is displayed.

18. Click Finish. The new role appears in the User Roles list.

Creating a User Role from an Existing User

To create a user role based on a user account that you have modified to your requirements, use the following procedure:

1. Log on to your Windows SBS 2008 primary server, using an account with network Administrator privileges. The Windows SBS Console appears.

2. Click Users And Groups, and make sure the Users tab is selected.

3. Select one of the user accounts on the page and, in the Tasks list, click Add A New User Role Based On This User Account's Properties. The Add A New User Role Based On *[User Name's]* Properties dialog box appears, as shown here.

4. In the User Role Name text box, type the name that you want to assign to the role. In the User Role Description text box, type a description of the role's capabilities, if desired.

5. Select the Display This User Role As An Option In The Add User Wizard check box if you intend to create user accounts based on this role.

6. Select the This User Role Displays As The Default Role In The Add A New User Account, Add Multiple New User Accounts Wizards check box if you intend to create all or most of your user accounts with this role.

7. Click OK. The new user role appears on the User Roles tab.

Working with Computers

Windows SBS 2008 includes the operating system for your server (or servers, if you purchased the Premium Edition), but you must purchase the Windows Vista SP1 or Windows XP SP2 operating system for your workstations separately. Once you have installed Windows Vista or Windows XP, you can join your workstations to the network by running the Connect Computer program on them.

> **NOTE** To run successfully, the Connect Computer program requires that you use Windows Vista SP1 or later or Windows XP SP2 or later.

Connecting Computers to the Network

When you click the Connect Computers To Your Network link in the Windows SBS Console's Getting Started Tasks list, a wizard appears that is primarily informational. After a page reminding you that you should create user accounts before you connect computers to the network, the wizard explains that you must run the Connect Computer program on each workstation that you want to connect to the network.

You can deploy the Connect Computer program to your workstations in two ways, as shown in the Connect Computers To Your Network Wizard (see Figure 5-15): by connecting to the Windows SBS 2008 server with Windows Internet Explorer and downloading the program, or by copying the program from the server to a removable medium, such as a USB flash drive, and moving it to the workstation.

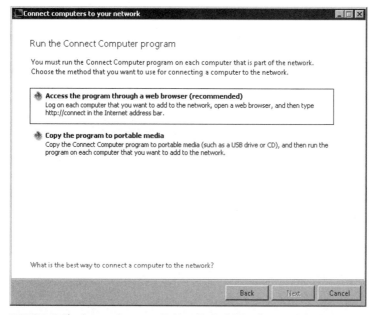

FIGURE 5-15 The Connect Computers To Your Network Wizard

When you select the Access The Program Through A Web Browser (Recommended) option, the wizard displays instructions for connecting to the server from the workstation, the same instructions found in the Getting Started pages for the user. Selecting the Copy The Program To Portable Media option displays the Specify

A Location To Copy The Connect Computer Program page, shown in Figure 5-16, which enables you to copy the Connect Computer program to any storage device recognized by the file system. The total size of the program is only 226 kilobytes (KB); you can therefore use a floppy disk or any USB flash drive. You can also copy the program to a folder on a hard disk and burn it to a CD-ROM.

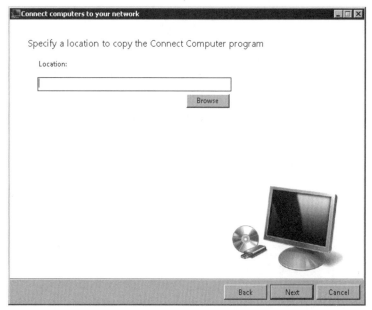

FIGURE 5-16 The Specify A Location To Copy The Connect Computer Program page in the Connect Computers To Your Network Wizard

Running the Connect Computer Program

To run the Connect Computer program on a workstation, use the following procedure:

1. Log on to your workstation using an account with network Administrator privileges.

2. Click Start, and then click Internet Explorer. An Internet Explorer window appears.

3. In the address box, type **http://connect** and press Enter. The Welcome to Windows Small Business Server 2008 page appears, as shown here.

4. Click the Start Computer Connect Program link. A File Download – Security Warning message box appears, asking if you want to run or save the program.

NOTE If you have the Connect Computer program on a removable medium, insert the disk or drive into the computer and run the Launcher.exe program.

5. Click Run. Then click Continue in the User Account Control dialog box. The Connect Computer Wizard appears, displaying the Choose How To Set Up This Computer page, as shown here.

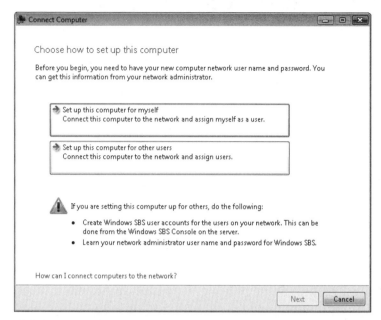

Choose how to set up this computer

Before you begin, you need to have your new computer network user name and password. You can get this information from your network administrator.

→ Set up this computer for myself
Connect this computer to the network and assign myself as a user.

→ Set up this computer for other users
Connect this computer to the network and assign users.

⚠ If you are setting this computer up for others, do the following:

- Create Windows SBS user accounts for the users on your network. This can be done from the Windows SBS Console on the server.
- Learn your network administrator user name and password for Windows SBS.

How can I connect computers to the network?

Next   Cancel

6. Click the Set Up This Computer For Myself option. The Verifying Computer Requirements page appears as the program checks the state of the computer. If the computer meets the requirements, the Computer Requirements Are Verified page appears.

> **NOTE** If the computer does not meet the requirements for running the program, such as if a Windows Vista workstation does not have Service Pack 1 or later installed, the wizard informs you what must be done before it can continue.

7. Click Next. The Type Your New User Name And Password page appears, as shown here.

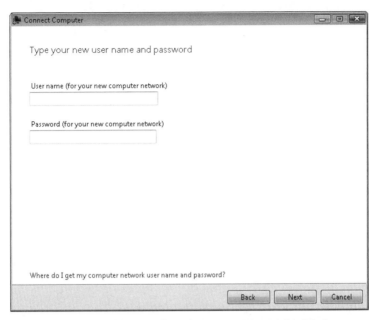

8. In the User Name and Password text boxes, type the credentials for your domain user account and click Next. The Verify Computer Description page appears, as shown here.

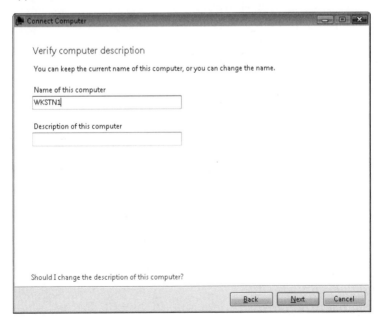

IMPORTANT The user name and password you supply on this page must be for a domain account created using the Windows SBS Console, not the local account created during the workstation installation.

9. The computer's current name appears in the Name Of This Computer text box. You can leave it as is or change the name and add a description, as desired. Then click Next. The Move Existing User Data And Settings page appears, as shown here.

    TIP Computer names can be no more than 15 characters long, are not case sensitive, and can consist only of letters, numbers, and the underscore and hyphen characters.

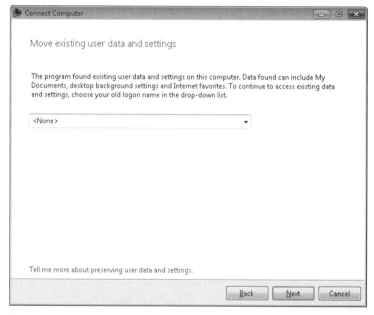

10. If the computer has documents and settings on it that you want to retain, select the local account name from the drop-down list and click Next. The Confirm Your User Data And Settings Selection page appears.

11. Click Next to continue. The Restart The Computer page appears, as shown here.

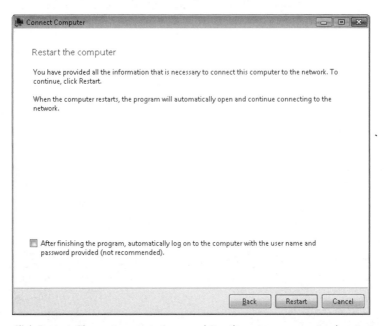

12. Click Restart. The system restarts, completes the setup process, and restarts again.

13. Log on using your domain user account. The Connect Computer Complete page appears.

14. Click Finish. The wizard closes, the computer appears in the Computers list on the Network page of the Windows SBS Console, and the workstation is now ready to use.

The Connect Computer Wizard performs a variety of configuration changes on the workstation, including the following:

- The wizard joins the computer to the AD DS domain, creating a new computer object in the MyBusiness\Computers\SBSComputers OU and adding it to the Domain Computers group.

- The wizard installs the Windows SBS 2008 ClientAgent and Windows Management Instrumentation (WMI) Provider components on the workstation.

- The wizard adds the domain user account to the local Administrators and Remote Desktop Users groups.

- Using Group Policy settings, the wizard configures the Automatic Updates client on the workstation to download new updates from WSUS on the Windows SBS 2008 server and install them automatically every day at 3 A.M.

- The wizard sets the Home page in Internet Explorer to the server's Share-Point Services Web site and adds links for the various Windows SBS 2008 internal Web sites to the Start menu and the Favorites list.

- The wizard opens selected ports in the Windows Firewall configuration to allow the workstation to send and receive the traffic associated with the Windows core networking, file and printer sharing, WMI, Remote Desktop, and Remote Assistance features.

- The wizard installs the Windows Small Business Server Desktop Links gadget, shown in the upper-right corner of Figure 5-17, onto Windows Vista computers. This gadget provides quick access to the user's e-mail account, the server's internal Web site, and the RWW site. However, users must add the gadget manually to the Windows Sidebar.

FIGURE 5-17 The Desktop Links gadget, installed in the Windows Sidebar application on a Windows Vista workstation.

MORE INFO For the procedure describing how to add the Windows Small Business Server Desktop Links gadget to the Windows Sidebar, see Chapter 10, "Working with Web Sites."

Assigning Computers to Users

Although Windows SBS 2008 recommends that you create user accounts for your network users before you connect their workstations, it is possible to assign a new user account to an existing workstation. To do this, you must grant the user account the permissions that it needs to access the computer.

The Windows SBS Console enables you to approach this task by modifying the properties of either the user or the computer. Modifying the user properties enables you to grant a single user access to multiple computers, while modifying the computer's properties enables you to grant access to multiple users.

Modifying a User's Computer Properties

To grant a user access to a computer, use the following procedure:

1. Log on to your Windows SBS 2008 primary server, using an account with network Administrator privileges. The Windows SBS Console appears.

2. Click Users And Groups, and make sure the Users tab is selected.

3. Select one of the user accounts on the page and, in the Tasks list, click Edit User Account Properties. The Properties sheet for the user account appears.

4. Select the Computers tab, as shown here.

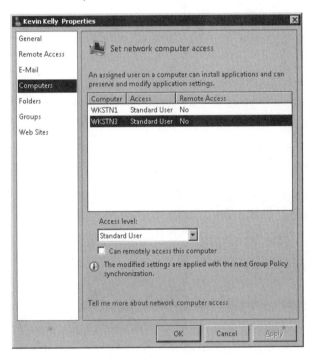

5. Select the computer that you want the user to access.

6. In the Access Level drop-down list, specify which of the following permissions you want the user to have:

   • Standard User   Enables the user to run most of the applications installed on the computer but prevents the user from making changes that can affect other users, including installing or uninstalling most hardware and software components, deleting system and application files, and modifying many configuration settings.

- Local Administrator   Enables the user to make changes that affect other users, such as creating and deleting local user accounts, modifying security settings, and installing and uninstalling hardware and software.

7. Select the Can Remotely Access This Computer check box if you want the user to be able to access the computer using RWW or a VPN connection.

8. Click OK to close the Properties sheet.

To assign a computer to a user immediately after you create the user account, you can also click the Assign An Existing Computer link on the final page of the Add A New User Account Wizard. This displays a stand-alone Assign Computer dialog box that contains the same interface as the Computers tab, as shown in Figure 5-18.

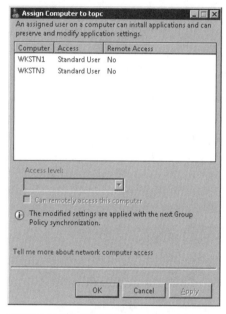

FIGURE 5-18 The Assign Computer dialog box

Modifying a Computer's User Properties

To approach the task from the computer side, use the following procedure:

1. Log on to your Windows SBS 2008 primary server, using an account with network Administrator privileges. The Windows SBS Console appears.

2. Click Network, and make sure the Computers tab is selected.

3. Select one of the computers on the page and, in the Tasks list, click View Computer Properties. The Properties sheet for the computer appears.

4. Select the User Access tab, as shown here.

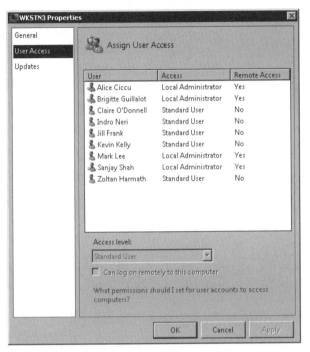

5. Select the user that you want to grant access to the computer.

6. In the Access Level drop-down list, specify which of the following permissions you want the user to have:

- Standard User   Enables the user to run most of the applications installed on the computer, but prevents the user from making changes that can affect other users, including installing or uninstalling most hardware and software components, deleting system and application files, and modifying many configuration settings.

- Local Administrator   Enables the user to make changes that affect other users, such as creating and deleting local user accounts, modifying security settings, and installing and uninstalling hardware and software.

7. Select the Can Log On Remotely To This Computer check box if you want the user to be able to access the computer using RWW or a VPN connection.

8. Click OK to close the Properties sheet.

Working with Groups

Internal security in Windows SBS 2008 is largely based on permissions. Permissions specify what Windows SBS 2008 resources a user is permitted to access and how much access the user receives. By the time you complete your Windows SBS 2008 deployment, the server and workstations have granted your users permissions for hundreds of files, folders, printers, AD DS objects, and registry settings automatically. Assigning permissions is a regular part of a network administrator's job, but fortunately, Windows SBS 2008 simplifies the process by enabling you to assign permissions to groups instead of individual users.

In Windows SBS 2008, a *group* is an AD DS object that functions as a proxy for all the other objects that the group has as its members. When you assign permissions to a group, all the group's members receive those permissions as well. The groups that Windows SBS 2008 creates by default are based on specific network functions and resources. For example, the Windows SBS Remote Web Workplace Users group has the permissions needed for users to access computers on the network using the RWW interface from a remote location. When you grant a user RWW access to a computer, the Windows SBS Console simply has to add the user object to the Windows SBS Remote Web Workplace Users group rather than assign all the necessary permissions to each individual user account.

Group memberships are completely independent of the AD DS hierarchy. You can add objects from any container in the domain to a group. If you choose to expand the AD DS tree by creating your own OUs, you can move user objects to other OUs as needed and they remain members of their groups.

Groups can also have other groups as members, a practice called *group nesting*. When you make one group a member of another group, the permissions you assign to the top-level group flow downwards through the second-level group to its members as well.

> **NOTE** Windows Server 2008 supports three group scopes: domain local, global, and universal. In a stand-alone Windows Server 2008 installation, group nesting is subject to certain limitations, based on the group scopes and other AD DS settings. However, Windows SBS 2008 simplifies the matter. All the groups that Windows SBS 2008 creates by default are universal groups, and any universal group can be a member of any other universal group. When you create groups in the Windows SBS Console, you have no choice but to create universal groups. To create domain local or global groups, you must use the Active Directory Users And Computers console.

Windows SBS 2008 supports two group types, as follows:

- **Security groups**   Administrators use security groups to control access to network resources. Assigning permissions to a security group gives every member of the group all those permissions.

- **Distribution groups**   Distribution groups, which are essentially mailing lists, enable users to send e-mail to all members of the group at once.

Creating a New Group

You can create your own groups to control access to your network resources as needed. For example, you might want to create a group with limited access permissions called New Hires, which you use for individuals that have just joined the company. Instead of having to assign permissions to each new user object, you can simply add the users to the New Hires group. Once a user passes the probationary stage, you can give them greater access by simply moving them to other groups.

To create a new group in the Windows SBS Console, use the following procedure:

1. Log on to your Windows SBS 2008 primary server, using an account with network Administrator privileges. The Windows SBS Console appears.

2. Click Users And Groups, and select the Groups tab, as shown here.

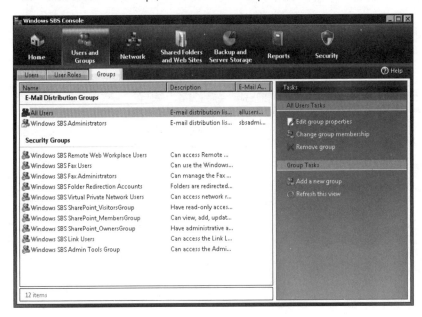

3. In the Tasks list, click Add A New Group. The Add A New Group Wizard appears, displaying the Getting Started page.

4. Click Next to continue. The Add A New Group page appears, as shown here.

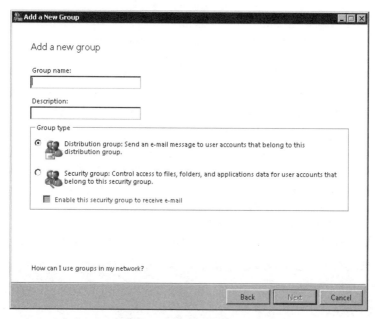

5. In the Group Name text box, type the name that you want to assign to the group. Type some informational text in the Description text box, if desired.

6. Select the type of group that you want to create. If you choose the Security Group option, specify whether you want to be able to send e-mail to the group by selecting the Enable This Security Group To Receive E-mail check box.

7. Click Next. The Select Group Members For New Users page appears, as shown here.

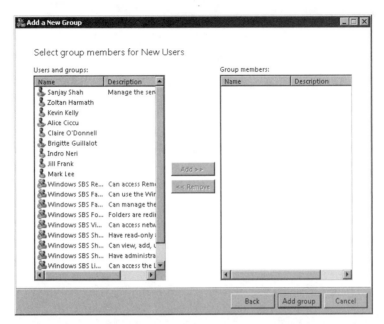

8. In the Users And Groups list, select the users and groups that you want to add as members of the new group and click Add.

9. Click Add Group. The wizard creates the group and the A New Group Has Successfully Been Added To The Network page appears.

10. Click Finish. The wizard closes.

Managing Group Memberships

Once you have created the user and group objects that you need, you can manage your group memberships in two ways: by opening the Properties sheet for a user object and selecting the desired groups, as shown earlier in this chapter, or by opening a group's Properties sheet and selecting the desired users, as shown in Figure 5-19.

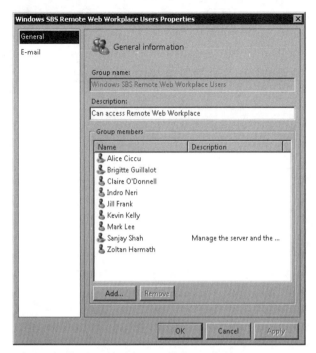

FIGURE 5-19 The General tab in a group's Properties sheet

Deploying Updates

Microsoft releases updates for its operating systems at least once per month, and while some are relatively minor, many of those updates are intended to address important issues. The classifications that Microsoft uses to describe its update releases are as follows:

- **Critical update** A bug fix that addresses a specific problem not related to security.

- **Definition update** An addition to the definition database that a product uses to detect viruses or other malware.

- **Driver** An update to a software component that enables the computer to use a specific hardware device.

- **Feature pack** An update providing new functionality between major product releases.

- **Security update** A bug fix that addresses a specific security-related problem. Security updates are further classified according to their severity— critical, important, moderate, or low.

- **Service pack** A cumulative, tested update package containing all the updates since the product release or the last service pack. Service packs might also include new features.

- **Tool** A new feature designed to perform a specific task or tasks.

- **Update rollup** A cumulative, tested collection of updates for a specific component, such as Windows Internet Explorer, or addressing a specific area, such as security.

- **Update** A bug fix that addresses a specific, noncritical problem not related to security.

Keeping servers and workstations updated is one of the most important jobs of a network administrator, and Microsoft Windows Small Business Server (SBS) 2008 includes features that simplify the process.

Understanding the Update Process

All the current Windows operating systems include an Automatic Updates client, which you can configure to connect to the Microsoft Update servers on the Internet at regular intervals, download the latest operating system updates, and install them, all without user intervention. However, in a network environment, Automatic Updates has several limitations in its default configuration, including the following:

- **Client configuration** In a network environment, configuring and activating the Automatic Updates client on each individual computer is a time- and labor-intensive task. The larger the network, the longer and more difficult the task.

- **Bandwidth utilization** When each computer on the network performs its own separate transactions from the Microsoft Update servers, as shown in Figure 6-1, your Internet connection can become saturated with multiple downloads of the same files. This can consume a great deal of bandwidth and slow down other processes, especially when large updates, such as service packs, are involved.

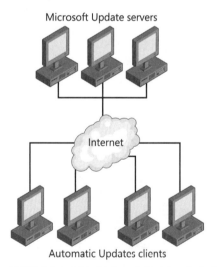

FIGURE 6-1 Individual Automatic Updates clients downloading updates from the Internet

- **Update evaluation** You can configure the Automatic Updates client to download updates and wait for a user to install them, but in a network environment, the decision of whether to install a specific update is never left to the network administrator. In the default configuration, this would be possible only if an administrator traveled to each computer and manually installed the updates.

Fortunately, Windows SBS 2008 includes tools that address all these problems.

Introducing Windows Server Update Services

Windows Server Update Services (WSUS) 3.0 SP1 is a free Microsoft product that enables network administrators to deploy what is essentially a Microsoft Update server on their local networks. When you install it on a server, WSUS downloads all the latest updates from the Microsoft Update servers on the Internet, and then the clients on the network download their updates from the WSUS server. To use WSUS with Windows Server 2008, an administrator must download the WSUS product, install it on a server, configure it to download updates, approve the updates for deployment, and configure the clients on the network to use WSUS. Fortunately for Windows SBS 2008 users, WSUS is incorporated into the product, and the Windows SBS setup program performs all the installation and configuration tasks automatically.

NOTE Windows SBS 2008 uses the simplest possible WSUS architecture, which consists of a single WSUS server that provides updates for all the network clients. However, it is also possible to create more complex WSUS installations for larger networks, in which one WSUS server functions as the source for other WSUS servers.

When you use WSUS, instead of each computer downloading the same files independently, only the WSUS server uses the Internet connection, as shown in Figure 6-2. The WSUS server downloads a copy of each available update and saves it in a local data store, making it available for access by all the computers on the network. Because the WSUS server has to download only one copy of each update, the amount of bandwidth consumed by the update process is reduced drastically. WSUS also provides administrators with the opportunity to research, evaluate, and test updates before deploying them to the network clients.

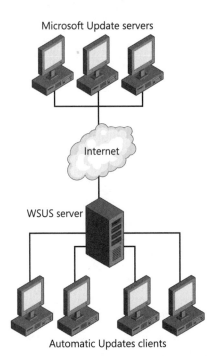

Microsoft Update servers

Internet

WSUS server

Automatic Updates clients

FIGURE 6-2 WSUS downloading a single copy of each update and distributing it to the network

By incorporating WSUS into its default installation, Windows SBS 2008 completes many of the configuration tasks that Windows Server 2008 administrators must perform manually. When the Windows SBS installation is finished, the WSUS server is ready to download a catalog of updates from the Internet, a process called *synchronization*. WSUS then automatically approves certain updates for distribution, downloads them, and prepares to deploy them to the clients on the network. You can also modify the default behavior of WSUS using the Windows SBS Console or the Update Services snap-in for the Microsoft Management Console (MMC). For example, If you want to evaluate or test updates before deploying them, you can configure WSUS to perform the downloads and store them until an administrator approves them for distribution.

Group Policy and Automated Updates

WSUS addresses the problems of bandwidth utilization and update evaluation, but not the client configuration problem. WSUS provides a service that clients can use, but it does not configure the clients to use it. To do this, Windows SBS 2008 uses Group Policy settings to configure the Automatic Updates client on network workstations.

MORE INFO For more information on Group Policy, see Chapter 5, "Working with Users, Computers, and Groups."

During the server installation, the Windows SBS 2008 setup program creates three Group Policy objects (GPOs). These GPOs contain settings that configure the Automatic Updates clients on all the network's servers and workstations to request updates from the WSUS server instead of from the Microsoft Update servers on the Internet.

Understanding the WSUS Default Settings

WSUS is essentially a Web application that uses a Microsoft SQL Server database to store information about the updates that it downloads from the Internet. The Windows SBS 2008 setup program creates a Web site for WSUS and installs the Windows Internal Database feature, which is a limited version of SQL Server included with Windows Server 2008. Clients connect to the server using a Uniform Resource Locator (URL) specified in their Group Policy settings and download all the updates that are approved for their use.

WSUS is a highly configurable application. When you deploy WSUS 3.0 SP1 on a server running Windows Server 2008, you have to run an installation program and then the Windows Server Update Services Configuration Wizard. These two procedures enable you to configure a variety of parameters, including what database to use, where to store the update files, what products and operating systems to update, and when to synchronize with the Microsoft Update servers.

Windows SBS 2008 configures all these options for you, though. Once the installation is completed, the server automatically synchronizes with the Microsoft Update servers, approves new updates, and deploys them to clients. You can reconfigure WSUS to conform to your organization's timetable and other needs, but first you must familiarize yourself with the application's default settings.

- **Synchronization** The setup program configures WSUS to synchronize with the Microsoft Update servers once daily at 10 P.M.
- **Products** By default, WSUS synchronizes updates for all the products that it supports, including server and workstation operating systems; server applications, such as Microsoft Exchange Server and SQL Server; and productivity applications, such as Microsoft Office.
- **Classifications** WSUS synchronizes, by default, all critical updates, definition updates, security updates, service packs, and update rollups. It does not synchronize drivers, feature packs, tools, and noncritical, nonsecurity updates.
- **Languages** WSUS synchronizes only updates in the language that you specified when installing Windows SBS 2008.
- **Approvals** By default, WSUS automatically approves all security, critical, and definition updates for servers. For clients, WSUS approves all security, critical, and definition updates, plus service packs.

- **Storage** WSUS downloads only the approved updates and stores them, in CAB format, in the C:\WSUS\WsusContent folder by default.
- **Server updates** Servers download the latest updates from the WSUS server and inform the administrator that they are ready to install. An administrator must install them manually using the Windows Update control panel.
- **Client updates** Clients connect to the WSUS server and download the latest updates for their respective operating systems, and then install them automatically each day at 3 A.M. If necessary, the Automatic Updates client restarts the computer when the update installations finish.

There is almost nothing you have to do to use WSUS in its default configuration. The server synchronizes itself, approves the most important updates, and downloads them. As you add clients to the network, they receive the Group Policy settings from the server that configure their Automatic Updates clients, causing the computers to download and install new updates as they become available.

Installing Server Updates Manually

The main WSUS-related task that administrators have to perform on a regular basis is to install updates on the servers manually. By default, servers receive Group Policy settings that configure the Automatic Updates client to download updates from the WSUS server but not to install them. There are several reasons for this arrangement.

The servers in a Windows SBS 2008 installation are critical to the operation of the network, and administrators should exercise more care in the maintenance of servers than they do with the maintenance of workstations. Although Microsoft tests updates before releasing them to the public, updates still can cause problems. Windows SBS 2008 administrators should evaluate each update intended for the servers by reading the documentation associated with them, and then decide whether to install them or not. You might also want to test an update on another computer before installing it on your production server or wait to see if other users experience any issues.

Another important factor is that many updates require a system restart before they take effect. The default Automatic Updates configuration permits client workstations to restart themselves if an update requires it. However, this action is not recommended for a server, which might be in the midst of a system backup or other important operation. WSUS therefore requires administrators to install manually any updates that WSUS supplies to them using the following procedure:

1. Log on to a Windows SBS 2008 server, using an account with network Administrator privileges.
2. Click Start. Then click Control Panel. The Control Panel window appears.
3. Double-click Windows Update. The Windows Update window appears, as shown here.

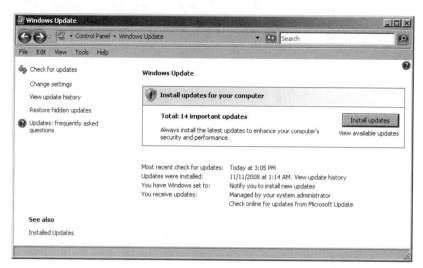

4. Click View Available Updates. The View Available Updates window appears, as shown here.

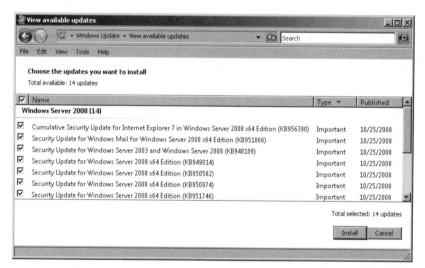

5. Clear the check boxes for the updates that you do not want to install. Then click Install. The Windows Update window reappears and displays the progress as the system installs the updates.

   When the installation is finished, the Windows Update window indicates the outcome of the installation and specifies which updates failed to install, if any, as shown here.

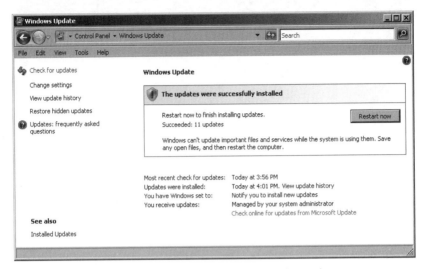

6. Click Restart Now, if the system prompts you to do so. The server restarts.

Monitoring WSUS Activity

The only other task that administrators should perform on a regular basis when running WSUS in its default configuration is to monitor the WSUS activities to make sure that all servers and workstations are receiving the updates they should on a regular basis.

In the Windows SBS Console, the Network Essentials Summary pane on the home page contains an Updates indicator, as shown in Figure 6-3, which displays the current overall status of WSUS operations. An OK status means that all the computers on the network have all the latest updates installed, while a Warning status means that there are updates yet to be installed on all or some of the network's computers.

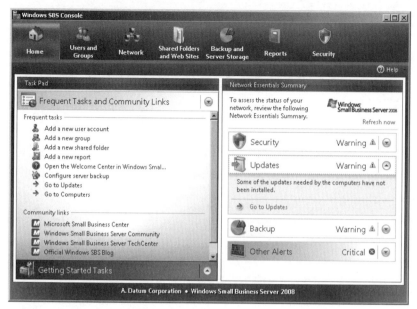

FIGURE 6-3 The Updates indicator in the Network Essentials Summary pane

When you click the Go To Updates link in the Network Essentials Summary pane or click the Security page and select the Updates tab, the display shown in Figure 6-4 appears. The main element on this page is a list of updates in the following four categories:

- **Updates With Microsoft Software License Terms That Are Pending Approval** Updates with special license terms to which you must agree before installing them
- **Updates With Errors** Updates that failed to install correctly on one or more computers
- **Optional Updates** Unapproved updates that are not essential to secure and efficient system operation
- **Updates In Progress** Updates that have been installed on some of the network's computers, but not all of them

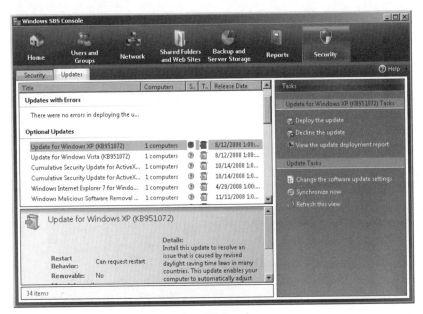

FIGURE 6-4 The Updates page in the Windows SBS Console

When you select an update from any of these four lists, the pane below the list displays information about that specific update, as shown in Figure 6-5, plus a link to the Microsoft Knowledge Base article containing documentation for the update.

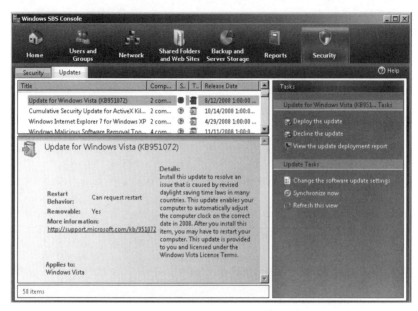

FIGURE 6-5 Update information, as displayed in the Windows SBS Console

When you select an update from the list and click View The Update Deployment Report in the Tasks pane, a Deployment Report window appears, as shown in Figure 6-6. This window provides the status of that update on each of the network's computers.

Computer Name	Status	Last Update Scan
servera	Not applicable	11/14/2008 12:55:56 PM
wkstn3	Not applicable	11/14/2008 12:35:06 PM
wkstn4	Not installed	11/14/2008 12:46:14 PM
wkstn2	Not applicable	11/14/2008 12:47:41 PM
wkstn5	Not installed	11/14/2008 12:38:04 PM

Deployment Report for Update for Windows XP (KB951072)

How do I fix an unsuccessful update?

Close

FIGURE 6-6 An update's Deployment Report window

Notice that the Updates page does not contain a list of the updates that all the computers on the network have installed successfully. The Windows SBS Console is more concerned with informing administrators of conditions that require their attention than providing complete documentation of background activities. However, it is possible to display the installed and missing updates for a specific computer by opening its Properties sheet from the Computers tab of the Network page and clicking Updates, as shown in Figure 6-7.

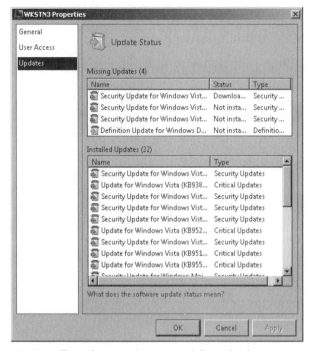

FIGURE 6-7 The Updates page in a computer's Properties sheet

Configuring WSUS Using the Windows SBS Console

Windows SBS 2008 provides a functional WSUS installation by default, but there are many possible reasons why administrators might want to modify those default settings. The following sections examine the various WSUS configuration settings that you can change using the Windows SBS Console, as well as the reasons why you might want to change them.

Moving the Update Repository

The Windows SBS 2008 setup program configures WSUS to store the updates that it downloads from the Internet on the computer's C: drive. This is largely because C: is often the only drive available during a new server installation. However, you might want to move the update repository to another drive later, for any of the following reasons:

- The C: drive is running low on disk space.
- You want to move the update repository to a fault-tolerant medium, such as a RAID-5 volume.
- You want to move the repository off the system volume to optimize system performance and simplify backups.

To move the WSUS update repository, use the following procedure:

1. Log on to your Windows SBS 2008 server using an account with network Administrator privileges. The Windows SBS Console appears.

2. Click Backup And Server Storage, and then select the Server Storage tab, as shown here.

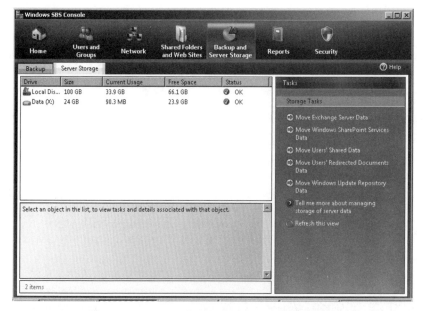

3. In the Tasks list, click Move Windows Update Repository Data. The Move Windows Update Repository Data Wizard appears, displaying the Getting Started page.

4. Click Next to continue. The Checking Your Server page appears as the wizard examines the server's backup status. If the system has had a recent backup, the Choose A New Location For The Data page appears, as shown here.

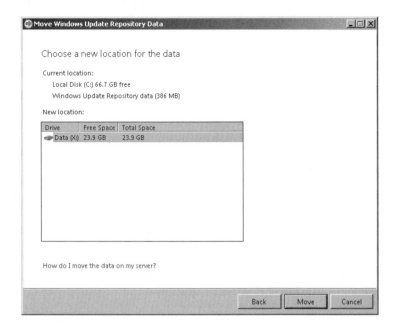

NOTE Windows SBS 2008 strongly recommends that you back up the server before moving a substantial data store. If you have not backed up the server recently, a message box appears with a warning to this effect. You can opt to proceed or cancel the wizard.

5.   In the New Location box, select the volume that you want to use to store the update repository and click Move. The wizard creates a folder called WSUS\WsusContent on the volume that you selected and moves the repository data there. Then the The Wizard Update Repository Data Was Moved Successfully page appears.

6.   Click Finish. The wizard closes.

Configuring Software Update Settings

The Windows SBS Console enables you to modify the default settings for some of the most basic WSUS and Automatic Updates parameters. To configure these settings, use the following procedure:

1.   Log on to your Windows SBS 2008 server, using an account with network Administrator privileges. The Windows SBS Console appears.

2.   Click Security, and then select the Updates tab.

3. In the Tasks list, click Change The Software Update Settings. The Software Update Settings dialog box appears.

4. Select one of the following tabs and use the controls to configure the following settings located there:

   • Server Updates   Specifies, by classification, which updates WSUS should automatically approve for servers, as shown here. The default Medium setting omits service packs, as shown here.

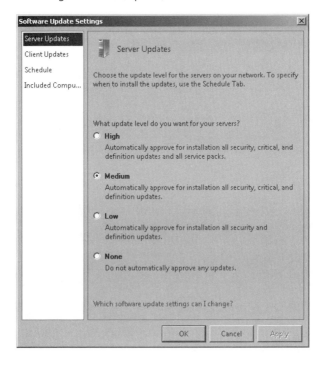

- **Client Updates**   Specifies, by classification, which updates WSUS should approve automatically for clients, as shown here. The default High setting includes all high-priority updates and service packs, as shown here.

- **Schedule** Specifies whether servers and clients should install updates automatically and, if so, how often and at what time the installations should occur, as shown here.

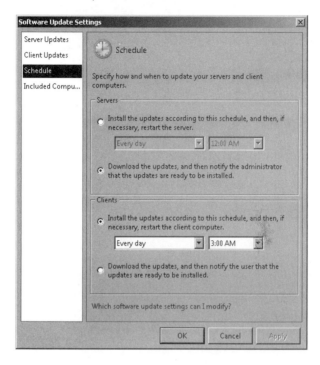

- **Included Computers**   Specifies which of the computers on the network should obtain their updates from the WSUS server, as shown here.

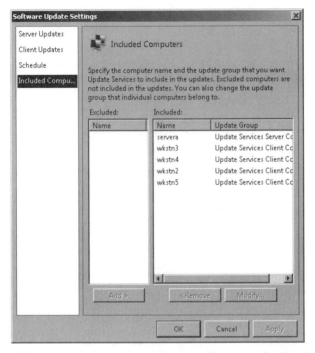

5. Click OK. The Software Update Settings dialog box closes.

Specifying Update Levels

The Server Updates and Client Updates pages in the Software Update Settings dialog box specify which types of updates WSUS should approve automatically for your servers and client workstations, respectively. In the default configuration, the only difference between the server and client settings is the inclusion of service packs for the clients.

Service packs are major updates, and many administrators do not like to install them as soon as they are released, preferring instead to wait to see if problems arise. The installation of a service pack requires a system restart and can also be a lengthy process, so you must be sure that the installation occurs at an appropriate time of day.

If you prefer to wait before installing service packs on your clients, you can change the Client Updates setting to Medium. This enables you to gauge the industry response to the service pack release and possibly install it manually on a single test computer before deploying it on the whole network.

Scheduling Update Installations

The installation of the updates on your network computers is controlled by the Automatic Updates client, not WSUS. Therefore, the Schedule tab of the Software Update Settings dialog box actually modifies the Group Policy settings that configure the Automatic Updates client.

Here again, servers and clients have their own separate settings. The default setting for clients is to install new updates automatically every day at 3 A.M. Depending on your organization's work schedule, you might want to change the time of the installation or even limit it to one day a week instead of every day. Microsoft typically releases new updates once a month, so you might feel that a daily schedule is not necessary. However, Microsoft does sometimes release updates that are particularly critical between the usual monthly cycles.

Another element to consider with client updates is whether your users are accustomed to shutting their computers down at the end of each workday. Obviously, an update installation cannot occur when a computer is turned off. If a scheduled installation does not occur, because the computer is shut down or for any other reason, the Automatic Updates client triggers the installation one minute after the computer's next startup. If this causes problems, you can change this behavior, but only by modifying the GPOs directly. For more information on modifying the Group Policy settings that control the Automatic Updates client, see the section entitled "Configuring Automatic Updates Using Group Policy," later in this chapter.

For servers, the default setting enables the computers to download new updates from the WSUS server, but the computers do not install them automatically. This enables administrators to exercise greater control over which updates the servers receive, and when. For information on how to install updates manually on servers running Windows SBS 2008, see the section entitled "Installing Server Updates Manually," earlier in this chapter.

Excluding Computers

The Included Computers page of the Software Update Settings dialog box enables you to specify which of the computers on your network you want to receive updates from WSUS. By default, all your computers are included, but if you want to change the default, you can select a computer and click Remove to disable its Automatic Updates client entirely.

You can also select a computer and click Modify to display the Change The Members Of An Update Group dialog box, as shown in Figure 6-8. This dialog box enables you to put a client workstation in the Update Services Server Computers group to prevent it from automatically installing updates, or to put a server in the Update Services Client Computers group to enable automatic installations.

FIGURE 6-8 The Change The Members Of An Update Group dialog box

Synchronizing WSUS

WSUS synchronizes with the Microsoft Update servers on the Internet once every day, but you can trigger a manual synchronization using the Windows SBS Console at any time by clicking Synchronize Now in the Tasks list on the Security/Updates page.

Approving Updates

WSUS automatically approves the most important updates by default, but the Security/ Updates page also contains a list of Optional Updates. WSUS does not approve these updates automatically. If you want to deploy them on your network, you must approve them manually, using the following procedure:

1. Log on to your Windows SBS 2008 server, using an account with network Administrator privileges. The Windows SBS Console appears.

2. Click Security, and then select the Updates tab.

3. Select one of the entries in the Optional Updates list and, in the Tasks list, click Deploy The Update. A Software Updates message box appears, prompting you to confirm your action, as shown here.

4. Click OK. Another Software Updates message box appears, informing you that the update is approved.

5. Click OK. The update moves from the Optional Updates list to the Updates In Progress list.

> **TIP** You can also remove an entry from the Optional Updates list and delete it permanently from the update repository by selecting it and clicking Decline The Update.

Configuring Automatic Updates Using Group Policy

The Windows SBS Console contains controls that enable you to configure only the most basic properties of the Automatic Updates client on your network computers, such as the time that installations should occur. To exercise more complete control over the client, you must modify the GPOs that contain the configuration settings for Automatic Updates.

Windows SBS 2008 creates three separate GPOs to configure Automatic Updates clients, as follows:

- **Update Services Common Settings Policy** Applies to all computers on the network

- **Update Services Client Computers Policy** Applies only to computers that are members of the Update Services Client Computers group

- **Update Services Server Computers Policy** Applies only to computers that are members of the Update Services Server Computers group

As part of its startup procedure, every computer on the network downloads and applies the Update Services Common Settings Policy GPO. This GPO contains most of the Automatic Updates policy settings that computers running Windows SBS 2008 need. The settings and default values for the Update Services Common Settings Policy GPO are listed in Table 6-1.

TABLE 6-1 Default Settings in the Update Services Common Settings Policy GPO

GROUP POLICY SETTING	DEFAULT VALUE	FUNCTION
Configure Automatic Updates	▪ Notify for download and notify for install ▪ 0 – Every day ▪ 03:00	Enables the Automatic Updates client, specifies whether the client should download and install updates with or without user intervention, and specifies the installation interval and time of day.
Specify intranet Microsoft update service location	http://*SERVER:* ####, where *SERVER* is the name of your server and #### is the port number assigned to the WSUS Web application	Specifies the URL that Automatic Updates clients use to access the WSUS server on the local network.
Automatic Updates detection frequency	1 hour	Specifies the interval at which Automatic Updates clients check the server for new updates.
Allow non-administrators to receive update notifications	Enabled	Enables users without administrative privileges to receive notifications of impending update downloads or installations from the Automatic Updates client.
Allow Automatic Updates immediate installation	Enabled	Specifies whether the Automatic Updates client should install updates that do not require a service interruption or system restart immediately.
No auto-restart with logged on users for scheduled automatic updates installations	Disabled	Specifies whether the Automatic Updates client can trigger a system restart when a user is logged on to the system. When set to Disabled, the computer can restart automatically while a user is logged on to the computer.

TABLE 6-1 Default Settings in the Update Services Common Settings Policy GPO

GROUP POLICY SETTING	DEFAULT VALUE	FUNCTION
Re-prompt for restart with scheduled installations	10 minutes	Specifies the time interval the Automatic Updates client should wait before restarting the computer after a user postponed a previous restart request.
Delay Restart for scheduled installations	5 minutes	Specifies the time interval the Automatic Updates client should wait before restarting the computer after an update installation.
Reschedule Automatic Updates scheduled installations	1 minute	Specifies the time interval the Automatic Updates client should wait after system startup before initiating an update installation that did not occur because the computer was offline.

After applying the Update Services Common Settings Policy GPO, each computer then applies either the Update Services Client Computers Policy or Update Services Server Computers Policy GPO, depending on its group membership. These GPOs contain only one policy setting, as listed in Tables 6-2 and 6-3, with each having a different default value. Because the computers apply these GPOs after the Update Services Common Settings Policy GPO, the client- or server-specific value for the Configure Automatic Updates policy setting overwrites the existing value from the first GPO.

TABLE 6-2 Default Settings in the Update Services Client Computers Policy GPO

GROUP POLICY SETTING	DEFAULT VALUE	FUNCTION
Configure Automatic Updates	■ Auto download and schedule the install ■ 0 – Every day ■ 03:00	Enables the Automatic Updates client, specifies whether the client should download and install updates with or without user intervention, and specifies the installation interval and time of day

GROUP POLICY SETTING	DEFAULT VALUE	FUNCTION
Configure Automatic Updates	■ Auto download and notify for install ■ 0 – Every day ■ 03:00	Enables the Automatic Updates client, specifies whether the client should download and install updates with or without user intervention, and specifies the installation interval and time of day

To modify the default settings for the Update Services Common Settings Policy GPO, use the following procedure:

1. Log on to your Windows SBS 2008 server, using an account with network Administrator privileges.

2. Click Start. Then click Administrative Tools, Group Policy Management. The Group Policy Management console appears, as shown here.

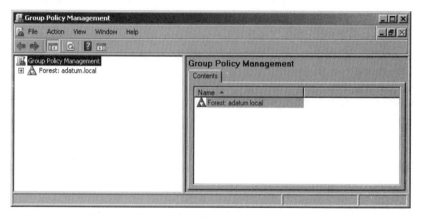

3. In the scope (left) pane, expand the Forest node and browse to the node representing your domain. The detail (right) pane lists the Group Policy objects linked to your domain object, including the three Update Services GPOs, as shown here.

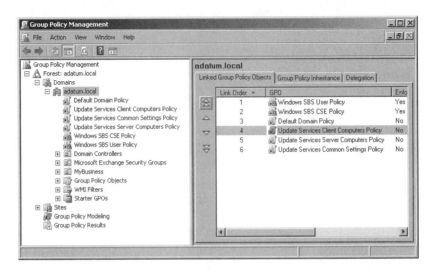

MORE INFO When a domain has multiple GPOs linked to it, the computers on the network apply the GPOs in order, beginning with the last GPO in the list and ending with the first. If the same policy settings appear in more than one GPO, the settings that the system applies last take precedence. Therefore, the GPO that is number one on the list has the highest priority.

4. Right-click the Update Services Common Settings Policy and, from the context menu, select Edit. The Group Policy Management Editor console appears, as shown here, displaying the contents of the GPO.

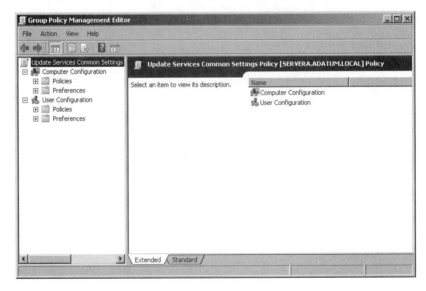

5. In the scope pane, shown here, browse to the Computer Configuration\
Policies\Administrative Templates\Windows Components\Windows Update
folder.

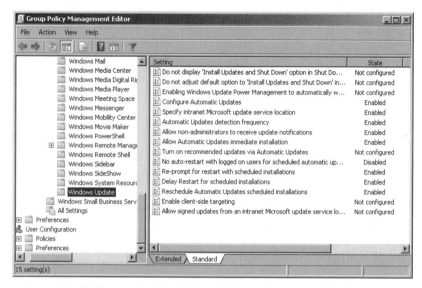

6. In the detail pane, double-click one of the policy settings listed in Table 6-1.
The Properties sheet for the policy setting appears, as shown here.

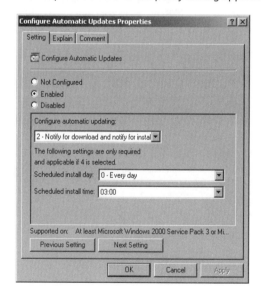

7. Modify the values for the policy setting as desired and click OK to close the Properties sheet.

8. Repeat steps 6 to 7 to modify additional policy settings.

9. Close the Group Policy Management Editor console.

10. Close the Group Policy Management console.

To modify the Configure Automatic Updates policy settings that your computers actually use, you must repeat the procedure and edit the Update Services Client Computers Policy and Update Services Server Computers Policy GPOs.

The most common modifications that administrators are likely to make to these GPOs is to change the installation time and frequency in the Configure Automatic Updates policy setting, or disable the automatic installation process for clients. Some of the other modifications you might consider are the following:

- Enabling the No Auto-restart With Logged On Users For Scheduled Automatic Updates Installations policy setting prevents users from being interrupted by an update installation if they are logged on when it is scheduled to occur. The potential drawback of this is that installations do not occur if a user leaves the computer logged on at the end of the day.

- The only situation in which you would want to modify the Specify Intranet Microsoft Update Service Location policy setting is if you deploy another WSUS server on your network and want your users to obtain their updates from that server.

- If you want to insulate your users from the update process, you can disable the Allow Non-administrators To Receive Update Notifications policy setting. When you do this, most Automatic Updates activities occur invisibly.

- Setting the Reschedule Automatic Updates Scheduled Installations policy setting to Disabled prevents missed update installations from occurring the next time the computer starts. Instead, the installation occurs at the next scheduled time. This modification can prevent users from facing what might be a lengthy and unexpected installation procedure during business hours.

When you modify the settings in these GPOs, the new values do not take effect until the next time the computer restarts.

Managing Storage

S hared storage is one of the primary reasons for the invention of the local area network (LAN), and Microsoft Windows Small Business Server (SBS) 2008 creates a number of shared folders as part of its default configuration. Once you have installed Windows SBS 2000, you can add more storage to your server and create as many shares as needed to support your users. You can also deploy additional servers on the network to provide even more file services.

Understanding the Default Windows SBS 2008 Storage Configuration

Before you can store data on a Windows SBS 2008 hard disk, you must create at least one volume on it. You create your first volume, which becomes the C: drive, during the operating system installation process, and Windows SBS 2008 uses that volume to store all the default system, application, and data files. While it is possible to create additional simple volumes from within the setup program, many administrators wait until after the installation process is complete. You must also wait if you want to create nonsimple volumes, such as mirror sets and RAID-5 arrays.

> **NOTE**   To create and manage volumes, you can use the Share and Storage Management Console or the Disk Management snap-in for Microsoft Management Console (MMC).

Using the Default Shares

Creating volumes makes a hard disk accessible to the operating system, but to make the volumes accessible to users on the network, you must create shared folders on them. Windows SBS 2008 creates a number of shares during the installation process. Some of these shares are intended for use by applications, such as Microsoft Exchange Server and Windows Server Update Services (WSUS), but the following three shares are meant for direct access by users:

- **Public**   Contains folders accessible to everyone for the purpose of storing files that individuals want to share with other users on the network
- **RedirectedFolders**   Contains the user profile folders for each account that has Folder Redirection enabled
- **UserShares**   Contains a subfolder for each user on the network, to which only that user has access permissions.

You can also create as many additional shares on your server as you need to support your users.

> **NOTE**   To create shares, you can use the Provision A Shared Folder Wizard, accessible from the Windows SBS Console or the Share and Storage Management Console. You can also create shares directly from a folder's Properties sheet.

Understanding Share Permissions

Shared folders have their own independent set of permissions, completely separate from the NTFS permissions you use to control access to files and folders. The main difference between share permissions and NTFS permissions is that share permissions apply only when a user attempts to access a protected resource from the network. NTFS permissions apply both over the network and on the local console. For example, users that have the NTFS permissions needed to access a server folder, but lack share permissions for that same folder, can access it from the server console but not over the network. Users that have share permissions but lack NTFS permissions cannot access the folder at all.

The share permission system functions just like the NTFS and other permission systems in Microsoft Windows, except that you can assign only three permissions. As with the other permission systems, you can allow or deny each of the permissions to any security principal available on the system. Table 7-1 lists the three share permissions and the tasks they enable users to perform.

TABLE 7-1 Share Permissions and Their Associated Tasks

SHARE PERMISSION	ALLOWS OR DENIES SECURITY PRINCIPALS THE ABILITY TO:
Full Control	• Change file permissions • Take ownership of files • Perform all tasks allowed by the Change permission
Change	• Create folders • Add files to folders • Change data in files • Append data to files • Change file attributes • Delete folders and files • Perform all actions permitted by the Read permission
Read	• Display folder names, file names, file data, and attributes • Execute program files • Access other folders within the shared folder

Because users must have both share and NTFS permissions to access a particular resource from the network, many administrators choose to avoid confusion by using only one of the permission systems. NTFS permissions are the logical choice because they provide more comprehensive and flexible protection. In fact, this is the approach that Windows SBS 2008 takes in its default shares. All three of the shares listed earlier have the Allow Full Control permission assigned to the Everyone special identity, which means that all network users can connect to them. To control access to the shares on a granular level, Windows SBS 2008 assigns NTFS permissions.

> **MORE INFO** A *security principal* is any object, such as a user, group, or computer, to which you can assign permissions. A *special identity* is a Windows element that stands for all objects sharing a specific trait or condition. For example, assigning permissions to the Authenticated Users special identity causes all users that are logged on to the domain to receive those permissions. For more information on Windows permissions, how they work, and how to assign them, see Chapter 12, "Optimizing Network Security."

Managing Disk Storage

You must create at least one volume during the Windows SBS 2008 installation, but after the installation is complete, you can create as many additional volumes as you need. You might have additional space to work with on the disk containing your C:

drive, and you might have additional disks already installed in the computer. You can also install additional disk storage on your server by adding internal disk drives, connecting external drives, or deploying network-based storage devices. Once your server recognizes the new storage devices, you can create and manage volumes using the tools and procedures discussed in the following sections.

Using the Disk Management Interface

The primary Windows tool for managing disk partitions and volumes is the Disk Management snap-in for MMC. Disk Management is not a Windows SBS 2008 tool; all Windows versions include it as part of the Computer Management console. As with all MMC snap-ins, however, you can create a custom MMC console that combines Disk Management with any other snap-ins you use regularly.

To access the Disk Management snap-in, you can use any of the following procedures:

- Click Start, Administrative Tools, Computer Management, and select the Storage/Disk Management node.
- Click Start, Administrative Tools, Server Manager, and select the Storage/Disk Management node.
- Click Start, Run, and execute the Diskmgmt.msc file.
- Click Start, Run, and execute the Mmc.exe file. Then click File, Add/Remove Snap-in, and add Disk Management to the console.

When you open the Disk Management snap-in, you see the interface shown in Figure 7-1.

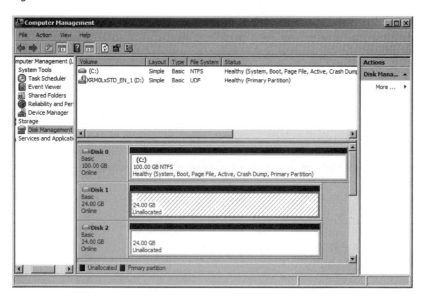

FIGURE 7-1 The Disk Management snap-in

The two center panes in the console, called Top and Bottom, can each display one of the following three views:

- **Disk list**   Lists the physical drives installed in the computer and displays the disk number; disk type, such as Basic or DVD; disk capacity; unallocated space; current status, such as online, offline, or no media; the device type, such as SCSI or IDE; and the partition style, such as MBR or GPT, as shown here.

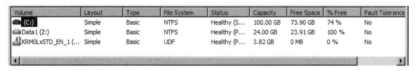

- **Volume list**   Lists the volumes on all the computer's disks, and displays the volume name; layout, such as Simple, Spanned, or Striped; the disk type, such as Basic or Dynamic; the file system, such as NTFS or Compact Disk File System (CDFS); the disk status, such as Healthy, Failed, or Formatting; and information about the disk's capacity and its current free space, as shown here.

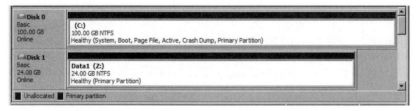

- **Graphical view**   Contains a graphical representation of the computer's physical disks, partitions, volumes, and logical drives. The disk status column (on the left) displays the disk number, plus its type, capacity, and status. The volume status column (on the right) displays the name, size, file system, and current status for each volume on the disk, as shown here.

The default interface contains the volume list in the top pane and the graphical view in the bottom. You can modify these defaults as desired. Right-clicking an element in any of the three panes displays a context menu containing commands for managing the selected element.

Initializing a Disk

When you install a new hard disk in your server, or access one for the first time, the first thing you must do is initialize it by selecting a partition style. To initialize a disk, perform the following procedure:

1. Click Start. Then click Administrative Tools, Computer Management. When the User Account Control dialog box appears, click Continue. The Computer Management console appears.

2. In the Scope (left) pane, select the Disk Management node. The Initialize Disk dialog box appears, as shown here.

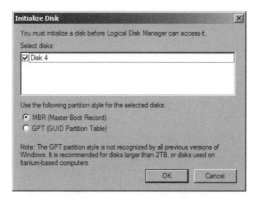

3. Select one of the following partition styles for the new disk:
   - MBR (Master Boot Record)   The default partition style, supporting up to four partitions and volumes up to 2 terabytes (TB) in size
   - GPT (GUID Partition Table)   Supports up to 128 partitions and volumes as large as 18 exabytes (18 x 2^{60} bytes)

4. Click OK. The Disk Management interface appears, with the new disk appearing as unallocated space.

Once you have initialized the disk, you can proceed to create volumes on it.

Creating Volumes

Windows SBS 2008 supports five volume types, as described in Table 7-2. These volume types provide varying amounts of fault tolerance and performance enhancement. The volume you created during the Windows SBS 2008 installation is a simple volume, and because the volume contains the computer's boot and system files, it must remain that way. However, you can use any unallocated space on the system disk, plus the space on your other disks, to create volumes of any type.

TABLE 7-2 Volume Types Supported by Windows SBS 2008

VOLUME TYPE	NUMBER OF DISKS REQUIRED	FAULT TOLERANCE	DESCRIPTION
Simple	1	None.	Consists of space from a single disk.
Spanned	2 to 32	None. The loss of one disk destroys the volume.	Consists of space from multiple dynamic disks, combined to create a single volume.
Striped	2 to 32	None. The loss of one disk destroys the volume.	Consists of space from multiple dynamic disks, combined to create a single volume. The system writes data one stripe at a time to each successive disk in the volume, increasing input/output (I/O) efficiency.
Mirrored	2	Yes. The volume survives the loss of one disk.	Consists of an identical amount of space on two disks. The system writes duplicate copies of all data to both of the disks, so that all the data remains available if one disk fails. The volume size therefore equals half of the total disk space.
RAID-5	3 or more	Yes. The volume survives the loss of one disk.	Consists of space on at least three disks. The system stripes data, along with parity information, across the disks. If one disk should fail, the system can reconstruct the missing data using the parity information on the other disks.

In addition to the volume types, Windows SBS 2008 supports two disk types: basic disks and dynamic disks. When you first initialize a disk, it appears as a basic disk. A *basic disk* can have up to four partitions: three primary partitions and one extended partition, with the extended partition hosting multiple logical drives. So long as you create only simple volumes on a disk, it remains a basic disk. The first three simple volumes you create on a basic disk are the primary partitions. When you create a fourth simple volume, the Disk Management snap-in creates an extended partition using all the remaining unallocated space on the disk, and a logical drive of the size you specified for the simple volume.

> **TIP** It is possible to create a fourth primary partition on a basic disk, but you cannot do it using the Disk Management snap-in. Instead, you must use the Diskpart.exe tool from the command prompt.

To create volumes other than simple volumes, you must convert the disks into dynamic disks. Technically, a *dynamic disk* has one partition that uses all its available space. You can then create multiple volumes within that single partition. When you use basic disks to create a spanned, striped, mirrored, or RAID-5 volume using the Disk Management snap-in, the tool converts the disks from basic to dynamic automatically. If you delete all the volumes on a dynamic disk (erasing the data on them), Disk Management converts it back to a basic disk.

> **IMPORTANT** The only drawback to using dynamic disks is that you cannot boot the computer from any dynamic disk other than the current boot volume. The only way to convert a dynamic disk back to a basic disk is to delete all the existing volumes, thereby erasing all the data on the disk.

Creating a Simple Volume

To create a simple volume with the Disk Management snap-in, perform the following procedure:

1. Click Start. Then click Administrative Tools, Computer Management. When the User Account Control dialog box appears, click Continue. The Computer Management console appears.
2. In the scope (left) pane, select the Disk Management node.
3. In the graphical view, right-click the unallocated space on any of your disks and, from the context menu, select New Simple Volume. The New Simple Volume Wizard appears.
4. Click Next to bypass the Welcome page. The Specify Volume Size page appears, as shown here.

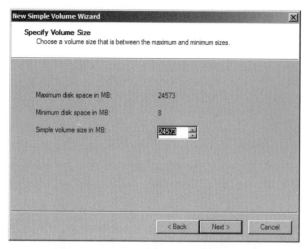

5. In the Simple Volume Size In MB box, specify the size of the volume you want to create and click Next. The Assign Drive Letter Or Path page appears, as shown here.

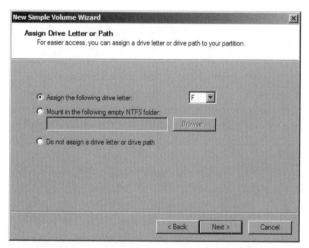

6. Select one of the following options and configure its properties:

- Assign The Following Drive Letter   Enables you to select the available drive letter you want to use to access the volume.

- Mount In The Following Empty NTFS Folder   Enables you to access the new volume from within a folder on another existing volume. This makes the new volume appear as though it is part of the existing volume.

- Do Not Assign A Drive Letter Or Drive Path   Enables you to create the new volume without any means of accessing it. You can assign a drive letter or mount the volume at a later time.

7. Click Next. The Format Partition page appears, as shown here.

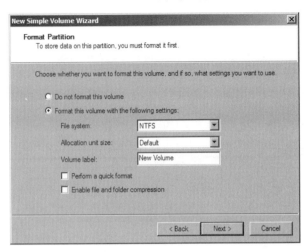

8. To format the volume, leave the Format The Volume With The Following Settings option selected and configure the following properties:

- **File System**   Specifies whether you want to format the volume using the NTFS, FAT, or FAT32 file system. NTFS provides many more features than FAT or FAT32, including access control, compression, and encryption. The only compelling reason to use FAT or FAT32 is if you must access the volume using an operating system that does not support NTFS.

- **Allocation Unit Size**   Specifies the size of the individual clusters the system uses when allocating space on the volume. For a volume that stores many small files, a smaller value provides more efficient use of space; for a volume that stores large files, a greater value provides better performance.

- **Volume Label** ⋅ Specifies a name, up to 32 characters long, that the system uses to identify the volume.

- **Perform A Quick Format**   Selecting this check box causes the wizard to format the volume without checking for errors. Clearing the check box causes the wizard to check the disk for errors as it formats the volume and mark bad sectors as inaccessible.

- **Enable File And Folder Compression**   Selecting this check box along with the NTFS file system causes the computer to store all the data it writes on the volume in a compressed form.

9. Click Next. The Completing The New Simple Volume Wizard page appears.

10. Click Finish. The wizard closes and the new volume appears in the unallocated space, as shown here.

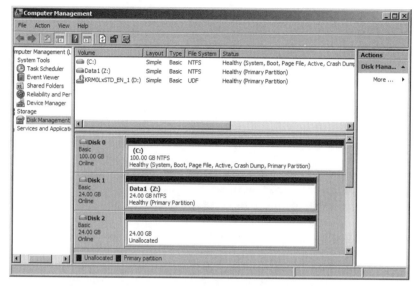

Depending on the computer's hardware, the size of the volume, and the settings you selected, it might take several minutes for the formatting to finish.

Creating Other Volume Types

The Disk Management snap-in also includes wizards for creating spanned, striped, mirrored, and RAID-5 volumes. These wizards are identical to the New Simple Volume Wizard, except for the addition of the Select Disks page, as shown in Figure 7-2. This page enables you to select the disks you want to use to create the volume and specify the amount of space you want to use on each disk.

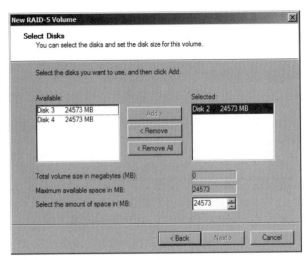

FIGURE 7-2 The Select Disks page in the New RAID-5 Volume Wizard

Depending on the type of volume you are creating, the Select Disks page imposes limits on your specifications, as follows:

- **Spanned**   You must select at least 2 and no more than 32 disks, and you can specify any amount of space on each disk.
- **Striped**   You must select at least 2 and no more than 32 disks, and you must specify the same amount of space on each disk.
- **Mirrored**   You can select only 2 disks, and you must specify the same amount of space on each disk.
- **RAID-5**   You must select 3 or more disks, and you must specify the same amount of space on each disk.

When the wizard finishes creating the volume, the space in all the disks involved changes color to reflect the properties of the new volume, as shown in Figure 7-3.

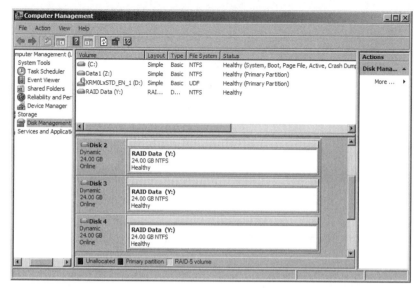

FIGURE 7-3 A new RAID-5 volume in the Disk Management snap-in

Shrinking and Extending Volumes

With certain limitations, Windows SBS 2008 also enables you to shrink and extend volumes after you have created them. When you right-click a volume and select Shrink Volume, a Shrink dialog box appears, as shown in Figure 7-4.

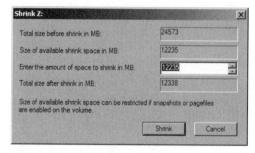

FIGURE 7-4 The Shrink dialog box

When you right-click a volume and select Extend Volume, the Extend Volume Wizard appears. The wizard consists of a Select Disks page just like the one you see when creating a spanned volume. This is because you can extend a volume onto one or more additional disks, creating a spanned volume in the process.

The ability to shrink and extend volumes is subject to the following limitations:

- You cannot shrink or extend volumes formatted using the FAT or FAT32 file systems; you can shrink or extend only NTFS or unformatted volumes.
- You can extend a boot volume or system volume only into contiguous space on the same disk; you cannot extend them onto other disks.

> **NOTE** In this context, the term *continuous space* refers to unallocated space immediately following the volume you want to extend.

- To extend a volume on a basic disk into noncontiguous space on the same disk, you must convert it to a dynamic disk.
- You cannot shrink or extend mirror or RAID-5 volumes, or shrink a striped volume.
- To shrink a volume, the amount of free space on the volume must be at least equal to the amount of space you want to reclaim.

Working with Shares

Once you have created volumes on your server disks, they are accessible from the server console, but network users can't access them until you create shares. The Windows SBS Console provides access to the Provision A Shared Folder Wizard, which is the same tool you can use to create shares in the Share and Storage Management Console, a tool included with Windows Server 2008. Once you have created shares, you can manage their basic properties from within the Windows SBS Console as well.

Creating a New Share

To create a new shared folder of volume with the Windows SBS Console, use the following procedure:

1. Log on to your Windows SBS 2008 server, using an account with network Administrator privileges. The Windows SBS Console appears.
2. Click Shared Folders And Web Sites, and then select the Shared Folders tab.
3. In the Tasks list, click Add A New Shared Folder. The Provision A Shared Folder Wizard appears, displaying the Shared Folder Location page, as shown on the next page.

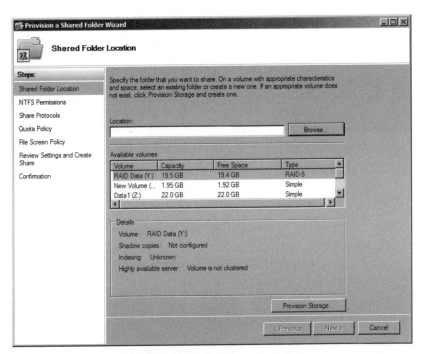

4. Click Browse. The Browse For Folder dialog box appears, as shown here.

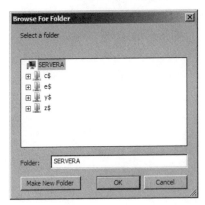

5. Select the volume on which you want to create the share. If you want to share a folder on the volume, browse to the folder and select it. You can also click Make New Folder to create and share a folder on the selected volume. Then click OK.

MORE INFO You can click Provision Storage to start the Provision Storage Wizard, which enables you to create new volumes. However, this wizard can create only simple volumes. To create a striped, spanned, mirrored, or RAID-5 volume, use the Disk Management snap-in.

6. Click Next. The NTFS Permissions page appears, as shown here.

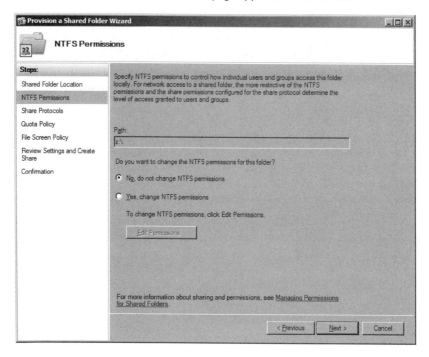

MORE INFO For more information on using NTFS permissions, see Chapter 9, "Administering E-mail".

7. Leave the default No, Do Not Change NTFS Permissions option selected and click Next. The Share Protocols page appears, as shown here.

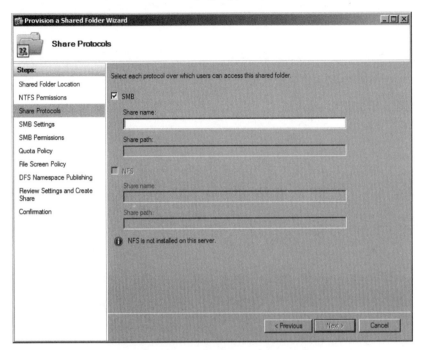

8. Leave the SMB check box selected and, in the Share Name text box, type the name under which the share will appear on the network.

> **MORE INFO** The NFS option is dimmed because the Services For Network File System role service is not installed on a server running Windows SBS 2008 by default. Network File System (NFS) is a file sharing protocol used by most UNIX and Linux distributions. If you have UNIX or Linux clients that need access to your Windows shares, you can install the role service and configure your shares to use NFS as well as Server Message Block (SMB) file sharing.

9. Click Next. The SMB Settings page appears, as shown here.

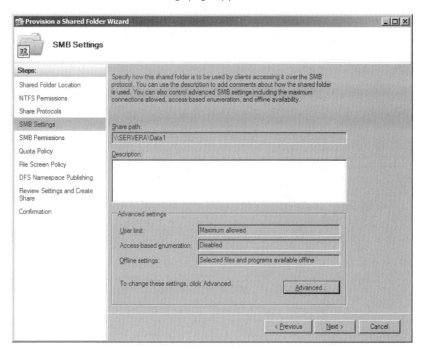

10. Click Advanced to open the Advanced dialog box, in which you can configure the following SBS settings:

- User limit   Specifies the maximum number of users allowed to access the share at one time, as shown here.

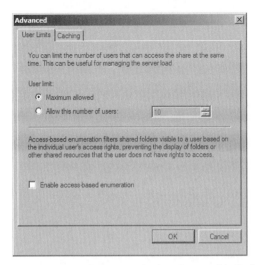

- Access-based enumeration   When enabled, allows only the users with access permissions to see the share on the network.

- Offline settings   Specifies whether users can save copies of the files in the share to local drives using Offline Files, as shown here.

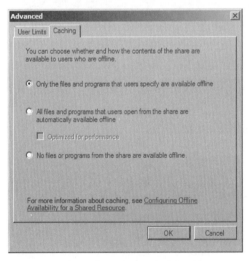

11. Click OK to close the Advanced dialog box.

12. Click Next. The SMB Permissions page appears, as shown here.

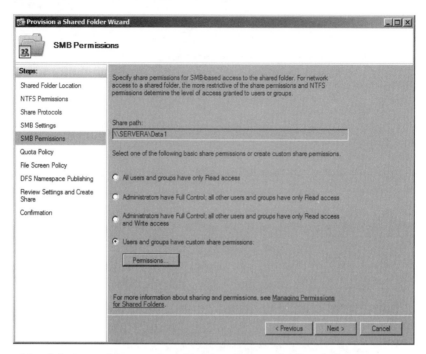

13. Select one of the preset permission options or click Permissions to open a Permissions dialog box, in which you can specify the share permissions you want to assign to your users, as shown here.

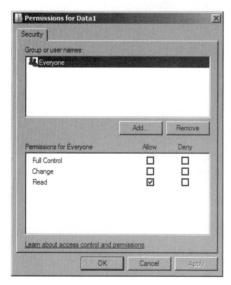

14. Click Next. The Quota Policy page appears, as shown here.

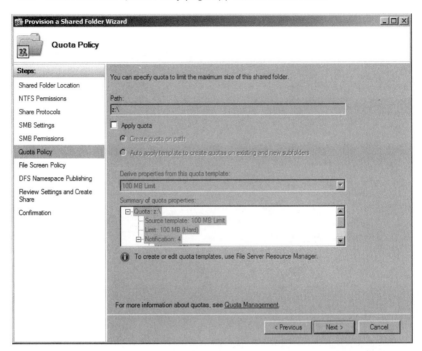

To set a quota on disk space consumption for each user, select the Apply Quota check box, and then select quota options and a quota template.

MORE INFO For more information on using quotas, see the section entitled "Enforcing Quotas," later in this chapter.

15. Click Next. The File Screen Policy page appears, as shown here.

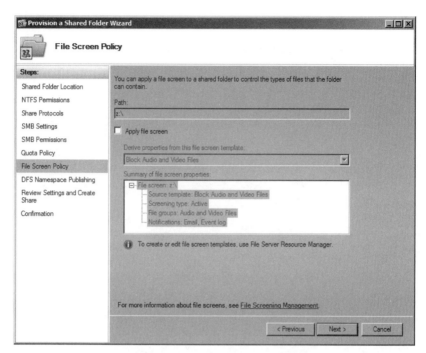

To use file screening, select the Apply File Screen check box, and then select a file screen template.

16. Click Next. The DFS Namespace Publishing page appears, as shown here.

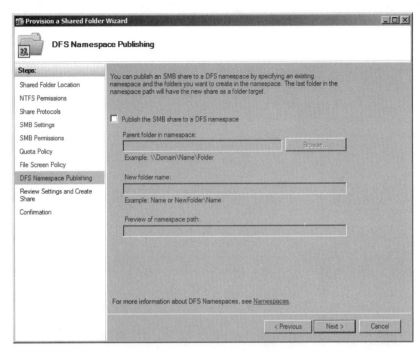

To add the share to a DFS namespace, select the Publish The SMB Share To A DFS Namespace check box and specify a namespace location and a folder name.

MORE INFO The Distributed File System (DFS) is a feature of Windows Server 2008 that enables you to combine shares from various locations into a single virtual namespace. To use DFS, you must install the File Services\Distributed File Services role service using the Server Manager console and then create and configure a DFS namespace.

17. Click Next. The Review Settings And Create Share page appears, as shown here.

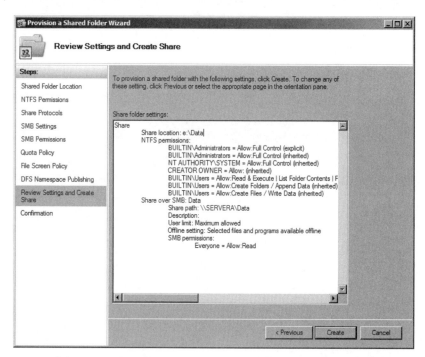

18. Click Create. The wizard creates the share and the Confirmation page appears, as shown here.

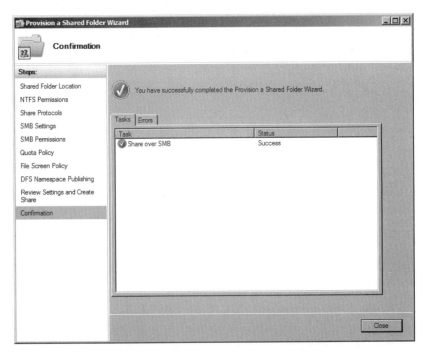

19. Click Close. The wizard closes.

Managing Shares

The Windows SBS Console, on the Shared Folders and Web Sites page, on the Shared Folders tab, displays the shared folders on your server, both the default shares and any new ones you have created, as shown in Figure 7-5. By selecting a share and using the controls in the Tasks list, you can stop sharing the folder or modify its properties, as described in the following sections.

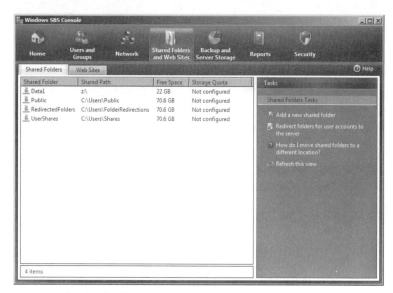

FIGURE 7-5 The Shared Folders tab in the Windows SBS Console

Configuring Share Permissions

When you select a share and, in the Tasks list, select Change Folder Permissions, the Properties sheet for the share appears, as shown in Figure 7-6. When you select an entry in the Users And Groups list, the dialog box displays the share permissions assigned to that entry.

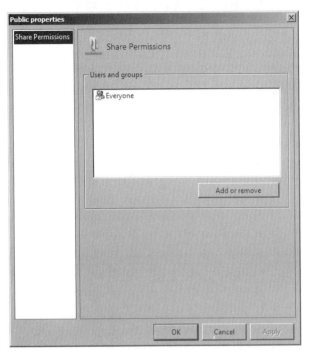

FIGURE 7-6 The Properties sheet for a shared folder in the Windows SBS Console

For the default shares, Windows SBS 2008 grants the Allow Full Control permission to the Everyone special identity. Changing the permissions for the default shares is not recommended. The shares you create yourself receive the permissions that you specify in the Provision A Shared Folder Wizard. You can modify these permissions by selecting an entry in the Users And Groups list and selecting the check boxes for the permissions you want to assign. To manage the entries in the list, click Add Or Remove to display the Shared Folders dialog box, as shown in Figure 7-7.

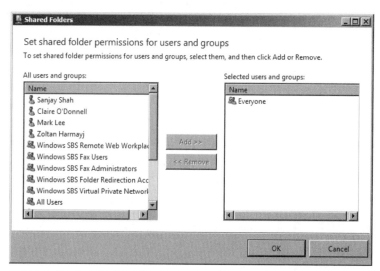

FIGURE 7-7 The Shared Folders dialog box in the Windows SBS Console

BEST PRACTICES Remember that, in addition to share permissions, users must have the appropriate NTFS permissions to access a shared folder. To simplify the administration of your shares, the recommended practice is to always grant Everyone the Allow Full Control share permission and use NTFS permissions to control access to the shared folders.

Moving Shares

Windows SBS 2008 includes wizards that enable you to move the shares containing the user folders and the folder redirection data to another volume. By default, these shares, called UserShares or RedirectedFolders, appear on the system volume, but you might want to move them to another location to reclaim disk space or store them on a fault-tolerant volume. The wizard preserves all the share and NTFS permissions as it moves the shares, and it also modifies the Group Policy settings needed to provide users with continued access to their data.

To move the UserShares share, perform the following procedure:

1. Log on to your Windows SBS 2008 server, using an account with network Administrator privileges. The Windows SBS Console appears.

2. Click Backup And Server Storage, and then select the Server Storage tab.

3. In the Tasks list, click Move Users' Shared Data. The Move Users' Shared Data Wizard appears.

4. Click Next to bypass the Getting Started page. The wizard checks the server for available disk space.

   If Windows SBS 2008 is not configured to perform regular backups, a message box appears, recommending that you perform a full backup before completing the wizard.

5. Click OK. The Choose A New Location For The Data page appears, as shown here.

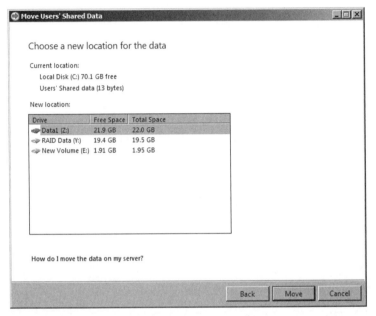

6. Select the volume where you want to store the share and click Move. The wizard moves the share and the The Users' Share Data Was Moved Successfully page appears.

7. Click Finish. The wizard closes.

   NOTE The process for moving the RedirectedFolders share is exactly the same as that for UserShares, except that you select Move Users' Redirected Documents Data in the Tasks list.

There is no wizard to move shares that you have created yourself. To move manually created shares, you must stop sharing them, move the folders to the new location, recreate the NTFS permissions, if necessary, and then share the folders again.

Using Folder Redirection

It is preferable to store user data on server drives rather than local workstation drives for several reasons, including the following:

- **Backups**   Backing up one or two servers is much faster, easier, and often cheaper than backing up multiple workstations.

- **Mobility**   With all data files stored on server drives, users can work from any computer and move to another location as needed.

- **Replacement**   Deploying new client computers in the place of older ones is a simple matter of replacing the hardware; no migration of data files is necessary.

Folder redirection is a Windows feature that enables client workstations to store the contents of their data folders on a server drive automatically. The process is completely invisible to the workstation user.

A Windows Vista workstation creates a folder for each person who logs on at the computer in the C:\Users folder. Each of these user folders contains a separate user profile for that person. A *user profile* is a set of folders and registry files that store the documents and configuration settings belonging to a particular user. A typical user profile consists of the folders listed in Table 7-3, some of which are hidden, plus a hidden registry file.

TABLE 7-3 User Profile Folders

VISIBLE FOLDERS	HIDDEN FOLDERS
Contacts	AppData
Desktop	Application Data
Documents	Cookies
Downloads	Local Settings
Favorites	My Documents
Links	NetHood
Music	PrintHood
Pictures	Recent
Saved Games	Send To
Searches	Start Menu
Videos	Templates

When a user logs on at the workstation using a local or domain account, the system loads that individual's profile and uses it throughout the session until the user logs off. During the session, the Documents folder in the user's profile becomes the operative Documents folder for the system, as do all the other folders in the profile. Folder redirection is simply a means of storing a copy of certain user profile folders on another computer, usually a file server. Once the folders are redirected to the server, that user can log on at any computer and the system copies the redirected folders to the user's local profile on that computer.

Windows SBS 2008 implements folder redirection using Group Policy settings that specify which folders to redirect and where to store them, as shown in Figure 7-8. During the operating system installation, the Windows SBS 2008 setup program creates a Group Policy object (GPO) called Small Business Server Folder Redirection Policy and links it to the *domain*/MyBusiness/Users/SBSUsers organizational unit object. This way, every user on the network loads the GPO during the domain logon process.

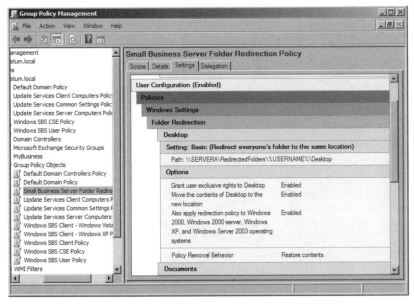

FIGURE 7-8 Policy settings in the Small Business Server Folder Redirection Policy GPO

> **TIP** If you have migrated your server from Windows SBS 2003 to Windows SBS 2008, and you had folder redirection enabled on your old server, then you will find a GPO called Small Business Server Folder Redirection in your domain. This is the Windows SBS 2003 folder redirection GPO, and you should delete it after you have demoted and disconnected your old server.

Understanding the Folder Redirection Defaults

The Group Policy settings for folder redirection are located in the GPO in the following container: User Configuration\Policies\Windows Settings\Folder Redirection, as shown in Figure 7-9. By default, Windows SBS 2008 redirects only the Desktops and Documents folders, along with the Music, Pictures, and Videos subfolders beneath the Documents folder.

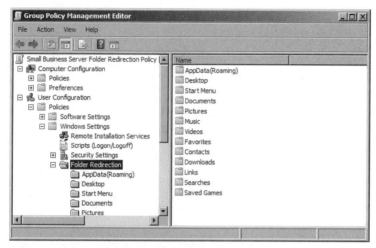

FIGURE 7-9 The Folder Redirection policies in a GPO

You can modify the settings in the Small Business Server Folder Redirection Policy GPO with the Group Policy Management Editor console by right-clicking one of the folders under the Folder Redirection node and opening its Properties sheet, as shown in Figure 7-10. The most common modification that administrators are likely to make is to redirect additional folders, such as Startup and Favorites, to provide users with a more complete server-based environment.

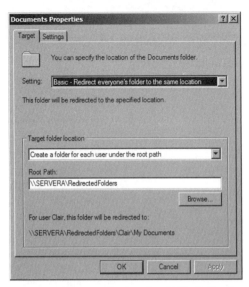

FIGURE 7-10 The Properties sheet for a Folder Redirection policy

Table 7-4 lists the default settings for the Desktop and Documents folders and explains their functions. The Music, Pictures, and Videos folders have only one setting: Follow The Documents Folder, which causes the workstation to treat them as subfolders beneath the Documents folder and redirect them using the Documents folder settings.

TABLE 7-4 Default Folder Redirection Group Policy Settings for the Desktop and Documents Folders

SETTING	DEFAULT VALUE	FUNCTION
Setting	Basic – Redirect Everyone's Folder To The Same Location	Causes workstations to redirect the Desktop or Documents folder for all users to the same server share. The alternative is to redirect the folders to different locations based on group memberships.
Target Folder Location	Create A Folder For Each User Under The Root Path	Causes workstations to create a separate folder for each user on the server share. The alternatives are to redirect the folders to each user's home directory, to a single folder for all users, or to the user's local userprofile location.

TABLE 7-4 Default Folder Redirection Group Policy Settings for the Desktop and Documents Folders

SETTING	DEFAULT VALUE	FUNCTION
Root Path	*SERVER*\Redirectedfolders	Specifies the server share where you want to store the redirected folders.
Grant The User Exclusive Rights To Desktop	Enabled	Prevents anyone except the user from receiving permission to access the redirected folder.
Move The Contents Of Desktop/ Documents To The New Location	Enabled	Causes the workstation to copy the contents of the redirected folders on its local drive to the target folder on the server share.
Also Apply Redirection Policy To Microsoft Windows 2000, Windows 2000 Server, Windows XP, And Windows Server 2003 Operating Systems	Enabled	Provides compatibility with earlier operating systems that use different folder names in their user profiles, such as My Documents.
Policy Removal	Redirect The Folder Back To The Local Userprofile Location When Policy Is Removed	Causes the workstation to copy the contents of the redirected folders back to the local drive in the event that an administrator disables the Folder Redirection Group Policy settings. The alternative is to direct the folders back to the local drives without copying their contents from the server, thus rendering those contents inaccessible.

Enabling Folder Redirection

Although Windows SBS 2008 creates the Small Business Server Folder Redirection Policy GPO by default, and even creates a folder for each user in the FolderRedirections share, it does not enable folder redirection for each user by default. To enable folder redirection, perform the following procedure:

1. Log on to your Windows SBS 2008 server, using an account with network Administrator privileges. The Windows SBS Console appears.
2. Click Users And Groups, and then select the Users tab.
3. Select one of the users in the list and, in the Tasks list, select Edit User Account Properties. The Properties sheet for the user account appears.
4. Click the Folders tab, as shown here.

5. Select the Enable Folder Redirection To The Server check box.

   Enabling folder redirection also imposes a 2-GB quota on the user's redirection folder by default. To disable this quota, clear the Enable Folder Redirection Quota check box.
6. Click OK to close the Properties sheet.

Moving Redirected Folders

Although you can change the location of your users' redirected folders by modifying the Root Path setting in the Small Business Server Folder Redirection Policy GPO, it is far easier to use the Move Users' Redirected Documents Data Wizard, in the Windows SBS Console. The wizard not only changes the Group Policy settings, it also modifies the permissions for the target folder and creates the necessary share for you, automatically.

To start the Move Users' Redirected Documents Data Wizard, in the Windows SBS Console, click Backup And Server Storage, select the Server Storage tab, and, in the Tasks list, click Move Users' Redirected Documents Data. The wizard then prompts you for a new location and moves the folders.

Enforcing Quotas

One of the longstanding rules of personal computing is that no matter how much disk space you have in a computer, you eventually end up filling it and needing more. In a server environment, the problem of disk space consumption is compounded by the number of users storing their files on the server drives. Windows SBS 2008 helps administrators to address this problem by establishing quotas that limit the amount of server disk space a user can consume.

For each user account you create, Windows SBS 2008 creates two quotas, one for the user's folder in UserShares and one for the user's folder in RedirectedFolders. The user's UserShares folder has a 2-GB hard quota, by default. A *hard quota* is one in which the system prevents the user from consuming more than a specified amount of disk space. When the user's disk space consumption reaches 85 percent of the 2 GB, the system sends a warning e-mail to the user and the administrator and records an event in the system log. If the user consumes the entire 2 GB, the server stops accepting data. To the user, it appears as though the server has run out of disk space, although it is in reality only that user's space that has been consumed.

As mentioned in the previous procedure, the quota for the user's folder in RedirectedFolders is a 2-GB soft quota. A *soft quota* generates the same warnings to the user and administrator as a hard quota, but it does not prevent the user from exceeding the allotted amount of disk space. A soft quota, therefore, is only a warning that serves to inform users and administrators of the user's current disk consumption.

As mentioned earlier, the Add A New User Account Wizard creates the two quotas for each user account, but it is up to you, the administrator, to enable them. You can also modify the default amount of disk space you allot to each user individually. To enable the quotas for an existing user account, use the following procedure:

1. Log on to your Windows SBS 2008 server, using an account with network Administrator privileges. The Windows SBS Console appears.
2. Click Users And Groups, and then select the Users tab.
3. Select one of the users in the list and, in the Tasks list, select Edit User Account Properties. The Properties sheet for the user account appears.
4. Click The Folders tab.
5. Select the Enforce Shared Folder Quota check box and modify the Maximum Shared Folder Size setting, if desired.

6. Select the Enable Folder Redirection To The Server check box and modify the Maximum Amount Of Data That Can Be Redirected To Server setting, if desired.

7. Click OK.

MORE INFO   For more detailed administration of quotas, and to create your own additional quotas, you must use the File Server Resource Manager console, accessible from the Administrative Tools program group. In addition to quotas, the console also enables you to create *file screens*, which specify the types of files that users are permitted to store on the server. For example, you can create file screens that prevent users from storing audio and video files on the server.

Sharing Printers

Printer sharing is one of the original applications for which local area networks (LANs) were invented. The ability to send jobs to printers over the network eliminates the need to purchase multiple, redundant printers and prevents users from having to bother the person who has the printer attached to his or her computer. Microsoft Windows Small Business Server (SBS) 2008 includes all the printer sharing capabilities of Windows Server 2008, as well as incorporating basic printer management capabilities into the Windows SBS Console.

Understanding Windows Printing

In addition to the hardware that actually does the printing, Microsoft Windows computers have a number of other components devoted to their print architecture. The main components of a shared printer solution in the Windows environment are as follows:

- **Print device**   In Windows, the term *print device* refers to the actual hardware that produces the hard copy output from a print job. Windows enables you to share a print device that is connected to any computer on the network using a Universal Serial Bus (USB), IEEE 1394 (FireWire), or other port, or connected directly to the network.

- **Printer**   Although the term is commonly used to refer to the hardware, the term *printer*, in Windows, actually refers to the logical representation of a print device that appears in the operating system and on the network. You can create a printer in Windows without there being an actual print device connected to the computer or the network, and it will appear in the Printers control panel just as though the hardware was present. A Windows printer specifies the port, or interface, that the system must use to connect to the print device, as well as what printer driver it must use to process its print jobs.

- **Print server**   A *print server* is the component responsible for holding print jobs in a queue and sending them, one at a time, to the print device. A print server can be a dedicated hardware device that connects the printer to the network, but more often, one or more of the computers on the network functions as the print server. In Windows printing, you can create a single print server that receives jobs from all the clients on the network and feeds them to the print device, or each client can function as its own print server, sending jobs directly to the print device.

- **Printer driver**   The *printer driver* is the software component that receives output from applications generating print jobs and converts it into a data stream using a *page description language (PDL)*, which generates commands that the print device understands. Windows printer drivers generate print jobs using an interim format called *Enhanced Metafile (EMF)*. The EMF data is then converted into a device-specific RAW format, either by the client or the print server, depending on the printer configuration. The print server then stores the RAW data in the print queue until the print device is ready to accept it.

NOTE   Although many sources, including Microsoft documents, use the term *printer* to refer to the printing hardware, this chapter uses the term *print device* to refer to the hardware, while *printer* refers to the Windows logical component.

Administrators can distribute these components around the network in various ways, to accommodate the printing strategy they want to create. Every computer that generates print jobs must have a printer and a printer driver, but you can locate print servers and print devices anywhere on the network.

Understanding the Windows Printing Process

The process by which a computer prints a document includes the following steps, as shown in Figure 8-1:

1. A user working with an application activates its print function, selects one of the printers installed on the computer, and configures application-related settings, such as what pages of the document to print.

2. The application calls the printer driver associated with the selected printer, enabling the user to configure printer-related settings, such as what size paper to use.

3. The printer driver converts the application's print output into XML Paper Specification (XPS) or EMF commands and data, which it sends to the print server.

4. The print server stores the job in a print queue called a *spooler*, where it waits until the print device is ready to accept the job.

5. When the print device is ready, the print server reads the job from the spooler, converts it from EMF to a Printer Control Language (PCL) format, if necessary, and sends it to the print device using the appropriate port.

6. The print device receives the job from the print server, processes the commands and data, and generates the hard copy output.

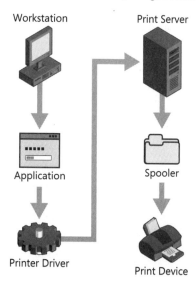

FIGURE 8-1 The Windows printing process

Designing a Network Printing Solution

The printing architecture on a small business network is not terribly complicated in most cases. Small businesses typically have, at most, two or three print devices, but administrators still have to make design decisions, such as the following:

- How to connect the print devices to the network
- Which computer(s) function as print servers
- Who has access to the print devices and when
- Who is responsible for daily printer maintenance

Connecting Print Devices

Before you can share a print device with your Windows SBS 2008 network, you must connect the hardware to one of the computers on the network or connect it directly to the network itself. Most of the print devices on the market today connect to a computer using a USB or IEEE 1394 port, and many also have an integrated network interface adapter, which enables you to connect the device directly to your Ethernet network. Older print devices might connect to a computer using a parallel or serial port, and, in some cases, you can purchase a network interface adapter as an expansion card that plugs into the printer. Finally, you can purchase an external print server that connects directly to the network and has a port for the printer.

The type of print device connection you use should depend on your network design, the layout of your office, and, as always, your budget. When you connect a print device to a computer, as shown in Figure 8-2, that computer functions as a print server, receiving jobs from other computers on the network and feeding them to the print device. Any Windows computer, whether server or workstation, can function as a print server. However, if your users do a lot of printing, the print server functions can impose a significant burden on a workstation that does not have the resources to support them. If at all possible, connecting the print devices to server computers is preferable to workstation connections unless the servers are in a location that would be inconvenient for users having to retrieve their printed documents.

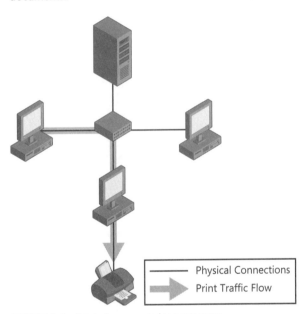

FIGURE 8-2 A print device connected to a computer

The best solution by far, however, is to connect your print devices directly to the network. This solution enables you to locate your print devices anywhere a network connection is available. You can also designate any computer on the network as a print server, which enables you to use your server computers for their intended purpose, no matter where they are located, as shown in Figure 8-3.

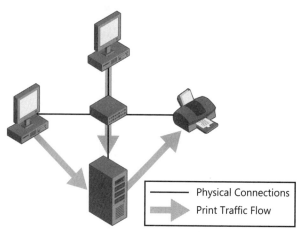

FIGURE 8-3 A print device connected to the network, with a single print server

It is also possible for each computer to function as its own print server, sending jobs directly to the print device, as shown in Figure 8-4. The only drawback to network-attached print devices is that units with network adapters tend to be more expensive than those without them.

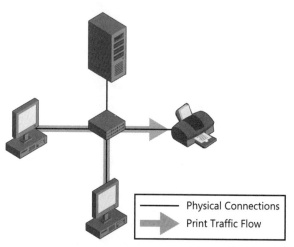

FIGURE 8-4 A print device connected to the network, with each computer acting as its own print server

Selecting a Print Server

The first deciding factor in selecting a computer to function as a print server is the type of print device connections you plan to use. As mentioned earlier, if you connect a print device directly to a computer, that computer must function as the print server. Network-attached printers provide greater flexibility.

In addition to the type of connections you plan to use, however, you should also base your selection of a print server on the following factors:

- **Print volume** The more printing your users do, the greater the burden on the print server. Large numbers of documents use more print server resources than small numbers, lengthy documents use more resources than brief ones, and graphical documents use more than plain text.

- **Print rendering** When a print server is running Windows Server 2008 or Windows Vista, you can specify whether the client or the print server should render the print jobs. Client-side rendering (CSR) reduces the burden on the print server.

- **Computer resources** Print volume and CSR both affect the resources used by print server functions. A workstation with the minimum recommended system requirements, for example, can function adequately as a print server, but its functionality as a workstation might be compromised.

Controlling Access to Print Devices

In many cases, administrators grant users unrestricted access to the print devices on the network. However, you might want to regulate access to color print devices, or other units with expensive consumables such as letterhead paper. Windows printers have their own permission system, which functions similar to NTFS and share permissions. You can specify which users can send jobs to a printer and also control access based on other factors, such as the time of day and the user's priority.

Providing Print Device Maintenance

Print devices are one of the few network hardware components that require maintenance on almost a daily basis. Part of your printing solution should included a decision as to who is responsible for the print devices' regular maintenance, including tasks such as loading media, clearing paper jams, and replacing toner or ink cartridges. These are thankless tasks that many people try to avoid, so it is important to delegate them decisively. Otherwise, you might find a huge backlog of print jobs left in the queue because the print device is out of paper or toner.

Deploying Network Printers

The process of deploying a printer on your Windows SBS 2008 network consists of the following basic steps:

- Connect the print device to the computer or network.

- Create a printer on the print server and install drivers.
- Share the printer.
- Configure clients to access the printer.

These steps are discussed in the following sections.

Connecting a Print Device

For most of the print devices on the market today, the process of connecting the device consists of simply plugging a cable into a USB or IEEE 1394 port on the computer you intend to use as a print server, or plugging a cable into any network connection. Keep in mind, however, that many print devices do not include a USB or network cable in the box, so you might have to purchase one separately.

Older print devices might use a parallel or serial port connection to connect to a computer. Parallel connections use a large, heavy cable that is limited to a maximum length of 6 to 9 feet. Serial cables are thinner and lighter, and can be longer, but print devices with serial connectors are relatively rare.

To connect a print device that does not have a built-in network adapter directly to the network, you can purchase a device that provides a network connection. Some print device models have an expansion slot that can accept a proprietary network adapter/print server made by the print device manufacturer, but external print server devices are also available that are not proprietary, which enable you to connect any print device to your network. Print server devices supporting either wired or wireless networks are available, providing you with virtually unlimited freedom in placing your computers.

> **MORE INFO** Hewlett-Packard is one of the largest manufacturers of print server devices. Its JetDirect line of products include internal print servers that plug into a modular *Enhanced Input/Output (EIO)* slot built into some of their print devices, and external print servers that can connect one or more print devices of any manufacturer to a network.

Creating a Printer

USB and IEEE 1394 are both Plug and Play interfaces, so when you connect a print device to a Windows computer using one of those ports and turn the print device on, the system typically detects it and automatically starts a Plug and Play hardware detection and installation sequence. During the installation process, Windows creates a printer, configures the port that provides access to the print device, installs printer drivers, and typically offers to share the printer with the network as well.

All the current Windows operating systems include a large collection of printer drivers, but if your print device is a newly released model, or a particularly obscure one, the system might prompt you to supply drivers. Print devices typically include a driver disk, and manufacturers usually have the latest drivers available on a Web site. Your print device might also include additional software, such as a print device management application. In most cases, Windows can access the print device without any special software other than drivers, so installing these other products is usually optional.

Installing a Local Printer Manually

If you have a print device that does not use a Plug and Play interface, such as one that connects to the computer's parallel or serial port, you have to run the Add Printer Wizard. The following procedure illustrates the process of installing a printer connected to a Windows SBS 2008 server using a parallel or serial port:

1. Click Start, and then click Control Panel. The Control Panel window appears.

2. Double-click Printers. The Printers control panel appears, as shown here.

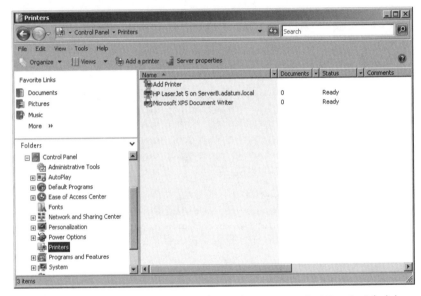

3. Right-click Add Printer and, from the context menu, select Run As Adminis-trator. When the User Account Control dialog box appears, click Continue. The Add Printer Wizard appears, displaying the Choose A Local Or Network Printer page, as shown here.

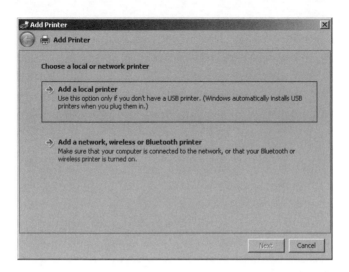

TIP When you install a printer on your Windows SBS 2008 server, if you do not elevate your access by selecting the Run As Administrator option, you can install only existing network printers. To create a new printer element for a locally attached print device, you must have Administrator access.

4. Click Add A Local Printer. The Choose A Printer Port page appears, as shown here.

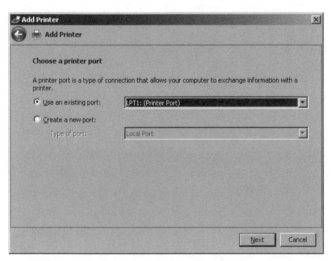

5. Leave the Use An Existing Port option selected and choose the correct port from the drop-down list. Then click Next. The Install The Printer Driver page appears, as shown here.

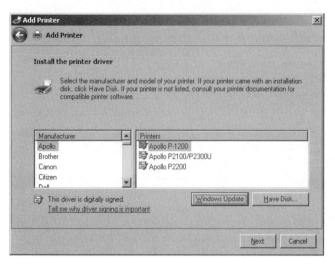

6. From the list on the left, select the manufacturer of the print device.

   NOTE If your printer does not appear in the list, you must obtain a printer driver from the manufacturer and click Have Disk to install it.

7. From the list of the manufacturers' printers on the right, select your print device and click Next. The Type A Printer Name page appears, as shown here.

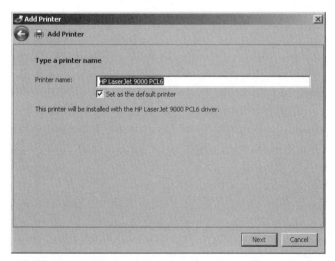

8. Specify the name that the system will use to identify the print device and click Next. The Printer Sharing page appears, as shown here.

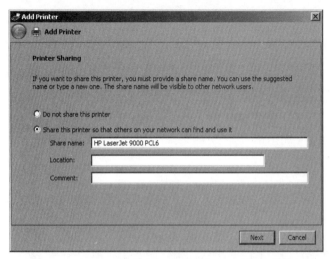

9. Leave the Share This Printer So That Others On Your Network Can Find And Use It option selected and, in the Share Name text box, specify the name by which the printer will be known on the network. Optionally, you can also specify additional information about the printer in the Location and Comment text boxes.

10. Click Next. The wizard installs the printer and the You've Successfully Added The Printer page appears.

11. Click Finish. The wizard closes and the printer appears in the Printers control panel.

IMPORTANT If you open the Windows SBS Console immediately after installing a printer using this procedure, the printer does not appear in the Printers list on the Network/Devices page. This is because although the Add Printer Wizard has shared the printer, it has not added it to your Active Directory Domain Services (AD DS) domain. To complete the installation, you must perform one of the procedures in 'Sharing a Printer,' later in this chapter.

Installing a Network-Attached Printer

The process of installing a print device that connects directly to the network and creating a printer for it is largely determined by the hardware manufacturer. In most cases, you simply connect the print device to the network and run an installation program on the computer that you want to function as the print server. The program detects the print device on the network, creates a Transmission Control Protocol/Internet Protocol (TCP/IP) port that points to the print device's IP address, creates a printer using that port, and installs the appropriate drivers. The program might also provide you with the opportunity to share the printer and install additional proprietary tools.

A print device that connects directly to a network has a network interface adapter, just like a computer, and like a computer, it must have an IP address. Most of the network print devices manufactured today include a Dynamic Host Configuration Protocol (DHCP) client, which enables them to obtain an IP address from the DHCP server on your network. Others might have a preconfigured IP address, which you can learn from the product documentation, or by printing out a test page.

As with most network peripherals, many network print devices have an integrated Web server, which provides a configuration interface, like the one shown in Figure 8-5. This interface typically enables you to specify whether you want the print device to obtain its IP address using DHCP, or use a specific address that you configure manually.

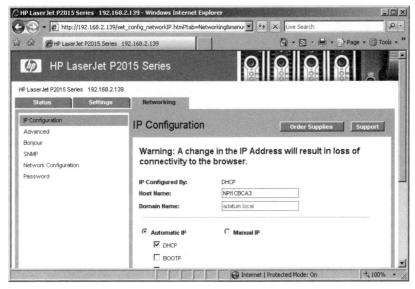

FIGURE 8-5 The configuration interface for a network-attached printer

Installing a Network Printer Manually

For a network-attached print device that does not have an installation program, or for a print device connected to a stand-alone print server that does not have an installation program, you can install a printer with a TCP/IP port manually using the following procedure:

1. Click Start, and then click Control Panel. The Control Panel window appears.

2. Double-click Printers. The Printers control panel appears.

3. Right-click Add Printer and, from the context menu, select Run As Administrator. When the User Account Control dialog box appears, click Continue.

The Add Printer Wizard appears, displaying the Choose A Local Or Network Printer page.

4. Click Add A Network, Wireless, Or Bluetooth Printer. The Select A Printer page appears, as shown here.

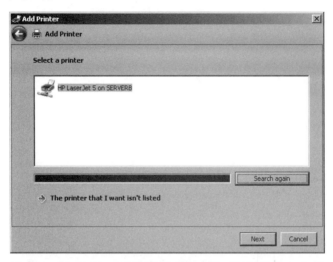

5. Click The Printer That I Want Isn't Listed. The Find A Printer By Name Or TCP/IP Address page appears, as shown here.

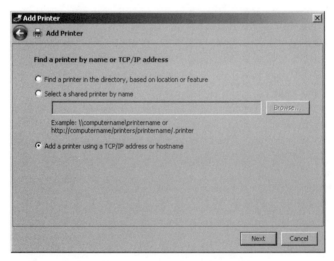

6. Leave the Add A Printer Using A TCP/IP Address Or Hostname option selected and click Next. The Type A Printer Hostname Or IP Address page appears, as shown here.

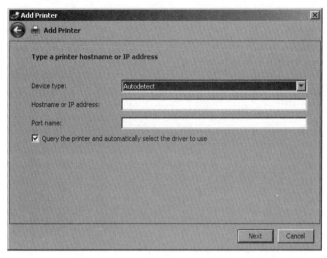

7. In the Device Type drop-down list, select TCP/IP Device.

8. In the Hostname Or IP Address text box, type the IP address of the print device or the stand-alone print server to which the print device is connected and click Next. The Install The Printer Driver page appears.

9. From the list on the left, select the manufacturer of the print device.

   NOTE If your printer does not appear in the list, you must obtain a printer driver from the manufacturer and click Have Disk to install it.

10. From the list of the manufacturers' printers on the right, select your print device and click Next. The Type A Printer name page appears.

11. Specify the name that the system will use to identify the print device and click Next. The Printer Sharing page appears.

12. Leave the Share This Printer So That Others On The Network Can Find And Use It option selected and, in the Share Name text box, specify the name by which the printer will be known on the network. Optionally, you can also specify additional information about the printer in the Location and Comment text boxes.

13. Click Next. The wizard installs the printer and the You've Successfully Added The Printer page appears.

14. Click Finish. The wizard closes and the printer appears in the Printers control panel.

Creating a DHCP Reservation for a Printer

DHCP client support is a common feature in network printer devices; it greatly simplifies the print device installation process. However, the *D* in *DHCP* stands for "Dynamic," meaning that it is possible for a client's IP address assignment to change.

If, for example, a network print device is disconnected or offline long enough for its DHCP lease to expire, the DHCP server might assign it a different address when you reconnect it to the network. The print device can communicate with the network, but the print clients might still have ports that reference the old IP address.

> **MORE INFO**   For more information on IP address assignment and DHCP, see Chapter 2, "A Networking Primer."

One of the best ways to ensure continued connectivity for a DHCP-equipped network print device is to create a reservation for it on the DHCP server. A *DHCP reservation* is an IP address that you permanently assign to a specific client, based on the Media Access Control (MAC) address encoded into its network interface adapter hardware. The print device still obtains its IP address from the DHCP server, but the server always assigns it the same address so long as the print device is connected to the same IP subnet.

> **BEST PRACTICES**   Although it might be possible to configure your print device manually to use a static IP address, creating a DHCP reservation is a better solution, so that all your IP address assignments are documented and managed in one place. If you manually assign an IP address in your DHCP scope to a device on your network, the DHCP server might attempt to assign that same address to another device later. DHCP servers check the network for IP address duplication before they complete each address assignment, but there is no way to know how the print device will react to an address conflict.

To create a DHCP reservation for your network print device, use the following procedure:

1. Connect your print device to the network and configure it to obtain its IP address using DHCP.

2. Log on to your Windows SBS 2008 server, using an account with network Administrator privileges.

3. Click Start, and then click Administrative Tools, DHCP. When the User Account Control dialog box appears, click Continue. The DHCP console appears, as shown here.

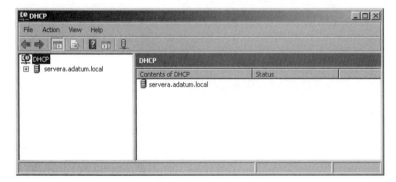

4. Expand the node representing your server and browse to the scope that the Connect To The Internet Wizard created on your server, as shown here.

5. Expand the scope and click the Address Pool node, as shown here.

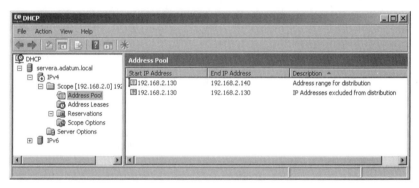

6. Note the range of addresses available for distribution. Then, right-click the Address Pool node and, from the context menu, select New Exclusion Range. The Add Exclusion dialog box appears, as shown here.

7. In the Start IP Address and End IP Address text boxes, specify a range of addresses at the end of your scope that is large enough to support all your network print devices. Click Add, and then click Close. The new exclusion range appears in the Address Pool list, as shown here.

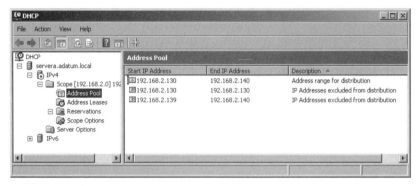

8. Click the Address Leases node.

9. Locate the lease for your print device in the list and adjust the column widths in the console so that you can see the entire Unique ID value for the lease, as shown here.

   TIP Your print device most likely has a host name that you do not recognize, one that is different from the names you have assigned to your network computers.

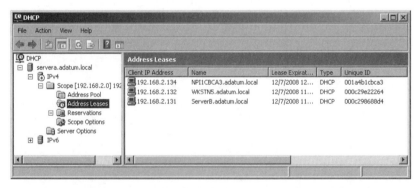

10. Click the Reservations node, which displays an empty list, and then click the Address Leases node again.

11. Right-click the Reservations node and, from the context menu, select New Reservation. The New Reservation dialog box appears, as shown here.

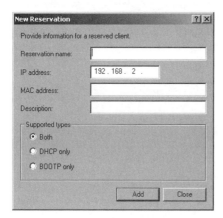

12. In the Reservation Name text box, type the name of your network print device.

13. In the IP Address text box, type one of the IP addresses in the exclusion range you just created.

14. In the MAC Address text box, type the Unique ID value for your print device's current address lease.

> **NOTE** The Unique ID value is the hardware address assigned to the print device's network interface adapter by the manufacturer.

15. Click Add, and then click Close. The reservation appears in the Address Leases list, with a Lease Expiration value of Reservation (Inactive), as shown here.

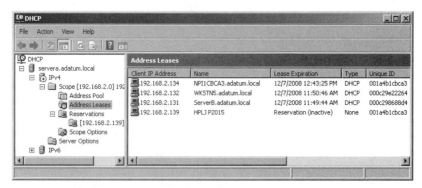

16. Turn the print device off or unplug it from its power source. Wait 30 seconds and then turn the print device back on or plug it back in. Wait another 30 seconds for the print device to initialize.

17. In the DHCP console, on the Action menu, click Refresh. The print device's original address lease disappears from the Address Leases list and the reservation you created now has a Lease Expiration value of Reservation (Active), as shown here.

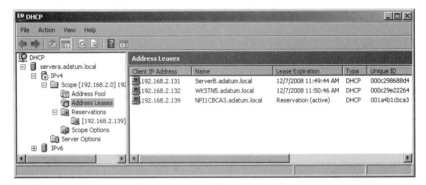

18. Close the DHCP console.

From now on, each time the DHCP server receives an IP address request from the print device containing the MAC address you specified, the server assigns the address in the reservation you created.

Sharing a Printer

Once you have installed a printer on one of your network computers, you must share it to make it accessible to all the other computers on the network. When you share a printer, Windows also enables you to add printer drivers for other Windows platforms. This way, when a client computer on the network installs the printer, it can download the correct driver from the print server automatically.

To share an existing printer on your Windows SBS 2008 server, use the following procedure:

1. Log on to your Windows SBS 2008 server, using an account with network Administrator privileges.

2. Click Start, and then click Control Panel. The Control Panel window appears.

3. Double-click the Printers icon. The Printers control panel appears.

4. Right-click the printer you want to share and, from the context menu, select Run As Administrator, Sharing. When the User Account Control dialog box appears, click Continue. The Properties sheet for the printer appears, displaying the Sharing tab, as shown here.

5. Select the Share This Printer check box.

6. In the Share Name text box, type the name by which the printer will be known on the network.

7. Select the Render Print Jobs On Client Computers check box, if you want to minimize the processing load on the print server.

8. Select the List In The Directory check box.

9. Click Additional Drivers. The Additional Drivers dialog box appears, as shown here.

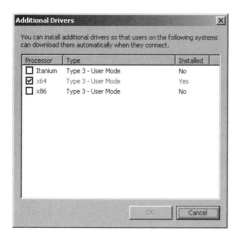

10. Select the check boxes for the platforms you want to install and click OK. A Printer Drivers dialog box appears for each platform you selected, as shown here.

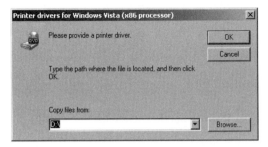

11. Type or browse to the location of the printer driver for each platform and click OK.

12. Click OK to close the Additional Drivers dialog box.

13. Click OK to close the printer's Properties sheet.

> **NOTE** In many cases, you do not have to perform this procedure, because the Add Printer Wizard includes a page that enables you to share the printer as you create it. However, the wizard's sharing page lacks one critical facility: it does not list the shared printer in AD DS.

When you share a printer without adding it to AD DS, computers on the network can send jobs to the printer, but they cannot search the directory for it, and, more importantly, administrators cannot manage the printer using the controls on the Network/Devices page of the Windows SBS Console. The console populates the Devices list by searching the AD DS database for printer objects, so if you have a shared printer on your network that does not appear in the console, you can add it to the directory in one of two ways:

- By clicking List A Shared Printer In This Console in the Tasks list on the Network/Devices page and specifying the path to the printer share, using the interface shown here.

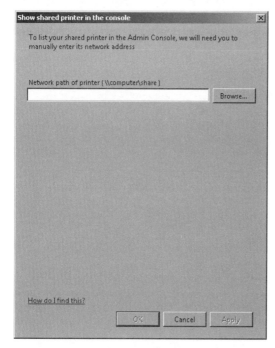

- By opening the Sharing tab in the printer's Properties sheet, as shown here, and selecting the List In The Directory check box.

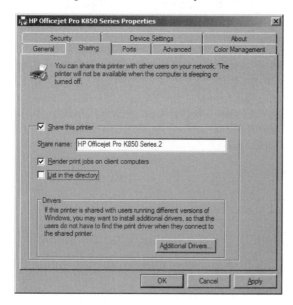

Deploying Printers on Clients

Once you have installed a print device, created a printer for it, and shared the printer with the network, client computers can install it as needed, using the following procedure:

1. Click Start, and then click Control Panel. The Control Panel window appears.
2. Double-click Printers. The Printers control panel appears, as shown here.

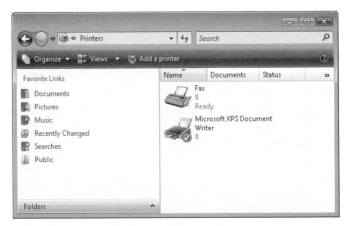

3. Click Add A Printer. The Add Printer Wizard appears, displaying the Choose A Local Or Network Printer page, as shown here.

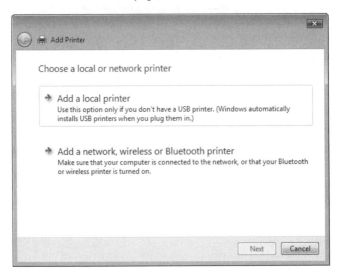

4. Click Add A Network, Wireless, Or Bluetooth Printer. The Searching For Available Printers page appears briefly, and then the Select A Printer page appears, as shown here.

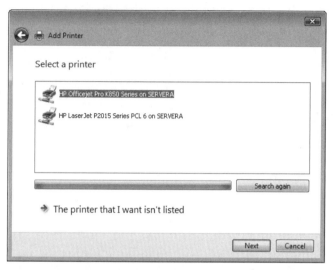

5. Select the printer you want to install and click Next. A Windows Printer Installation progress indicator box appears as the system installs the printer. Then the Type A Printer Name page appears, as shown here.

6. Modify the default printer name, if desired, and click Next. A You've Successfully Added The Printer page appears.

7. Click Finish. The wizard closes and the printer appears in the Printers control panel, as shown here.

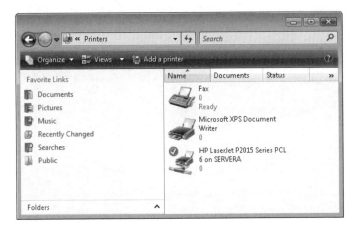

MORE INFO In addition to installing printers on client computers manually, you can also deploy a printer to all the clients on the network using Group Policy settings. For more information, see Chapter 16, "Managing Infrastructure Services."

Managing Printers Using the Windows SBS Console

Once you have deployed your print devices, created printers for them, shared them, and listed them in the AD DS directory, you can manage them all from the Windows SBS Console on your primary server, no matter which computers you are using as print servers. When you click the Network button in the console and select the Devices tab, you see a list of the shared printers on the network, as shown in Figure 8-6.

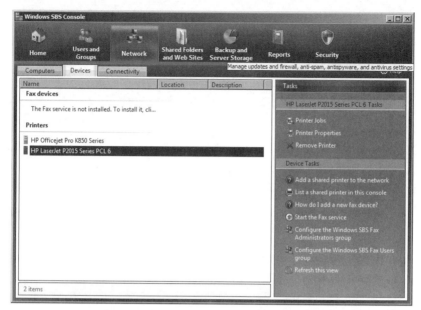

FIGURE 8-6 Installed and shared printers in the Windows SBS Console

By selecting a printer and clicking one of the items in the printer-specific Tasks list, you can perform the management tasks described in the following sections.

Managing Queued Print Jobs

When you select a printer and click Printer Jobs in the Tasks list, a window appears, named for the printer and containing a list of the jobs currently waiting in the print queue, as shown in Figure 8-7. With the appropriate permissions, you can pause, resume, and cancel individual print jobs, as well as pause and cancel the entire queue.

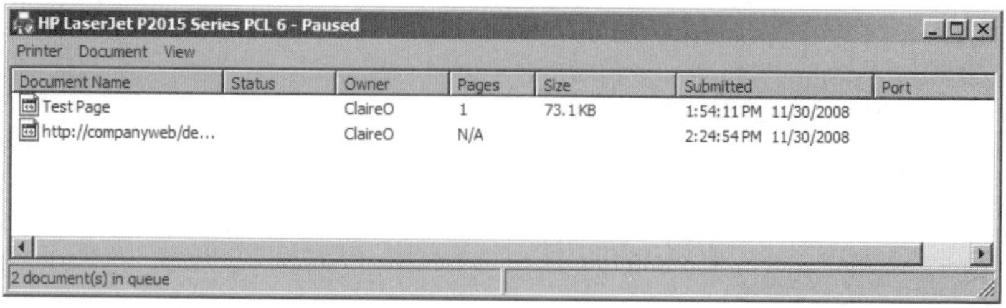

FIGURE 8-7 The print queue window for a shared printer

Controlling Printer Access

As mentioned earlier in this chapter, Windows printers have their own system of permissions, which you can use to specify who is allowed to access and manage your shared printers. By default, Windows grants the Allow Print permission to the Everyone special identity on all printers. This enables all users to send jobs to the printers. The other permission assignments, and the capabilities provided by the various print permissions, are listed in Table 8-1.

TABLE 8-1 Windows Printer Permissions

PERMISSION	CAPABILITIES	DEFAULT ASSIGNMENTS
Print	• Connect to a printer • Print documents • Pause, resume, restart, and cancel the user's own documents	• Everyone • Administrators • Server Operators • Print Operators
Manage Printers	• Cancel all documents • Share a printer • Change printer properties • Delete a printer • Change printer permissions	• Administrators • Server Operators • Print Operators
Manage Documents	• Pause, resume, restart, and cancel all users' documents • Control job settings for all documents	• Creator Owner • Administrators • Server Operators • Print Operators

To limit printer access to specific users, you must revoke the permissions from the Everyone special identity and then grant the Allow Print permission to the users or groups that you want to give access to the printer. To modify the default print permissions, use the following procedure:

1. Log on to your Windows SBS 2008 server, using an account with network Administrator privileges. The Windows SBS Console appears.

2. Click Network, and then select the Devices tab.

3. Select the printer that you want to manage and, in the Tasks list, click Printer Properties. The Properties sheet for the printer appears, as shown here.

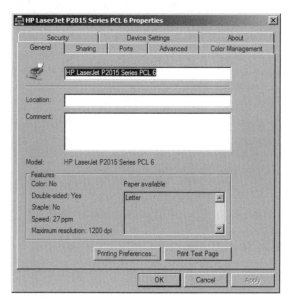

4. Click the Security tab, as shown here.

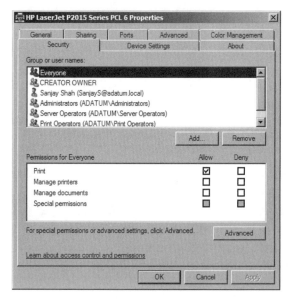

The Group Or User Names list in the top half of the tab specifies all the security principals possessing permissions to the selected printer. The Permissions list in the bottom half of the tab specifies the permissions assigned to the selected security principal.

5. To revoke existing permissions, select one of the security principals in the Group Or User Names list and clear any or all of the Allow check boxes in the Permissions list.

6. To grant new permissions, click Add. The Select Users, Computers, Or Groups dialog box appears, as shown here.

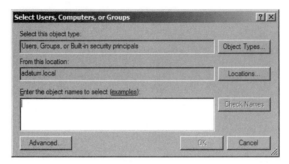

7. In the Enter The Object Names To Select text box, type the name of the user or group you want to add to the list and click OK. The user or group appears in the list.

8. Select the security principal you just added and, in the Permissions list, select the check boxes for the permissions you want to assign.

9. Click OK. The Properties sheet closes.

Administering E-Mail

E-mail is an all-but-essential tool in today's business world, and Microsoft Exchange Server 2007 is one of the most powerful e-mail server products on the market. Exchange Server is a highly flexible product, designed to support networks of virtually any size, and as a result, it can be complicated to install and configure. However, Microsoft Windows Small Business Server (SBS) 2008 integrates the Exchange Server installation into its primary setup procedure and completes most of the configuration tasks for you. The Windows SBS Console enables you to configure the e-mail settings that small businesses use most often, but you still have access to the full power of the Exchange Management Console and the other tools included with Exchange Server 2007.

An E-Mail Primer

A basic understanding of how e-mail works is critical to managing an e-mail system efficiently. E-mail is a client/server application that enables a client to send messages to any other client with only a simple identifying address. Between the sending and receiving clients is a system of e-mail servers that communicate with each other using specialized protocols, such as the Simple Mail Transfer Protocol (SMTP). As with most networking subjects, e-mail communication can be extremely complicated, but the typical small business network administrator does not need to delve into the technical details too deeply. The following sections examine some of the most basic concepts, however, and describe how they pertain to Windows SBS 2008.

Understanding E-Mail Addresses

As all e-mail users know, an e-mail address consists of a single user name, followed by an @ character and a domain name, as shown in Figure 9-1. The first part of the address, the part before the @ sign, is the *local part*, which need be understood only by the destination mail server. The part after the @ sign identifies the domain on the Internet where the destination client is located.

sanjays@adatum.com

Local Part   Domain Name

FIGURE 9-1 The parts of an e-mail address

In Chapter 2, "A Networking Primer," you learned how Internet Protocol (IP) addresses consist of two parts: a host identifier and a network identifier. Routers on the Internet use the network identifier to forward IP datagrams to a particular destination network, and then the router on the destination network uses the host identifier to forward the datagrams to the correct computer on that network. In the same way, the Domain Name System (DNS) uses fully qualified domain names (FQDNs), which consist of two parts: a host name and a domain name. When a DNS server tries to resolve an FQDN into an IP address, it forwards the name resolution request to the authoritative server for the domain, which looks up the IP address of the specified host.

E-mail communications function in much the same way. The SMTP servers on the Internet read only the second part of the e-mail address and forward the e-mail message to the server for the appropriate domain. Then, the domain server reads the first part of the address and deposits the e-mail message in the mailbox for the appropriate user.

Because the domain name of an e-mail address must be understandable to all the servers on the Internet, it must conform to the same standards as all DNS domain names. The domain name part of an e-mail address is subject to the following limitations:

- The domain name can be no more than 255 characters long.
- Domain names can consist only of the letters *A* to *Z*, the numbers 0 to 9, and the hyphen (-) character.
- Domain names are not case-sensitive. The addresses *sanjays@adatum.com* and *sanjays@ADATUM.COM* are delivered to the same mail server.

Because the local part of an e-mail address has to be read and understood only by the destination mail server, its specifications are less stringent. The local part of an e-mail address is subject to the following limitations:

- The local part of the name can be no more than 64 characters long.
- Local part names can consist of the letters *A* to *Z*, the numbers 0 to 9, and the following characters: ! # $ % & ' * + - / = ? ^ _ ` { | } ~
- Local part names can also contain the period (.) character, so long as it does not appear as the first or last character and so long as it does not appear twice in succession.
- Local part names can conceivably be case-sensitive, but in Exchange Server 2007, they are not. Exchange Server delivers the addresses *sanjays@adatum.com* and *SanjayS@adatum.com* to the same mailbox.

Local part names can be case-sensitive because their interpretation is left solely to the destination e-mail server. If a particular server implementation supports case-sensitive local part names, and the destination server is running that implementation, then the distinction of two local part names that differ only in their case is possible. However, on the Internet, senders rarely know what server implementations their recipients are using, so most e-mail servers, including Exchange Server 2007, follow the recommendation of the SMTP standard and treat all local part names as case-insensitive. Windows SBS 2008 does not allow you to create two user accounts with e-mail addresses that differ only in case.

MORE INFO Some e-mail servers impose other restrictions on local part name construction. For example, the Windows Live Hotmail system limits local part names to letters, numbers, and the period (.), hyphen (-), and underscore (_) characters. You cannot create a Hotmail account name using any other characters, and the Hotmail system does not send e-mail to any address using other characters.

Despite the limitations listed earlier, one of your primary goals when assigning e-mail addresses should always be user-friendliness. An e-mail address like *hknjv!fgjyc8*pi09r65q34^47iponi0-v665q{436y@xyucu6ysxxgfu7opm83opdx5z-w56iyb.com* would be technically legal, but it would be nothing but trouble for the individuals forced to use it, or anyone trying to remember it.

Understanding E-Mail Server Functions

E-mail clients have two basic functions: they send outgoing mail to one kind of server and they retrieve incoming mail from another. The servers conduct the rest of the e-mail communication process, including the transmission of messages to computers hundreds or thousands of miles away. The following sections discuss the main e-mail server types.

IMPORTANT It is critical to realize that in this discussion of e-mail communications, the term *server* does not necessarily refer to a separate computer, but rather to a process running on a computer, in the form of an application or service. A single computer can perform multiple server functions, as in the case of an Exchange Server 2007 computer, which can perform all the e-mail server roles simultaneously.

Simple Mail Transfer Protocol (SMTP)

SMTP is the primary e-mail communication protocol, responsible for the majority of e-mail traffic on the Internet. Every e-mail client has the name or IP address of an SMTP server in its configuration settings, to which it transmits its outgoing mail messages. E-mail servers can use SMTP for both incoming and outgoing traffic.

SMTP is a text-based application layer protocol that e-mail clients use to send their outgoing messages to a server, and which e-mail servers use to forward the messages to other servers. Windows SBS 2008 servers function as SMTP servers, as can all Exchange Server 2007 computers. Whichever e-mail client your users choose to run, it sends its outgoing e-mail messages to the Windows SBS 2008 server using SMTP. If the intended recipient of a message is another user on your network, the Windows SBS server deposits the message in the recipient's mailbox. If the message is addressed to a user in another domain, the server transmits the message to another SMTP server on the Internet.

An SMTP server is a relatively simple mechanism, but its role has been complicated over the years by the increasing prevalence on the Internet of unsolicited e-mail traffic, also known as *spam*. In earlier days, Internet service providers (ISPs) set up SMTP servers for their customers, connected them to the Internet, and left them open for use by anyone. The well-known port number for the SMTP protocol is 25, and those servers willingly accepted anyone's outgoing SMTP e-mail messages, so long as they were addressed to that port.

However, it was not long before spammers began using these open servers to send millions of messages. By using the SMTP servers belonging to other ISPs, the spammers made it difficult, if not impossible, to trace their spam e-mails back to them. As a result of the enormous amounts of bandwidth consumed by the spam, ISPs were forced to add various forms of protection to their SMTP servers.

Most Internet SMTP servers today require users to authenticate before they can submit outgoing traffic, and many of them refuse all traffic addressed to port number 25. E-mail clients typically enable users to specify the credentials they should use to log on to the SMTP server, as shown in Figure 9-2, as well as an alternative to port number 25. Port number 587 has been standardized as the port for authenticated outgoing mail submissions, but some ISPs use nonstandard ports instead.

FIGURE 9-2 The Outgoing Server configuration settings in Microsoft Office Outlook 2007

Post Office Protocol Version 3 (POP3)

SMTP is strictly a "push" protocol. E-mail clients and other e-mail servers send messages to SMTP servers; they do not retrieve messages from them. To retrieve their incoming messages from a server, clients use one of two "pull" protocols: *Post Office Protocol version 3 (POP3)* or *Internet Message Access Protocol version 4 (IMAP4)*. POP3 is the more popular of these protocols.

MORE INFO The standard for version 3 of POP was published in 1996. POP1 and POP2 have long since become obsolete, and any reference to POP without a version identifier almost certainly refers to POP version 3. There is a Post Office Protocol version 4 (POP4) server in development, but the protocol has not yet been standardized, nor is it commercially available.

POP3 is a relatively simple protocol that is designed to provide clients with offline access to their e-mail messages. A POP3 server maintains a separate mailbox for each user, where the server stores the incoming e-mail messages it receives through SMTP connections. E-mail clients periodically connect to the server, authenticate the user, and download the messages in the user's mailbox. In most cases, the server deletes the messages once the client has downloaded them, but many POP3 implementations provide users with the ability to leave the downloaded messages on the server, as shown in Figure 9-3.

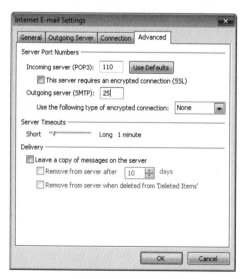

FIGURE 9-3 The Advanced configuration settings in Outlook 2007

The design of the POP3 mechanism enables clients to connect to the server, download messages, and then disconnect, after which the user can work with the messages offline. Because of this, the client's message store is said to be authoritative in a POP3 application. When dial-up connections were the prevalent form of Internet access, POP3 provided the most bandwidth-efficient method of accessing incoming e-mail.

POP3 is designed to keep the server side of the application as simple as possible, leaving the majority of the messaging tasks to the client. There are, however, two potential areas of server complexity. One involves the numbering of the messages in a mailbox when a user downloads and deletes some, but not all of the waiting messages. Instead of numbering the messages consecutively, and renumbering the messages when the client deletes some of them, most POP3 implementations use a technique called *Unique Identification Listing (UIDL)* to assign a permanent, unique identifier to each message in the mailbox.

The other potential problem is one of authentication security. The POP3 standard contains no provision for the use of encrypted passwords, and some implementations still require clients to transmit passwords in plain text. There are, however, a number of POP3 implementations that use security extensions to protect passwords and prevent unauthorized access to e-mail accounts.

POP3 servers use the well-known port number 110 for client connections, and many implementations can use *Secure Sockets Layer (SSL)* or *Transport Layer Security (TLS)* to encrypt the contents of the e-mail messages during download.

Internet Message Access Protocol 4 (IMAP4)

IMAP4 is another "pull" protocol that clients can use to obtain their e-mail messages from a server. However, unlike POP3, IMAP4 is designed to leave the messages stored on the server and enable users to work with them there. An IMAP4 client is able to store copies of e-mail messages on the local drive, but the authoritative message store resides on the server.

Most e-mail clients can support both IMAP4 and POP3 connections to a server. IMAP4 connections use well-known port number 143. ISPs tend to provide their customers with POP3 mailboxes because they require fewer server resources and much less server storage. Web-based e-mail implementations, on the other hand, often use IMAP4 to display a user's message store in a Web browser interface.

IMAP4 places a much greater burden on the server than POP3, not only because the server must maintain a message store for each user but also because the IMAP4 server provides more functions than a POP3 server. IMAP4 clients can create folders to organize e-mail messages, move messages around between folders, and run searches for specific messages. Searching, in particular, can be a highly resource intensive task, depending on the size of the mailbox.

IMAP4 also provides distinct advantages for the user. When a client connects to a server using IMAP4, access to the user's message store is almost immediate because the client is displaying the contents of the mailbox as it exists on the server. By contrast, a POP3 client must check the server for new messages, download them, and integrate the messages into the client's data store before the user can begin working with them.

Because IMAP4 stores messages on the server, users can access their mailboxes from different locations without causing problems. For this reason, IMAP4 is a popular solution on college campuses, where students in a computer center might use a different system each time they access their e-mail. IMAP4 also enables multiple users to access the same mailbox simultaneously, while a POP3 mailbox can support only one connected user at a time. This can be highly useful in a business environment, such as a help desk that has several people servicing a single e-mail help line.

Exchange Server 2007 Functions

Exchange Server 2007, although based on industry standards, is a proprietary mail and scheduling product that is designed to provide clients with access to local and Internet e-mail, shared calendars and scheduling, task management, and a unified messaging interface that can route other types of traffic, such as voice mail and faxes, to a user's inbox. Windows SBS 2008 automatically installs Exchange Server 2007 with the operating system and configures it to provide these services to your network users.

When you run the Add A New User Account Wizard in the Windows SBS Console, the wizard creates an Exchange Server mailbox for each of your new users using the e-mail address you specify. By default, the e-mail address consists of the user's account name and the name of the Internet domain you specified in the Internet Address Management Wizard, as in the example *sanjays@adatum.info*.

Users can access their mailboxes using the Office Outlook Web Access (OWA) site, shown in Figure 9-4, which Windows SBS 2008 creates by default. Users can also access their Exchange Server mailboxes with Outlook 2007, but this client is not included with Windows SBS 2008. You must purchase Office 2007 for your client computers to obtain the Outlook client.

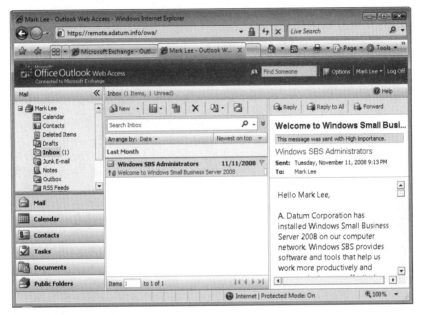

FIGURE 9-4 The OWA interface

The Exchange Server 2007 implementation in Windows SBS 2008 includes POP3 and IMAP4 servers among its capabilities, but by default, the server does not start the Exchange POP3 and Exchange IMAP4 services, which prevents clients from using these protocols to access their Exchange Server mailboxes. If desired, you can start the POP3 or IMAP4 service on your Windows SBS 2008 server, enabling users to access their mailboxes using clients such as Windows Mail in Windows Vista and Outlook Express in Windows XP. However, this solution provides users only with e-mail access. These clients do not support the scheduling and task management features in Exchange Server.

Understanding E-Mail Client Functions

An e-mail client performs two basic functions: it sends outgoing e-mail messages to a server, and it retrieves the incoming messages from a server. Virtually all e-mail clients are capable of sending messages to an SMTP server and accessing incoming messages using POP3, IMAP4, or both. Some clients, such as Outlook, can also connect to proprietary mail server products, such as Exchange Server 2007.

Many e-mail clients are available, in two major forms: stand-alone applications and Web-based interfaces. All the Windows client operating systems include an Internet e-mail client. Windows Vista has Windows Mail, and Windows XP and earlier versions have Outlook Express. Both of these clients include support for SMTP, POP3, and IMAP4 connections, but they cannot connect to Exchange Server except by using these protocols.

To configure an e-mail client to access Internet e-mail, you typically have to specify settings for the following parameters:

- **User name**   The name of the user that appears in the client interface.
- **E-mail address**   The address associated with the mailbox that the client accesses.
- **Account name**   The name that the client uses to log on to the POP3 or IMAP4 server containing the user's mailbox. This name might or might not be the same as the local part of the e-mail address.
- **Password**   The password that the client uses to log on to the POP3 or IMAP4 server.
- **Outgoing server name**   The name of the SMTP server to which the client sends outgoing Internet e-mail messages.
- **Outgoing server port number**   The port number that the SMTP server uses to receive client transmissions. The default value is 25, and the use of port number 587 is common. However, some servers use nonstandard port numbers.
- **Outgoing server user name and password**   Some SMTP servers require clients to log on before they can send outgoing messages. These fields contain the client credentials for the SMTP logon and usually have an option to use the same credentials as the POP3 or IMAP4 server.
- **Incoming server name**   The name of the POP3 or IMAP4 server from which the client receives incoming Internet e-mail messages.
- **Incoming server port number**   The port number that the POP3 or IMAP4 server uses to receive client transmissions. The default value for POP3 is 110; for IMAP4, the default is 143. The use of nonstandard port numbers for POP3 and IMAP4 is possible, but rare.
- **Server message retention settings**   For POP3 server connections, this specifies whether the server should delete messages that the client has finished downloading.

Web-based clients are applications that run on a Web server, usually a server belonging to the e-mail service provider. ISPs often provide their customers with both POP3 access, which requires a stand-alone client, and a Web-based interface, which runs on their own servers. Other mail providers, such as Windows Live Hotmail, provide only a Web interface, although there are stand-alone clients that can access these Web mail servers using a Hypertext Transfer Protocol (HTTP) connection and download messages to the local drive.

Proprietary clients and server mail solutions can use any communications protocol the developers want. Outlook, for example, is designed primarily to connect to Exchange Server computers on the same local network and uses a proprietary protocol called *Messaging Application Programming Interface/Remote Procedure Call (MAPI/RPC)*. However, you can also configure Outlook to access a POP3 or IMAP4 server on the Internet and an Internet-based SMTP server for outgoing messages.

Understanding Internet E-Mail Communications

For internal e-mail, clients on your Windows SBS network simply send their outgoing messages to the server, which places them in the appropriate destination mailboxes. For users connecting with OWA, the messages never actually leave the server because the OWA site and Exchange Server are running on the same computer. However, e-mail communications involving the Internet are somewhat more complex.

An Internet e-mail transaction consists of the following basic steps:

1. A user on your network creates an e-mail message with an address on another domain in a client and sends it.

2. The client sends the e-mail message to an SMTP server. In the case of a client on your Windows SBS 2008 network, Exchange Server 2007, running on your Windows SBS 2008 server, can provide the outgoing SMTP service.

3. The SMTP server reads the destination e-mail address from the outgoing message.

4. The SMTP server generates a DNS request containing the destination domain name and sends it to its DNS server (on a Windows SBS 2008 network, this is the same computer).

5. The DNS server forwards the request to other DNS servers on the Internet as needed until it locates the authoritative DNS server for the destination domain.

   MORE INFO   For more information on DNS servers and resource records, see Chapter 2.

6. The destination domain's DNS server responds by sending the Mail Exchanger (MX) record for the domain to the DNS server on your network.

7. The SMTP server receives the FQDN of the destination mail server from the DNS server.

8. The SMTP server initiates another DNS transaction, this time to resolve the destination mail server's name into an IP address.

9. The SMTP server receives the IP address of the destination mail server from its DNS server.

10. The SMTP server transmits the e-mail message to the IP address of the mail server for the destination domain using the SMTP protocol.

11. The destination mail server, which can be another Exchange Server computer or a POP3 or IMAP4 server, receives the message, reads the local part of the destination address, and places the message in the mailbox for the appropriate user.

12. At some future time, the recipient connects to his or her e-mail server using a client, and accesses the message, either by downloading it or reading it in place.

Connecting an Exchange Server to the Internet

Thus far, this chapter has discussed two e-mail systems that are essentially separate. SMTP, POP3, and IMAP4 servers are designed to send and receive e-mail over the Internet, and Exchange Server 2007 is a proprietary solution initially designed for internal messaging on a private network. How, then, do you bring the two together so that your users can send messages to and receive them from users both on the local network and on the Internet?

There are several ways to answer this question, as Exchange Server 2007 is a highly flexible application. However, as with most of the powerful technologies it includes, Windows SBS 2008 selects and implements a configuration that is acceptable to most small business administrators.

The default Exchange Server 2007 configuration in Windows SBS 2008 is, firstly, an internal e-mail server that enables the users on the network to communicate amongst themselves. When users log on to the Active Directory Domain Services (AD DS) domain, they receive access to their Exchange Server mailboxes on the primary Windows SBS server. Remote users working from home or any other location can use the Remote Web Workplace site to access their Exchange Server mailboxes through the Internet. This internal network access provides users with the full e-mail, scheduling, and task management capabilities of Exchange Server.

When a network user sends an e-mail message to an addressee on the Internet, the Windows SBS server receives the message by default and uses the SMTP server capabilities in Exchange Server 2007 to locate the destination mail server and transmit the message over the Internet. When an Internet user sends an e-mail message to one of your network users, using an address in the Internet domain you registered with the Internet Address Management Wizard, your server receives the message and deposits it in the user's mailbox.

Your Windows SBS server is accessible to mail servers on the Internet because the Internet Address Management Wizard automatically creates an MX resource record on the DNS server for your domain name, as shown in Figure 9-5. The MX record contains the FQDN of your server, with the host name *remote*, plus your Internet domain name, as in *remote.adatum.info*. As a result, other SMTP servers on the Internet are able to forward messages to your server.

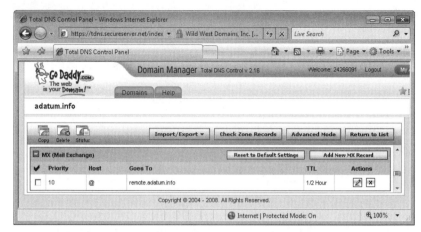

FIGURE 9-5 The MX resource record created by the Internet Address Management Wizard

The Internet Address Management Wizard also configures your router to forward the SMTP traffic on port 25 to your server, as shown in Figure 9-6. These two settings (the MX record and the router configuration) complete the route from the mail servers on the Internet to your mail server on your private network.

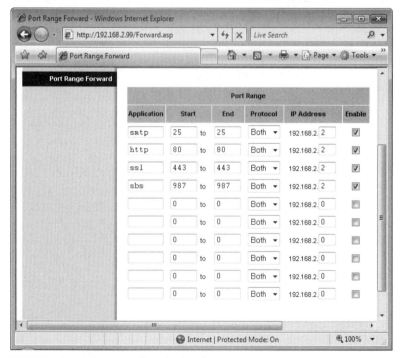

FIGURE 9-6 A typical router configuration interface

MORE INFO There are situations in which you might have to configure both of these settings manually, such as when you register your domain name with a registrar not supported by the Internet Address Management Wizard, or when the wizard cannot automatically configure your router. These manual configuration tasks are not difficult, but they depend on the interfaces provided by your domain registrar and your router. For more information on the tasks performed by the Internet Address Management Wizard, see Chapter 4, "Getting Started."

Configuring E-Mail Settings in Windows SBS 2008

Although the Windows SBS 2008 setup program automatically installs and configures Exchange Server 2007, you might want to perform some additional configuration tasks, which are described in the following sections.

Configure a Smart Host for Internet E-Mail

The Internet e-mail transmission process, as described earlier in this chapter, might seem quite complicated, but it actually is quite efficient under ideal conditions. However, if a destination mail server is not available to receive messages, Exchange Server must keep retrying the transmission until it reaches its timeout interval. This means that the transmission of a single e-mail message could require the server to transmit dozens of messages over the network's Internet connection. Multiply this by the hundreds or thousands of e-mail messages that the server sends every day, and you can see how this can bog down the server's performance and consume a significant amount of Internet bandwidth.

Another problem with this arrangement is the fact that many Internet servers assume that messages originating from dynamic IP addresses are spam. Most ISPs assign dynamic IP addresses to their clients, including the broadband routers that most Windows SBS 2008 networks use to access the Internet. Therefore, you might find that all your outgoing e-mail messages are failing to reach their destinations because intermediate servers are discarding them as spam.

One way to overcome these problems is to use a smart host to transmit your Internet e-mail. A *smart host* is an SMTP server, typically supplied by your ISP, that functions as an interim mail stop for your domain. You configure Exchange Server to send all its outgoing mail to the smart host, and the smart host is then responsible for transmitting and retransmitting the individual messages to their destinations as needed. In addition, because the smart host has a static IP address, its traffic is less likely to be perceived as spam.

The Getting Started Tasks list in the Windows SBS Console provides access to a wizard that configures Exchange Server 2007 to use a smart host. To run this wizard, use the following procedure:

1. Log on to your Windows SBS 2008 primary server using an account with network Administrator privileges. The Windows SBS Console appears.

2. On the Home page of the Windows SBS Console, click Configure A Smart Host For Internet E-Mail. The Configure Internet Mail Wizard appears, displaying the Before You Begin page, as shown here.

    TIP The Configure Internet Mail Wizard is also accessible from the Network/ Connectivity page of the Windows SBS Console. To start the wizard, click Smart Host For Internet E-Mail, in the Internet E-Mail section.

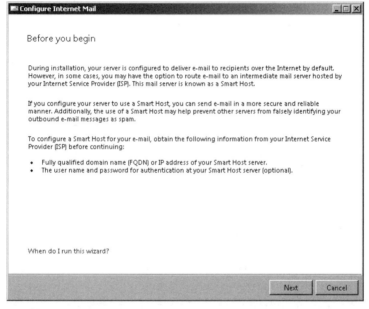

The Before You Begin page lists the resources you must have to complete the wizard, which include the FQDN or IP address of the smart host you intend to use. You obtain this information from your ISP or other provider. In most cases, ISPs require authentication to access the mail server, so you need a user name and password as well.

3. Click Next. The Specify Settings For Outbound Internet Mail page appears, as shown here.

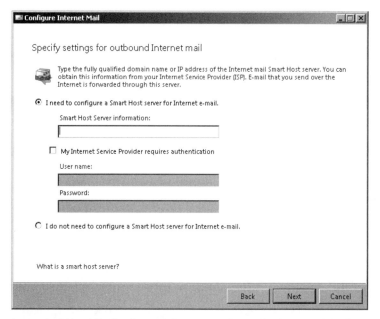

4. Leave the I Need To Configure A Smart Host Server For Internet E-Mail option selected and, in the Smart Host Server Information text box, type the name or IP address of the server you want to use.

5. If necessary, select the My Internet Service Provider Requires Authentication check box and, in the User Name and Password text boxes, type the credentials for the server, as supplied by your ISP.

6. Click Next. The Configuring Internet E-Mail Settings page appears as the wizard attempts to contact the server you specified. If the attempt succeeds, the Configure Internet Mail Settings Is Complete page appears.

If the wizard cannot connect to the server, it specifies the nature of the problem, such as a nonexistent server or rejected credentials, allows you to correct your settings, and tries again. Keep altering your settings until the wizard connects.

7. Click Finish. The wizard closes.

Using the POP3 Connector

One of the by-products of the e-mail-enabled age is the proliferation of e-mail addresses that people tend to gather. The Add A New User Account Wizard creates a new mailbox for each user on the network, but he or she might already have other e-mail addresses as well, addresses from personal accounts or other affiliations. To incorporate e-mail from other sources into users' Exchange Server mailboxes, there are two possible solutions:

- Configure the Office Outlook client on each individual workstation to access the external accounts.
- Use the POP3 Connector in Windows SBS 2008 to access the external accounts.

In addition to functioning as an Exchange Server client, Office Outlook is a POP3 and IMAP4 client. When you add a POP3 account to an Outlook client that is already configured to access an Exchange Server mailbox, you can integrate the messages downloaded from the POP3 server into the mailbox so that the program permanently stores them on the Exchange Server computer. With this arrangement, you must configure each individual client with the appropriate configuration settings for the POP3 account, and the system can check the POP3 server for new messages only while the client is running on the workstation.

The POP3 Connector is essentially a multiuser POP3 client that runs on Exchange Server, which you configure with the account information for each of your users. The POP3 connector checks each of the POP3 accounts at scheduled intervals, downloads new messages, and deposits them in the correct users' mailboxes. With the POP3 Connector, server administrators manage the account information, and the connector runs all the time, downloading new messages even when the clients are not logged on to the network.

To use the POP3 connector, you must have the server name and user credentials for each POP3 account you want the server to access. To configure the POP3 Connector, use the following procedure:

1. Log on to your Windows SBS 2008 primary server using an account with network Administrator privileges. The Windows SBS Console appears.
2. Click Network, and then select the Connectivity tab, as shown here.

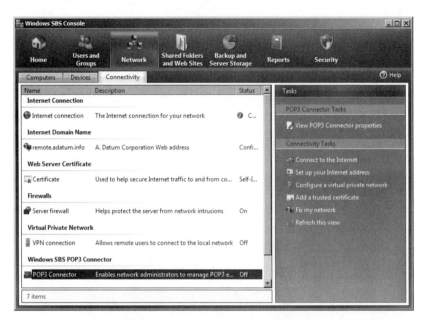

3. Under Windows SBS POP3 Connector, select the POP3 Connector item, and in the Tasks list, click View POP3 Connector Properties. The Windows SBS POP3 Connector dialog box appears, as shown here. You must add each POP3 account you want the connector to access to the POP3 Mailboxes list.

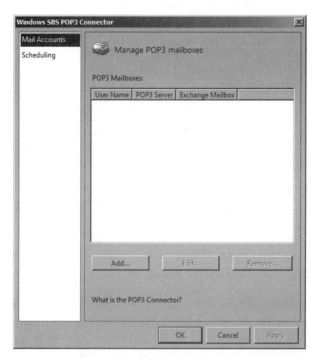

Windows SBS POP3 Connector

Mail Accounts
Scheduling

Manage POP3 mailboxes

POP3 Mailboxes:

User Name	POP3 Server	Exchange Mailbox

Add...   Edit...   Remove...

What is the POP3 Connector?

OK   Cancel   Apply

4. With the Mail Accounts tab selected, click Add. The POP3 Mailbox Accounts dialog box appears, as shown here.

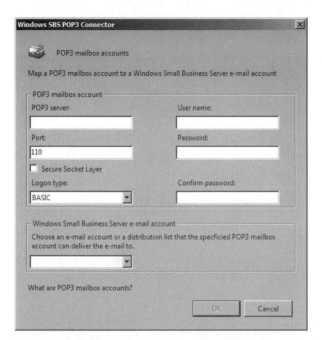

5. In the POP3 Mailbox Account box, configure the following settings:

- **POP3 Server**   Specifies the name or IP address of the Internet server hosting the POP3 mailbox you want to access.

- **Port**   Specifies the port number the server is using for POP3 traffic. The default value is 110.

- **Secure Socket Layer**   Configures SSL encryption for the POP3 connection, if the server supports it.

- **Logon Type**   Specifies which of the following authentication methods you want the server to use when connecting to the POP3 server: Basic, Secure Password Authentication (SPA), or Authenticated Post Office Protocol (APOP).

MORE INFO   The Basic option uses plain text authentication, SPA encrypts the password before transmission, and APOP combines the password with a timestamp before encrypting it. This is done to create a unique value during each logon. APOP is more secure than SPA, because it prevents potential attackers from capturing the encrypted passwords and replaying them. However, you must make sure that the POP3 server supports SPA or APOP authentication before you select these options.

- **User Name**   Specifies the account name you want the server to use when logging on to the POP3 server.
- **Password and Confirm Password**   Specifies the password associated with the user name.

6. In the Windows Small Business Server E-Mail Account drop-down list, select the mailbox to which the connector should deposit the downloaded messages.

7. Click OK. The new account appears in the POP3 Mailboxes list.

8. Repeat steps 4 to 7 to configure additional POP3 mailboxes.

9. Click the Scheduling tab, as shown here.

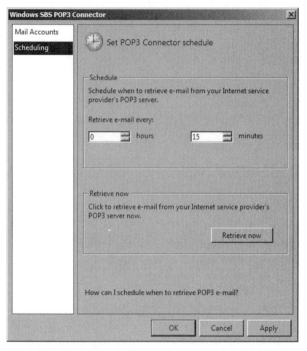

10. In the Schedule box, specify the interval at which the server should check the POP3 accounts for new mail.

   TIP   You can also trigger an immediate check of the POP3 accounts by clicking Retrieve Now.

11. Click OK.

Setting Mailbox Quotas

User mailboxes can grow to an enormous, unwieldy size, especially when e-mail messages carry attachments. To prevent mailboxes from growing too large, Windows SBS 2008 has the ability to impose quotas that issue warnings and ultimately stop saving incoming mail when a mailbox reaches a specified size. Windows SBS enables mailbox quotas by default and sets them to a maximum size of 2 gigabytes (GB). When a user's mailbox is within 100 megabytes (MB) of the quota limit, Exchange Server issues a warning. When the mailbox reaches the quota limit, Exchange Server stops sending and receiving mail for that user.

To reduce the size of a mailbox that has reached its quota limit, the user can delete some of the messages or archive them to another location using the capabilities of the client program. The administrator can also choose to increase the quota.

MORE INFO In Windows SBS 2008, mailbox quotas are a function of Exchange Server 2007, not the File Server Resource Manager, which implements the default user share and folder redirection quotas. To modify mailbox quotas with greater precision, you must use the Exchange Management Console.

To enable, disable, or modify quotas for specific mailboxes, use the following procedure:

1. Log on to your Windows SBS 2008 primary server using an account with network Administrator privileges. The Windows SBS Console appears.

2. Click Users And Groups, and then select the Users tab, as shown here.

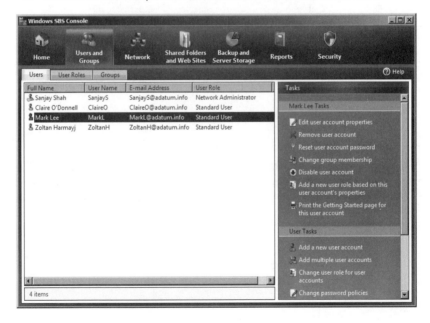

3. Select the user whose quota you want to modify and, from the Tasks list, select Edit User Account Properties. The Properties sheet for the user appears.

4. Click the E-Mail tab, as shown here.

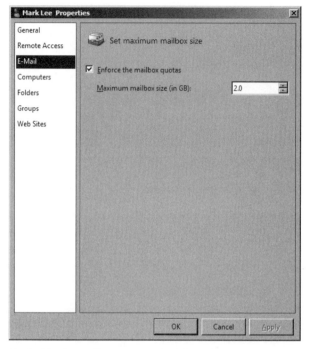

5. To disable the mailbox quota, clear the Enforce The Mailbox Quotas check box. To modify the quota size, change the value in the Maximum Mailbox Size box.

6. Click OK to close the Properties sheet.

Moving Exchange Server Data

Because the Windows SBS 2008 setup program installs Exchange Server 2008 along with the operating system, you cannot choose the disk where Exchange Server creates its message stores. However, Windows SBS 2008 does provide a wizard that enables you to move the message stores at any time. Therefore, if you want to put the mailboxes on a fault-tolerant volume, or even if you just need more disk space for them, you can move the message stores using the following procedure:

1. Log on to your Windows SBS 2008 primary server using an account with network Administrator privileges. The Windows SBS Console appears.

2. Click Backup And Server Storage, and then select the Server Storage tab, as shown here.

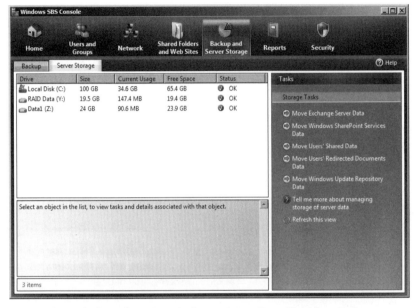

3. In the Tasks list, select Move Exchange Server Data. The Move Exchange Server Data Wizard appears.

4. Click Next to bypass the Getting Started page. The wizard checks your server's backup status and searches for available volumes. If your server is not configured to perform regular backups, the Server Backup Is Not Configured dialog box appears.

5. Click OK to close the Server Backup Is Not Configured dialog box. The Choose A New Location For The Data page appears, as shown here.

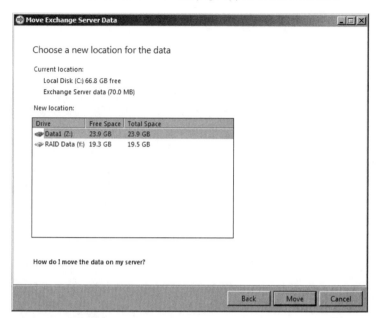

6. Select the volume where you want to move the Exchange Server data and click Move. The wizard moves the data to the volume you selected, and the The Exchange Server Data Was Moved Successfully page appears.

7. Click Finish. The wizard closes.

Working with Web Sites

Microsoft Windows Small Business Server (SBS) 2008 relies heavily on Web-based applications for many of its client communication and administration tasks. One of the biggest favors that the setup program does for you during the Windows SBS 2008 installation is to create and configure your server to host many different internal Web sites, tasks that would take hours if you had to perform them manually. Once created and configured, these Web sites need little attention from administrators, but you can customize them to accommodate the needs of your users.

Introducing Internet Information Services 7.0

Internet Information Services (IIS) 7.0 is the Web server application supplied with Windows Server 2008 and Windows SBS 2008. In the early days of the Web, a Web server was nothing more than an application that listened for incoming requests from browsers and responded to those requests by sending *Hypertext Markup Language (HTML)* files in return, using an application layer protocol called *Hypertext Transfer Protocol (HTTP)*. Today, however, Web servers are far more complex. They can supply browsers with many other types of files, including images, audio, and video. Web servers can also host applications that are designed to use a browser as a client, using a variety of protocols. Over the years, IIS has evolved into a comprehensive Web server product that can host multiple Web sites and applications simultaneously, providing a wide variety of client and administrative services.

Introducing the Windows SBS 2008 Default Web Sites

Windows SBS 2008 uses IIS to provide clients with a variety of services, including the following:

- **Client deployment** When you join a client workstation to your Windows SBS 2008 network, you use Windows Internet Explorer to access a site called *Connect*, as shown here. Connect is an intranet Web application hosted by IIS on your Windows SBS server. The application checks the client computer for the necessary prerequisites and enables the user to download and run a program called Launcher.exe, which starts the Connect Computer Wizard. This wizard joins the computer to the domain and performs a large number of workstation setup tasks that would otherwise require an administrator's presence.

  MORE INFO For more information on the Connect Web site and the tasks performed by the Connect Computer Wizard, see the section entitled "Working with Computers," in Chapter 5, "Working with Users, Computers, and Groups."

- **Windows Server Update Services (WSUS)** WSUS provides the computers on your Windows SBS network with operating system and application updates that it obtains from the Microsoft Update servers on the Internet. Although it is not visible to the network users, WSUS does this by creating an alternative to the Microsoft Updates Web site on your Windows SBS server.

MORE INFO For more information about WSUS, see Chapter 6, "Deploying Updates."

- **Remote Web Workplace (RWW)** RWW is a portal site that provides network users at remote locations with access to your Windows SBS network resources via the Internet, using the interface shown here.

- **Office Outlook Web Access (OWA)** OWA is a Web-based client for the Microsoft Exchange Server 2007 mail server incorporated into Windows SBS 2008. Unlike earlier versions of Windows SBS, which include Microsoft Office Outlook, OWA is the only Exchange Server client supplied with the Windows SBS 2008 product. Users on the internal network can access the OWA site directly, as shown here, and remote users on the Internet can access it through the Remote Web Workplace site.

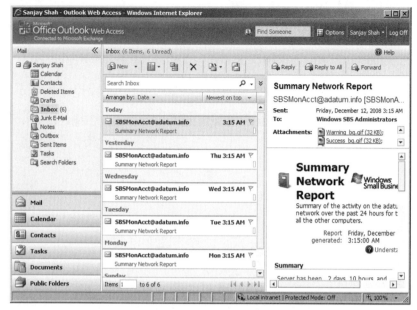

- **Windows SharePoint Services (WSS)** WSS, shown here, is a database-enabled Web application that provides Windows SBS users with several collaboration tools, such as document storage, discussion groups, shared calendars, and task lists. Using the host name *companyweb*, this is the main internal Web site for Windows SBS 2008 users.

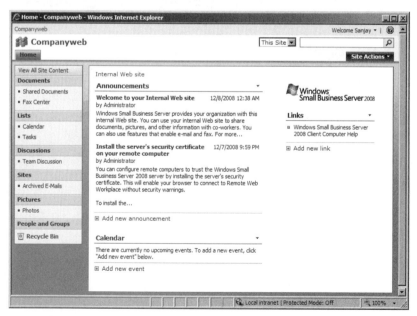

- **SharePoint Central Administration** SharePoint Central Administration, shown here, creates a separate Web site that provides administrative control over the main SharePoint site.

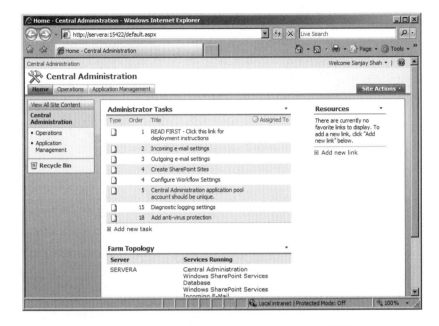

MORE INFO For more information on using and managing the WSS sites, see Chapter 11, "Creating and Customizing Web Sites."

Understanding the IIS Architecture

IIS takes the form of a role in the Windows Server 2008 operating system. *Roles* are a form of modular software management that enable you to install and uninstall specific operating system components. To work with the roles on your server, you use the Server Manager console, shown in Figure 10-1.

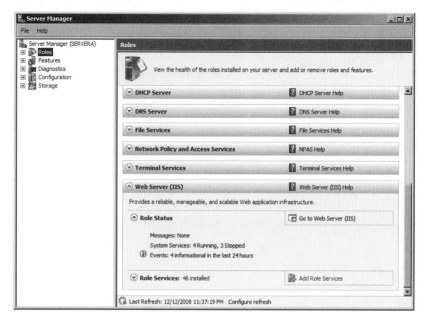

FIGURE 10-1 The Server Manager console

The Windows SBS 2008 setup program installs and configures eight different roles on your server during the installation process, among them the *Web Server (IIS)* role. The Web Server (IIS) role is itself a modular service that has 46 components called *role services*, as shown in Figure 10-2, which provide IIS with various security, management, logging, and application capabilities. Windows SBS 2008 installs all the role services, although it does not necessarily require all of them.

In a Windows Server 2008 installation, IIS has one default Web site with a placeholder splash screen, which uses the standard port for HTTP communications, port 80. This site and the splash screen are still accessible on a Windows SBS 2008 server, if you use a Uniform Resource Locator (URL) containing only the server's name or Internet Protocol (IP) address, as shown in Figure 10-3. However, the default IIS installation in Windows SBS 2008 also includes several other sites, which are accessible using various other URLs.

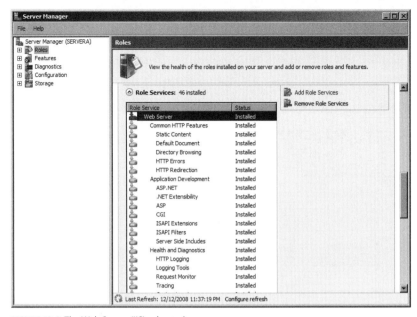

FIGURE 10-2 The Web Server (IIS) role services

FIGURE 10-3 The default IIS Web site

In IIS, a *site* is an individual set of Web pages that is separate from the other sites running on the computer. In Windows SBS 2008, the default IIS sites are all intended for use by a single organization, but it is also possible to use IIS to create completely separate sites for different companies, each with its own content and configuration settings. With IIS, you can create as many additional sites as your server hardware can support. You create and manage sites using the Internet Information Services (IIS) Manager application, as shown in Figure 10-4.

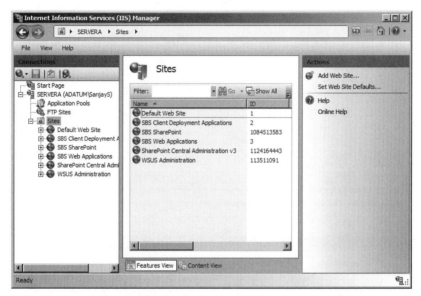

FIGURE 10-4 The default Windows SBS sites in the Internet Information Services (IIS) Manager

Each site points to a location on a local drive that holds the files containing the site's content, such as HTML and image files. Working with the content is a matter of creating and editing files at this location.

IIS also supports the use of *virtual directories*, which are pointers to other locations on the same computer or on the local network. For example, if you have a site with its home directory on the local drive, but you want to publish some files located on another computer, you can either copy those files to the home directory (which creates version synchronization problems), or just create a virtual directory on the site that points to the folder on the other computer. The files appear on the site and yet remain in their original location.

Running Multiple Sites

Hosting multiple Web sites on a single server presents a small problem for IIS. When Web browsers connect to a site, they do so by sending an HTTP request message to the Web server's IP address using the well-known HTTP port number 80. When requests for different sites arrive at the server, how is IIS supposed to differentiate them and forward each request to the correct site?

The answer is by configuring each site with a different set of bindings. *Bindings* are essentially rules that tell IIS how to associate incoming requests with specific sites. IIS supports three types of bindings, as follows:

- **IP address**   It is possible to assign more than one IP address to a single computer. By doing this, you can configure IIS to use a different address for each site. However, you must also register a different name in a Domain Name System (DNS) domain for each address.

- **Port number**   Web browsers send all their HTTP requests to port 80 on the destination server unless the user specifies a different port number in the URL. You can create bindings that assign a different port number to each site on an IIS server, enabling the server to distinguish among the incoming requests. However, to access a site that uses a nonstandard port number, users must specify that number in their URLs, following the server name and a colon, as in the example *www.adatum.com:1024*. In Windows SBS 2008, the WSUS site uses port number bindings because the URL that clients use to access the Web server, which contains the port number 8530, is hidden from users in a Group Policy object (GPO). In a situation like this, in which users do not have to remember the port number and type it in a URL, port number bindings are a viable option. Another reason to use port number bindings is to keep a site hidden from the average user. The SharePoint Central Administration site on your server uses a nonstandard port number, which is unknown to the network users, but which administrators can access through the Windows SBS Console.

- **Host header**   Communications between browsers and Web servers are based on IP addresses, not server names, but HTTP messages have a Host field that contains the server name that the user specified in the browser. A host header binding associates a particular Host field value with one of the sites on the IIS server, even if all the host names resolve into the same IP address. In Windows SBS 2008, the client deployment, SharePoint, and RWW sites all use host header bindings.

To configure or modify the bindings for a site, you select a site in Internet Information Services (IIS) Manager and open its Site bindings dialog box, as shown in Figure 10-5.

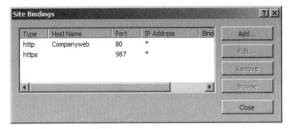

FIGURE 10-5 A Site Bindings dialog box in the Internet Information Services (IIS) Manager

Running Web Applications

When software developers create stand-alone client/server applications, they have to design both the server and the client components from scratch, including the client user interface. Web applications for Windows SBS 2008 simplify the software design and deployment process by using the existing mechanisms of IIS on the server and Internet Explorer on the browser. Internet Explorer provides the basic functions that simplify the design of the user interface, and IIS includes role services that provide support for a number of application development environments, including Active Server Pages (ASP), ASP.NET, and Internet Server Application Programming Interface (ISAPI).

Originally, the Web consisted of static pages written in HTML, and the only function of the Web server was to transmit those pages to browsers on request. Today, however, Web applications enable sites to do much more than simply display static information. Application-enabled Web sites can generate pages on demand, using information provided by the user or extracted from a database.

The WSS site included with Windows SBS 2008 is a perfect example of this arrangement. Clients connect to the SharePoint site, and IIS runs the SharePoint Web application that generates pages using content stored in a Microsoft SQL Server database. Windows SBS uses a single computer for the Web server and the database server, but with Windows Server 2008, it is also possible to deploy the components on separate computers.

IIS is capable of running multiple applications, each associated with a different site, and it can do so without one application jeopardizing the stability of the others or of the entire computer. IIS does this by using individual address spaces called *application pools*. Each application pool runs in its own protected space, so that if an application crashes, it cannot have any effect outside the pool. This is called *worker process application mode*. The Windows SBS 2008 setup program creates 13 separate application pools for the various sites in IIS, as shown in Figure 10-6.

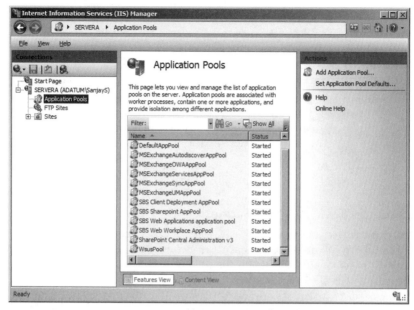

FIGURE 10-6 The default IIS application pools in Windows SBS 2008

Accessing the Windows SBS Web Sites

The Web sites hosted by IIS on your Windows SBS 2008 server are accessible like any other Web site—by typing a URL in a browser window. However, Windows SBS provides a number of tools that make the sites more readily accessible to users and administrators.

Accessing the Client Deployment Site

The first site that each workstation accesses on the Windows SBS server is the client deployment site, which joins the computer to the domain and configures it to access the network resources. To connect to this site, a user or administrator simply has to type the word **connect** in the browser's address box. This works for two reasons:

- The Windows SBS 2008 setup program creates an Alias (CNAME) resource record in the Active Directory Domain Services (AD DS) domain that equates the name *connect* with the name of the server. When the workstation performs a DNS name resolution on the name *connect*, it receives the IP address of the server in return.

- The client deployment Web site has a host header binding that associates the name *connect* with the site. As a result, IIS forwards HTTP requests containing *connect* in the Host field to the client deployment site.

Using Shortcuts and Links

In addition to joining the workstation to the network, the Connect Computer Wizard configures the workstation so that users have various ways to access the Web sites on the Windows SBS 2008 server, including the following:

- On the Start menu, the wizard creates a Windows Small Business Server 2008 program group that contains an Internal Web Site shortcut pointing to the WSS site, *companyweb*.
- In the Internet Explorer Favorites list, the wizard creates links to the Internal Web Site and to the RWW site.
- On Windows Vista workstations, the wizard installs the Windows Small Business Server Desktop Links gadget, as discussed in the following section.

Using the Windows SBS Gadget

Windows Vista includes a desktop utility called Windows Sidebar, which enables users to display miniature applications called *gadgets*. Gadgets can display system information or pull content from the Internet and display it on the desktop. The default Windows Sidebar configuration contains three gadgets, which display a clock, a slide show, and selected news headlines. The Windows SBS 2008 Connect Computer Wizard installs a new gadget on Windows Vista workstations called Windows Small Business Server Desktop Links, as shown in Figure 10-7. This gadget displays a small window containing the following links:

- **Check E-Mail**   Connects to the OWA site
- **Internal Web Site**   Connects to *companyweb*, the default WSS site
- **Remote Web Workplace**   Connects to the RWW site in your AD DS domain

FIGURE 10-7 The Windows Small Business Server Desktop Links gadget

Although the wizard installs the Windows Small Business Server Desktop Links gadget, it does not add it to the Windows Sidebar display. To add the gadget manually to the desktop on a Windows Vista workstation, use the following procedure:

1. Click Start, and then click Control Panel. The Control Panel window appears.
2. Click Appearance And Personalization. The Appearance And Personalization window appears, as shown here.

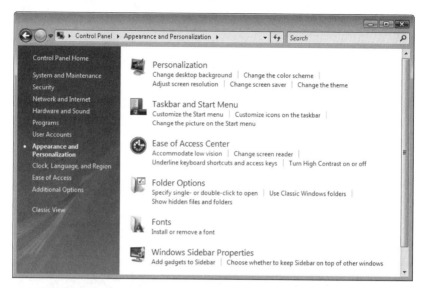

3. Under Windows Sidebar Properties, click Add Gadgets To Sidebar. A window appears, as shown here, containing the gadgets installed on the computer.

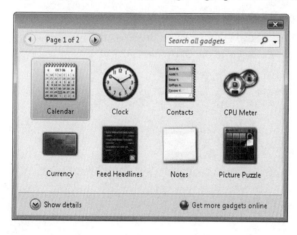

TIP You can also add gadgets by clicking the plus sign (+) on the Windows Sidebar toolbar.

4. Click the right arrow to switch to Page 2 of 2, as shown here.

5. Double-click the Windows Small Business Server Desktop Links gadget. The gadget appears in the Windows Sidebar, as shown here.

6. Close the window containing the installed gadgets.

7. Close the Appearance And Personalization window.

Using RWW

As mentioned earlier, RWW is a portal site that contains no content of its own but provides users with access to the other Windows SBS 2008 Web sites, as well as other internal network resources. RWW is unique among the default Windows SBS Web sites in that it is available both to internal network users and to Internet users at remote locations. For internal users, RWW provides a convenient central access point for the Windows SBS network resources. For users at remote locations, however, RWW also provides the unique ability to log on to the AD DS domain from outside the physical network.

Once connected to the RWW site, a user with the correct permissions can perform the following tasks:

- Connect to the OWA site
- Connect to the Internal *companyweb* Web site
- Establish a Terminal Services connection to a workstation on the internal network
- Change the user's password
- View the Windows Small Business Server 2008 Client Computer Help pages

Users with administrative credentials can perform the following additional tasks:

- Establish a Terminal Services connection to a the network server
- Access the Windows Small Business Server (SBS) Community page on the Internet
- Manage Office Live Small Business sites, accounts, and reports

To provide this remote access, your Windows SBS 2008 server, your Internet access router, and your Internet domain must be configured properly. This configuration consists of the following elements:

- The Windows SBS 2008 setup program creates the RWW site in IIS and configures it with a host header binding that associates the site with the name *remote.*

- The Internet Address Management Wizard creates a DNS resource record in your Internet domain, pointing the host name *remote* to your router's external (Internet) address.

- The Internet Address Management Wizard configures your router to admit Internet traffic through ports 25, 80, 443, 987, and 3389 and forward the traffic to your server.

- The Windows SBS 2008 setup program creates a certificate installation package that enables you to distribute your server's self-signed certificate to remote computers.

- The Windows SBS setup program installs the Terminal Services Gateway role service, which enables RWW users to establish Terminal Services connections from the Internet.

NOTE Terminal Services connections created through the RWW site use the Remote Desktop capabilities built into the Windows Server 2008 operating system; therefore, no additional licensing is required. Windows SBS 2008 does not install the Terminal Server role service on the primary server, nor is that server capable of functioning as a fully licensed Terminal Services server.

Connecting to the RWW Site

The RWW Web site is accessible to users, both on the internal Windows SBS network and on the Internet, through the URL *http://remote.domain_name.com*, where *domain_name.com* is the name of the Internet domain name you registered using the Internet Address Management Wizard. The server name in this URL resolves to the external address of your router, and the router forwards the traffic to your Windows SBS server. Internal users on the Windows SBS network can connect to the RWW site more easily by using the Favorite that the Connect Computer Wizard creates in Internet Explorer or by using the Windows Small Business Server Desktop Links gadget.

TROUBLESHOOTING If computers on the Internet are unable to connect to your server using RWW, the most likely causes of the problem are a missing or incorrect DNS resource record for the host name remote in your domain, or an improperly configured router that is not forwarding all the required port traffic to the server.

When a user on the internal network connects to the RWW site, a sign-in page appears, as shown in Figure 10-8. The user must log on using his or her AD DS domain account to enter the site.

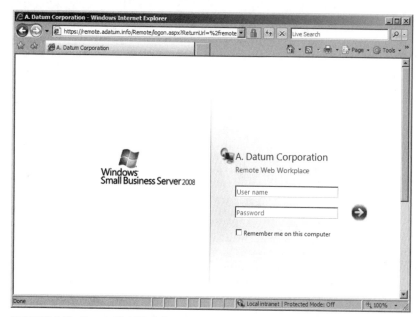

FIGURE 10-8 The Remote Web Workplace sign-in page

For Internet users, the process might be slightly more complicated in some cases. The RWW site uses Secure Sockets Layer (SSL) encryption, which uses digital certificates to confirm the identity of the server. If, during your initial Windows SBS 2008 server configuration, you used the Add A Trusted Certificate Wizard to purchase a certificate from a third-party provider and install it on your server, as described in Chapter 4, "Getting Started," then clients on the Internet trust the server's certificate and allow the browser to access the RWW site.

If you did not purchase a certificate from a trusted third-party provider, then your server is using a self-signed certificate. Computers on the local network trust the server's self-signed certificate because they are members of the same AD DS domain. However, computers on the Internet are not members of the domain and have no reason to trust the server's certificate. As a result, when Internet computers attempt to connect to the RWW site, a Certificate Error page appears, as shown in Figure 10-9.

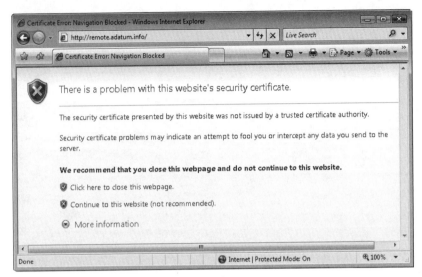

FIGURE 10-9 A certificate error page in Internet Explorer

Installing a Server Certificate

The appearance of the Certificate Error page does not prevent the computer from accessing the site. Users can click the Continue To This Website link to proceed to the RWW logon page, but unless they are aware of the reason for the error, they might be reluctant to do so. To prevent the error page from appearing, you can either obtain a certificate from a commercial provider or install your server's self-signed certificate on each Internet computer that will access the RWW site.

Windows SBS 2008 provides a certificate installation package that simplifies the process of deploying the server certificate to remote clients. To deploy the server certificate, use the following procedure:

1. On your Windows SBS 2008 server, open Windows Explorer and browse to the Public\Public Downloads folder.

2. Copy the Install Certificate Package archive file to a removable medium, such as a flash drive or a writable CD or DVD.

3. On the computer where you want to deploy the certificate, insert the drive or disk.

4. Open Windows Explorer and copy the Install Certificate Package file to a local folder.

5. Browse to the Install Certificate Package file, right-click it and, from the context menu, select Extract All. The Extract Compressed (Zipped) Folders Wizard appears.

6. Click Extract. The wizard extracts the files from the archive and displays them in Windows Explorer.

7. Double-click the InstallCertificate program. An Open File – Security Warning dialog box appears.

8. Click Run. The Certificate Installation dialog box appears, as shown here.

9. Select the Install The Certificate On My Computer option and click Install. The User Account Control dialog box appears.

10. Click Continue. A Certificate Installation message box appears, as shown here, indicating that the certificate is installed.

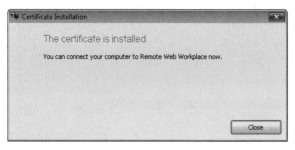

11. Click Close.

Once the certificate is installed, the user can access the RWW site without receiving a Certificate Error page.

Accessing the WSUS Web Site

Unlike the other Windows SBS 2008 Web sites, users do not access the WSUS site using a Web browser. Because the site is a local replacement for the Microsoft Updates site on the Internet, the Automatic Updates client on the network computers is responsible for accessing it. The Group Policy settings that configure the Automatic Updates clients contain a URL pointing to the Windows SBS 2008 server by name, with the port number 8530, to distinguish it from the server's other Web sites.

MORE INFO For information on accessing and managing the *companyweb* site on your Windows SBS 2008 server, see Chapter 11.

Managing the Windows SBS Web Sites

The Internet Information Services (IIS) Manager provides full control over all the Windows SBS 2008 Web sites and also enables you to create and configure new sites on your server. However, for everyday maintenance, the Windows SBS Console provides controls that enable you to manage the basic properties of the three main Web sites: OWA, RWW, and the Internal Web site.

Enabling and Disabling Web Sites

By default, Windows SBS 2008 enables all three of its main Web internal Web sites, but you can disable them from the Windows SBS console, if you wish. To disable a Web site, use the following procedure:

1. Log on to your Windows SBS 2008 server using a domain account with administrative privileges. The Windows SBS Console appears.

2. Click Shared Folders And Web Sites, and then select the Web Sites tab, as shown here.

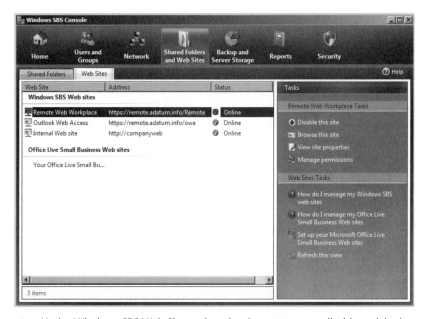

3. Under Windows SBS Web Sites, select the site you want to disable and, in the Tasks list, click Disable This Site. The Status indicator for the site changes from Online to Offline.

Configuring General Settings

Each of the three Windows SBS Web sites has a Properties sheet, which you open by selecting a site on the Shared Folders And Web Sites/Web Sites page and clicking View Site Properties in the Tasks list. The General tab on each Properties sheet, as shown in Figure 10-10, has a check box that provides an alternative way to disable or enable the site. The Internal Web Site sheet also contains fields that enable you to modify the default Site Title and Description values.

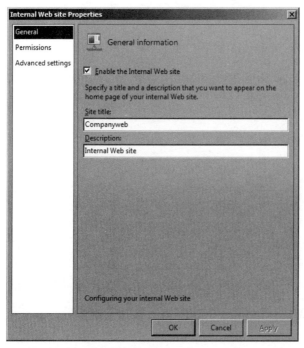

FIGURE 10-10 The General tab of the Internal Web Site Properties sheet

Configuring Web Site Permissions

Although the Windows SBS Console refers to them as *permissions,* most IIS Web sites actually use group memberships to specify who can access them. For example, to access the RWW site, users must be members of the Windows SBS Remote Web Workplace Users group. To modify the membership of this group, use the following procedure:

1. Log on to your Windows SBS 2008 server using a domain account with administrative privileges. The Windows SBS Console appears.

2. Click Shared Folders And Web Sites, and then select the Web Sites tab.

3. Under Windows SBS Web Sites, select the Remote Web Workplace site and, in the tasks list, click Manage Permissions. The Remote Web Workplace Properties sheet appears, as shown here, displaying the Permissions tab.

4. Click Modify. The Change Group Membership dialog box appears, as shown here.

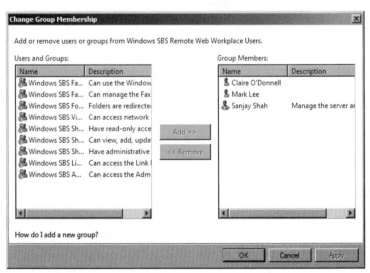

5. In the Users And Groups list, select the users and groups that you want to add to the Windows SBS Remote Web Workplace Users group and click Add.

6. In the Group Members list, select the users and groups that you want to remove from the Windows SBS Remote Web Workplace Users group and click Remove.

7. Click OK to close the Change Group Membership dialog box.

8. Click OK to close the Properties sheet

The Internal Web site uses group memberships as well, as shown in Figure 10-11, but it has three levels of access, represented by the following three groups:

- **Windows SBS SharePoint_MembersGroup**   Provides users with read and write access to the site

- **Windows SBS SharePoint_OwnersGroup**   Provides users with administrative access to the site

- **Windows SBS SharePoint_VisitorsGroup**   Provides users with read-only access to the site

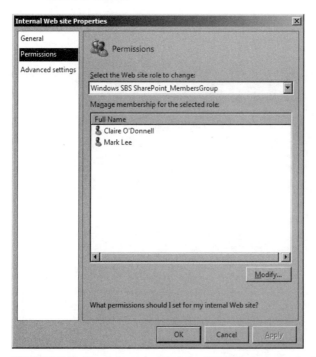

FIGURE 10-11 The Permissions tab of the Internal Web Site Properties sheet

The OWA site uses the same basic interface to manage permissions, but in this case, the Windows SBS Console is modifying a property of the user's Exchange Server mailbox rather than a group membership. You can also grant a user access to the OWA site by selecting the Outlook Web Access tab on the Web Sites tab of the user's Properties sheet.

Configuring RWW

The Windows SBS Console enables you to specify what items appear in the RWW interface and how the site appears to users.

Customizing the RWW Site

To customize the appearance of the RWW site, use the following procedure:

1. Log on to your Windows SBS 2008 server using a domain account with administrative privileges. The Windows SBS Console appears.

2. Click Shared Folders And Web Sites, and then select the Web Sites tab.

3. Under Windows SBS Web Sites, select the Remote Web Workplace site and, in the tasks list, click View Site Properties. The Remote Web Workplace Properties sheet appears.

4. Click the Customization tab, as shown here.

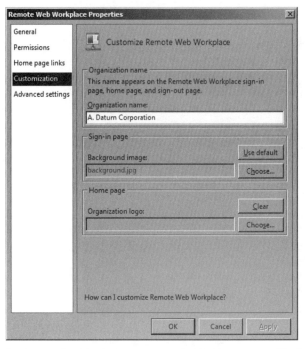

5. To change the title that appears on the site's pages, modify the value in the Organization Name text box.

6. To change the background of the sign-in page, click the Choose button next to the Background Image text box. The Choose An Image dialog box appears, as shown here.

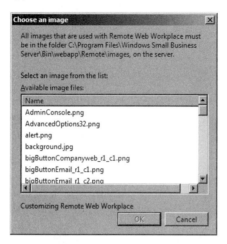

7. Select one of the image files in the list and click OK. The file you selected appears in the Background Image text box.

8. To change the logo on the RWW home page, click the Choose button next to the Organization Logo text box. The Choose An Image dialog box appears.

9. Select one of the image files in the list and click OK. The file you selected appears in the Organization Logo text box.

TIP To add your own images to the Available Image Files list in the Choose An Image dialog box, you must copy them to the C:\Program Files\Windows Small Business Server\Bin\Webapp\Remote\Images folder on your Windows SBS server.

10. Click OK to close the Remote Web Workplace Properties sheet.

Configuring RWW Site Content

To specify the items that should appear on the RWW site, use the following procedure:

1. Log on to your Windows SBS 2008 server using a domain account with administrative privileges. The Windows SBS Console appears.

2. Click Shared Folders And Web Sites, and then select the Web Sites tab.

3. Under Windows SBS Web Sites, select the Remote Web Workplace site and, in the tasks list, click View Site Properties. The Remote Web Workplace Properties sheet appears.

4. Click the Home Page Links tab, as shown here.

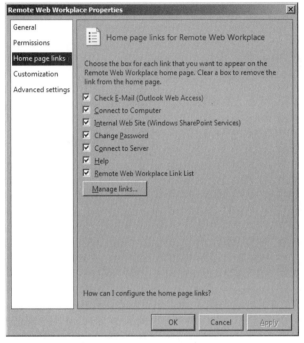

5. To remove elements from the RWW home page, clear some or all of the check boxes on the Home Page Links tab.

6. Click Manage Links. The Remote Web Workplace Link List Properties sheet appears, as shown here.

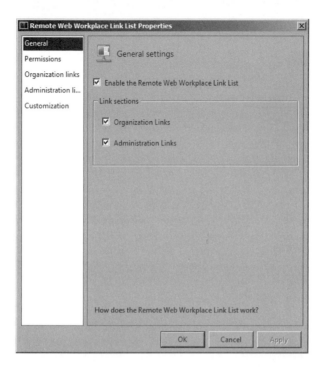

MORE INFO The Remote Web Workplace Link List is the collection of hyperlinks that appear below the three main buttons on the RWW home page. The list on the left contains organization links, and the list on the right contains administration links.

7. On the General tab, clear any of the following check boxes, as desired:
- Enable The Remote Web Workplace Link List
- Organization Links
- Administration Links

8. Click the Permissions tab, as shown here.

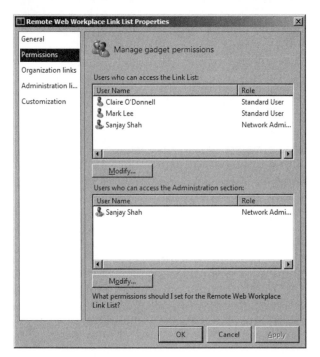

9. In the Users Who Can Access The Link List section, click Modify to open a Change Group Membership dialog box, in which you can specify which users and groups are able to access the Remote Web Workplace Link List.

10. In the Users Who Can Access The Administration Section area, click Modify to open a Change Group Membership dialog box, in which you can specify which users and groups are able to access the administration links in the Remote Web Workplace Link List.

11. Click the Organization Links tab, as shown here.

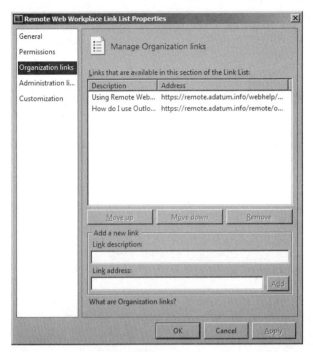

12. To add a link to the organization links list, type a descriptive title in the Link Description text box and a URL in the Link Address text box. Then click Add. The new link appears in the list.

13. Click the Administration Links tab and repeat step 12 to add a hyperlink to the administration links list, if desired.

14. Click the Customization tab, as shown here.

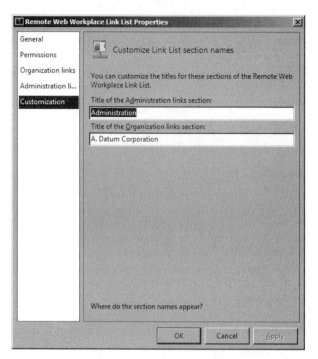

15. To modify the titles of the organization links and administration links sections, modify the values in the two text boxes.

16. Click OK to close the Remote Web Workplace Link List Properties sheet.

17. Click OK to close the Remote Web Workplace Properties sheet.

Configuring Advanced Settings

The Properties sheet for each of the Windows SBS Web sites has an Advanced Settings tab, which contains only a button providing access to a tool that provides more comprehensive access to the site's configuration, as shown in Figure 10-12. The Properties sheets for the Remote Web Workplace and Outlook Web Access sites provide access to IIS Manager, while the Internal Web Site Properties sheet provides access to the WSS 3.0 Central Administration site.

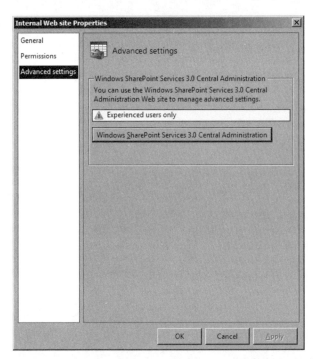

FIGURE 10-12 The Advanced Settings tab of the Internal Web Site Properties sheet

CHAPTER 11

Creating and Customizing Web Sites

■ Working with Windows SharePoint Services   **351**

I n Chapter 10, "Working with Web Sites," you learned how Microsoft Windows Small Business Server (SBS) 2008 uses Internet Information Services (IIS) 7.0 to implement multiple Web sites for use by internal and remote network users. Most of these Web sites require only minimal administrative attention because the Windows SBS 2008 setup program creates and configures them during the operating system installation. However, many administrators want to customize the internal Windows SharePoint Services Web site or create their own additional sites, using IIS or Microsoft Office Live Small Business. For these administrators, this chapter examines some of the more advanced Web site creation and management features found in Windows SBS 2008.

Working with Windows SharePoint Services

The primary intranet Web site on your Windows SBS network is a Windows SharePoint Services site, which is created by default during the installation of Windows SBS 2008. Windows SharePoint Services (WSS) 3.0 is a Web application that provides browser-based clients with an interface that enables them to share, collaborate on, and discuss documents, using a variety of tools. At the server, the WSS application stores user-contributed documents and information in a Microsoft SQL Server database.

WSS can function as a distributed application, with the Web site running on one server and the database on another. However, in Windows SBS 2008, everything runs on your primary server. IIS hosts the WSS Web site, and the Windows Internal Database feature hosts the database.

NOTE Windows SharePoint Services 3.0 is included with all versions of Windows SBS 2008. The SQL Server database that WSS creates is located on the primary server and has no connection to the SQL Server 2008 product included with Windows SBS 2008 Premium. Although it is possible for Windows SBS 2008 Premium networks to use the secondary server to host a WSS database, you cannot use the Windows Internal Database to host a third-party application.

Although the WSS site is usable as is, administrators can improve its appearance and functionality by configuring and customizing it in many ways.

Accessing the Internal Web Site

By default, Windows SBS 2008 configures the internal Web site to use the standard port number 80 with a host header binding containing the name *Companyweb*. Your internal Domain Name System (DNS) domain has an Alias (CNAME) resource record equating the name *Companyweb* with the name of your Windows SBS server.

MORE INFO For more information on Web site bindings, see the section entitled "Running Multiple Sites" in Chapter 10.

Internal network users can therefore access the site from any browser by using the Uniform Resource Locator (URL) *http://companyweb*. Users can also access the site using the shortcut that the Connect Computer Wizard creates on client workstations, the favorite in Windows Internet Explorer, or the Windows Small Business Server Desktop Links gadget in Windows Vista. Finally, both internal and remote users can access the site through the Remote Web Workplace (RWW) interface or by using the URL *http://remote.domain_name.com:987*, where *domain_name.com* is your Internet domain name.

Managing the Internal Web Site Properties

The Windows SBS Console provides the same basic control over the internal Web site that it does over the other default Web sites that IIS hosts. To configure the internal Web site's properties, use the following procedure:

1. Log on to your Windows SBS 2008 server using a domain account with administrative privileges. The Windows SBS Console appears.

2. Click Shared Folders And Web Sites, and then select the Web Sites tab.

3. Under Windows SBS Web Sites, select Internal Web Site, and, in the tasks list, click View Site Properties. The Internal Web Site Properties sheet appears, as shown here.

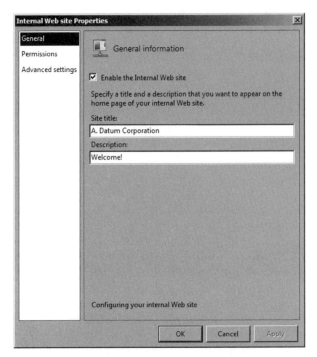

4. On the General tab, configure the following properties, if desired:

   - Enable The Internal Web Site   Clear this check box to disable the Web site entirely.

   - Site Title   Modify this value to change the title displayed on the upper left of each page on the site.

   - Description   Modify this value to change the descriptive text displayed at the top of the site's home page.

   NOTE Changing the Site Title field from its default *Companyweb* value does not change the host header binding or the DNS record associated with the site. Users can still type the URL *http://companyweb* to access the internal Web site.

5. Click the Permissions tab, as shown here.

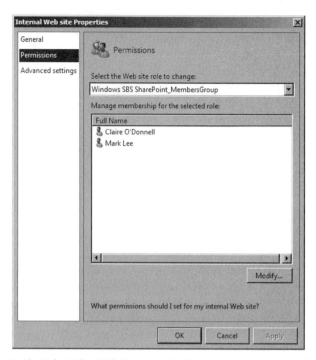

6. In the Select The Web Site Role To Change drop-down list, select the group whose membership you want to change and click Modify. The Change Group Membership dialog box appears, as shown here.

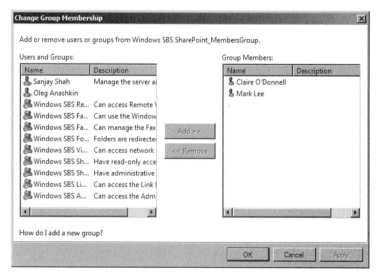

7. In the Users And Groups list, select the users and groups that you want to add to the Windows SBS Remote Web Workplace Users group and click Add.

8. In the Group Members list, select the users and groups that you want to remove from the Windows SBS Remote Web Workplace Users group and click Remove.

9. Click OK to close the Change Group Membership dialog box.

10. Repeat steps 6 to 9 to modify the memberships of the other groups, if desired.

11. Click OK to close the Properties sheet.

Understanding the Default WSS Permissions

Unlike the other Windows SBS 2008 sites, the Internal Web site uses three separate groups to provide three levels of access to the site, as follows:

- **Windows SBS SharePoint_OwnersGroup**   Provides users with full administrative access to the site. All new user accounts you create with the Network Administrator role are members of this group.

- **Windows SBS SharePoint_MembersGroup**   Enables users to read and write content on the site. Users can add documents to the site and edit existing ones, but they cannot create document libraries or make other modifications to the structure of the site. All new user accounts you create with the Standard User role are members of this group.

- **Windows SBS SharePoint_VisitorsGroup**   Enables users to read content on the site.

These three groups are Active Directory Domain Services (AD DS) security groups, which the Windows SBS 2008 setup program creates during the operating system installation. However, Windows SharePoint Services also has its own system of groups, and each of the AD DS groups is a member of one of the SharePoint groups. SharePoint has its own system of permissions as well. SharePoint groups can have any of the following SharePoint permissions:

- **Full Control**   Provides unlimited administrative access to the site

- **Design**   Provides the ability to view, add, update, delete, approve, and customize site content

- **Contribute**   Provides the ability to view, add, update, and delete content

- **Read**   Provides the ability to view content only

By creating the AD DS groups and adding them to the SharePoint groups, Windows SBS 2008 simplifies the process of working with the site's permissions. Using the Windows SBS Console, administrators can control access to the site simply by altering the AD DS group memberships. The actual relationships between the AD DS security groups, the SharePoint groups, and the SharePoint permissions is shown in Table 11-1.

TABLE 11-1 Relationships between AD DS and SharePoint Groups

AD DS GROUP NAME	SHAREPOINT GROUP NAME	SHAREPOINT PERMISSION
Windows SBS SharePoint_OwnersGroup	CompanyWeb Owners	Full Control
Windows SBS SharePoint_MembersGroup	CompanyWeb Members	Design
Windows SBS SharePoint_VisitorsGroup	CompanyWeb Visitors	Read

Using the SharePoint Central Administration Site

The Advanced Settings tab of the Internal Web Site Properties sheet contains a button that opens the Windows SharePoint Services 3.0 Central Administration Web site, shown in Figure 11-1. This is a completely separate, administrative site, which uses a random port number binding to distinguish it from the main site.

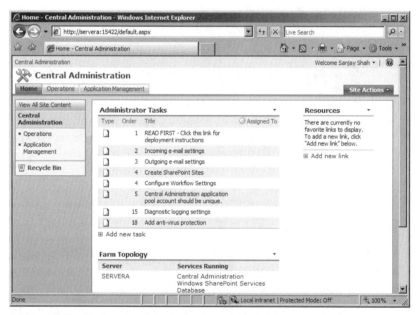

FIGURE 11-1 The Windows SharePoint Services 3.0 Central Administration Web site

When you select the Operations tab, you see a page containing links to many of the configurable WSS settings, as shown in Figure 11-2.

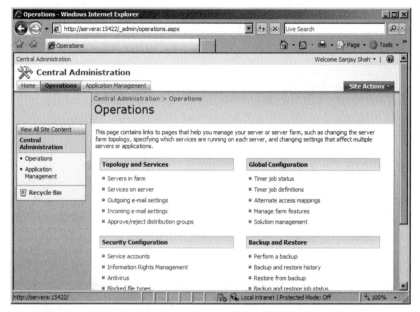

FIGURE 11-2 The Operations tab on the Windows SharePoint Services 3.0 Central Administration Web site

Some of the settings that Windows SBS administrators might configure are as follows:

- **Antivirus** Provides configuration settings, as shown here, that enable administrators to control how a third-party virus scanner product should interact with WSS.

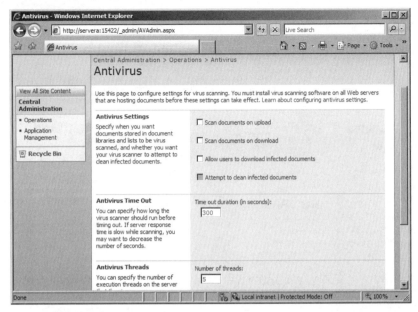

- **Blocked File Types** Enables administrators to specify file types that users cannot save to or retrieve from the WSS site, using the interface shown here.

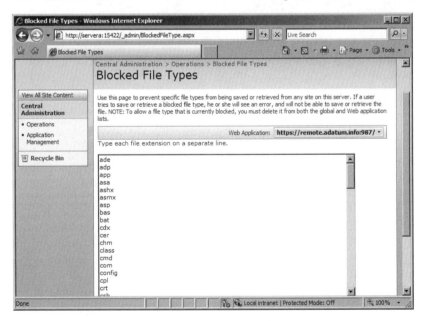

- **Diagnostic Logging** Provides controls, as shown here, that enable administrators to specify when and where WSS should create log entries.

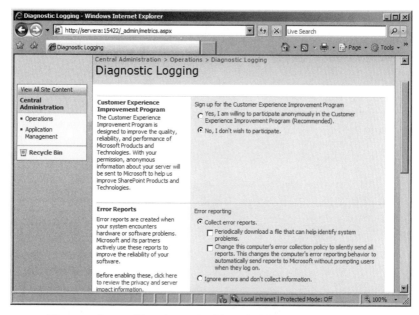

- **Alternate Access Mappings** Enables administrators to specify the URLs that provide access to the WSS site, using the interface shown here.

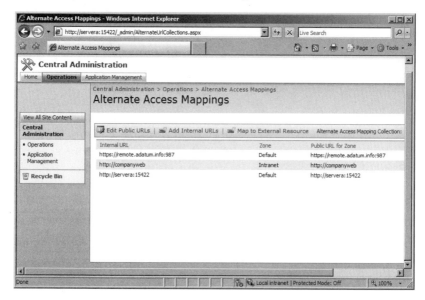

- **Perform A Backup**   WSS has its own backup capability, as shown here, that enables administrators to copy the sites and their content to another location.

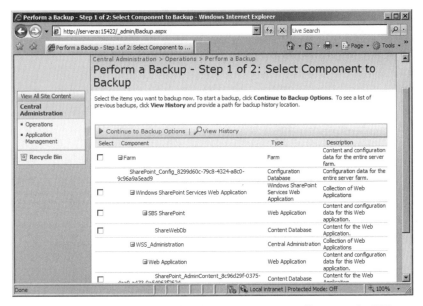

- **Restore From Backup**   Administrators can restore all or part of a WSS installation from a previously completed backup, using the interface shown here.

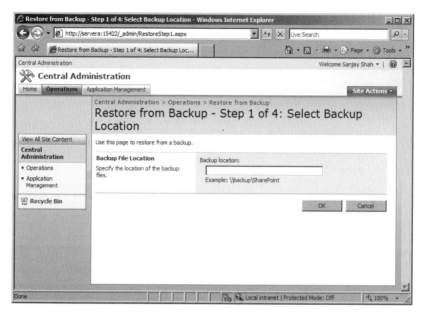

- **Default Database Server** To use a SQL Server database other than the Windows Internal Database for WSS, administrators can specify the server name and the credentials needed to access it, using the interface shown here.

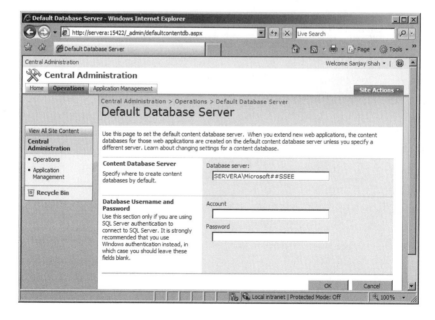

Moving the WSS Data Store

As with all its other services, Windows SBS 2008 configures Windows SharePoint Services to store its data on the system drive during the operating system installation. If you create additional storage volumes after the installation, you might want to move the WSS data to another drive using the following procedure:

1. Log on to your Windows SBS 2008 server using a domain account with administrative privileges. The Windows SBS Console appears.

2. Click Backup And Server Storage, and then select the Server Storage tab.

3. In the Tasks list, select Move Windows SharePoint Services Data. The Move Windows SharePoint Services Data Wizard appears.

4. Click Next to bypass the Getting Started page. The wizard checks your server's backup status and searches for available volumes. If your server is not configured to perform regular backups, a Server Backup Is Not Configured dialog box appears.

5. Click OK to close the Server Backup Is Not Configured dialog box. The Choose A New Location For The Data page appears, as shown here.

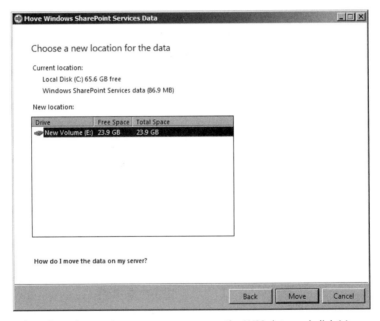

6. Select the volume where you want to move the WSS data and click Move. The wizard moves the data to the volume you selected and a The Windows SharePoint Services Data Was Moved Successfully page appears.

7. Click Finish. The wizard closes.

Migrating a SharePoint Web Site

If you are migrating to Windows SBS 2008 from Windows SBS 2003 and you have been using WSS on your old server, you probably want to migrate your existing WSS database to your new server. Unfortunately, the process of migrating the Share-Point database is manual. When you run the Migrate To Windows Small Business Server 2008 Wizard on your Windows SBS 2008 server, Migrate SharePoint Web Site appears as one of the optional tasks. Selecting this task displays a Help file that provides instructions for the migration process.

> **MORE INFO** For more information on the process of migrating from Windows SBS 2003 to Windows SBS 2008, see Chapter 3, "Installing Microsoft Windows Small Business Server (SBS) 2008," and Chapter 4, "Getting Started." To see where the SharePoint migration falls in the overall migration procedure, see the section entitled "Running the Migration Wizard" in Chapter 4.

The process of migrating the WSS site from your Windows SBS 2003 server to your Windows SBS 2008 server consists basically of detaching the SQL Server database from the old site, copying it to your new server, and creating a new Web site using the copied database. The process consists of multiple procedures on both the old server and the new one, as detailed in the following sections.

> **IMPORTANT** Before you begin the WSS migration process, be sure that you have applied all the latest service packs and updates on both servers.

Prescanning the Database

Before you copy the WSS database from your Windows SBS 2003 server to your new server, you must scan it using a program called Prescan.exe, which is included with Windows SBS 2008. To perform this scan, use the following procedure:

1. Log on to your Windows SBS 2008 server using a domain account with administrative privileges. The Windows SBS Console appears.

2. Open Windows Explorer and browse to the C:\Program Files\Common Files\ Microsoft Shared\Web Server Extensions\12\BIN folder.

3. Copy the Prescan.exe file from the BIN folder to the C:\Program Files folder on your Windows SBS 2003 server. You can do this by browsing to the other server in the network, or by using a flash drive or other removable medium.

4. Log on to your Windows SBS 2003 server using a domain account with administrative privileges.

5. Click Start. Then click All Programs, Accessories, Command Prompt. A command-prompt window appears.

6. At the command prompt, type **cd\"Program Files"** and press Enter to switch to the C:\Program Files folder.

7. Type **prescan /v http://companyweb** and press Enter. The Prescan.exe file scans the database.

8. If the scan completes successfully, as shown here, close the command-prompt window and begin the next procedure. If the scan generates an error, check the error log files specified in the program output, correct the problem causing the error, and repeat the scan.

IMPORTANT You must complete the prescan successfully on your Windows SBS 2003 server before you can use the database on your Windows SBS 2008 server.

Copying the Database

Once you have completed the prescan, you can copy the WSS database from your Windows SBS 2003 server to your Windows SBS 2008 server. However, before you can do this, you must stop the database service, so that the files are not in use. To stop the service and copy the database, use the following procedure:

1. Log on to your Windows SBS 2003 server using a domain account with administrative privileges.

2. Click Start. Then click Administrative Tools, Services. The Services console appears, as shown here.

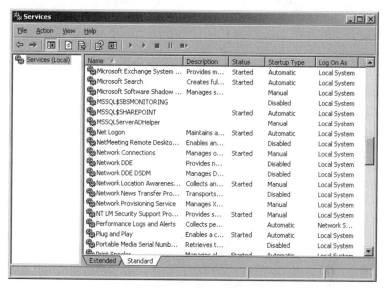

3. In the list of services, right-click the MSSQL$SHAREPOINT service and, from the context menu, select Stop. The database service stops.

4. Open Windows Explorer and browse to your Windows SBS 2008 server on the network.

5. Create a new folder called C:\Sbs2003 on your Windows SBS 2008 server.

6. On your Windows SBS 2003 server, browse to the C:\Program Files\Microsoft SQL Server\MSSQL$SHAREPOINT\Data folder, as shown here.

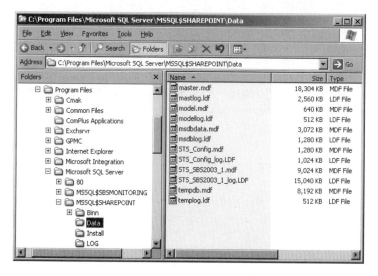

7. Copy the STS_*servername*_1.mdf and STS_*servername*_1_log.ldf files (where *servername* is the name of your Windows SBS 2003 server) from the Data folder to the C:\Sbs2003 folder you created on your new server.

8. Switch to the Services console and restart the MSSQL$SHAREPOINT service.

9. Log off the Windows SBS 2003 server.

Attaching the Database

Before you can create a Web site that uses the database files you copied from the Windows SBS 2003 server, you must attach the files to the SQL Server database engine using the following procedure:

1. Log on to your Windows SBS 2008 server using a domain account with administrative privileges.

2. Click Start. Then click All Programs, Microsoft SQL Server 2005. Right-click SQL Server Management Studio Express and, from the context menu, select Run As Administrator. When the User Account Control dialog box appears, click Continue. The Connect To Server dialog box appears, as shown here.

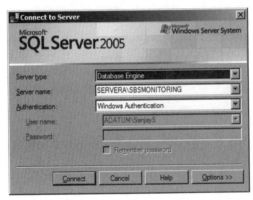

3. In the Server Name text box, type **\\.\pipe\mssql$microsoft##ssee\sql\ query** and click Connect. The Microsoft SQL Server Management Studio Express window appears, as shown here.

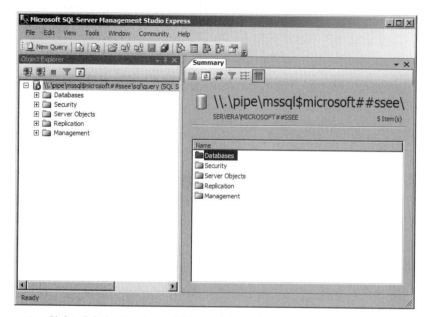

4. Right-click the Databases folder and, from the context menu, select Attach. The Attach Databases dialog box appears, as shown here.

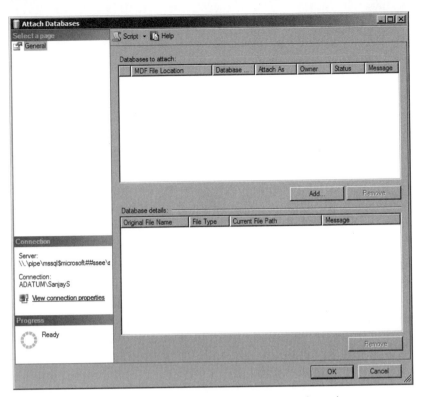

5. Click Add. The Locate Database Files dialog box appears, as shown here.

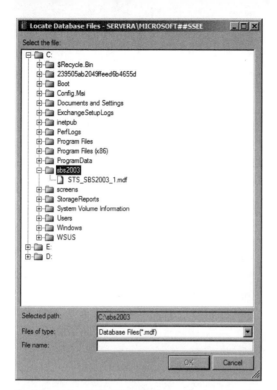

6. Browse to the C:\Sbs2003 folder and select the STS_*servername*_1.mdf file. Then click OK. The database appears in the Attach Databases dialog box, as shown here.

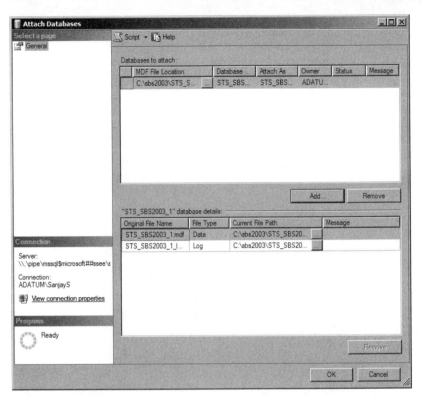

7. Click OK. The database appears in the Databases folder, as shown here.

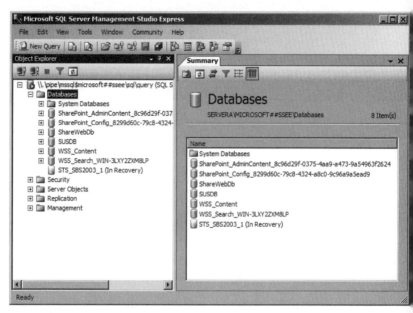

8. Close the Microsoft SQL Server Management Studio Express window.

Creating a New Web Site

Once you have attached the database you copied from your Windows SBS 2003 server to the SQL Server database engine in Windows SBS 2008, you can create a new Web site to host that database using the following procedure:

1. Log on to your Windows SBS 2008 server using a domain account with administrative privileges.

2. Click Start. Then click Administrative Tools, Internet Information Services (IIS) Manager. When the User Account Control dialog box appears, click Continue. The Internet Information Services (IIS) Manager console appears, as shown here.

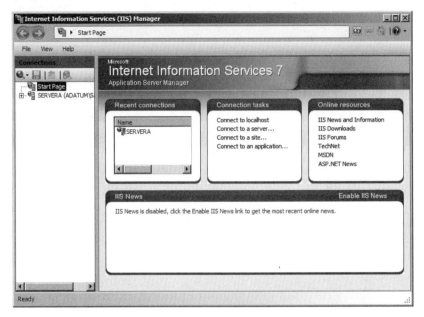

3. Expand the mode representing your server.

4. Right-click the Sites folder and, from the context menu, select Add Web Site. The Add Web Site dialog box appears, as shown here.

5. In the Site Name text box, type **OldCompanyweb**.

6. In the Physical Path text box, click the browse (...) button. The Browse For Folder dialog box appears, as shown here.

7. Browse to the C:\Inetpub folder and click Make New Folder. Give the new highlighted folder the name **OldCompanyweb** and click OK.

8. Click OK to close the Browse For Folder dialog box.

9. In the Host Name text box, type **OldCompanyweb** and click OK. The new site is added to the Sites folder, as shown here.

Creating a Web Application

With the old database in place on your new server and a Web site in place to use it, you can now create the Web application that will tie the two together using the following procedure:

1. Log on to your Windows SBS 2008 server using a domain account with administrative privileges.

2. Click Start. Then click Administrative Tools, SharePoint Services 3.0 Central Administration. When the User Account Control dialog box appears, click Continue. An Internet Explorer window appears, containing the Central Administration page, as shown here.

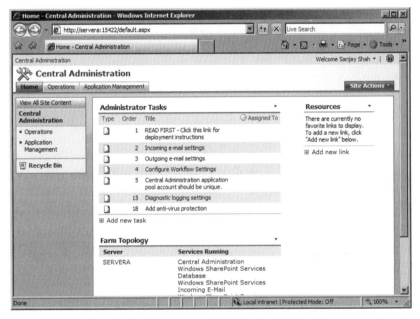

3. Click the Application Management tab. The Application Management page appears, as shown here.

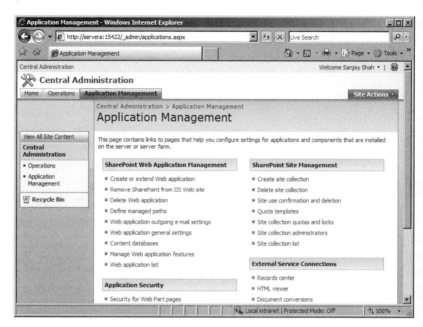

4. In the SharePoint Web Application Management section, click Create Or Extend Web Application. The Create Or Extend Web Application page appears, as shown here.

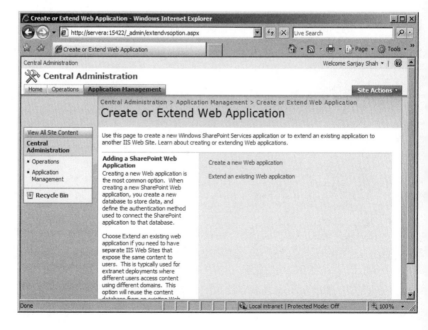

5. Click Create A New Web Application. The Create New Web Application page appears, as shown here.

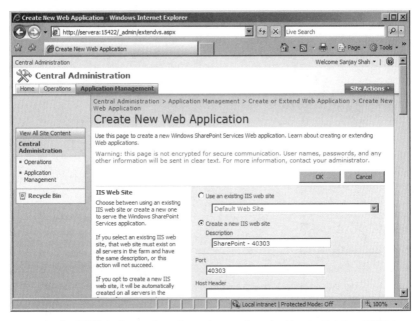

6. In the IIS Web site section, shown here, select the Use An Existing IIS Web Site option and, from the drop-down list, select the OldCompanyweb site you created in the previous procedure.

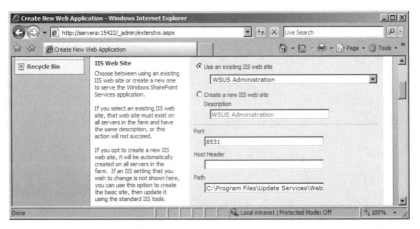

7. In the Security Configuration section, shown here, for the Authentication Provider setting, select the NTLM option.

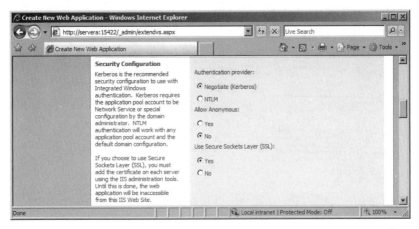

8. In the Application Pool section, shown here, select the Use Existing Application Pool option and, in the drop-down list, select the OldCompanyweb application pool.

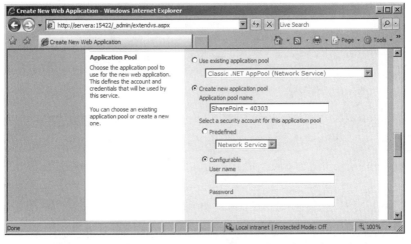

9. In the Database Name And Authentication section, shown here, in the Database Name text box, type **STS_*servername*_1**, where *servername* is the name of your Windows SBS 2003 server.

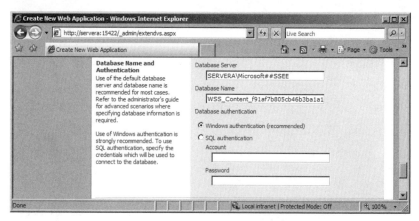

10. In the Search Server section, shown here, from the Select Windows Share-Point Services Search Server drop-down list, select your Windows SBS 2008 server name.

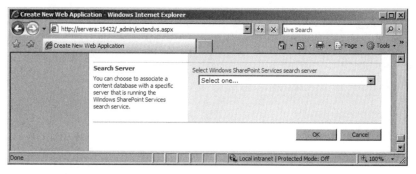

11. Leave the default values in place for all the other settings on the page and click OK.

12. Click OK to confirm that you want to change the Authentication Provider setting to NTLM.

An Operation In Progress page appears as the program upgrades the database and creates the new Web application, which can take as long as 30 minutes, after which the Application Created page appears, as shown here.

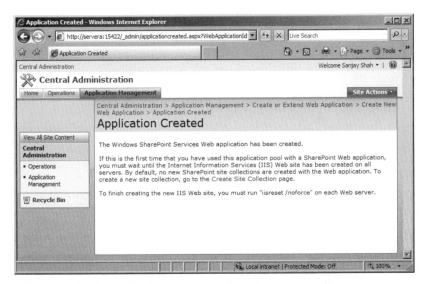

13. Click the Application Management tab again.

14. In the SharePoint Site Management section, click Site Collection Administrators. The Site Collection Administrators page appears, as shown here.

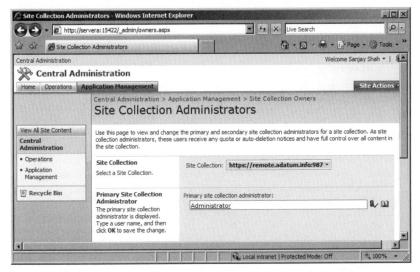

15. If the Site Collection section does not contain the *http://OldCompanyweb* value, click the Site Collection drop-down list and select Change Site Collection. The Select Site Collection page appears, as shown here.

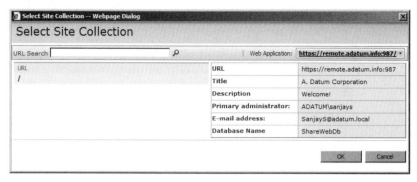

16. Click the Web Application drop-down list and select Change Web Application. The Select Web Application page appears, as shown here.

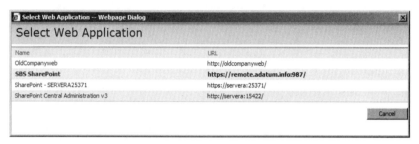

17. Click the *OldCompanyweb* application, and then click OK. The Site Collection Administrator page reappears with the *http://OldCompanyweb* value in the Site Collection setting.

18. In the Primary Site Collection Administrator section, click Browse. The Select People dialog box appears.

19. Find and select an account with network administrator privileges, and click OK to close the Select People dialog box.

    IMPORTANT The Administrator account is disabled by default in Windows SBS 2008. If your Windows SBS 2003 database uses the Administrator account for the Primary Site Collection Administrator setting, you must change it to an active account with network Administrator privileges.

20. Click OK, and then close the Central Administration window.

Updating the DNS

To access the OldCompanyweb site you have just created, you must create an Alias resource record in your DNS server, as shown in the following procedure:

1. Log on to your Windows SBS 2008 server using a domain account with administrative privileges.

2. Click Start. Then click Administrative Tools, DNS. When the User Account Control dialog box appears, click Continue. The DNS Manager console appears, as shown here.

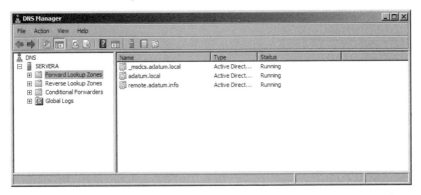

3. Expand the Forward Lookup Zones folder and select the zone named after your domain.

4. Right-click the zone and, from the context menu, select New Alias (CNAME). The New Resource Record dialog box appears, as shown here.

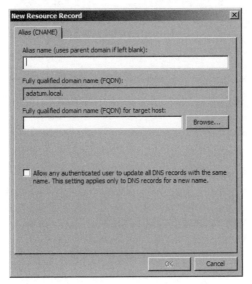

5. In the Alias Name (Uses Parent Domain If Left Blank) text box, type **OldCompanyweb**.

6. In the Fully Qualified Domain Name (FQDN) For Target Host text box, type the FQDN for your Windows SBS 2008 server and click OK. The new resource record appears in the zone.

MORE INFO For more information on DNS servers and resource records, see Chapter 2, "A Networking Primer."

Resetting IIS

Before you can access your new site, you must reset the IIS service using the following procedure:

1. Log on to your Windows SBS 2008 server using a domain account with administrative privileges.

2. Click Start. Then click All Programs, Accessories. Right-click Command Prompt and, from the context menu, select Run As Administrator. When the User Account Control dialog box appears, click Continue. A command-prompt window appears.

3. At the command prompt, type **iisreset** and press Enter. The program resets the IIS service, as shown here.

4. Close the command-prompt window.

Exporting and Importing

Once you have completed all the previous procedures, you have an operational WSS Web site on your Windows SBS 2008 server that you can access with the URL *http://OldCompanyweb*. You can now use the Stsadm.exe command-line program to export the data from the OldCompanyweb site and import it into the Companyweb site, as shown in the following procedure:

1. Log on to your Windows SBS 2008 server using a domain account with administrative privileges.

2. Click Start. Then click All Programs, Accessories. Right-click Command Prompt and, from the context menu, select Run As Administrator. When the User Account Control dialog box appears, click Continue. A command-prompt window appears.

3. At the command prompt, type **cd\"Program Files\Common Files\ Microsoft Shared\Web Server Extensions\12\BIN"** and press Enter.

4. To back up your existing Companyweb site to a file called Newdb.bak, type **stsadm -o export -url http://companyweb -filename Newdb.bak –includeusersecurity** and press Enter. The program backs up the site.

5. To export the contents of the OldCompanyweb site to a file called Olddb. bak, type **stsadm -o export -url http://OldCompanyweb -filename olddb.bak –includeusersecurity** and press Enter.

6. To import the OldCompanyweb content into your Companyweb site, type **stsadm -o import -url http://companyweb -filename olddb.bak –includeusersecurity** and press Enter.

7. Close the command prompt window.

CHAPTER 12

Optimizing Network Security

S ecurity is one of the primary concerns of any network administrator, of course, and Microsoft Windows Small Business Server (SBS) 2008 is designed to help administrators keep their networks secure without the need for extensive training in security principles. As mentioned in previous chapters, Windows SBS 2008 is based on the open architecture of Windows Server 2008 and other Microsoft products, but instead of leaving the user to design an effective and secure configuration, the product arrives preconfigured. The designers of Windows SBS have made many of the decisions that are ordinarily left up to administrators, and in doing so, they have created a networking environment that takes advantage of the software's security capabilities.

Network security is not just a matter of design and deployment, however. It is an ongoing concern, and administrators must be aware of the Windows SBS security architecture and the tools they can use to maintain and enhance it.

Understanding Windows SBS Security Principles

Security is essentially a matter of controlling access to network resources. In theory, one can create a perfectly secure system simply by denying everyone access to it, but this is hardly a feasible solution for a data network. Some of the basic security principles for the small business network administrator to consider are as follows:

- Allow users to access the network resources they need to perform their jobs
- Prevent unauthorized network users from accessing administrative tools and settings

- Allow network users to access the Internet without providing Internet users unrestricted access to the network

The following sections examine the mechanisms and design decisions in Windows SBS 2008 that enable administrators to realize these goals.

Authenticating Users

Authentication, one of the two fundamental security functions, is the process of verifying a user's identity in preparation for granting that user access to a protected resource. To authenticate a user, a system requires one of the following:

- **Something the user *knows*** The most common form of authentication requires users to supply a piece of information, such as a password, that the system already possesses. The complicating factor in this type of authentication is the security of the passwords themselves, which can conceivably be intercepted during transmission or compromised by the user. Windows SBS 2008 uses password-based authentication by default, with authentication protocols that protect the passwords from capture during network transmission.

- **Something the user *has*** Some security systems require users to possess a smart card or other identifying device that they must scan before they can access protected resources. Windows SBS 2008 can support smart card authentication, but it is not configured to do so by default. The main drawback of this authentication method is the additional cost for the card reader hardware. Smart cards can also be easily lost or stolen, so users are nearly always required to provide a password as well.

- **Something the user *is*** Some security systems require users to confirm their identities by scanning physiological characteristics, such as fingerprints. This technology is known as *biometrics*. Biometrical authentication is one of the most secure systems available because fingerprints and other physiological characteristics are difficult to spoof or steal. Windows SBS 2008 does not include direct support for biometrical authentication, but it does support modular authentication protocols that enable the system to interact with third-party hardware and software authentication solutions.

Active Directory Domain Services (AD DS) is responsible for authenticating network users in Windows SBS 2008. When you create user accounts, you specify passwords for them, which AD DS stores in its database. When users log on from their workstations, they type their passwords as part of the authentication process.

The biggest problem with password-based authentication is the tendency of the passwords to be compromised. There are two potential avenues of compromise: the network and the users themselves. If client applications transmit passwords over the network in clear text, it is possible for someone to capture the network packets and read the passwords inside them. Even if a client application encrypts the passwords before transmitting them, a potential intruder can often identify the data string that contains the encrypted password and use it to create an illicit logon by replaying it back to a server, still in its encrypted form. However, to protect the user passwords, AD DS uses *Kerberos*, an authentication protocol that enables clients to log on without transmitting passwords over the network in any form, clear or encrypted.

MORE INFO Kerberos, named for the three-headed dog of Greek mythology that guards the entrance to Hades, is a highly complex protocol that requires three elements to function: the client attempting to access a protected resource, the server hosting the protected resource, and an authentication provider. In Windows SBS 2008, the AD DS domain controller is the authentication provider, and it is involved in every security transaction. To avoid transmitting passwords over the network, Kerberos uses cryptographic values derived from the passwords to create unique *tickets* that clients and servers exchange to gain access to protected resources. Because the tickets are generated for a specific use at a specific time, intruders capturing the packets cannot replay them or derive user passwords from them.

Passwords are also vulnerable to low-tech forms of compromise, typically resulting from users' sloppy or naive security habits. Users often write passwords down, give them to coworkers for the sake of convenience, or are duped into supplying them through social engineering. To address these problems, Windows SBS 2008 uses Group Policy settings to compel users to change their passwords at regular intervals. You can modify these settings to suit the security needs of your organization.

MORE INFO *Social engineering* is the term used to define the process by which intruders gain access to protected resources by manipulating users into providing their credentials or other information. For example, a friendly stranger claiming to be from the company's IT department calls a user on the phone and says that he has been instructed to upgrade the user's account, but he needs the user's password to do so. The user, without verifying the caller's identity, supplies the password and thinks no more of it. In many cases, social engineering is a far easier and more effective tactic for penetrating a network's security than other high-tech alternatives.

Authorizing Users

The other fundamental security function is *authorization*, which is defined as the process of specifying which protected resources an authenticated user is permitted to access. Authentication confirms the user's identity, but authorization actually provides access to the network resources. In Windows SBS 2008, various permission systems authorize users to access protected resources.

Although they function in much the same way, Windows SBS 2008 has separate permission systems for each of the following resources:

- NTFS files and folders
- Folder shares

- Printer shares
- AD DS objects
- Registry keys

Permissions are basically flags that enable a particular user or group of users to perform specific actions on a specific resource. For example, a user that possesses the Read permission for an NTFS file is allowed to read the contents of the file, but the user cannot modify the file or do anything other than reading it without additional permissions.

Permissions are stored as a part of the objects they protect. Each protected element has an *access control list (ACL)* that consists of individual *access control entries (ACEs)*. Each ACE consists of a *security principal*, which is the user, group, or computer receiving access, and the permissions assigned to that security principal. In Windows SBS 2008, when you open the Properties sheet for a file, the Security tab contains the interface you can use to modify the file's ACL, as shown in Figure 12-1. Other elements, such as folder and printer shares, AD DS objects, and registry keys, have different permissions, but you use the same interface to manage them.

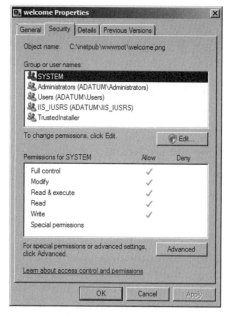

FIGURE 12-1 The Security tab on a file's Properties sheet

In Windows SBS 2008, as with all the other Microsoft Windows operating systems, permissions are always a part of the protected element, not the entity receiving access to that element. Each file on an NTFS volume, for example, has an ACL specifying the users and groups that can access it. If you move the file to another NTFS drive, the ACL goes with it. However, user and group objects in the AD DS database do not have a list of the files and other resources they are permitted to access.

Providing Internet Access

Authentication and authorization are intended primarily to limit the access to network resources that you grant to internal users. Allowing a user to read a file, but not modify it, is not necessarily a matter of suspicion; permissions also prevent accidental damage to documents and systems. However, providing your network users with access to the Internet is a lot like leaving your front door unlocked. Unless you have appropriate security measures in place, anybody can walk in, and the danger from Internet intruders is far greater than that from your internal users.

By itself, a small business network is a private arrangement, designed for internal use. However, virtually all small business network administrators want to provide their users with access to the Internet as well, and this means connecting your private network to another network owned by an Internet service provider (ISP). The ISP's network is connected to other networks in turn, and together, all these connected networks form the Internet.

Understanding Windows SBS Defaults

The default Windows SBS 2008 configuration is designed for the private internal network to have an Internet connection, but it handles it differently from previous Windows SBS versions. In its default configuration, Windows SBS 2003 calls for a primary server that has two network interface adapters: one to connect to the private, internal network, and one to connect to an ISP's network. The product also includes Microsoft Internet Security and Acceleration (ISA) Server, which has firewall functions that protect the internal network from Internet intrusion.

The problem with this arrangement is that the same server providing access to the Internet is also functioning as a domain controller, an internal mail server, and an intranet Web server, among other things. Running these internal functions on a server with a direct Internet connection is a violation of basic Windows security practices, which Microsoft strongly discourages.

Windows SBS 2008 uses a different configuration, which expects and allows the server to have only one network interface. Instead of connecting the Windows SBS server directly to the Internet, the default network configuration calls for a stand-alone router that provides Internet access to the entire network. The Internet Address Management Wizard, which you run after the Windows SBS 2008 installation, configures the server to use the router and, in many cases, can configure the router to accommodate the Internet capabilities of the applications and services running on the server.

MORE INFO A *router* is a device that connects two networks and relays traffic between them. For more information about routers, see Chapter 2, "A Networking Primer." For more information about the Internet Address Management Wizard and the tasks it performs, see Chapter 4, "Getting Started."

Understanding Network Address Translation

In addition to providing the network with Internet access, the router also functions as a firewall, protecting the network from unauthorized access by network users. Internet access routers rely on a technique called *Network Address Translation (NAT)* to protect the internal network. A Windows SBS network uses private Internet Protocol (IP) addresses for its computers, addresses that are, by definition, inaccessible from the Internet. Because of this, it is not possible for a computer on the Internet to initiate access to a computer on your private network. All Internet access must originate from within the private network, and the computers on the Internet can respond only to the requests they receive.

When a computer on your Windows SBS network attempts to access an Internet resource, it generates a message destined for an Internet server and transmits it to its Default Gateway address. The Default Gateway address identifies the router on the local network that provides access to other networks. However, the messages generated by the computers on your network have private IP addresses. Were these messages to reach an Internet server unaltered, the server would attempt to reply to the private IP addresses, and those attempts would fail. This is where the NAT capabilities of your stand-alone router come in.

A NAT router, like all routers, has two network interfaces. One of these is connected to your private network and has a private IP address; the other is connected to your ISP's network and has a registered IP address that is accessible from the Internet. When your network computers send messages to the Internet, the NAT router receives them and modifies the Source IP Address value in each message from the private IP address of the source computer to the registered IP address of the router itself. The router then forwards the messages to their original destinations on the Internet, as shown in Figure 12-2.

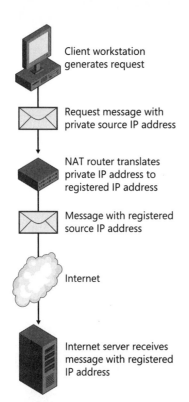

Client workstation
generates request

Request message with
private source IP address

NAT router translates
private IP address to
registered IP address

Message with registered
source IP address

Internet

Internet server receives
message with registered
IP address

FIGURE 12-2 A NAT router translates outgoing traffic and forwards it to the destination.

When the Internet servers respond, they send their replies to the NAT router's registered address. When it receives the replies, the router replaces their Destination IP Address values with the private addresses of the computers that originally generated the requests, as shown in Figure 12-3. The NAT router maintains a translation table that enables it to associate outgoing messages with incoming replies.

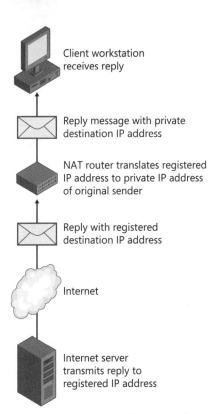

Client workstation
receives reply

Reply message with private
destination IP address

NAT router translates registered
IP address to private IP address
of original sender

Reply with registered
destination IP address

Internet

Internet server
transmits reply to
registered IP address

FIGURE 12-3 Incoming traffic is addressed to the NAT router and forwarded to the recipient.

The end result is that the computers on the Internet are aware of only the NAT router; they cannot communicate with the computers on your private network directly. Because the router is not a Windows computer, it is relatively immune to many types of software-based attacks. However, this does not mean that the computers on your network are invulnerable to attacks from the Internet.

Some of the greatest dangers to computers on a private network are "Trojans," or "Trojan horses," which are programs that appear to perform one function but which are actually designed to perform another. If a user on your network can be duped into downloading and installing a program of this type, the program can send transmissions to computers on the Internet, signaling its readiness to perform certain illicit tasks. Because the private computer is initiating the communication, computers on the Internet are capable of responding, and the NAT router forwards their messages to the private network in the usual manner.

To protect the computers on your private network from threats such as this, you can configure Windows Firewall to limit the types of traffic your computers are permitted to receive.

Using Password Policies

For the majority of small business networks, complex authentication mechanisms such as smart cards and biometric scanners are not necessary, so they rely on passwords to identify their users. However, you can maximize the security that the default authentication system provides by requiring users to supply passwords that are not easy to guess or break. By modifying the default Group Policy settings for your domain, you can require your users to specify passwords of a given length and complexity and to change their passwords at regular intervals.

Specifying password policies for your network is always a balance between what degree of protection you feel your network needs and what amount of inconvenience your users tolerate. For example, you could conceivably create what appears to be a highly secure password system by assigning each of your users a long, randomly generated password, such as *j;8&3sFv5)81@sgGts20*sOt5*. However, your users would probably hate you for making them type in such a password every day. You can bet that they would change the password at the first opportunity. Even if they didn't (or couldn't) do that, most of them would probably write the password on a note and stick it to their monitors—which can be as bad as not having a password at all.

Password-based authentication systems are susceptible to dictionary attacks when the passwords are relatively weak. A *dictionary attack* is a type of brute-force technique that attempts to guess a password by running automatically through a list of common words. Weak passwords are those that consist of single words that are likely to be found in the list used by attackers. To strengthen passwords, users can make them longer, use uncommon words or phrases, or add numerals, symbols, or both.

Allowing users to select their own passwords is a better solution, and with Group Policy settings, you can increase the security of the passwords by enforcing the following requirements:

- **Passwords of a specific length** The longer a password is, the more difficult it is to crack. Given a choice, users tend to prefer short passwords that are easy to type, so requiring passwords of at least seven characters is a good way to strengthen the authentication system.

- **Frequent password changes** Given a sufficient amount of time, it is possible to crack any password, but every time the password changes, the penetration process has to start all over again. Requiring users to change their passwords frequently makes them more difficult to penetrate.

- **Complex passwords** Adding capital letters, numerals, and symbols makes it far more difficult to penetrate passwords using dictionary attacks.
- **Unique passwords** Even when you require them to change their passwords frequently, people tend to use the same two or three passwords over and over. To prevent this, you can require users to supply a new value each time they change their passwords.

Modifying Password Policy Settings

To modify the default password policy settings, you use the Group Policy Management console, as shown in the following procedure:

1. Log on to your Windows SBS 2008 server using a domain account with administrative privileges.

2. Click Start. Then click Administrative Tools, Group Policy Management. When the User Account Control dialog box appears, click Continue. The Group Policy Management console appears, as shown here.

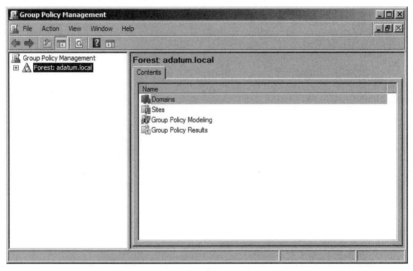

3. Browse to the Forest/Domains/*domainname*/Group Policy Objects folder (where *domainname* is the name of your AD DS domain), as shown here.

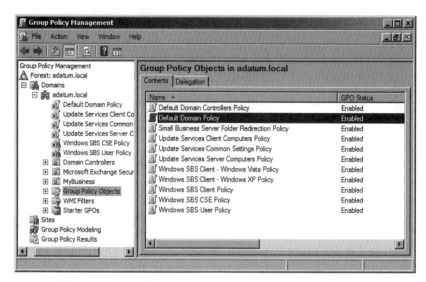

4. Right-click the Default Domain Policy object and, from the context menu, select Edit. The Group Policy Management Editor console appears, as shown here.

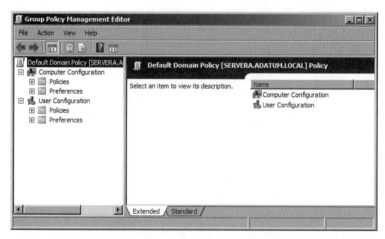

5. Browse to the Computer Configuration/Policies/Windows Settings/Security Settings/Account Policies/Password Policy node, as shown here.

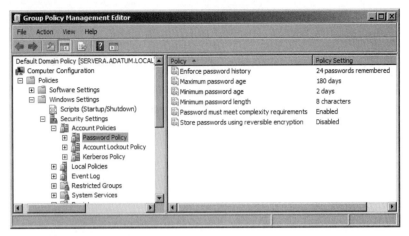

6. Double-click the policy whose value you want to modify. The Properties sheet for the policy appears, as shown here.

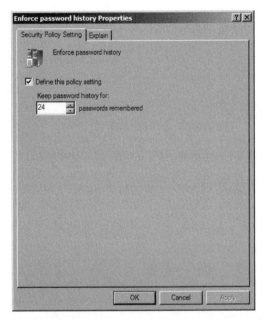

7. Modify the policy value using the box provided. You can also disable the policy entirely by clearing the Define This Policy Setting check box.

8. Click OK to close the Properties sheet.

9. Repeat steps 6 to 8 to modify other policy settings.

10. Close the Group Policy Management Editor console.

11. Close the Group Policy Management console.

Selecting Password Policy Values

The password policies you can modify, along with their Windows SBS 2008 default settings, are listed in Table 12-1.

TABLE 12-1 Windows SBS 2008 Password Policy Settings

SECURITY POLICY SETTING	DEFAULT VALUE	DESCRIPTION
Enforce Password History	24 passwords	Stores the passwords that users have previously supplied and prevents them from reusing those same passwords.
Maximum Password Age	180 days	Specifies how often users are required to change their passwords.
Minimum Password Age	2 days	Determines how long a user must keep a password before changing it.
Minimum Password Length	8 characters	Determines the minimum length of a password.
Password Must Meet Complexity Requirements	Enabled	Forces users to specify passwords that <ul><li>Do not contain all or part of the user's account name</li><li>Are at least six characters in length</li><li>Contain characters from three of the following four categories: uppercase characters (*A* through *Z*), lowercase characters (*a* through *z*), base 10 digits (0 through 9), and nonalphabetic characters (such as *!*, *$*, *#*, and *%*)</li></ul>
Store Passwords Using Reversible Encryption	Disabled	Causes the system to store passwords in a form that can be easily decrypted by applications that require access to them.

The values you select for the password policy settings should be a compromise between network security and user convenience. Some of the factors you should consider for these settings are as follows:

- **Minimum Password Length** As mentioned earlier, longer passwords are more secure than shorter ones, but they can also be more difficult for users to remember. The default value of 8 is typical, but you might want to consider implementing a password rule for your organization that calls for users to select a password and increase its length by appending a suffix to it. For example, if your users must change their passwords each month, you can have them append a suffix containing the name of the month. A password such as *foxtrot!Nov2008* is relatively easy to remember and far more difficult to break than *foxtrot*, even if the attacker is aware of the suffix.

- **Maximum Password Age** Ideally, you should set this policy to a value that is shorter than the time a typical password-cracking program takes to penetrate passwords of the length and complexity you require for your organization. The default value of 180 days (six months) is relatively long; you might want to consider altering this value to 30 (monthly) or 60 (bimonthly) to increase security. However, too low a value can increase the irritation factor for your users and increase the number of forgotten password support calls you receive.

- **Minimum Password Age** This setting is designed to prevent users from changing their passwords when compelled to do so and then immediately changing them back to the their previous values. The default value of two days is usually sufficient to prevent users from abusing their password changing capabilities.

- **Enforce Password History** Users have a tendency to gravitate toward the same passwords, and if possible, they alternate between the same two passwords indefinitely. This setting enables you to force the use of different passwords for a specified number of changes. The default value of 24, combined with the 180-day Maximum Password Age value, means that it will be 12 years before a user can repeat a password.

- **Password Must Meet Complexity Requirements** This policy setting is one of the most effective ways to increase the security of your network. Forcing users to include uppercase, numeric, and symbolic characters in their passwords compounds the mathematical difficulty of cracking them. To make complex passwords easier to remember, users can substitute comparable numbers or symbols for letters, but this is only advisable when the password is reasonably strong to begin with. For example, substituting characters to change the password *mason* to *M@s0n* is not particularly effective if Mason is the user's name, because attackers trying to guess the password are likely to try those character substitutions. However, if a user selects a less-obvious word or phrase and then substitutes numbers and symbols for equivalent letters in it, the result can be a very strong password indeed.

- **Store Passwords Using Reversible Encryption** Enabling this setting severely compromises the effectiveness of the Windows SBS 2008 authentication system. You should leave the default Disabled setting in place unless you have a specific reason to change it.

Setting Account Lockout Policies

It is common for users to mistype their passwords when logging on, forcing them to try two or more times before the system authenticates them successfully. However, a system that allows unlimited logon attempts provides attackers with an unrestricted opportunity to guess user passwords. In addition to its password policies, Windows SBS 2008 has account lockout policies that enable you to specify how many unsuccessful logon attempts the system should allow and what actions it should take when users exceed the specified limit.

To modify the default account lockout policy settings, use the following procedure:

1. Log on to your Windows SBS 2008 server using a domain account with administrative privileges.

2. Click Start. Then click Administrative Tools, Group Policy Management. When the User Account Control dialog box appears, click Continue. The Group Policy Management console appears.

3. Browse to the Forest/Domains/*domainname*/Group Policy Objects folder, where *domainname* is the name of your AD DS domain.

4. Right-click the Default Domain Policy object and, from the context menu, select Edit. The Group Policy Management Editor console appears.

5. Browse to the Computer Configuration/Policies/Windows Settings/Security Settings/Account Policies/Account Lockout Policy node, as shown here.

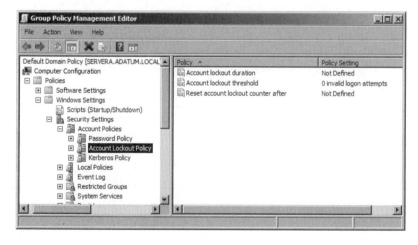

6. Double-click the policy whose value you want to modify. The Properties sheet for the policy appears, as shown here.

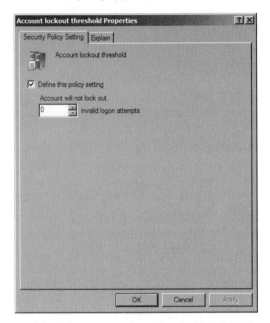

7. Modify the Account Lockout Threshold policy value using the Invalid Logon Attempts box provided and click OK. When you select a value other than zero, a Suggested Value Changes dialog box appears, as shown here.

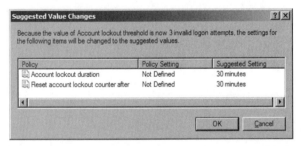

8. Click OK to close the Properties sheet. The system resets the other two policies to the suggested values.

9. Repeat steps 6 to 8 to modify the suggested settings for the Account Lockout Duration and Reset Account Lockout Counter After policies, if desired.

10. Close the Group Policy Management Editor console.

11. Close the Group Policy Management console.

The account lockout policies you can modify, along with their default settings, are listed in Table 12-2.

TABLE 12-2 Windows SBS 2008 Account Lockout Policy Settings

SECURITY POLICY SETTING	DEFAULT VALUE	DESCRIPTION
Account Lockout Duration	Not defined	Specifies how long a locked-out account will remain disabled before the system automatically re-enables it. A value of 0 requires an administrator to unlock the account manually.
Account Lockout Threshold	0 invalid logon attempts	Specifies how many unsuccessful logon attempts users can make before the system locks their accounts. A value of 0 provides an unlimited number of logon attempts.
Reset Account Lockout Counter After	Not defined	Specifies the amount of time that must elapse after an unsuccessful logon attempt before the counter is reset to 0 unsuccessful logon attempts.

The default values for the account lockout policy settings place no limitation on the number of logon attempts the system allows a user. This means that potential intruders can try as many times as they want to guess users' passwords. To protect your accounts from this type of attack, you can specify a different value for the Account Lockout Threshold policy setting. A value of 3 is usually a sensible setting because most users should be able to type their passwords successfully in three attempts or fewer.

When you impose a limit on the number of logon attempts your users can make, you should also consider what happens when a user exceeds the limit. In most cases, the objective is to configure the system to require as little administrator intervention as possible, but your organization might require a different policy.

When you specify a value other than 0 for the Account Lockout Threshold policy, the system automatically sets the Account Lockout Duration and Reset Account Lockout Counter After policies to values of 30 minutes. The Account Lockout Duration value means that any users that exceed the threshold and are locked out by the system will remain locked out for 30 minutes, after which the system automatically unlocks their accounts. To increase the security of the system, at the expense of administrator convenience, you can set the Account Lockout Duration value to 0, which causes the system to leave the account locked until an administrator manually unlocks it.

When a user mistypes a password, the system sets the user's account lockout counter to 1. A second unsuccessful logon increases the account lockout counter value to 2. The system continues to augment the counter each time the user fails to log on successfully until one of the following events occurs:

- The user logs on successfully, in which case the system resets the counter to 0.
- The number of unsuccessful logons reaches the Account Lockout Threshold value, in which case the system locks the account and resets the counter to 0.
- The user stops attempting to log on for the time interval specified in the Reset Account Lockout Counter After value, in which case the system resets the counter to 0.

Working with Permissions

In Chapter 7, "Managing Storage," you learned how to create a new shared folder and, in the process, configure the share permissions for that folder. Share permissions, you recall, specify which users are allowed to access shared folders over the network and what degree of access those users should receive. Assuming that the shared folder is on an NTFS volume, it is also necessary for users to have NTFS permissions before they can access the files in the shared folder.

NTFS permissions provide more detailed access control than share permissions, and they are effective on the local console, not just over the network. For this reason, many administrators give all their users the Allow Full Control share permission to all shared folders and rely on NTFS permissions for user- and group-specific access control. This minimizes the confusion between share and NTFS permissions for both users and administrators.

Assigning Share Permissions

When you create a new share using the Provision A Shared Folder Wizard, the SMB Permissions page, shown in Figure 12-4, enables you to select from four share permission assignments, none of which is equivalent to the Allow Full Control For Everyone assignment that Windows SBS 2008 uses for its default shares. However, when you select the Users And Groups Have Custom Share Permissions option and click Permissions, a Permissions dialog box for the share appears, enabling you to assign any permissions you wish.

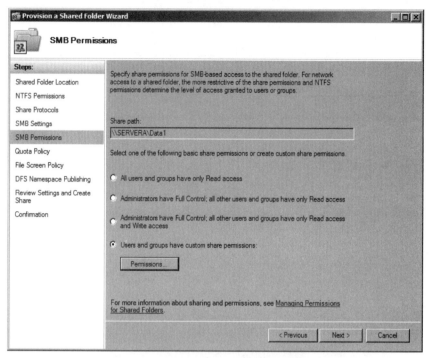

FIGURE 12-4 The SMB Permissions page of the Provision A Shared Folder Wizard

This same Permissions interface is accessible from the shared folder's Properties sheet. To assign the Allow Full Control permission to a folder share that you have already created, use the following procedure:

1. Log on to your Windows SBS 2008 server using a domain account with administrative privileges.

2. Open Windows Explorer and browse to the shared folder you want to manage, as shown here.

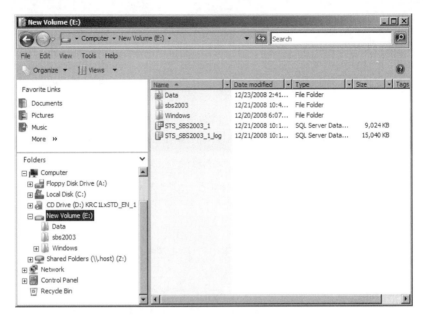

3. Right-click the shared folder and, from the context menu, select Properties. The Properties sheet for the folder appears, as shown here.

4. Click the Sharing tab, as shown here.

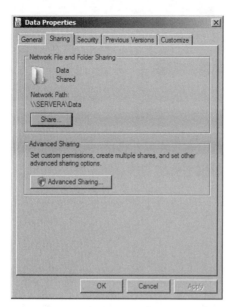

5. Click Advanced Sharing. When the User Account Control dialog box appears, click Continue. The Advanced Sharing dialog box appears, as shown here.

6. Click Permissions. The Permissions dialog box for the share appears, as shown here.

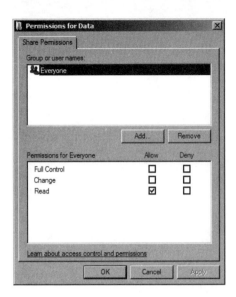

NOTE This is the same Permissions dialog box that appears when you select the Users And Groups Have Custom Share Permissions option in the Provision A Shared Folder Wizard.

7. In the Group Or User Names list, select Everyone.

8. In the Permissions for Everyone box, select the Allow Full Control check box and click OK.

   MORE INFO For an explanation of the share permissions and the capabilities they provide, see the section entitled "Understanding Share Permissions" in Chapter 7.

9. Click OK to close the Advanced Sharing dialog box.

10. Click OK to close the Properties sheet.

11. Close Windows Explorer.

Introducing NTFS Permissions

Once you grant the Everyone special identity the Allow Full Control share permission, anyone can access the shared folder over the network. However, users cannot access the files in the shared folder unless they have appropriate NTFS permissions. NTFS permissions apply whether the user is accessing the files over the network or is seated at the computer where the files are stored.

Unlike the relatively simple share permissions system, NTFS permissions provide much more detailed control over the access granted to a specific user or group. You might limit some users to reading a file while granting others permission to modify the contents of the same file. Still others might be able to create new files in the same folder.

BEST PRACTICES Windows SBS 2008 supports the NTFS, FAT, and FAT32 file systems for its hard disks, but only NTFS has a system of permissions. In addition, NTFS provides other advanced capabilities, including file compression and file encryption. At this time, the only reason not to choose the NTFS file system for your disks is that you must boot the computer using another operating system that does not support NTFS. Given that all the current versions of Windows and most UNIX and Linux distributions have NTFS support, the use of FAT or FAT32 is unnecessary for virtually all installations.

Standard Permissions and Special Permissions

The NTFS file system includes two types of permissions: standard permissions and special permissions. *Standard permissions* are the ones that most administrators use on an everyday basis. The six NTFS standard permissions and the privileges they provide when you apply them to files and folders are listed in Table 12-3.

TABLE 12-3 NTFS Standard Permissions

STANDARD PERMISSION	WHEN APPLIED TO A FOLDER, ENABLES A SECURITY PRINCIPAL TO:	WHEN APPLIED TO A FILE, ENABLES A SECURITY PRINCIPAL TO:
Full Control	■ Modify the folder permissions ■ Take ownership of the folder ■ Delete subfolders and files contained in the folder ■ Perform all actions associated with all the other NTFS folder permissions	■ Modify the file permissions ■ Take ownership of the file ■ Perform all actions associated with all the other NTFS file permissions
Modify	■ Delete the folder ■ Perform all actions associated with the Write and the Read & Execute permissions	■ Modify the file ■ Delete the file ■ Perform all actions associated with the Write and the Read & Execute permissions

TABLE 12-3 NTFS Standard Permissions

STANDARD PERMISSION	WHEN APPLIED TO A FOLDER, ENABLES A SECURITY PRINCIPAL TO:	WHEN APPLIED TO A FILE, ENABLES A SECURITY PRINCIPAL TO:
Read & Execute	■ Navigate through restricted folders to reach other files and folders ■ Perform all actions associated with the Read and List Folder Contents permissions	■ Perform all actions associated with the Read permission ■ Run applications
List Folder Contents	■ View the names of the files and subfolders contained in the folder	■ Not applicable
Read	■ See the files and subfolders contained in the folder ■ View the ownership, permissions, and attributes of the folder	■ Read the contents of the file ■ View the ownership, permissions, and attributes of the file
Write	■ Create new files and subfolders inside the folder ■ Modify the folder attributes ■ View the ownership and permissions of the folder	■ Overwrite the file ■ Modify the file attributes ■ View the ownership and permissions of the file

When you open the Properties dialog box for an NTFS file or folder, select the Security tab, and click Edit. When the User Account Control dialog box appears, click Continue. You see the interface shown in Figure 12-5, which is quite similar to the share permission interface you worked with earlier. In fact, all the Windows SBS 2008 permissions systems use the same basic interface, the differences being the names of the permissions you can select and the number of available permissions.

Standard permissions are easy to use, but they are not the most detailed form of permissions available on NTFS volumes. In actuality, standard permissions are preconfigured combinations of special permissions. *Special permissions* provide the finest possible control over your NTFS files and folders. There are 14 special permissions, as listed in Table 12-4.

FIGURE 12-5 The Security tab of an NTFS file

TABLE 12-4 NTFS Special Permissions

SPECIAL PERMISSION	FUNCTIONS
Traverse Folder/ Execute File	▪ The Traverse Folder permission allows or denies security principals the ability to move through folders that they do not have permission to access so they can reach files or folders that they do have permission to access. This permission applies to folders only. ▪ The Execute File permission allows or denies security principals the ability to run program files. This permission applies to files only.
List Folder/ Read Data	▪ The List Folder permission allows or denies security principals the ability to view the file and subfolder names within a folder. This permission applies to folders only. ▪ The Read Data permission allows or denies security principals the ability to view the contents of a file. This permission applies to files only.
Read Attributes	▪ Allows or denies security principals the ability to view the NTFS attributes of a file or folder.

TABLE 12-4 NTFS Special Permissions

SPECIAL PERMISSION	FUNCTIONS
Read Extended Attributes	■ Allows or denies security principals the ability to view the extended attributes of a file or folder.
Create Files/ Write Data	■ The Create Files permission allows or denies security principals the ability to create files within the folder. This permission applies to folders only.
	■ The Write Data permission allows or denies security principals the ability to modify the file and overwrite existing content. This permission applies to files only.
Create Folders/ Append Data	■ The Create Folders permission allows or denies security principals the ability to create subfolders within a folder. This permission applies to folders only.
	■ The Append Data permission allows or denies security principals the ability to add data to the end of the file but not to modify, delete, or overwrite existing data in the file. This permission applies to files only.
Write Attributes	■ Allows or denies security principals the ability to modify the NTFS attributes of a file or folder.
Write Extended Attributes	■ Allows or denies security principals the ability to modify the extended attributes of a file or folder.
Delete Subfolders and Files	■ Allows or denies security principals the ability to delete subfolders and files, even if the Delete permission has not been granted on the subfolder or file.
Delete	■ Allows or denies security principals the ability to delete the file or folder.
Read Permissions	■ Allows or denies security principals the ability to read the permissions for the file or folder.
Change Permissions	■ Allows or denies security principals the ability to modify the permissions for the file or folder.
Take Ownership	■ Allows or denies security principals the ability to take ownership of the file or folder.
Synchronize	■ Allows or denies different threads of multithreaded, multiprocessor programs to wait on the handle for the file or folder and synchronize with another thread that might signal it.

When you assign a standard permission to a user or group, you are actually assigning a combination of special permissions. The standard permissions and their corresponding special permissions are listed in Table 12-5. However, it is also possible to work with special permissions directly.

TABLE 12-5 NTFS Standard Permissions and Their Special Permission Equivalents

STANDARD PERMISSIONS	SPECIAL PERMISSIONS
Read	■ List Folder/Read Data ■ Read Attributes ■ Read Extended Attributes ■ Read Permissions ■ Synchronize
Read & Execute	■ List Folder/Read Data ■ Read Attributes ■ Read Extended Attributes ■ Read Permissions ■ Synchronize ■ Traverse Folder/Execute File
Modify	■ Create Files/Write Data ■ Create Folders/Append Data ■ Delete ■ List Folder/Read Data ■ Read Attributes ■ Read Extended Attributes ■ Read Permissions ■ Synchronize ■ Write Attributes ■ Write Extended Attributes
Write	■ Create Files/Write Data ■ Create Folders/Append Data ■ Read Permissions ■ Synchronize ■ Write Attributes ■ Write Extended Attributes

STANDARD PERMISSIONS	SPECIAL PERMISSIONS
List Folder Contents	▪ List Folder/Read Data
	▪ Read Attributes
	▪ Read Extended Attributes
	▪ Read Permissions
	▪ Synchronize
	▪ Traverse Folder/Execute File
Full Control	▪ Change Permissions
	▪ Create Files/Write Data
	▪ Create Folders/Append Data
	▪ Delete
	▪ Delete Subfolders and Files
	▪ List Folder/Read Data
	▪ Read Attributes
	▪ Read Extended Attributes
	▪ Read Permissions
	▪ Synchronize
	▪ Take Ownership
	▪ Write Attributes
	▪ Write Extended Attributes

When you open the Properties sheet for an NTFS file or folder, click Advanced on the Security tab, and then click Edit. When the User Account Control dialog box appears, click Continue. The Advanced Security Settings dialog box appears, as shown in Figure 12-6. This dialog box is the closest you can come to working directly with the access control entries in the file or folder's ACL.

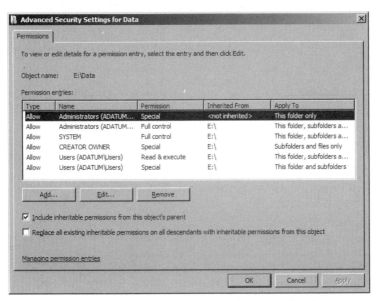

FIGURE 12-6 The Advanced Security Settings dialog box for an NTFS file or folder

Using Group Permissions

Although it is possible to assign permissions to individual users, the general rule of thumb for network administrators is to assign permissions to groups instead. You can then grant permissions to users simply by adding them to a group. This way, when creating accounts for new users, or when a user changes jobs within the organization, you only have to manage group memberships instead of assigning and revoking a large number of permissions to different resources.

Understanding Permission Inheritance

Permissions always flow downward through a tree hierarchy by default. In the case of an NTFS volume, the permissions you assign to a folder are inherited by all the files and subfolders in that folder. Therefore, if you grant a user permission to access the root of a disk, that user receives the same permission for all the subordinate files and folders on that disk.

As a general rule, administrators design the directory structures of their disks to accommodate this phenomenon by placing the more restricted folders lower in the directory tree. For example, if you want to create a folder for each of your users and assign permissions allowing only each user full access to his or her own folder, you might first create a folder called UserData and grant the Allow Read and Allow List Folder Contents permissions to the Everyone special identity. Then, you can create a separate folder for each user beneath UserData and grant each user the Allow Full Control permission to that folder. The result is that your users have complete control over their own folders and the ability to view the contents of and read files in everyone else's folder.

It is possible to prevent folders from inheriting permissions from their parent folders if necessary. One way to do this is to assign Deny permissions for a particular folder to a particular user or group. As you can see in the permission interfaces shown earlier, Windows SBS 2008 enables you to allow permissions or deny them. Deny permissions always override Allow permissions, so even if a user inherits permissions to a particular folder from a parent, an explicit Deny permission for that folder takes precedence. Another way to prevent permission inheritance is to open the Advanced Security Settings dialog box and clear the Include Inheritable Permissions From This Object's Parent check box.

Both of these methods are effective ways of controlling permission inheritance, but they can complicate the access control process enormously, particularly if you have more than one administrator managing permissions for your users. Most administrators avoid using Deny permissions entirely and leave the default permission inheritance policies in place.

Understanding Effective Permissions

As you have seen, Windows SBS 2008 users can receive NTFS permissions for a particular file or folder in a variety of ways, including the following:

- From explicit user assignments
- Inherited from parent folders
- Through group memberships

In many cases, users receive permissions for a specific file or folder from multiple sources, and those permissions can sometimes conflict. In a case like this, it is important for administrators to understand how Windows SBS resolves these permission conflicts. The combination of Allow and Deny permissions for a file or folder that a user receives from all possible sources is called the user's *effective permissions* for that resource. The three basic rules to remember when evaluating permission combinations are as follows:

- **Allow permissions are cumulative.** When a user receives different Allow permissions from various sources, the system combines them to form the effective permissions. For example, if a user inherits the Allow Read and Allow List Folder Contents permissions for a file from its parent folder, and receives the Allow Write and Allow Modify permissions for the same file from a group membership, the user's effective permissions for the file are the combination of all four permissions.

- **Deny permissions override Allow permissions.** When a user receives both Allow and Deny permissions from any single source, the Deny permissions take precedence over the Allow permissions. For example, if a user receives the Allow Full Control permission for a file from one group membership and the Deny Full Control permission for the same file from another group membership, then the Deny Full Control permission overrides the Allow Full Control permission, preventing the user from accessing the file in any way.

■ **Explicit permissions take precedence over inherited permissions.** When you explicitly assign a user permissions to a file or folder, these permissions override any permissions that the user inherits from a parent folder or receives from group memberships. For example, if a user inherits the Deny Full Control permission for a file from its parent folder, assigning the user the Allow Full Control permission for that file overrides the inherited permission and provides the user with full access.

Because the interactions of the various permission sources can be difficult to evaluate, the Advanced Security Settings dialog box for an NTFS file or folder enables you to view the effective permissions for a specific user or group. To view effective permissions, use the following procedure:

1. Log on to your Windows SBS 2008 server using a domain account with administrative privileges.

2. Open Windows Explorer and browse to the parent folder of the folder you want to access.

3. Right-click the file or folder whose effective permissions you want to view and, from the context menu, select Properties. The Properties sheet for the file or folder appears.

4. Click the Security tab, as shown here.

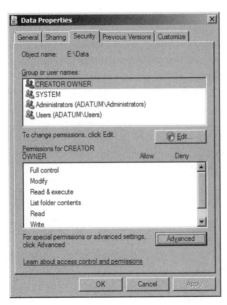

5. Click Advanced. The Advanced Security Settings dialog box for the file or folder appears.

6. Click the Effective Permissions tab, as shown here.

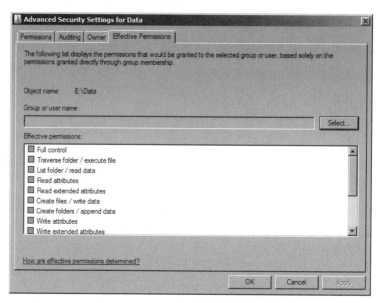

7. Click Select. The Select Users, Computers, Or Groups dialog box appears, as shown here.

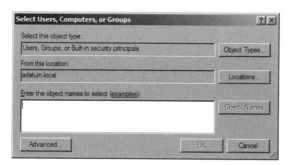

8. In the Enter The Object Names To Select text box, type the name of the user or group whose effective permissions you want to view and click OK. The user or group appears in the Group Or User Name text box and the Effective Permissions box displays the permissions that the user or group currently possesses, as shown here.

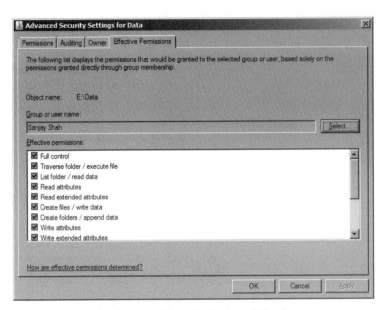

9. Click OK to close the Advanced Security Settings dialog box.

10. Click OK again to close the Properties sheet.

11. Close Windows Explorer.

Assigning NTFS Permissions

When you create a new share using the Provision A Shared Folder Wizard, the NTFS Permissions page, shown in Figure 12-7, provides access to the Permissions dialog box for the folder you intend to share. You can also modify the NTFS permissions for any file or folder using its Properties sheet.

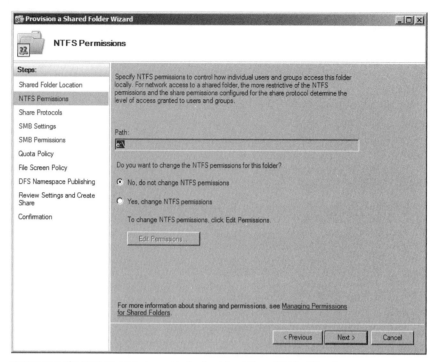

FIGURE 12-7 The NTFS Permissions page in the Provision A Shared Folder Wizard

To assign NTFS permissions to a folder, use the following procedure:

1. Log on to your Windows SBS 2008 server using a domain account with administrative privileges.

2. Open Windows Explorer and browse to the parent folder of the folder you want to manage.

3. Right-click the folder whose NTFS permissions you want to manage and, from the context menu, select Properties. The Properties sheet for the folder appears.

4. Click the Security tab.

5. Click Edit. When the User Account Control dialog box appears, click Continue. The Permissions dialog box for the folder appears, as shown here.

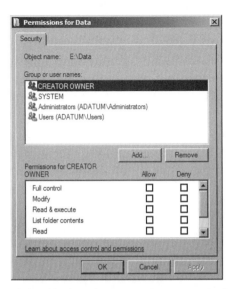

6. Click Add. The Select Users, Computers, Or Groups dialog box appears.

7. In the Enter Object Names To Select text box, type the name of the user or group to which you want to assign permissions and click OK. The user or group appears in the Group Or User Names list, as shown here.

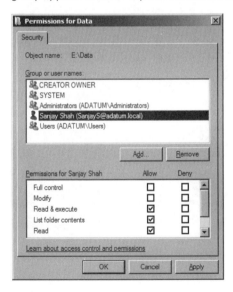

8. With the user or group you added selected, select the check boxes for the permissions you want to allow or deny. Then click OK.

9. Click OK again to close the Properties sheet.

10. Close Windows Explorer.

Understanding Resource Ownership

One of the peculiarities of the NTFS permission system is that it is possible to revoke all permissions from all users, leaving no one with the ability to access a particular file or folder. To prevent files and folders from being so orphaned, every NTFS element has an owner. The owner of a file or folder always has the ability to modify the permissions for that file or folder, even if the owner does not possess any permissions himself or herself. By default, the owner of a file or folder is the user who created it. However, any user who possesses the Allow Take Ownership special permission or the Allow Full Control standard permission can assume ownership of a file or folder.

Backing Up and Restoring

B acking up data is a critical administrative function for every network, one that many administrators tend to neglect. In many cases, hard disk contents are an organization's most precious possession. Their loss can cause production to cease, commerce to falter, and businesses to fail.

As the primary moving parts in a computer, hard disk drives operate at incredibly close tolerances. The platters on which hard drives store data spin at anywhere from 5,000 to 15,000 revolutions per minute (RPM), with read and write heads floating over the moving surface at distances measured in millionths of an inch. The traditional analogy is to imagine storing your most valuable possessions on an airliner flying at 600 miles per hour, 10 feet over the ground.

When a hard disk drive fails, whether due to a power interruption, a physical shock, a manufacturer's defect, or just simple wear and tear, it is common for the drive heads to come in contact with the platter surface and scratch the recording medium, destroying data in the process. This is called a *head crash*. Hard drive failures are inevitable; it's just a matter of when they occur. In addition to hardware malfunctions, computers are also susceptible to other disasters, such as fire and theft, which can be equally destructive to your data. Performing regular backups enables you to replace your data at the same time that you replace a drive or computer, and resume productivity as quickly as possible.

Creating a Backup Strategy

In large-enterprise network environments, creating an effective backup strategy can require a huge investment of time, effort, and money. Backing up large numbers of servers often requires additional software and an extensive amount of specialized hardware. However, for small business networks, the task is usually far less difficult.

The Windows SBS Console in Microsoft Windows Small Business Server (SBS) 2008 incorporates backups into the Getting Started Tasks list, which you perform after completing the operating system installation. The Server Storage wizards in the console, which you can use to move specific data stores to new locations, even check to make sure that you have performed a backup before they complete their tasks. The Windows SBS Console also has a Backup And Server Storage page, as shown in Figure 13-1, which you can use to create and modify a backup job.

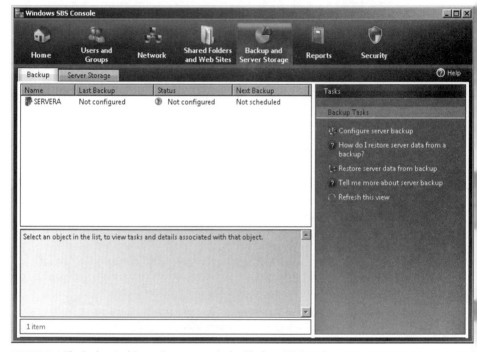

FIGURE 13-1 The Backup And Server Storage page in the Windows SBS Console

The backup interface in the Windows SBS Console provides access to some of the features of the Windows Server Backup program, but not all of them. The console's backup controls enable you to create and manage a scheduled backup job that copies the entire system volume, and selected other volumes, to an external hard drive connected to the server. The result is basic disaster control, enabling you to restore entire volumes lost due to drive failure or loss of an entire computer.

Although Windows SBS 2008 includes a backup software package, Windows Server Backup is relatively limited in its capabilities. Depending on your needs, you might want to consider using a third-party software product as part of your backup solution.

The following sections examine some of the factors you should consider when planning a network backup strategy.

Selecting a Backup Medium

A *backup* is simply a copy of your data, saved to another storage medium. Any medium can provide protection again data loss due to a hard drive failure, but to protect against fire, theft, and other disasters, a removable backup medium that you can store off-site is preferable. The traditional backup medium is magnetic tape, but external hard drives are an increasingly popular solution.

There are three factors to consider when evaluating the suitability of a storage medium for use as a backup device:

- **Storage capacity** The ideal capacity for a backup medium is large enough to hold an entire backup job without having to change media. This enables you to run your backup jobs unattended, preferably at night or during other offline hours. This usually rules out DVDs and other optical disks. Magnetic tape drives are available with capacities as high as 1,000 gigabytes (GB) or 1 terabyte (TB), but these can be extremely expensive. Inexpensive, external hard disk drives are available in sizes up to 1 TB.

- **Data transfer speed** The speed of your backup device might or might not be a major issue, depending on how much data you have to back up and how much time you have available to perform your backups. Hard disk drives are generally the fastest backup solution. There are high-speed magnetic tape drives available, but here again, their prices can be prohibitive for small business.

- **Hardware cost** Price is always a consideration. As a general rule, the price of high-performance magnetic tape equipment goes steadily up as capacity and performance levels increase, while the price of hard disk storage has been going steadily down for years. Prices for high-end tape drives can easily run into five figures (in U.S. dollars), plus you must consider the price of the tape cartridges themselves, while 1-TB external hard drives are available for as little as $100.

If you plan to use the Windows Server Backup software included with Windows SBS 2008, selecting a backup medium is less of a problem. The Configure Server Backup Wizard in the Windows SBS Console supports only external hard drives. You can use the Windows Server Backup console to perform interactive backups to writable optical disks or to network shares, but the software includes no support for magnetic tape drives whatsoever.

Using External Hard Disk Drives

In addition to the standard hard disk unit, an external hard drive consists only of a case, a power supply, and an interface to your computer. You can remove the hard disk from the case and install it in a computer if you want to. You can also purchase an empty external drive housing and install a hard disk you already own into it. External hard disk drives make excellent backup solutions. They are inexpensive, fast, hold a lot of data, and disconnect easily from the computer.

External hard drives have been available for many years, but until recently, they were Small Computer System Interface (SCSI) drives that required a special host adapter in the computer and an expensive cable. Today, there are three external interfaces that are suitably fast for hard disk connections. They are listed in Table 13-1.

TABLE 13-1 External Hard Drive Interface Specifications

INTERFACE	OTHER NAMES	MAXIMUM TRANSFER SPEED (MB/SEC)	BANDWIDTH (MB/SEC)	MAXIMUM CABLE LENGTH (METERS)
Universal Serial Bus 2.0	USB 2.0	60	480	5
IEEE 1394a	FireWire 400, i.LINK, Lynx	49.13	393.216	4.5
IEEE 1394b	FireWire 800	98.25	786.432	100
External Serial Advanced Technology Attachment	eSATA 300	300	3000	2 (or 1, with a passive host adapter)

Virtually all the PCs on the market today include USB ports, and some have IEEE 1394 ports as well. Computers with ports on the front of the case are particularly attractive for backup devices, so that you can remove them easily. The External Serial AT Attachment interface is not yet widely available as standard computer equipment, but you can install a host bus adapter card that provides the interface. The maximum cable length for an eSATA device is shorter than USB or IEEE 1394—only 2 meters, or 1 meter with a passive host adapter. All these interfaces support *hot swapping*, which enables you to attach and detach devices without powering down the computer.

Nearly all the external hard drives on the market support USB, and most have at least one additional interface, such as IEEE 1394a, IEEE 1394b, or eSATA. Some products include support for all the interfaces. Most external hard drive products use Serial AT Attachment hard drives, with a bridge circuit that enables them to connect to a USB or IEEE 1394 interface. The eSATA interface eliminates the need for the bridge, which can enable certain advanced drive technologies to function as in an internal installation, and provides a far faster transfer rate. Cable length for eSATA devices is limited to 1 or 2 meters, however, depending on the interface in the computer.

Although the USB specification indicates a better level of performance than IEEE 1394a, IEEE 1394a devices tend to outperform USB ones in real-world implementations, but only marginally. IEEE 1394b is decidedly faster than USB 2.0, but eSATA can provide substantially better performance then either. However, USB 2.0 and IEEE 1394a are both adequate backup solutions for most situations. If your server has an integrated eSATA port, you would be well to use it, but unless you have a need for the fastest possible interface, an integrated USB or IEEE 1394 connection is likely to be more reliable at this time than an after-market eSATA card.

Most external hard drives have their own power supply, but there are a few models that draw power from the USB or IEEE 1394 interface. These latter devices are generally designed as portable solutions for notebook computers. For server backups, an independent power supply is preferable. Apart from these factors, the only other specifications to consider are those of the hard drive itself. More RPMs and a larger cache are certainly preferable for a backup solution, but they can add to the cost.

Using Magnetic Tape Drives

Magnetic tape has long been the industry standard backup medium. Tape capacities and transfer speeds have kept pace with hard disk characteristics over the years, they can store data for years, and the media cost per gigabyte of storage is relatively low. With magnetic tape, because the storage medium is separate from the drive mechanism, there is far less that can go wrong. If you drop a tape cartridge on the floor, it is probably still usable; not so with a hard disk drive, in most cases.

Magnetic tape drives are different from the other types of storage media that computers use, in that they are not random access devices. You cannot immediately access any file on a tape by moving the drive heads to a specific location or by accessing a specific memory address, as you can with other media. With magnetic tape, the drive must spool through the reel of tape until it locates the desired file, a process that can take several minutes.

Because of this, you cannot use a magnetic tape drive for anything other than backups. You can't mount a tape as a volume and assign it a drive letter, as you can with other media. Instead, computers use a special software driver to address the tape drive and send data to it. When you purchase a backup software product, you must make sure that it supports the magnetic tape drive you plan to use.

There are a variety of magnetic tape drive technologies available, with varying tape capacities, transfer speeds, and prices. At one time, there were relatively low-cost tape systems on the market, intended for backups of stand-alone computers and small networks. However, these have been made almost entirely obsolete by writable optical disks, flash drives, and external hard drives. Today, the magnetic tape drive market is concentrated on high-end network backup solutions, using technologies such as Digital Linear Tape (DLT), Linear Tape-Open (LTO) Ultrium, Advanced Intelligent Tape (AIT), and Digital Data Storage/Digital Audio Tape (DDS/DAT).

The question then is whether a magnetic tape solution is suitable for a small business network. In most cases, the answer is no. The combination of a magnetic tape drive and the software you need to use it provides far more capability than Windows Server Backup and an external hard drive, but with prices that start at $1,000 and climb steeply into the stratosphere, most small business owners find the cost to be prohibitive.

Using a Redundant Medium

As mentioned earlier, one of the requirements for full backup protection is a removable storage medium that you can take off-site. If you use magnetic tape, this is easy. Most tape backup software packages implement a rotation scheme that makes copies of your data to store off-site.

With external hard drives, storing data off-site means removing the entire device, not just the storage medium. Fortunately, the devices are not so expensive that it is impractical to purchase more than one, and Windows Server Backup provides the ability to perform simultaneous backups to multiple devices. Therefore, if you plan to use external hard drives for your backup medium, you should purchase at least two, so that you can create two copies of your data and store one off-site, preferably in a secure location, such as a safe deposit box. For organizations that require a permanent archive of their data, you might want to purchase a new backup drive each month, perform an additional Backup, and store those drives off-site.

Selecting Backup Targets

A *backup target* is a file, folder, or volume that you select to be copied to your backup device. Two of the most critical questions you should consider when devising a backup strategy are:

- How much data is there to back up?
- Where is the data stored?

The amount of data you have to back up dictates how long your backup jobs take and what the capacity of your backup medium has to be. The location of the data to be backed up dictates the type of backup software you need.

Windows Server Backup is capable of backing up only the volumes on the computer running the program. When you create a backup job on your server using the Configure Server Backup Wizard, you must back up the entire system volume, and you can select all or any of the other volumes on the computer as well. For the wizard to create the job, your external hard drive must have sufficient storage space to accommodate all the data on the volumes you select.

> **BEST PRACTICES** To accommodate the future growth of your data, Microsoft recommends that you use an external hard drive with 2.5 times the capacity of the data you plan to back up.

Unlike most third-party backup software products, Windows Server Backup can back up only entire volumes. If you want to select targets by choosing individual files and folders, you must use a third-party software product. Windows Server Backup is also unable to back up data stored on other computers. Third-party network backup solutions enable you to select targets from any computer on the network and back them up to a device connected to your server.

NOTE Although Windows Server Backup can back up only entire volumes, you can restore individual files and folders from a backup.

Network administrators often configure their client computers to store all data files on a server, rather than a local drive. One of the main reasons for this is to facilitate backups. If you plan to use Windows Server Backup on your primary Windows SBS server, you should arrange to store all your network data on that server. This means redirecting all critical folders from your client computers to a server volume so that there is no need to back up the local drives on your workstations.

Creating a Backup Schedule

Another important question you should ask when planning your backup strategy is when the backups should occur. Most administrators schedule backups to run when the network is not in use, such as when the organization is closed. This is because backup software programs are often unable to back up files that are open or currently in use.

Windows Server Backup schedules its jobs by adding them to the Task Scheduler application in Windows. Some third-party backup software products do this as well, while others have their own schedulers, which typically run as a service, triggering jobs at the times you specify.

The object of scheduling backups is to simplify the administrator's daily role in the process as much as possible. Once you have created and scheduled your backup jobs, all you have to do is see to it that the correct medium is available each day. For magnetic tape users, this means swapping the tapes in the drive on a daily basis, while external hard drive users have to reconnect their off-site drives.

Selecting Backup Software

Although Windows SBS 2008 includes a backup software program, it has relatively limited capabilities. As part of your backup strategy planning process, you should consider whether you need any of the features that Windows Server Backup does not provide, and if so, look for a backup software product that does provide them.

Using Windows Server Backup

The Microsoft Windows operating systems have long included a backup software program, but Windows Server Backup, the program included with Windows SBS 2008 and Windows Server 2008, is different from the previous Windows backup utilities in many ways. Chief among these differences is the fact that Windows Server Backup uses a different format for the backup files it creates. Therefore, if you have files you created with the Windows Server 2003 NTBackup utility, you cannot restore them using the Windows Server Backup program in Windows SBS 2008.

TIP For users who must restore files they backed up with the NTBackup utility from a previous version of Windows, Microsoft has released a restore-only version of NTBackup, which is available from their Web site at *http://go.microsoft.com/fwlink/?LinkId=82917.*

Some of the other differences between Windows Server Backup and previous Windows backup utilities are as follows:

- **Backup media** Windows Server Backup is designed primarily to perform backups to external hard drives. The program does not include any support for magnetic tape drives and can back up to optical disks and network shares only during interactive jobs, not scheduled ones.

- **Volume formatting** When you select an external hard drive volume as your backup medium, Windows Server Backup reformats the volume (destroying any data it finds there) and dedicates it exclusively to backup use. After the reformat, the volume no longer has a drive letter and no longer appears in Windows Explorer.

- **System volume backup** When you create a backup job through the Windows SBS Console, Windows Server Backup always backs up the entire system volume, including the boot files, the registry, the Active Directory Domain Services (AD DS) database, and other system resources that do not appear as files in Windows Explorer.

- **Target selection** Windows Server Backup creates block-based images of your volumes and therefore can back up only entire volumes. You cannot include or exclude individual files or folders, as you can with file-based backup software products.

- **Job scheduling** Windows Server Backup can schedule only one backup job, which you can configure to run once or several times per day.

- **Job types** Windows Server Backup does not enable you to create incremental, differential, and full backup jobs on a per-job basis. The scheduled job you create with the Configure Server Backup Wizard performs incremental backups by default, to save space on the backup drive, but it does so in a way that is different from traditional backup software products.

  MORE INFO For more information on the incremental backup mechanism in Windows Server Backup, see the section entitled "Configuring Performance Settings," later in this chapter.

- **Backup format** Windows Server Backup creates image-based backup files using the virtual hard disk (VHD) format. This enables you to open the files in a virtual machine, using the Hyper-V server role included in Windows Server 2008.

- **Application support** Windows Server Backup is capable of backing up and restoring both your Exchange Server message stores and your Windows SharePoint Services database. The program automatically stops the required services before backing up these applications and automatically restarts them afterwards.

Using Third-Party Backup Software

There are two basic classes for backup software products: those that are intended for stand-alone computers and those intended for network use. The main difference between the two is the ability to use one computer as a backup server that can back up data from other computers on the network. For a single-server small business network, it might not be worth the additional time and expense required to purchase and deploy a full-featured network backup product. If you configure your workstations to store all their data files on the server, you can simply back up that one computer with a stand-alone product. If you have to back up other servers or workstation drives, however, a network backup software product might be preferable.

Some of the features that differentiate third-party network backup software products from Windows Server Backup are as follows:

- **Backup media** Third-party backup products typically provide support for a variety of backup media, including magnetic tape drives. Because a software product that supports magnetic tape must include hardware-specific drivers, be sure that the product you select supports the drive you plan to purchase.

- **Target selection** Third-party backup software products usually allow you to select backup targets using a tree display similar to that of Windows Explorer. This enables you to create backup jobs that include or exclude specific files, folders, or volumes.

- **Job scheduling** Third-party backup software products enable you to create as many interactive or scheduled backup jobs as you need. Scheduling capabilities typically let you create jobs that run on a daily, weekly, or monthly basis.

- **Job types** Most third-party backup software products support incremental and differential backup jobs, as well as full backups. Incremental and differential jobs enable you to back up only the data that has changed since the last backup. This complicates the restore process somewhat but saves space on the backup medium and executes backups in far less time.

> **MORE INFO** In a traditional backup software package, a *differential backup* is a job that backs up only the files that have changed since the last full backup. To perform a full restore from differentials, you must restore the most recent full backup and then the most recent differential backup. An *incremental backup* is a job that backs up only the files that have changed since the last incremental backup. To perform a full restore from incrementals, you must restore the most recent full backup and then restore each of the incrementals you performed since that full backup in the order you performed them.

- **Cataloging backups** Most third-party backup software products use a database to maintain a catalog of the jobs they perform and the files they save to the backup media. If you use magnetic tape, for example, the catalog enables you to search for a specific version of a specific file and locate the exact tape containing that file.

- **Media rotation** Third-party backup software products that support magnetic tape drives can usually implement a media rotation scheme that corresponds to your schedule of backup jobs. A media rotation scheme specifies the name you should use to label each tape and tells you which tape to insert in the drive for each daily job. This allows you to keep track of your tape usage and simplifies the daily administration of your backup regimen.

- **Application support** Many third-party backup software manufacturers produce add-on modules (at extra cost) that enable their products to back up network applications and services, such as mail servers and databases, while they are running. This prevents you from having to shut down critical services to back them up.

- **Restoring data** Third-party backup software products that enable you to select individual files and folders as backup targets also enable you to restore selected files or folders. This way, you can also use your backups to protect individual files against accidental damage or deletion.

Some of these capabilities are far more than the typical small business network needs, but for organizations with special security requirements, they can provide extra protection.

Configuring Server Backups

The Windows SBS Console simplifies the creation of scheduled backup jobs by supplying a wizard that steps you through the process. Once you have created the job, the console provides controls that enable you to modify its properties. Windows SBS 2008 also includes the Windows Server Backup console, which provides more comprehensive control over the backup process and provides the means to restore data from a backup medium.

Creating a Scheduled Backup Job

To create a scheduled backup job with the Windows SBS Console, use the following procedure:

1. Connect your external hard drives to the computer by plugging them into a USB, IEEE 1394, or eSATA port.

2. Log on to your Windows SBS 2008 server using a domain account with administrative privileges. The Windows SBS Console appears.

3. Click Backup And Server Storage, and then select the Backup tab.

4. In the Tasks list, click Configure Server Backup. The Configure Server Backup Wizard appears, as shown here.

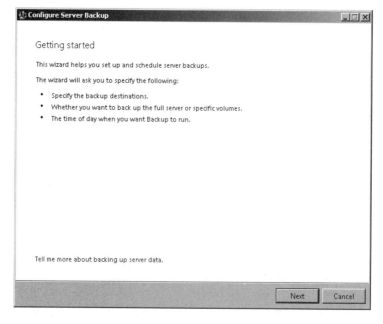

TIP Alternatively, you can start the Configure Server Backup Wizard by clicking Configure Server Backup in the Getting Started Tasks list in the Windows SBS Console.

5. Click Next to bypass the Getting Started page. The Specify The Backup Destination page appears, as shown here.

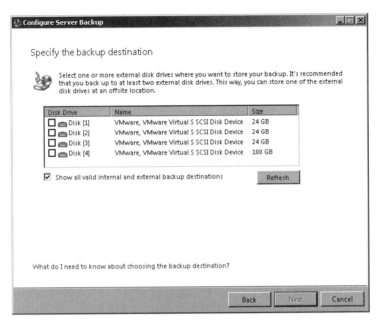

6. Select the check boxes for your external hard drives and click Next. The Label
   The Destination Drives page appears, as shown here.

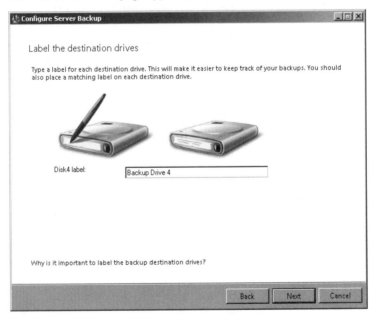

7. Specify an alternative label for each drive, if desired, in the text box provided
   and click Next. The Select Drives To Back Up page appears, as shown here.

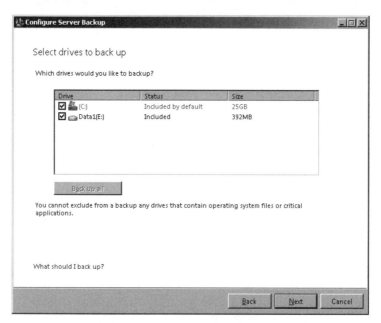

8. In addition to the default C: drive, select the check boxes for any other drives that you want to include in the backup job and click Next. The Specify The Backup Schedule page appears, as shown here.

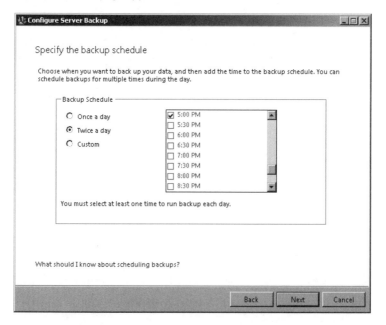

9. Select one of the following scheduling options:
   - Once a day   The backup occurs once daily at 11:00 P.M.
   - Twice a day   The backup occurs twice daily at 5:00 P.M. and 11:00 P.M.
   - Custom   The backup occurs as many times as you wish each day, at the times you select.

10. Click Next. The Confirm Backup Details page appears, as shown here.

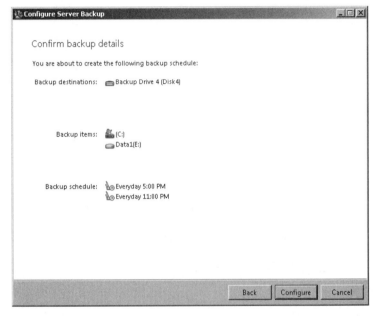

11. Click Configure. A Configure Server Backup message box appears, warning you that the wizard is about to format the drives you selected as the backup destination.

12. Click Yes. The wizard prepares the backup drive, configures the backup job, and displays the Server Backup Configured page, as shown here.

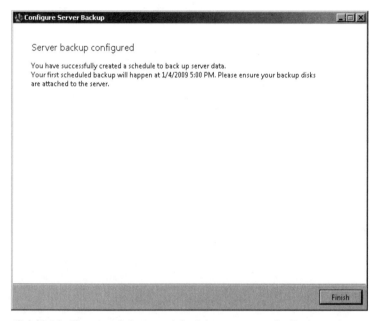

13. Click Finish. The wizard closes and the job appears on the Backup tab.

When the scheduled time for the backup arrives, the Task Scheduler application starts the job, which runs in the background as the server continues to function normally. When the backup finishes, its status appears in the console as Successful, as shown in Figure 13-2.

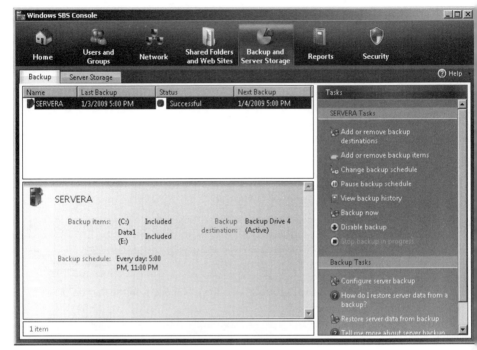

FIGURE 13-2 A successful backup job, as displayed in the Windows SBS Console

Modifying a Backup Job

Once you have created a backup job using the Configure Server Backup Wizard, the Tasks list on the Backup And Server Storage page provides controls that enable you to modify the parameters of the job as needed. Most of the items in the task list open the various tabs of the Server Backup Properties sheet, as follows:

- **Add or remove backup destinations**   Enables you to specify the devices you want to use to perform backups.

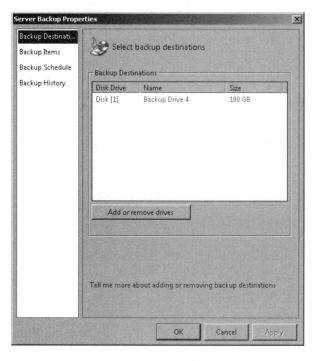

- **Add or remove backup items** Enables you to specify the targets for your backups.

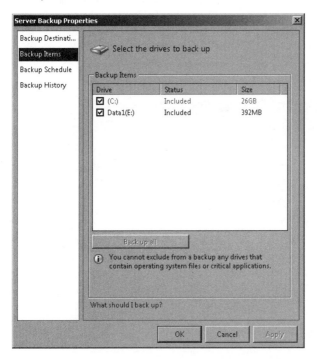

- **Change backup schedule** Enables you to modify the times at which the backup jobs should occur.

- **View backup history**   Displays a full record of all previous backups the system has performed, as shown here.

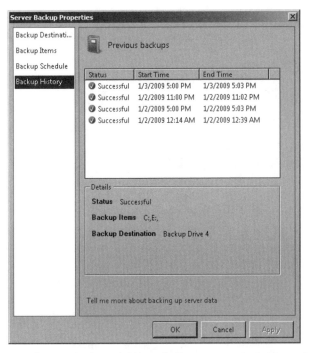

You can also use the items in the tasks list to pause the backup schedule, disable the backup job entirely, or start a backup immediately, regardless of the schedule.

Creating a Backup Administrator Role

Once you have devised a backup strategy and created a scheduled backup job, the hard part of the process is over. What remains are the mundane tasks of swapping out backup media and checking to make sure that the backup job completes successfully each day. Network administrators often delegate these tasks to other users, and not necessarily to users to whom they want to grant full administrative privileges. Fortunately, Windows SBS 2008 includes a built-in group called Backup Operators, which provides the rights and permissions a user needs to manage backup jobs, and no more.

Backup Operators is not a Windows SBS group, so you cannot use the Windows SBS Console to add an existing user account to the group. However, you can create a user role that includes the group membership and then create user accounts based on that role. Alternatively, you can use the Active Directory Users And Computers console to add an existing user to the Backup Operators group.

MORE INFO   To create the user role, follow the procedure in the section entitled "Creating a New User Role" in Chapter 5, "Working with Users, Computers, and Groups." Base your new role on the Network Administrator role and, on the Choose User Role Permissions (Group Membership) page, remove all the default groups and add the Backup Operators group.

Backing Up a Second Server

As mentioned earlier, Windows Server Backup is capable of backing up only volumes on the computer running the program. If you have purchased Windows SBS 2008 Premium Edition and installed a second server on your network, you cannot back up your secondary server using the Windows Server Backup program and the backup medium on your primary server. However, your second server has its own copy of Windows Server Backup, which leaves you with two possible ways to facilitate the backup process:

- Connect a separate set of backup drives to the secondary server and create a separate, independent backup job on that server.
- Create a shared folder on your primary server and configure your secondary server to back itself up to the network share. Then use your backup media on the primary server to back up the shared folder.

Windows Server Backup is a feature that your primary Windows SBS 2008 server installs by default. However, you must install the feature yourself on your secondary server, using the Server Manager console.

Using the Windows Server Backup Console

You can create and modify backup jobs using the Windows SBS Console, but when you click Restore Server Data From Backup in the Tasks list, the console opens a Windows Server Backup console window, shown in Figure 13-3. You can also use this console to monitor backup activity, configure backup performance settings, and perform single backups with different parameters from your scheduled backup job.

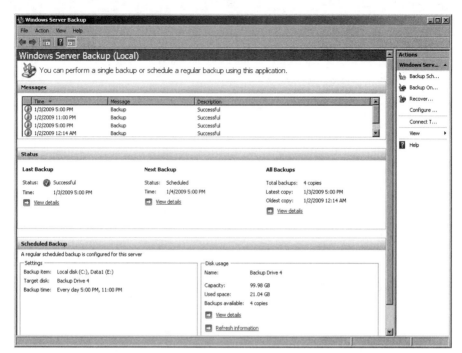

FIGURE 13-3 The Windows Server Backup console

When you open the Windows Server Backup console, whether from the Windows SBS Console or from the Administrative Tools program group, you see a display divided into the following sections:

- **Messages** Displays a list of event messages providing detailed results of each backup the system has performed, as shown here.

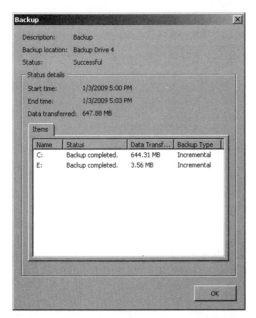

- **Status** Displays the results of the most recent backup, the scheduled time of the next backup, and a summary of all the backups available for restoration, as shown here.

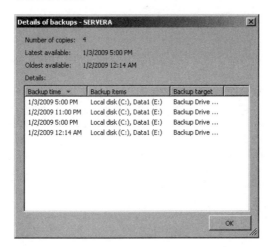

- **Scheduled Backup** Displays the settings for the next scheduled backup and disk usage information for the backup medium, as shown here.

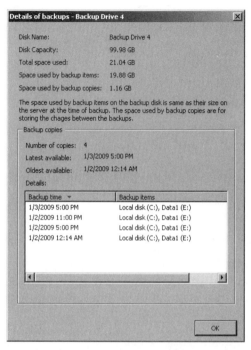

In addition to viewing information about the system's backup activities, you can perform additional tasks, as described in the following sections.

Configuring Performance Settings

When you click Configure Performance Settings in the action pane of the Windows Server Backup console, the Optimize Backup Performance dialog box appears, as shown in Figure 13-4. This dialog box enables you to specify whether Windows Server Backup should perform incremental backups.

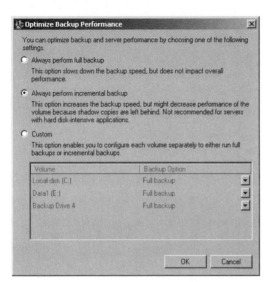

FIGURE 13-4 The Optimize Backup Performance dialog box

Traditional backup software products are designed for use with magnetic tape drives. Incremental and differential backups save storage space by copying only the files that have changed since the last backup. Each job, however, uses a separate tape, and to fully recover a lost volume, you must perform multiple restores from different tapes: first the most recent full backup, and then one or more of the incremental or differential tapes you have made since that full backup.

When Windows Server Backup performs incremental backups, it takes advantage of the hard disk's random access capabilities and updates the full backup on the disk by replacing the files that have changed since the last backup. The software then saves the previous versions of those changed files to another location on the disk, along with metadata that indicates its original location and when the system backed it up.

As a result of using incrementals, the backup drive always contains a full backup image that represents the most recent version of the target volumes. If you perform a restore and select the most recent version of a volume, the program simply accesses that full backup image. If you restore an earlier version of a volume, the software accesses the displaced files and integrates them into the full backup image to create a replica of the volume as it existed at the time that the system performed the earlier backup.

By default, the Optimize Backup Performance dialog box has the Always Perform Incremental Backup option selected. By saving only the files that have changed, incremental backups not only save space on the backup disk, they also finish much faster. If you select the Always Perform Full Backup option instead, Windows Server

Backup creates a full image of the selected volumes during each backup, consuming more storage space and taking more time to complete. You can also select the Custom option to specify different settings for each of the volumes in your backup job. In most cases, there is no compelling reason to perform full backups each time a job runs.

Performing Restores

As mentioned earlier, when you click Restore Server Data From Backup in the Windows SBS Console, the Windows Server Backup console appears. As with most backup software products, Windows Server Backup lets you select the elements you want to restore and specify whether to copy them to their original locations or to an alternative folder or volume.

> **IMPORTANT** One of the most crucial elements of any backup strategy is the need to perform regular test restores to ensure that your backups are viable. Even when your backup software indicates the successful completion of your backup jobs, there is no way to be absolutely sure you are protected against data loss other than actually performing a restore.

To perform a restore, use the following procedure:

1. Log on to your Windows SBS 2008 server using a domain account with administrative privileges. The Windows SBS Console appears.

2. Click Backup And Server Storage, and then select the Backup tab.

3. In the Tasks list, click Restore Server Data From Backup. The Windows Server Backup console appears.

4. In the Actions pane, click Recover. The Recovery Wizard appears, displaying the Getting Started page, as shown here.

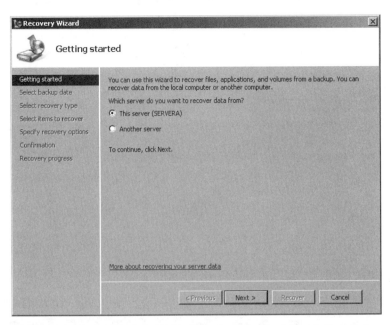

5. Click Next to accept the default This Server option. The Select Backup Date page appears, as shown here.

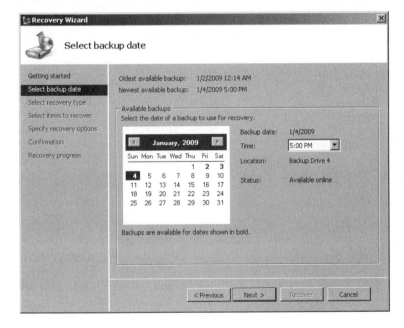

6. In the Available Backups box, select the date and time of the backup you want to restore and click Next. The Select Recovery Type page appears, as shown here.

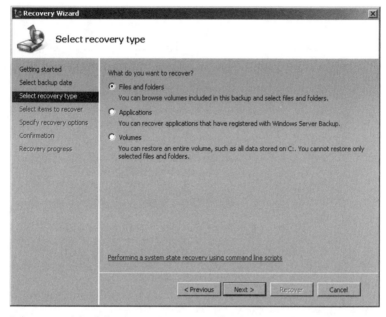

7. Select one of the following options to specify what type of restore you want to perform:

- Files And Folders   Displays the Select Items To Recover page, as shown here, on which you can select the files or folders you want to restore, and the Specify Recovery Options page, on which you can select a destination for the restored files or folders and configure the program's overwrite behavior.

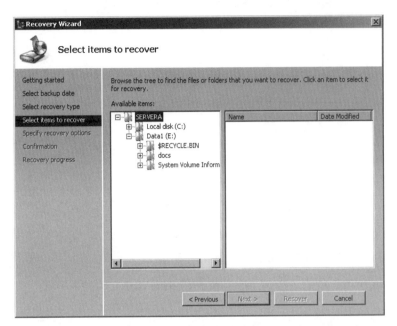

- Applications   Displays the Select Application page, as shown here, on which you can select the application you want to restore, and the Specify Recovery Options page, on which you can select a destination for the restored application.

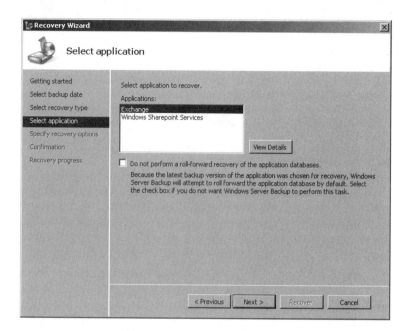

NOTE Windows Server Backup is capable of performing only full restores of the system's Microsoft Exchange Server and Windows SharePoint Services data. For example, you cannot select a particular Exchange Server mailbox for restoration.

- Volumes   Displays the Select Volumes page, as shown here, on which you can select the volumes you want to restore and specify a destination for each one.

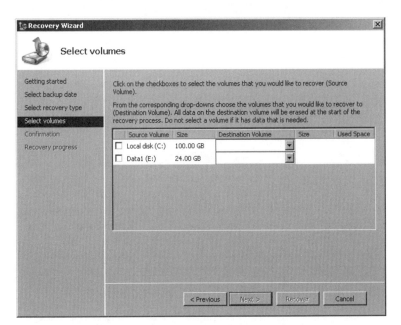

8. Configure the required settings for the type of restore you intend to perform. If you selected the Files And Folders option or the Applications option,
   use the controls on the Specify Recovery Options page, like the one shown
   here, to select the destination for the restored elements and, if necessary,
   specify whether the program should overwrite existing files with the same
   names. If you selected the Volumes option, use the Destination Volume
   drop-down lists on the Select Volumes page to specify the destinations for
   the restored volumes.

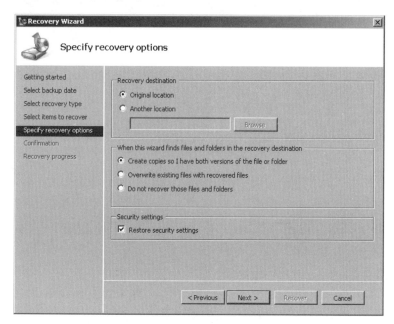

9. Click Next. The Confirmation page appears.

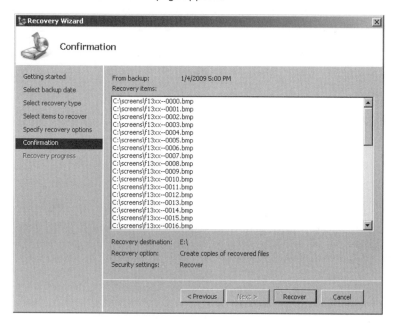

10. Click Recover. The Recovery Progress page appears, as shown here, as the wizard restores the items you selected and places them in your specified destination.

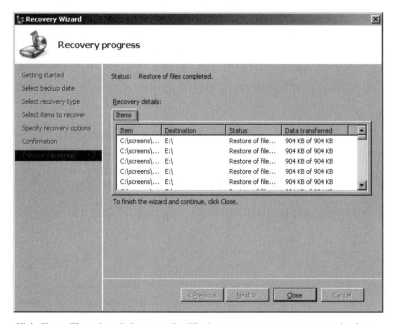

11. Click Close. The wizard closes and a File Recovery message appears in the Windows Server Backup console.

Recovering an Entire System

Because your backup job includes the system volume by default, along with the system recovery elements, you can recover an entire server if the internal hard disk or the computer containing it is lost or destroyed. Because all the system data, including the boot files, has been lost, you must start the computer using your Windows SBS 2008 installation disk. However, you do not have to perform a complete reinstallation of the operating system. Your Windows SBS 2008 disk includes the Windows Recovery Environment (RE), a bare-bones version of the operating system that provides you with tools you can use to diagnose and repair system problems, as well as the ability to perform a full restore from a backup located on an external hard drive.

To perform a complete restore of your primary server, use the following procedure:

1. Start your computer and insert the Windows SBS 2008 installation disk into the DVD-ROM drive.

2. If necessary, press a key to boot from the DVD rather than the internal hard disk. The Install Windows page appears, as shown here.

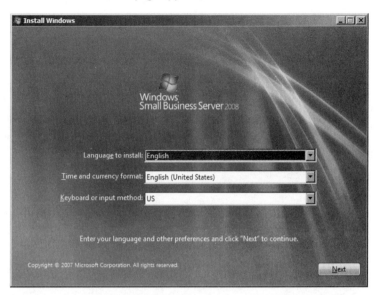

3. Select the appropriate Language, Time and Currency, and Keyboard or Input Method values and click Next. The Install Now page appears, as shown here.

4. Click Repair Your Computer. The System Recovery Options Wizard appears, as shown here.

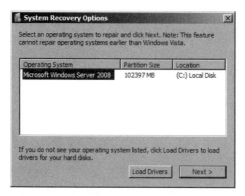

5. Select Microsoft Windows Server 2008 and click Next. The Choose A Recovery Tool page appears, as shown here.

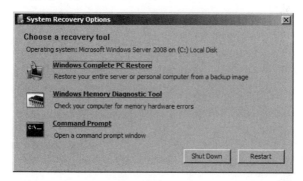

NOTE If your computer needs special drivers to access the hard disk drives, click Load Drivers and insert a flash drive or other medium containing the driver installation files.

6. Click Windows Complete PC Restore. The Windows Complete PC Restore Wizard appears, displaying the Restore Your Entire Computer From A Backup page, as shown here.

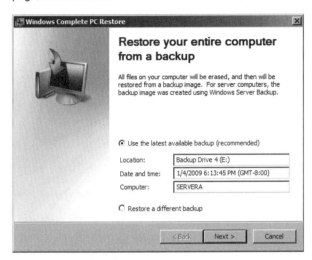

7. Confirm that the system has located the most recent backup on your drive and click Next. The Choose How To Restore The Backup page appears, as shown here.

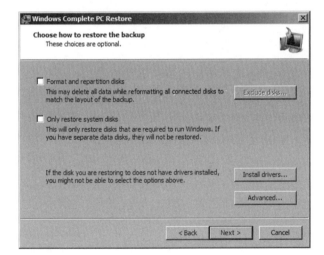

8. Select the Format And Repartition Disks check box. If necessary, click Exclude Disks and select any drives that you want to exclude from the restore. Then click Next. An untitled summary page appears, as shown here.

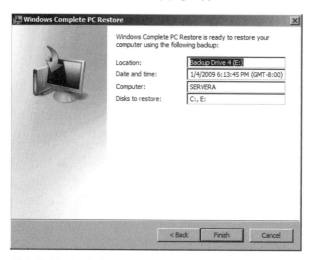

9. Click Finish. A Windows Complete PC Restore message box appears, prompting you to confirm your actions.

10. Select the I Confirm That I Want To Format The Disks And Restore The Backup check box and click OK. A message box appears, as shown here, displaying the progress of the restore.

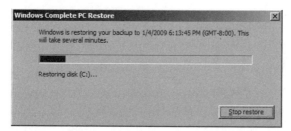

When the restore is finished, a Do You Want To Restart Your Computer Now? message box appears, offering you the ability to abort the default 60-second restart interval.

11. Remove the Windows SBS 2008 installation disk from the DVD-ROM drive and click Restart Now. The computer restarts and boots from the newly restored system drive.

CHAPTER 14

Adding a Second Server

When you purchase Microsoft Windows Small Business Server (SBS) 2008 Premium Edition, you receive the software and the license needed to install a second server on your network running Windows Server 2008. You also receive a copy of Microsoft SQL Server 2008 Standard for Small Business, to run on your additional server. Microsoft designed the Windows SBS Premium Edition package to accommodate customers who want to deploy a SQL-based application on their networks.

The Windows SBS 2008 primary server is already performing many different roles, so adding another major application would, in most cases, be unwise. A secondary server provides a better platform for SQL-based applications and can perform other roles as well. You can use the second server as an additional file or print server, or even as a domain controller for a branch office. This chapter examines the process of deploying an additional server on your network and describes some of the ways you can use it.

Expanding Your Network

Windows SBS 2008 is designed primarily for networks consisting of one or two servers and up to 75 workstations. However, a Windows SBS network is more expandable than many people think. First, although you can add a second server by purchasing Windows SBS 2008 Premium Edition, you don't have to implement your second server in this way. If you purchase Windows SBS 2008 Standard Edition when you initially set up your network, you can always add a second server later by purchasing a copy of Windows Server 2008.

The operating system for the second server in Windows SBS 2008 Premium Edition is Windows Server 2008 Standard Edition, with no additional components. No Windows SBS 2008 additions or restrictions are incorporated into the operating system. The Premium Edition product includes both 32-bit and 64-bit editions of Windows Server 2008, of which you can use one. SQL Server 2008 Standard for Small Business is not incorporated into the second server operating system either. You receive it as a separate application, which can run on either the 32-bit or 64-bit platform.

TIP In Windows Server 2008 Premium Edition, the installation of SQL Server Standard for Small Business on the second server is completely optional; you can use the second server for any purpose you wish. Depending on the type of license you choose and current prices, you might find that even if you do not need SQL Server 2008, purchasing the Windows SBS 2008 Premium Edition package is less expensive than purchasing Windows SBS 2008 Standard Edition plus a copy of Windows Server 2008.

Understanding Windows SBS 2008 Limitations

Running Windows SBS 2008 on your network is not the same as running Windows Server 2008 plus Microsoft Exchange Server 2007 and (optionally) SQL Server 2008 Standard, even if you disregard the differences in software costs. Windows SBS 2008 imposes certain limitations on the network with regard to the additional servers and workstations you can add to the network, although they are not as stringent as some people think. These limitations include the following:

- Your Windows SBS 2008 network can consist of only one Active Directory Domain Services (AD DS) domain, with the Windows SBS primary server as the first domain controller in this root domain.

- You cannot install more than one Windows SBS 2008 primary server in a single AD DS domain, even if you purchase an additional license.

- You cannot create subdomains, such as newyork.adatum.local, beneath the AD DS domain you create on your Windows SBS 2008 server.

- You cannot establish trusts between your Windows SBS 2008 domain and any other AD DS domain, whether running on Windows SBS 2008, Windows Server 2008, or any other operating system.

- You can install only one Windows SBS 2008 secondary server on your network using either the 32-bit or 64-bit version supplied with the product, but not both.

- You can install only the second server included with Windows SBS 2008 Premium Edition on your Windows SBS 2008 network. You cannot install it on another network or use it as the domain controller for another AD DS domain.

- You can install only the copy of SQL Server 2008 Standard for Small Business included with Windows SBS 2008 Premium Edition on the Windows SBS 2008 primary or secondary server.

    CAUTION Although you can install SQL Server 2008 on your primary server, you must not use it to host the SBSMONITORING or Windows Server Update Services databases that Windows SBS 2008 creates. You can move the Windows SharePoint Services (WSS) content database to SQL Server 2008, running on either your primary or secondary server, but you cannot move the WSS configuration or search databases.

- You cannot install the copy of Exchange Server 2007 included with Windows SBS 2008 on any server other than the Windows SBS 2008 primary server.
- You cannot use more than 75 Client Access Licenses (CALs) on your Windows SBS 2008 network.

With these limitations in mind, this means that you can do either of the following:

- You can add as many additional servers as you want to your Windows SBS 2008 network, so long as you purchase appropriate licenses for any servers other than the secondary server included with the Premium Edition package.
- You can add as many domain controllers as you want to your Windows SBS 2008 domain, using the Windows SBS secondary server or any additional Windows Server 2008 computers.

Understanding Licensing for Additional Servers

When you purchase Windows SBS 2008 Premium Edition, you receive an additional license for a secondary server, running either the 32-bit or 64-bit version of Windows Server 2008 included with the product. You also receive a license to install SQL Server 2008 Standard for Small Business on that secondary server. The terms for the secondary server licenses are the same as those for the primary server.

However, you are not required to install SQL Server 2008 on the secondary server, nor are you required to install the secondary server at all. If you prefer to hold off on deploying the secondary server until later, you can do so, but, as mentioned earlier, you cannot use the license to deploy the secondary server on another network.

If you want to install additional servers on your Windows SBS 2008 network other than the one supplied with Standard Edition or the two supplied with Premium Edition, you are free to do so. However, you must purchase an appropriate license for each copy of Windows Server 2008 you plan to deploy, using any of the standard Microsoft licensing options. For example, you can purchase a new computer with an original equipment manufacturer (OEM) license included, or purchase a retail copy of Windows Server 2008 and install it on an existing computer. You can also purchase a license through Microsoft Open Value Licensing (MOVL) or Microsoft Open License Program (MOLP). The type of license you choose does not have to match that of your Windows SBS 2008 license.

It is important to understand, however, that many vendors bundle the Windows Server 2008 server license with a number of CALs, which adds to the cost. You do not need to purchase additional CALs when you add a server to your Windows SBS 2008 network. The Windows SBS 2008 CAL Suite and CAL Suite for Premium licenses you have purchased for your Windows SBS 2008 users or devices enable them to access any additional Windows Server 2008 computers, so long as you join those servers to your Windows SBS domain.

IMPORTANT If you plan to use the Terminal Services or Rights Management Services capabilities built into Windows Server 2008, you must purchase the appropriate Terminal Services CALs or Rights Management Services CALs for the users that will be accessing those services.

Deploying a Second Server

As discussed earlier in this chapter, Windows SBS 2008 Premium Edition enables you to install a second server on your network for any purpose you wish. What you plan to do with the server determines what hardware the computer requires and how the installation should proceed. Some of the roles you might use a second server to perform are as follows:

- **File and print server**   If your users have heavy file storage and printing requirements, if might be beneficial to move your file and print services to a second server.

- **Second domain controller**   A second domain controller can provide redundancy on a local network, but it can also enable a branch office to access AD DS resources without having to connect to a remote domain controller over a wide area network (WAN) link.

- **Secondary Web server**   The primary Windows SBS 2008 server uses Internet Information Services (IIS) to host WSS and perform a variety of administrative tasks. You can use IIS on a secondary server to deploy additional Web sites and Web-based intranet applications that might overwhelm the primary server.

- **Terminal Services application server**   The primary server on a Windows SBS 2008 network cannot function as a terminal server, but you can use a secondary server for this purpose, eliminating the need to install applications on individual workstations.

- **SQL Server–based application server**   Using SQL Server, the secondary server can provide services to your network using a wide variety of applications, either existing or custom-developed.

Planning a Second Server Deployment

The role or roles you want your second server to perform determines what type of computer you should buy and what hardware and software you should install. As discussed in Chapter 3, "Installing Microsoft Windows Small Business Server (SBS) 2008," planning is a crucial part of the network deployment process, and your plan for your secondary server should be no less detailed than that for your primary one.

Determining System Hardware Requirements

The first step of the deployment process is selecting the server hardware. The first decision to make is that of the processor platform. Unlike the Windows SBS 2008 primary server, which requires a computer with a 64-bit processor, your secondary server can be a 32-bit or 64-bit computer. If you are buying a new computer for this purpose, then it can probably run either version of Windows Server 2008. If you plan to repurpose a computer you already own, you might be limited to the 32-bit version. Before you make this decision, however, be sure that all the applications you plan to use on the secondary server run on the platform you select.

> **TIP** If you are migrating from an earlier version of Windows SBS to Windows SBS 2008 Premium Edition, you might want to consider buying a new computer for your primary server and, after the migration process is complete, reinstalling your old server to make it the secondary server on your Windows SBS 2008 network.

Adding Role-Specific Hardware

The base system requirements for the secondary server are listed in Chapter 3, but you must also determine if you need additional hardware, which depends on the details of the server's role. For example, if you plan to deploy a file server, you must decide how much storage you need for your users, in addition to that required for the operating system, and what type of storage you want to use. You should also plan for future growth and purchase a computer to which you can add more storage and more memory later.

A modest file server for a very small network might just have one or two Serial ATA (SATA) hard disks. For a slightly larger network that has all its users constantly accessing server files, you might want to move up to Small Computer System Interface (SCSI) disks, and, if your applications require fault tolerance, you might want use redundant array of independent disks (RAID). The amount of storage you have in the server will also influence the amount of memory it needs.

> **MORE INFO** For more information on choosing a server configuration, see the section entitled "Selecting Server Hardware," in Chapter 3.

For an application server, the planning process should begin by selecting the applications you intend to run. For example, if you are going to deploy a Terminal Services application server, you should list all the applications you want to provide to network users, along with the maximum number of users that will access each application at the same time. These factors affect the server's storage configuration, and more importantly, its memory capacity.

For business-specific Web and SQL Server–based applications, you must select the exact applications you plan to run before you begin shopping for hardware. If you intend to purchase an existing application, the manufacturer usually has specific hardware requirements that you must observe. If you intend to work with software developers to create your own custom application, the selection of the server hardware should be a collaborative effort between your organization and the developers.

Installing a Second Server

To install a secondary server running Windows Server 2008 on your network, use the following procedure:

1. Turn on the computer and insert the appropriate additional server disk for your hardware platform from the Windows SBS 2008 package into the DVD-ROM drive.

2. Press a key to boot from the DVD if the system prompts you to do so. The computer reads from the DVD and displays the first page of the Install Windows Wizard, as shown here.

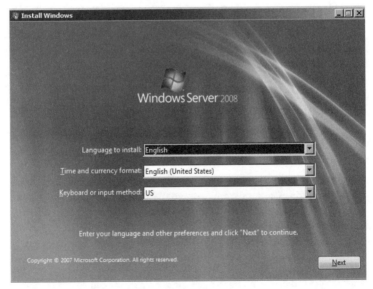

3. If you plan to use language, time and currency format, or keyboard settings other than the defaults, select your preferences from the three drop-down

lists on this page. Then click Next. The Install Now page appears, as shown
here.

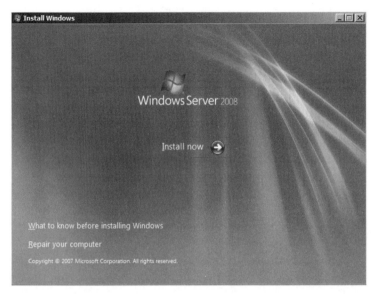

4. Click Install Now. The Type Your Product Key For Activation page appears, as shown here.

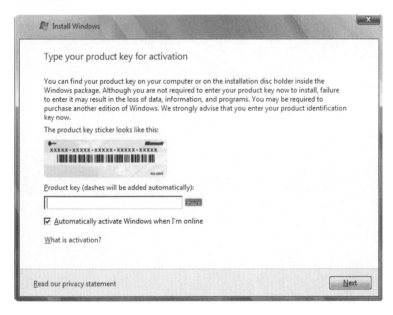

5. In the Product Key text box, type the 25-character product key for your additional server, supplied with your Windows SBS 2008 product. Leave the Automatically Activate Windows When I'm Online check box selected and click Next. The Please Read The License Terms page appears, as shown here.

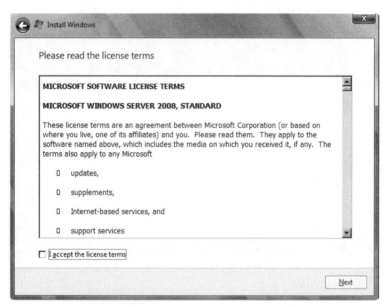

6. Select the I Accept The License Terms check box and click Next. The Which Type Of Installation Do You Want? page appears, as shown here.

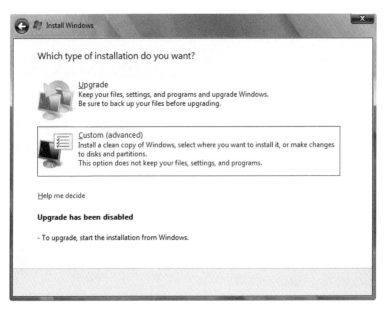

7. Click Custom (Advanced). The Where Do You Want To Install Windows? page appears, as shown here.

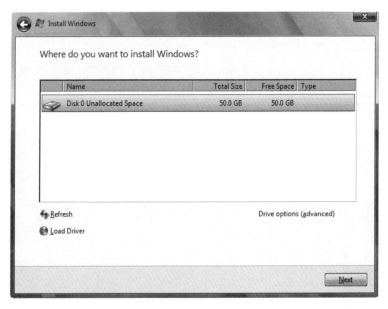

8. To create a partition on a disk, click Drive Options (Advanced) to display additional controls, as shown here.

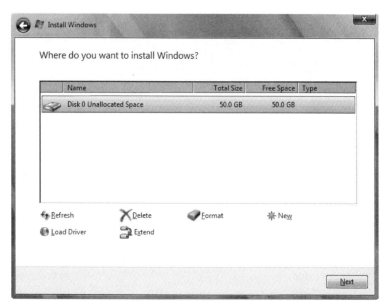

9. Select the disk on which you want to create the partition and click New. In the Size box that appears, specify a size greater than 12,740 megabytes (MB) for the partition and click Apply. The new partition appears in the list, as shown here.

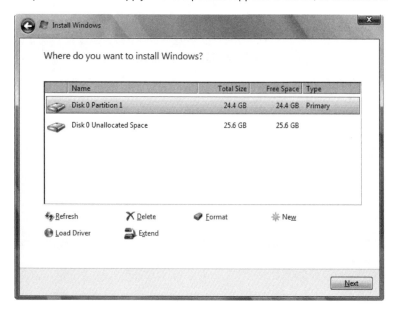

10. Select the partition on which you want to install Windows Server 2008 and click Next. The Installing Windows page appears, as shown here, and the setup program proceeds through the various stages of the operating system installation.

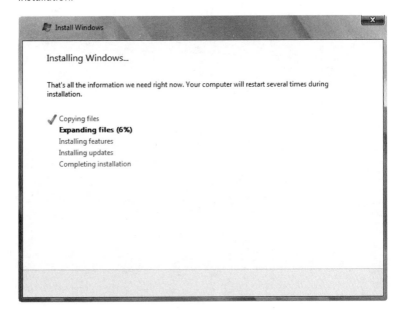

When this phase of the installation process is completed, the computer restarts, and a message appears, stating that you must change the password, as shown here.

11. Click OK. A Windows logon page appears, as shown here.

12. Type a password for the local Administrator account in the New Password and Confirm Password text boxes, and click the right arrow button. A message appears, stating that the password has been changed.

13. Click OK. The Windows desktop appears.

Performing Post-Installation Tasks

Once the Windows Server 2008 installation process is finished, you see the Initial Configuration Tasks window, as shown in Figure 14-1. Unlike the primary server installation, which automatically configures many of the computer's settings, the secondary server installation is a bare-bones affair. You must configure the server yourself and add the roles and features it needs to provide the services you want.

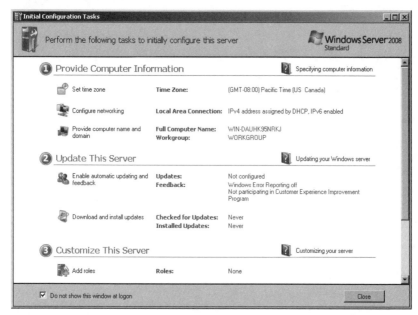

FIGURE 14-1 The Initial Configuration Tasks window

The following sections describe the procedures you must perform on a newly installed secondary server.

Adjusting Time Zone Settings

By default, new Windows Server 2008 computers are configured to use the Pacific time zone. To change the computer to another time zone, use the following procedure:

1. Log on to Windows Server 2008 using the local Administrator account. The Initial Configuration Tasks window appears.

2. In the Provide Computer Information section, click Set Time Zone. The Date And Time dialog box appears, as shown here.

3. Click Change Time Zone. The Time Zone Settings dialog box appears, as shown here.

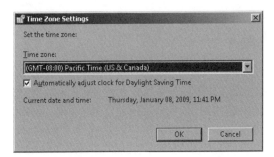

4. In the Time Zone drop-down list, select the correct time zone for your location and click OK.

TIP If you are installing a server that you will move to another location later, such as a branch office, select the time zone for the server's final location.

5. Click OK to close the Date And Time dialog box.

Configuring Network Settings

By default, a newly installed computer running Windows Server 2008 attempts to obtain an Internet Protocol (IP) address and other Transmission Control Protocol/Internet Protocol (TCP/IP) settings from a Dynamic Host Configuration Protocol (DHCP) server on the local network. If you have configured your primary server to function as a DHCP server, as described in Chapter 4, "Getting Started," then the secondary server automatically configures its network interface using TCP/IP settings it obtains from the primary server.

> **MORE INFO** For more information on IP addressing and DHCP, see Chapter 2, "A Networking Primer."

Depending on the tasks you expect your secondary server to perform, this default arrangement might not be satisfactory. When a computer obtains its IP address using DHCP, it is possible that the address might change someday. For standard Windows server functions, such as file and printer sharing, this is usually not a problem because the DHCP server changes the domain's Domain Name System (DNS) records when it changes the IP address. This enables the other computers on the network to locate the secondary server, no matter how often its address changes.

However, certain roles and applications require a server to have a static IP address. For example, if you intend to configure the secondary server to function as a domain controller or as a second DHCP server, you must reconfigure the network settings with a static IP address.

When you ran the Connect To The Internet Wizard on your primary server, the wizard configured the DHCP Server service by creating a scope and excluding certain IP addresses from that scope, including the addresses of your router and of the primary server itself. This prevents DHCP from assigning those addresses to other computers. If you plan to assign a static IP address to your secondary server, you should use one of these excluded addresses or create a new exclusion, if necessary.

There are two ways to configure your server to use a static IP address: you can create a DHCP reservation that permanently associates the server's hardware address with a specific IP address assignment, or you can configure the TCP/IP client manually on the server.

CREATING A DHCP RESERVATION

The procedure for creating a DHCP reservation for your server is the same as the one described in the section entitled "Creating a DHCP Reservation for a Printer" in Chapter 8, "Sharing Printers." When you look at the Address Leases node in the DHCP console, you see your secondary server's lease, as shown in Figure 14-2. As with a printer, the server has an arbitrary name specified by the device. The Unique ID value displayed in the lease entry is the hardware address you use when creating the reservation.

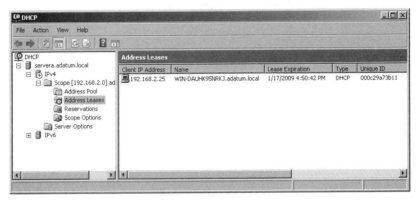

FIGURE 14-2 The IP address lease of a newly installed secondary server, as displayed in the Address Leases node of the DHCP console

> **TIP** To confirm that you are using the correct Unique ID value when creating your DHCP reservation, check the computer name selected by your secondary server during the operating system installation, which appears in the Initial Configuration Tasks window, in the Provide Computer Information section.

Once you have created the DHCP reservation, restart the secondary server to force its DHCP client to reconfigure the computer's TCP/IP settings using the address you reserved.

CONFIGURING THE TCP/IP CLIENT

If you choose to configure your server's TCP/IP client manually, you must still use an IP address that is excluded from your DHCP scope. Once you have determined an appropriate address, use the following procedure to complete the configuration:

1. Log on to your secondary server using the local Administrator account. The Initial Configuration Tasks window appears.

2. In the Provide Computer Information section, click Configure Networking. The Network Connections window appears, as shown here.

3. Right-click the Local Area Connection icon and, from the context menu, select Properties. The Local Area Connection Properties sheet appears, as shown here.

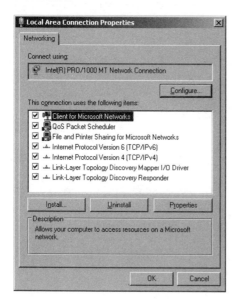

4. Select the Internet Protocol Version 4 (TCP/IPv4) component and click Properties. The Internet Protocol Version 4 (TCP/IPv4) Properties sheet appears, as shown here.

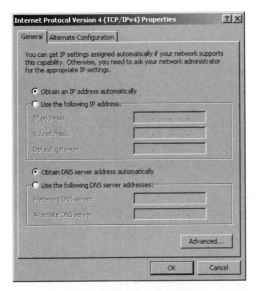

5. Select the Use The Following IP Address option.

6. In the IP Address text box, type the excluded address you want to use for your server, and in the Subnet Mask text box, type the appropriate mask for your network.

7. In the Default Gateway text box, type the IP address of your Internet access router.

8. In the Preferred DNS Server text box, type the IP address of your primary Windows SBS 2008 server and click OK.

9. Click OK to close the Local Area Connection Properties sheet.

10. Close the Network Connections window.

Changing the Computer Name and Joining the Domain

During the operating system installation on your secondary server, the Windows Server 2008 setup program selects an arbitrary computer name, one that no other computer on the local network possesses. During the initial planning phase of your network deployment, you should have devised a computer naming scheme that enables you to select an appropriate name for your server easily. You also have to join the server to your AD DS domain manually.

MORE INFO For more information on computer naming, see the section entitled "Selecting Names," in Chapter 3.

To change your server's computer name and join it to your domain, use the following procedure:

1. Log on to Windows Server 2008 using the local Administrator account. The Initial Configuration Tasks window appears.

2. In the Provide Computer Information section, click Provide Computer Name And Domain. The System Properties sheet appears, as shown here.

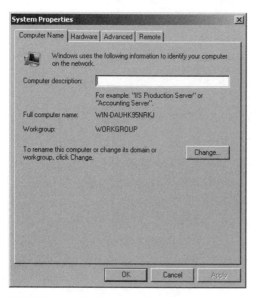

3. Click Change. The Computer Name/Domain Changes dialog box appears, as shown here.

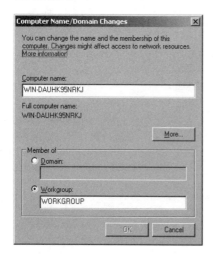

4. In the Computer Name text box, type the name you selected for your server.

5. In the Member Of box, select the Domain option and type the full name of your AD DS domain

6. Click OK. A Windows Security dialog box appears, as shown here.

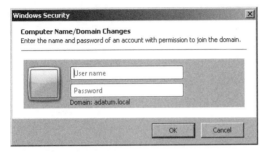

7. In the User Name text box, type the name of the network Administrator account you created when installing your primary server.

8. In the Password text box, type the password associated with the account and click OK. A Computer Name/Domain Changes message box appears, welcoming you to the domain, as shown here.

9. Click OK. Another message box appears, informing you that you must restart the computer.

10. Click OK. Then click Close to close the System Properties sheet. A Microsoft Windows message box appears, prompting you to restart the computer.

11. Click Restart Now. The computer restarts.

Once the computer has restarted, you can log on using a domain account instead of the local administrator account.

Moving the Computer Object

Once you have joined the secondary server to your AD DS domain, the server appears in the Windows SBS Console, on the Network/Computers tab, as shown in Figure 14-3. However, notice that the server appears in the Client Computers section, not the Servers section. This is because during the process of joining the server to the domain, the domain controller has no way of distinguishing a server from a workstation.

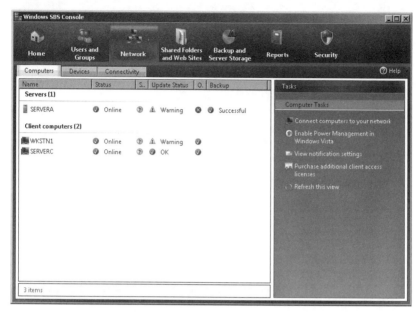

FIGURE 14-3 A newly joined secondary server, as shown in the Windows SBS Console

To move the secondary server to the Servers section and configure it to receive the Group Policy settings intended for servers, use the following procedure:

1. Log on to your Windows SBS 2008 primary server using the local Administrator account. The Windows SBS Console appears.

2. Click Start. Then click Administrative Tools, Active Directory Users And Computers. When the User Account Control dialog box appears, click Continue. The Active Directory Users And Computers console appears.

3. Expand the node named for your domain and browse to the My Business/ Computers/SBSComputers organizational unit, as shown here.

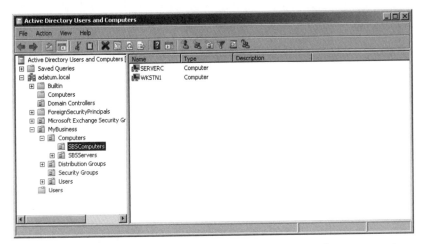

4. Right-click the computer object representing your secondary server and, in the context menu, select Move. The Move dialog box appears, as shown here.

5. In your domain, browse to and select the My Business/Computers/SBSServers organizational unit and click OK. The console moves the computer object to the SBSServers container.

6. Close the Active Directory Users And Computers console.

7. In the Windows SBS Console, click Network and select the Computers tab.

8. In the Tasks list, click Refresh This View. Your secondary server moves from the Client Computers section to the Servers section, as shown here.

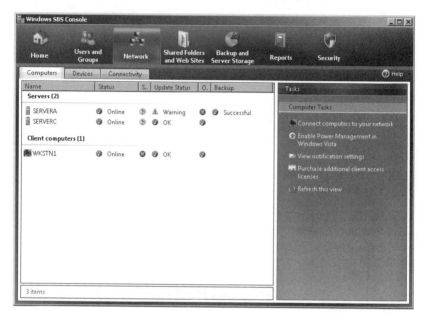

Deploying a Second Domain Controller

As mentioned earlier, you cannot use your secondary server to create another AD DS domain, whether in the same forest or in a different one. You can, however, configure it to function as a second domain controller in your existing Windows SBS 2008 domain. A second domain controller provides redundancy, for times when your primary server is offline, and if your organization has a branch office at a remote location, a second domain controller provides users at that location with local access to AD DS services.

> **TIP** If you are installing a domain controller that you will be moving to another location later, you should use an IP address on the local network for this procedure. Just before you shut down the computer prior to moving it, change the network settings to an IP address on the network that will be the server's final destination.

Promoting a server to a domain controller is a two-stage process. First you must install the AD DS role, and then you must run the Active Directory Domain Services Installation Wizard. To configure your secondary server to function as a domain controller, use the following procedure:

1. Log on to your Windows SBS 2008 secondary server using a domain account with network Administrator privileges.

2. Click Start. Then click Administrative Tools, Server Manager. When the User Account Control dialog box appears, click Continue. The Server Manager console appears, as shown here.

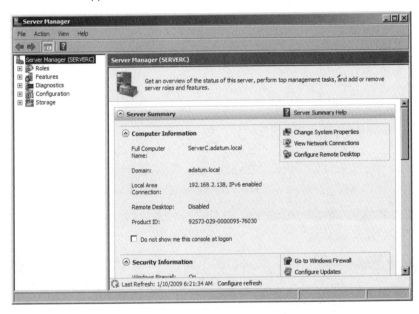

3. In the scope (left) pane, select the Roles node, as shown here.

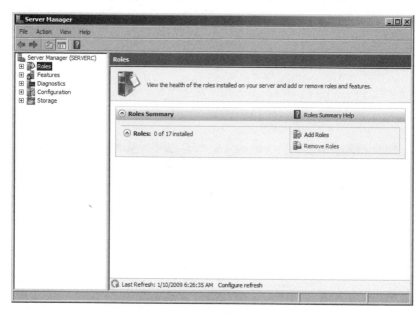

4. Click Add Roles. The Add Roles Wizard appears, as shown here.

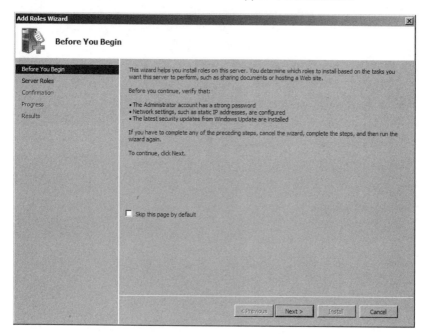

5. Click Next to bypass the Before You Begin page. The Select Server Roles page appears, as shown here.

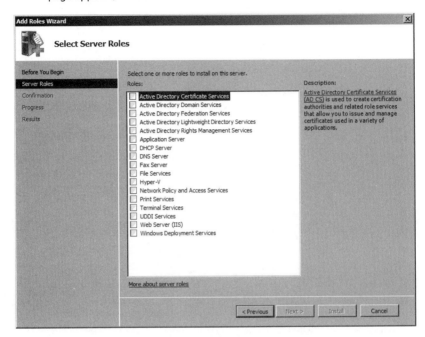

6. Select the Active Directory Domain Services check box and click Next. The Active Directory Domain Services page appears, as shown here.

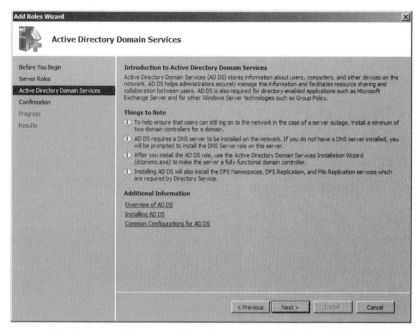

7. Click Next to continue. The Confirm Installation Selections page appears, as shown here.

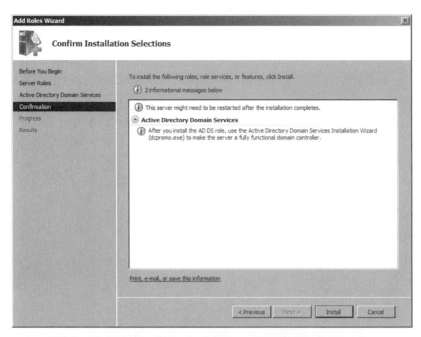

8. Click Install. The wizard installs the role and the Installation Results page appears, as shown here.

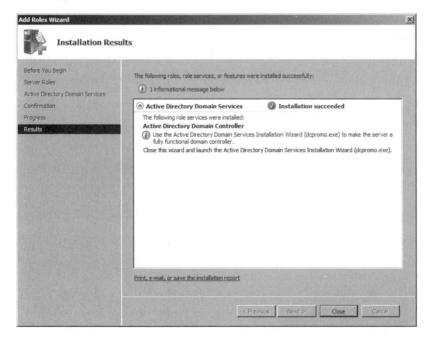

9. Click the Close This Wizard And Launch The Active Directory Domain Services Installation Wizard (Dcpromo.exe) link. The Active Directory Domain Services Installation Wizard appears, as shown here.

10. Click Next to bypass the Welcome page. The Operating System Compatibility page appears.

11. Click Next. The Choose A Deployment Configuration page appears, as shown here.

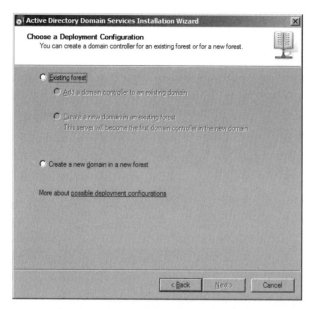

12. Select the Existing Forest option, and then leave the Add A Domain Controller To An Existing Domain option selected and click Next. The Network Credentials page appears, as shown here.

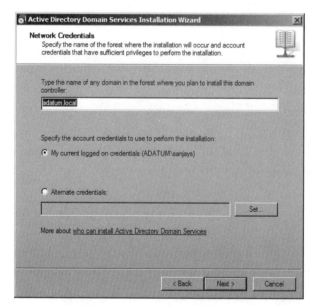

13. Make sure that the full name of your AD DS domain appears in the Type The Name Of Any Domain In The Forest Where You Plan To Install This Domain Controller text box and click Next. The Select A Domain page appears, as shown here.

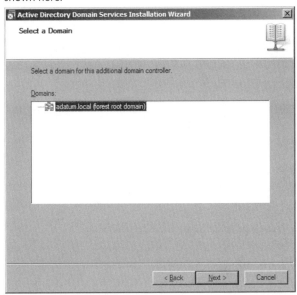

14. Click Next to accept the default forest root domain. The Select A Site page appears, as shown here.

15. Click Next to accept the Default-First-Site-Name site. The Additional Domain Controller Options page appears, as shown here.

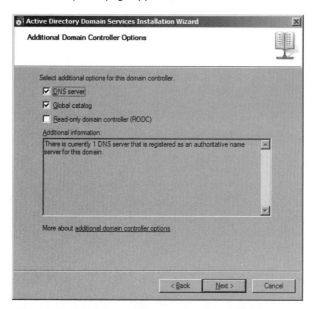

16. Click Next to accept the default settings. A Static IP Address Assignment message box appears, warning you that the computer has a dynamically assigned IP address.

NOTE If you have already configured your server to use a static IP address, as described in the section entitled "Configuring Network Settings," earlier in this chapter, this message refers to the computer's IPv6 address, which you can safely leave as a dynamically assigned address.

17. Click Yes, The Computer Will Use A Dynamically Assigned IP Address (Not Recommended). An Active Directory Domain Services Installation Wizard message box appears, advising you to create a delegation to the DNS server in the parent zone.

18. Click Yes. The Location For Database, Log Files, and SYSVOL page appears, as shown here.

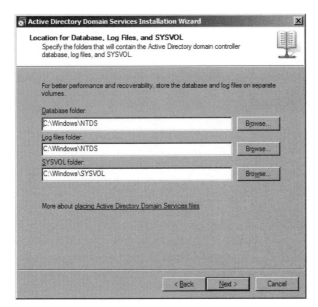

19. Click Next to accept the default values. The Directory Services Restore Mode Administrator Password page appears.

20. In the Password and Confirm Password text boxes, type the password you want to use when starting the computer in Directory Services Restore Mode and click Next. The Summary page appears, as shown here.

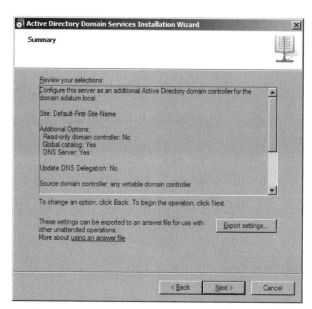

21. Click Next. The Wizard configures the server to function as a domain controller, and the Completing The Active Directory Domain Services Installation Wizard page appears, as shown here.

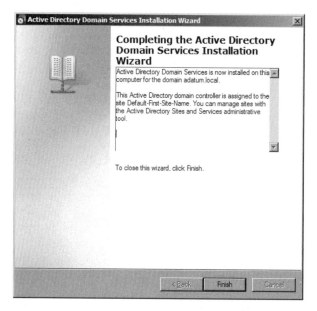

22. Click Finish. An Active Directory Domain Services Installation Wizard message box appears, prompting you to restart the computer.

23. Click Restart Now. The computer restarts.

Deploying SQL Server 2008 Standard for Small Business

Windows SBS 2008 Premium Edition includes SQL Server 2008 Standard for Small Business, a database management application that enables you to run a variety of line-of-business applications on your secondary server. The Windows SBS 2008 package includes SQL Server on a separate disk, which you must install manually. SQL Server is not a self-contained application in itself; rather, it is an environment that enables applications to store information in and retrieve information from SQL databases. How you install and configure SQL Server on your secondary server depends completely on the applications you plan to run.

Selecting Applications

There are two basic ways to obtain an application that uses SQL Server databases: you can purchase a product that already exists or you can work with a developer to create a custom application for your business. SQL-based applications are available for many vertical markets, including packages designed to manage professional offices, such as medical practices and legal firms, as well as utilities that can be valuable to any business, such as time-clock and payroll software.

Purchasing an application of this type is not the same as going to the computer store and selecting a commercial software product off the shelf. In most cases, you are dealing with a vendor that has designed and developed applications for specific markets or that is prepared to custom-design an application to your needs. In either situation, your relationship with the vendor is probably more personal, and you should plan to pay more for that privilege. Retail software prices are based on the product's attraction to a large market. A large company that creates a word processor program that appeals to millions of users can afford to sell it for far less than a company that creates a semi-customized application for a niche market with only hundreds or thousands of potential customers.

Selecting a SQL application for your business, or having one developed, is a major part of your network planning process. The requirements of the application dictate what hardware you need in your secondary server and how you install SQL Server 2008 on the computer. The application selection process should include the following elements:

- Meetings with your staff, including department managers or supervisors, as well as key employees that actually will be using the product. Use these meetings to compile a list of features that your application must have and a wish list of features you would like to have.

- Discussions with multiple vendors of software solutions appropriate for your organization. In addition to gathering product collateral and other information about the software, try to ascertain what kind of support the vendor supplies and how they respond to requests for new features and custom software modifications.

- Detailed system requirements for the software products you are considering. Determine whether you can run each product on your version of SQL Server 2008 and whether your budget can support the purchase of the required hardware.

- Live demonstrations of the applications, if possible, attended by the managers and users with whom you developed your list of requirements.

- Communications with other users of each software package you are considering to determine whether they are satisfied with the product and with the vendor's service.

Determining SQL Server Requirements

Hardware requirements for SQL-based applications often go far beyond just a specific processor and a certain amount of memory. Many applications base their hardware requirements on the number of users that access the application or on the size of the database. For example, as you add more users, you might need a faster processor, additional memory, and more disk space.

Some applications also have specific requirements for the computer's storage subsystem. For example, an application might require a certain RAID configuration or specify that you place the database files on drives that are separate from the database log files and the system files.

Finally, applications might also call for the installation of certain SQL Server features and specify configuration settings for certain parameters. Obviously, requirements like these can affect not only your server hardware purchasing decisions but also the process of installing and configuring SQL Server 2008.

> **TIP** Because SQL Server 2008 Standard is a relatively new release and some applications might not support it yet, Microsoft is including a copy of SQL Server 2005 Standard Edition, in both 32-bit and 64-bit versions, with Windows SBS 2008, for a period of one year from the initial Windows SBS 2008 release.

Installing SQL Server 2008

Although the requirements of your selected applications might require special handling, a typical example of a basic SQL Server 2008 installation proceeds as follows:

1. Log on to your secondary server using a domain account with network Administrator privileges.

2. Insert your SQL Server 2008 Standard disk into the DVD-ROM drive and run the Setup.exe file on the disk when the system prompts you to do so. When the User Account Control dialog box appears, click Continue. The SQL Server Installation Center window appears, as shown here.

If your server does not have the latest versions of Microsoft .NET Framework and Windows Installer installed, the setup program offers to install them for you. This process takes several minutes and requires you to restart the computer. After the computer restarts, run the Setup.exe program on the SQL Server 2008 disk again.

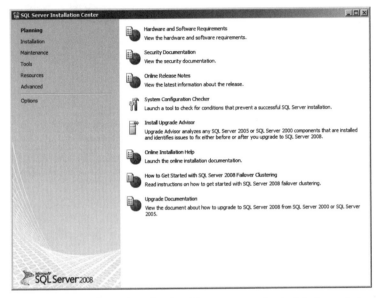

3. Click System Configuration Checker. The program checks 14 elements to determine whether your server is ready to install SQL Server, and then displays a Setup Support Rules dialog box containing the results, as shown here.

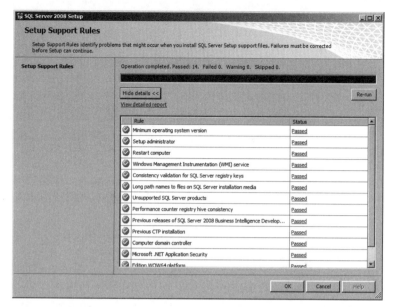

If your system fails to pass any of the tests, correct the problem and rerun the System Configuration Checker.

4. Once the system has passed all the tests, click OK to return to the SQL Server Installation Center window.

5. In the left column, click Installation. The Installation page of the SQL Server Installation Center appears, as shown here.

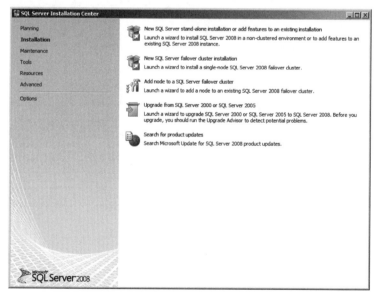

6. Click New SQL Server Stand-Alone Installation Or Add Features To An Existing Installation. The SQL Server 2008 Setup Wizard appears and displays the Setup Support Rules dialog box again, this time checking six elements that are required before the installation can proceed.

7. If your system passes all six tests, click OK. If not, correct the problems indicated and click Re-Run until the system passes all six tests. Then click OK. The Product Key page appears, as shown here.

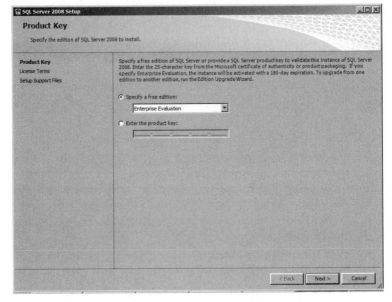

8. Click the Enter The Product Key option and type the SQL Server 2008 product key supplied with your Windows SBS 2008 package.

9. Click Next. The License Terms page appears, as shown here.

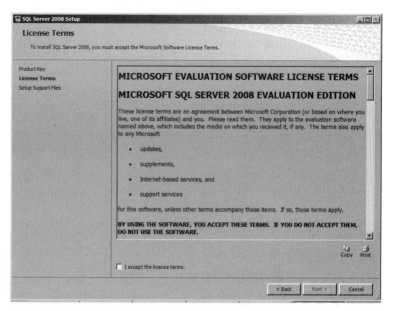

10. Select the I Accept The License Terms check box and click Next. The Setup Support Files page appears.

11. Click Next to continue. The wizard installs the setup support files and displays the Setup Support Rules page, which contains the results of the installation, as shown here.

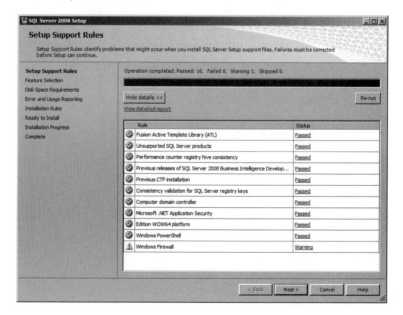

12. Click Next. The Feature Selection page appears, as shown here.

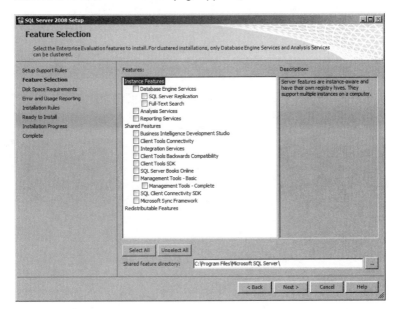

13. Select the check boxes for the following components:

- Database Engine Services
- Analysis Services
- Reporting Services
- Management Tools – Basic

14. Click Next. The Instance Configuration page appears, as shown here.

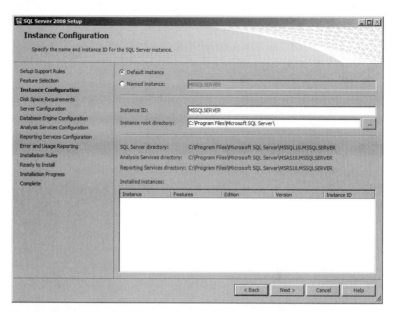

15. Click Next to accept the default settings. The Disk Space Requirements page appears, as shown here.

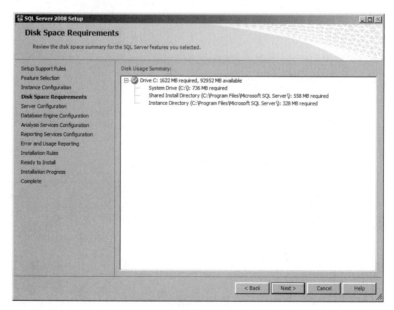

16. Click Next. The Server Configuration page appears, as shown here.

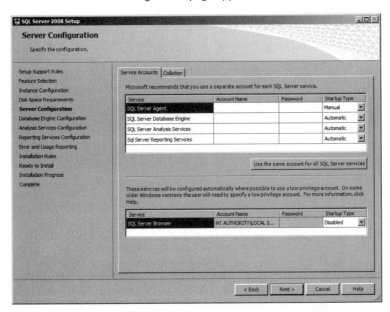

17. Specify an account name and password for each of the SQL Server services and click Next. The Database Engine Configuration page appears, as shown here.

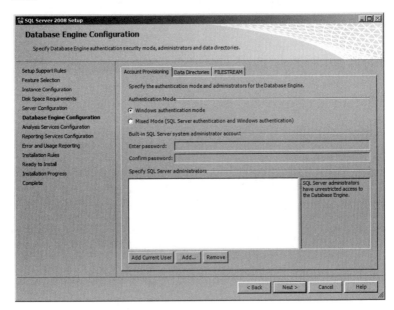

18. Click Add Current User and then click Next to accept the default Windows Authentication Mode option. The Analysis Services Configuration page appears.

19. Click Add Current User and then click Next. The Reporting Services Configuration page appears.

20. Click Next to accept the default Install The Native Mode Default Configuration option. The Error And Usage Reporting page appears.

21. Click Next to accept the default settings. The Installation Rules page appears and checks to see if an installation can proceed based on the settings you supplied.

22. Click Show Details to display the test results, as shown here.

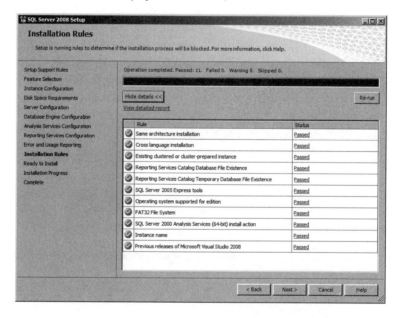

23. Click Next. The Ready To Install page appears, as shown here.

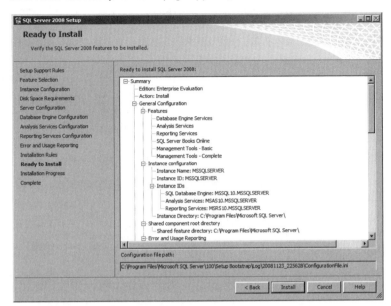

24. Click Install. The wizard installs SQL Server 2008 and displays the results of the installation process, as shown here.

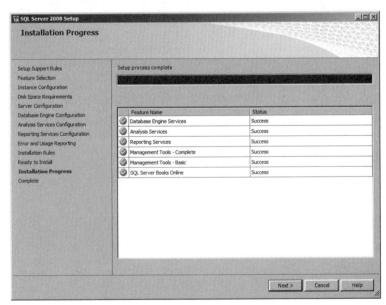

25. Click Next. The Complete page appears, as shown here, showing the overall results of the installation.

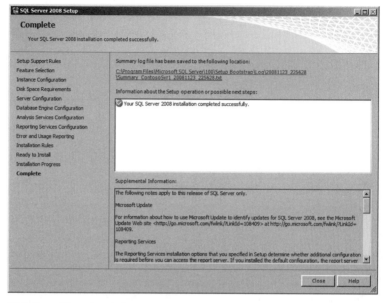

26. Click Close. The wizard closes.

CHAPTER 15

Monitoring Microsoft Windows Small Business Server (SBS) 2008

- Using Windows SBS Console Monitoring **507**
- Using the Windows SBS 2008 Best Practices Analyzer **523**
- Using WSUS Reports **529**

Keeping track of how your computers are performing is part of the job of every network administrator, and Microsoft Windows Small Business Server (SBS) 2008 provides many tools that enable you to manage your network computers and monitor their activities without having to leave your workstation.

Using Windows SBS Console Monitoring

As you have seen in previous chapters, Windows SBS Console provides administrators with many of the most vital Windows SBS controls and settings, leaving the details and comprehensive access to the standard Windows Server 2008 tools. The same is true when it comes to monitoring and reporting. The console can provide administrators with basic real-time monitoring, programmed alerts, and reports that it generates on a regular basis.

Using the Network Essentials Summary

On the Home page of the Windows SBS Console, as shown in Figure 15-1, the Network Essentials Summary pane provides a high-level, real-time view of four basic performance areas, as follows:

- **Security** Checks for the presence of virus and spyware protection, as well as active firewalls, on both your servers and workstations

- **Updates** Makes sure that Windows Server Update Services (WSUS) is running and that all the network servers and workstations have the latest updates installed

- **Backup** Checks to see that the server is configured to perform regular backups and whether the backups are completing successfully

- **Other Alerts** Checks for a variety of other conditions, including Error events in the System log, required services that are not running, and other important system status alerts

FIGURE 15-1 The Home page of the Windows SBS Console

Each of the four areas in the Network Essentials Summary pane has a status indicator with a colored icon specifying the current status of the area: OK (green check mark), Warning (yellow exclamation point), or Critical (red X). There is also an arrow in each area that you can click to display more information about the network's current condition and expose a link to a console page providing more detailed information, as shown in Figure 15-2.

FIGURE 15-2 An expanded Networking Essentials Summary area display

Unfortunately, the conditions that trigger a change in these status displays are not configurable. If, for example, you have deliberately stopped one of the services on your server that Windows SBS considers to be essential, the Other Alerts status always appears as Critical, and clicking the arrow only tells you that one of your servers has reported an alert. You have to click the Go To Computers link and seek more information about the problem before you can determine whether the alert concerns the stopped service you know about or a new condition.

Using Notification Settings

When you click Network in the Windows SBS Console and select the Computers tab, as shown in Figure 15-3, you see a list of the computers on your network, a column specifying whether each computer is online, and indicators providing the same four categories of information as the Network Essentials Summary pane. The difference here is that you have a separate set of indicators for each computer, while the Network Essentials Summary pane condenses the information for the entire network into four indicators.

FIGURE 15-3 The Network/Computers tab in the Windows SBS Console

From this page, you can also configure Windows SBS 2008 to send e-mail notifications to you, or anyone else, when certain events occur. To set up e-mail notifications, use the following procedure:

1. Log on to your Windows SBS 2008 primary server, using an account with network Administrator privileges. The Windows SBS Console appears.

2. Click Network, and then select the Computers tab.

3. From the Tasks list, select View Notification Settings. The Notification Settings dialog box appears.

4. On the Services tab, as shown on the following page, select the system services that should trigger an e-mail notification when they shut down.

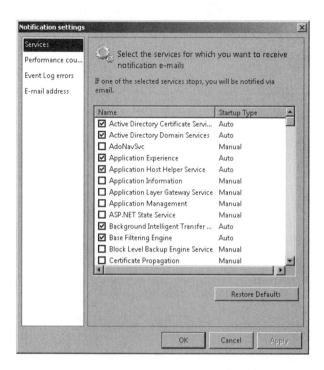

NOTE Of course, certain service failures can render the server unable to send any e-mail messages at all, in which case the system sends no e-mail notifications.

5. Click the Performance Counters tab, as shown here, and specify whether you want the system to send an e-mail notification when the amount of free disk space on the server drops below 10 percent of its capacity. You can also modify the default threshold by clicking Edit and specifying a different value in the Change Threshold To text box.

MORE INFO In Microsoft Windows, performance counters are registers that track specific statistics pertaining to certain hardware or software components. Unfortunately, this interface supports only one of the hundreds of counters available. To track other counter values, you must use the Reliability And Performance Monitor console, as described later in this chapter.

6. Click the Event Log Errors tab and specify which event types should trigger an e-mail notification, as shown here.

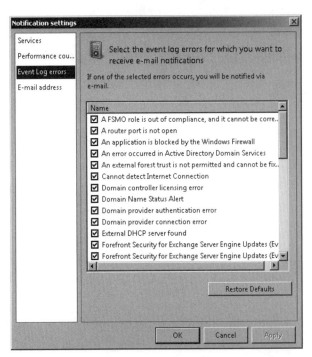

7. Click the E-Mail Address tab, as shown here, and in the E-Mail Address text box, specify the addresses of the individuals you want to receive notifications. You can use local or Internet e-mail addresses, separating multiple addresses with semicolons.

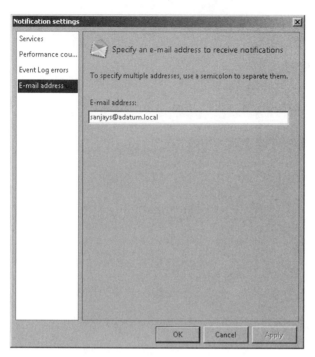

8. Click OK to close the Notification Settings dialog box.

Creating and Viewing Reports

Another way to monitor Windows SBS network activity is to create reports. When you click Reports in the Windows SBS Console, you see the interface shown in Figure 15-4, which displays the two reports that Windows SBS 2008 creates by default.

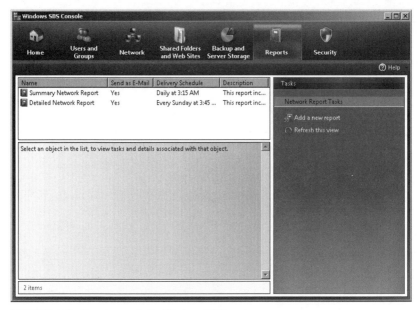

FIGURE 15-4 The Reports page in the Windows SBS Console

The reports that the Windows SBS Console generates are essentially expanded versions of the Network Essentials Summary that appears on the console's Home page, captured at a specific time. By default, Windows SBS runs a Summary Network Report each day at 3:15 A.M. and a Detailed Network Report each Sunday at 3:45 A.M. and e-mails them both to the Windows SBS Administrators distribution group. You can modify the schedule for these reports as needed, as well as their contents and their recipients. You can also create your own reports.

The Summary Network Report, as shown in Figure 15-5, displays the status of six system areas. These areas include the same Security, Updates, Backup, and Other Alerts areas as the Network Essentials Summary, plus two more: E-mail Usage And Mailbox Sizes and Server Event Logs. For each area that has an Error status, the report includes a one-line summary of the basic problem. In nearly all cases, the summary report can indicate that a problem exists, but administrators must consult other server resources to determine the source and nature of the problem.

FIGURE 15-5 A Summary Network Report generated by Windows SBS 2008

The Detailed Network Report, as shown in Figure 15-6, covers the same six areas but provides more information for each one, regardless of its status. The detailed report includes statistics, policy settings, and key error messages that can often provide administrators with enough information to diagnose a problem without having to consult other resources.

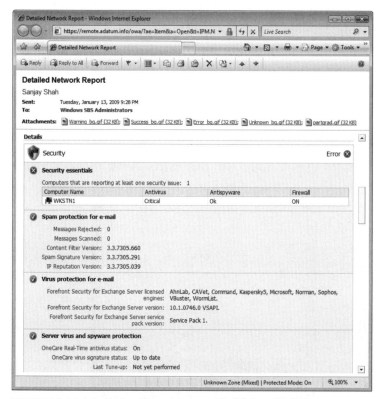

FIGURE 15-6 A Detailed Network Report generated by Windows SBS 2008

IMPORTANT Remember that both of these reports reflect the condition of the network at the time that the system generated them. By the time you read the reports, some conditions might have changed.

MODIFYING THE DEFAULT REPORTS

The Detailed Network Report begins with a Summary section that is identical to the Summary Network Report, followed by a Details section. Because the system does not take very long to generate either report, you might want to consider modifying the default schedules to generate the detailed report every day, instead of once per week.

To modify the schedule of the Detailed Network Report, use the following procedure:

1. Log on to your Windows SBS 2008 primary server, using an account with network Administrator privileges. The Windows SBS Console appears.

2. Click Reports.

3. Select Detailed Network Report and, from the Tasks list, click View Report Properties. The Detailed Network Report Properties sheet appears, as shown here.

4. Click the Schedule tab, as shown here.

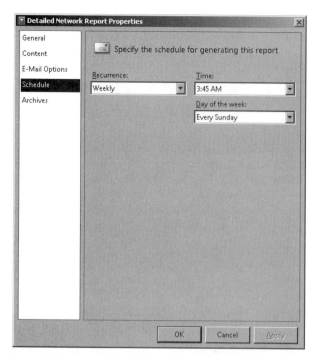

5. From the Recurrence drop-down list, select Daily. From the Time drop-down list, select a different time for the report to run, if desired.

6. Click OK.

CREATING NEW REPORTS

In addition to modifying the default reports, you can create new reports that contain information on specific areas and run at specified times, which the system supplies to specific users via e-mail. To create a new report, use the following procedure:

1. Log on to your Windows SBS 2008 primary server, using an account with network Administrator privileges. The Windows SBS Console appears.

2. Click Reports.

3. From the Tasks list, select Add A New Report. The New Report Properties sheet appears, as shown here.

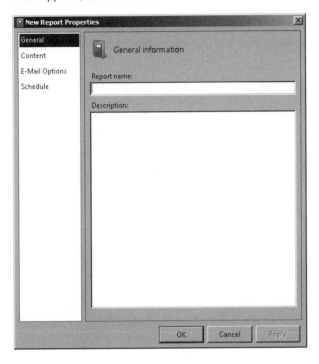

4. In the Report Name text box, type the name you want to assign to the report. Then, click the Content tab, as shown here.

5. Select the check boxes for the areas that you want to include in the report and click the E-Mail Options tab, as shown here.

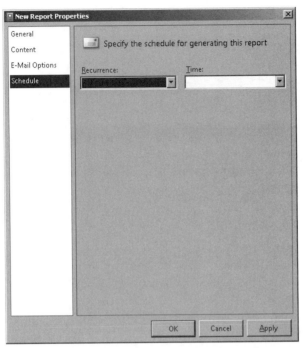

6. Select the E-Mail This Report At Its Scheduled Time check box and select the check boxes for the internal users or groups that you want to receive the report. You can also type other e-mail addresses in the Other E-Mail Addresses (Separated By A Semi-Colon) text box, if desired. Then, click the Schedule tab, as shown here.

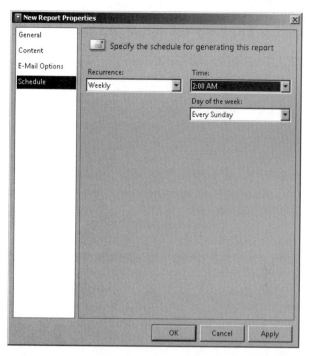

New Report Properties

General
Content
E-Mail Options
Schedule

Specify the schedule for generating this report

Recurrence:
Weekly

Time:
2:00 AM

Day of the week:
Every Sunday

OK   Cancel   Apply

7. In the Recurrence drop-down list, specify whether you want the system to run the report daily or weekly. Then, from the Time drop-down list, select the time of day that you want the system to generate the report. If you chose the Weekly option, select a value in the Day Of The Week drop-down list.

8. Click OK. The new report appears on the Reports page.

Using the Windows SBS 2008 Best Practices Analyzer

As discussed in Chapter 1, "Introducing Microsoft Windows Small Business Server 2008," the designers of Windows SBS 2008 have made many of the installation and configuration decisions that Windows Server 2008 administrators must make themselves. The default server configuration implements a series of *best practices* by installing certain roles and features and configuring them to create a standard Windows SBS server configuration.

These best practices are not required to run Windows SBS 2008; you can make whatever changes to the operating system and its applications you want. However, you should be conscious of the repercussions that deviations from the standard configuration can have. The Windows SBS 2008 Best Practices Analyzer (BPA) is a tool that can examine your current network configuration and create a report listing the differences between it and the recommended Windows SBS 2008 settings.

The Windows SBS 2008 BPA is not supplied with the Windows SBS 2008 product. You must download it from the Microsoft Download Center at *http://www.microsoft.com /downloads/details.aspx?FamilyID=86a1aa32-9814-484e-bd43-3e42aec7f731* and install it on your Windows SBS primary server. The BPA is packaged as a Microsoft Installer (.msi) file, which you must execute on your primary server. A standard installation wizard then takes you through the process of approving the license agreement and specifying a location for the program. You can also choose to integrate the Windows SBS 2008 BPA into the Windows SBS Console, which enables you to view the results of the BPA scan in the Detailed Network Report.

Once you have installed the software, use the following procedure to run the Windows SBS 2008 BPA and perform your first scan:

1. Log on to your Windows SBS 2008 primary server, using an account with network Administrator privileges.

2. Click Start. Then click All Programs, Windows Small Business Server Tools, Windows Small Business Server 2008 Best Practices Analyzer. When the User Account Control dialog box appears, click Continue. The Windows Small Business Server 2008 Best Practices Analyzer window appears, as shown here.

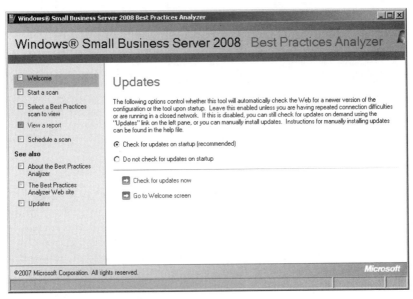

3. On the Updates page, leave the Check For Updates On Startup (Recommended) option selected and click Go To Welcome Screen. The Welcome To The Best Practices Analyzer page appears, as shown here.

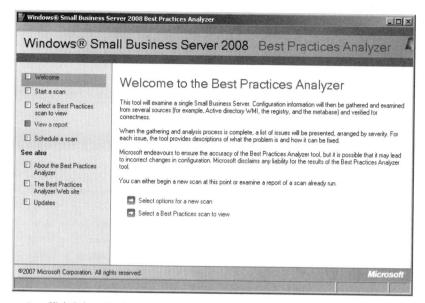

4. Click Select Options For A New Scan. The Start A Scan page appears, as shown here.

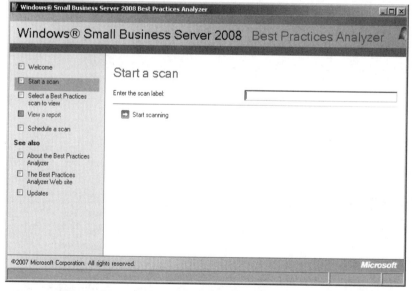

5. In the Enter The Scan Label text box, type a descriptive name for the scan.

6. Click Start Scanning. The program begins scanning your server, as shown here. This process can take several minutes.

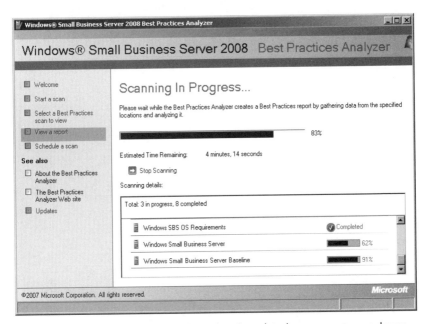

When the scan is finished, a Scanning Completed page appears, as shown here.

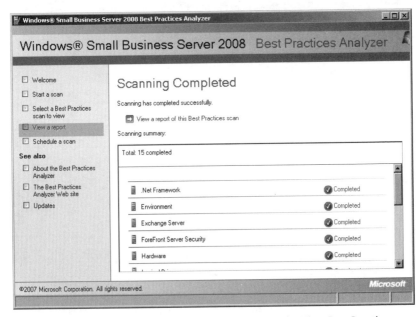

7. Click View A Report Of This Best Practices Scan. The View Best Practices Report page appears.

TIP you can also configure the Windows SBS 2008 BPA program to perform scans at regular intervals, by clicking Schedule A Scan, as shown here, and specifying details for a daily, weekly, or monthly schedule.

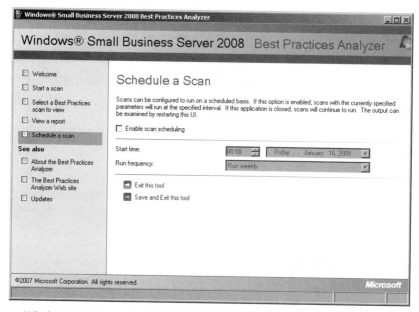

Windows SBS 2008 BPA enables you to view its reports in several formats. By default, the program uses a list format, which displays warnings in one tab and informational items in another. Clicking one of the warnings, as shown in Figure 15-7, displays additional information about the issue and instructions for restoring it to the default Windows SBS configuration.

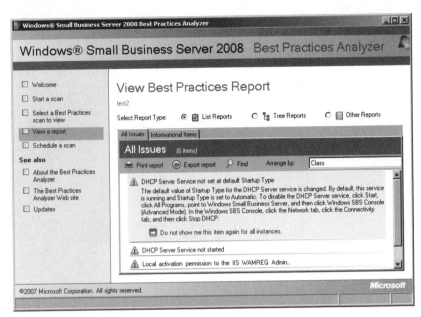

FIGURE 15-7 A Windows SBS 2008 BPA list report

Clicking the Tree Reports option enables you to concentrate on specific areas of the operating system, displaying the same information using a different organizational paradigm, as shown in Figure 15-8. Clicking the Other Reports option displays a time-stamped log of the BPA program's activities.

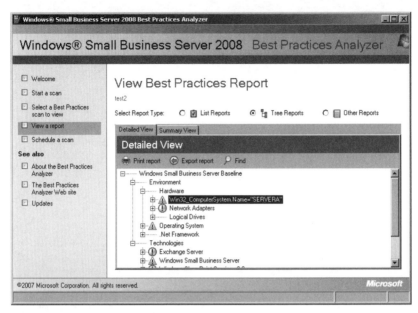

FIGURE 15-8 A Windows SBS 2008 BPA tree report

Using WSUS Reports

The Windows SBS Console enables you to view a list of the updates that WSUS has furnished to each computer on your network, but it does not provide any more detailed WSUS statistics. You can obtain additional information about WSUS activities, however, by using the Update Services console.

To generate WSUS reports, use the following procedure:

1. Log on to your Windows SBS 2008 primary server, using an account with network Administrator privileges.

2. Click Start, and then click Administrative Tools, Microsoft Windows Server Update Services 3.0 SP1. When the User Account Control dialog box appears, click Continue. The Update Services console appears, as shown here.

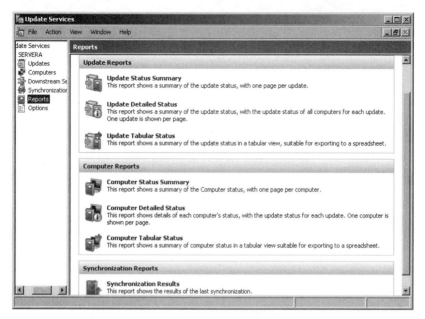

3. Expand the node named for your server and select Reports. The Reports pane appears, as shown here.

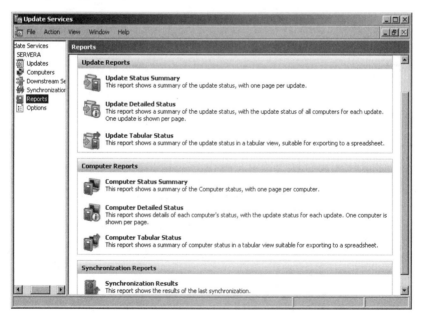

4. To check the status of your WSUS synchronizations, click Synchronization Results. The Synchronization Report window for your server appears, as shown here.

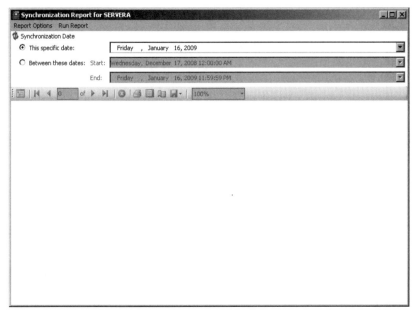

5. Select the Between These Dates option and then choose Start and End dates.
6. On the menu bar, select Run Report. The console generates a report that begins with a summary of each synchronization performed during the selected dates, as shown here.

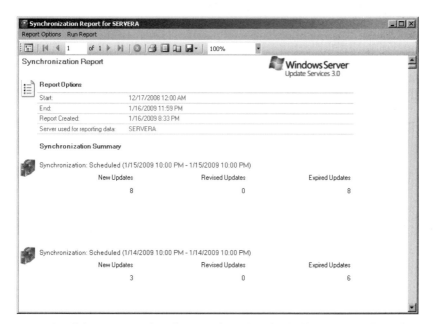

7. Scroll down to see a list of new updates downloaded by WSUS, as shown here.

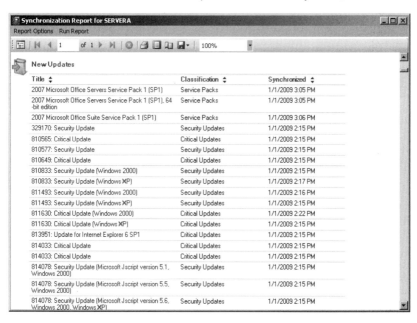

8. Print or save the report, if needed, and close the Synchronization Report window.

9. To generate a detailed report of all WSUS updates, click Update Detailed Status. The Updates Report window for your server appears, as shown here.

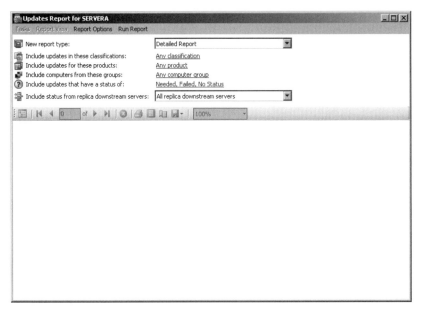

10. Make sure the New Report Type drop-down list is set to Detailed Report and configure the following options as needed:

- Include Updates In These Classifications   Enables you to specify the types of updates for which you want a report, using the interface shown here.

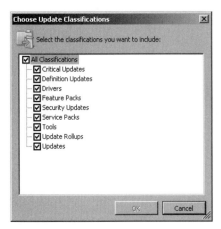

- **Include Updates For These Products** Enables you to specify the operating systems and applications for which you want a report, using the interface shown here.

- **Include Computers From These Groups** Enables you to select the WSUS computer groups on which you want to report, using the interface shown here.

- **Include Updates That Have A Status Of** Enables you to specify which updates you want included in the report, based on their completion status, using the interface shown here.

11. On the menu bar, select Run Report. The console generates a report like the one shown here, which lists each selected update, provides detailed metadata for it, and lists its approval and deployment history.

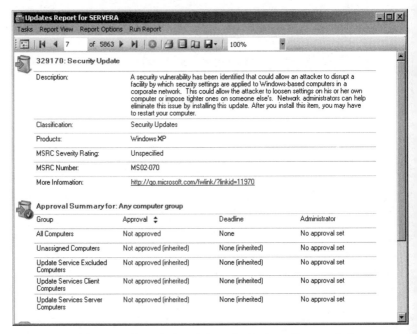

12. Print or save the report, if needed, and close the Updates Report window.

13. To generate a detailed report for each computer, click Computer Detailed Status. The Computers Report window for your server appears, as shown here.

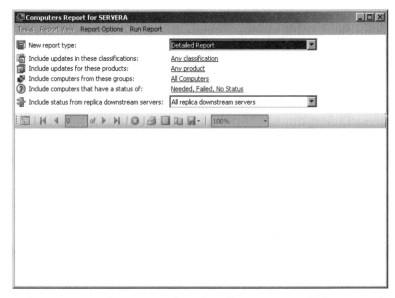

14. Make sure the New Report Type drop-down list is set to Detailed Report and configure the options that follow as needed.

15. On the menu bar, select Run Report. The console generates a report like the one shown here, which lists each selected computer, and summarizes its update status.

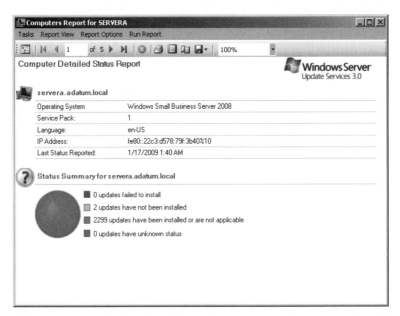

16. Click Next Page to display a list of the updates corresponding to your selected options, as shown here.

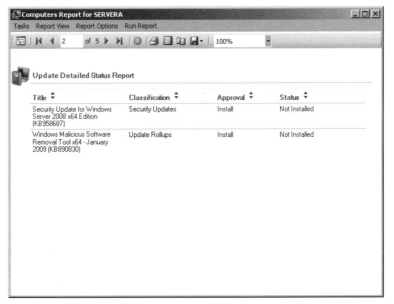

17. Print or save the report, if needed, and close the Computers Report window.

18. Close the Update Services console.

Managing Microsoft Windows Small Business Server (SBS) 2008

The Windows SBS Console enables administrators to manage many of the most important elements of Microsoft Windows Small Business Server (SBS) 2008, but it does not do everything. A Windows SBS administrator must use the other tools supplied with the operating system in many situations. This chapter covers some of these tools and the tasks commonly associated with them.

Accessing Remote Computers

Depending on the layout of the network, it might be difficult, or even impossible, for administrators to physically access the computers they need to manage. Servers might be stored in a locked closet or even located in a branch office. Windows SBS 2008 includes a number of tools that enable administrators to access remote computers, as described in the following sections.

Using Remote Desktop

Remote Desktop is a client/server implementation of Terminal Services technology that enables a user on one computer to log on to another computer and perform virtually any task possible from the local console. The Remote Desktop server capability is built into most Microsoft Windows operating systems, and any Windows computer can run a Remote Desktop client program.

As the name implies, the Remote Desktop client functions strictly as a terminal,
controlling the activities of the server from a distance. The client computer runs
a program called *Remote Desktop Connection (RDC)*, which sends keystrokes and
mouse commands to the server and receives output in the form of display elements.
When you log on to a computer using Remote Desktop and start an application, the
application actually runs on the server using the server's processor, memory, and
other resources. In the same way, configuring system settings with Remote Desktop
means that you are reconfiguring the server, not the client.

Remote Desktop is a limited version of Terminal Services, a Windows Server role
that enables multiple users to access applications running on a server instead of
installing them on a local drive. Terminal Services requires the purchase of additional Client Access Licenses (CALs) and cannot run on a Windows SBS 2008 primary
server, but the Remote Desktop version is operable on all servers without additional
licensing, although it is limited to two connections.

To administer a computer running Windows SBS 2008 or Windows Server 2008
using Remote Desktop, you must complete the following tasks:

- Enable Remote Desktop on the server.
- Establish a connection between the client and the server.

Enabling Remote Desktop

By default, computers running Windows Server 2008 have their Remote Desktop
server functions disabled. This is to prevent access by unauthorized users before all
the computer's security precautions are in place. However, because the Windows
SBS 2008 installation process secures the computer, the setup program enables
Remote Desktop on the primary server. To enable Remote Desktop manually on a
server running Windows Server 2008, use the following procedure:

1. Log on to your server, using an account with network Administrator privileges. The Initial Configuration Tasks window appears, as shown here.

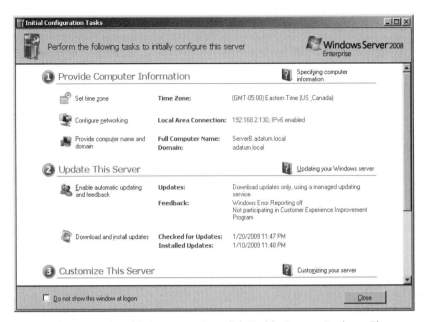

2. In the Customize This Server section, click Enable Remote Desktop. The System Properties sheet appears, as shown here.

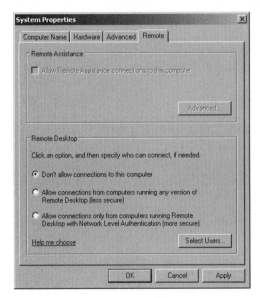

TIP If the server is a domain controller, the Server Manager console appears instead, and you can open the System Properties sheet by clicking Configure Remote Desktop in the Server Summary section of the Server Manager console.

3. In the Remote Desktop section, select the Allow Connections From Computers Running Any Version Of Remote Desktop (Less Secure). A Remote Desktop message box appears, informing you that the system will open a firewall exception for Remote Desktop communications.

4. Click OK. Then click Select Users. The Remote Desktop Users dialog box appears, as shown here.

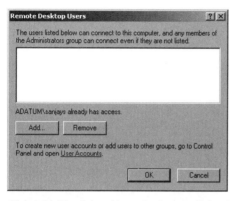

5. Click Add. The Select Users Or Groups dialog box appears, as shown here.

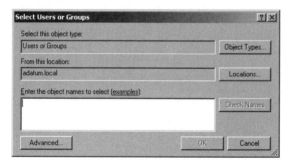

6. In the Enter The Object Names To Select text box, type the names of the user accounts and groups to which you want to grant Remote Desktop access, and then click OK. The users and groups you specify appear in the Remote Desktop Users dialog box.

MORE INFO The Remote Desktop Users dialog box adds the objects you specify to the Remote Desktop Users local group on the server, which enables them to access the server from a remote location. Administrators have Remote Desktop access by default; you do not have to add them to the Remote Desktop Users group.

7. Click OK to close the Remote Desktop Users dialog box.

8. Click OK to close the System Properties sheet.

Using the Remote Desktop Connection Client

Once you have enabled Remote Desktop on the computer that functions as the server, you can run the Remote Desktop Connection program on the client and establish a connection to it, using the following procedure:

1. Log on to a Windows Vista workstation using a domain user account.

2. Click Start. Then click All Programs, Accessories, Remote Desktop Connection. The Remote Desktop Connection dialog box appears, as shown here.

3. In the Computer text box, type the name or IP address of the computer to which you want to connect.

4. Click Options. The dialog box expands, as shown here.

5. Click the Display tab, as shown here.

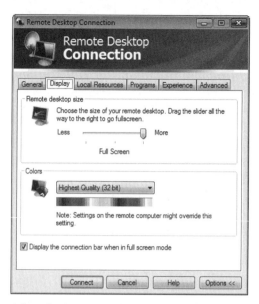

6. Adjust the Remote Desktop Size slider to a value smaller than that of your current screen resolution.

7. Click Connect. A Windows Security dialog box appears, as shown here.

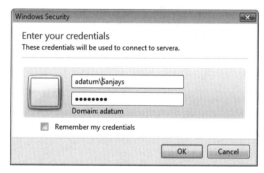

8. In the User Name and Password text boxes, type the credentials for an account that has Remote Desktop connection privileges on the server and click OK. A Remote Desktop window appears, containing the server's desktop, as shown here.

At this point, any activity you perform within the Remote Desktop window is taking place on the remote computer, using that computer's resources. The RDC client program uses the Remote Desktop Protocol (RDP) to send your keystrokes and mouse movements to the server and receive the screen display elements that appear on your monitor. Closing the Remote Desktop window disconnects the client from the server.

Using Microsoft Management Console

Microsoft Management Console (MMC) is the primary administration tool for Windows computers. The MMC program itself is a shell application that can load individual components called *snap-ins*. Many of the administration tools in the Windows server and workstation operating systems take the form of MMC snap-ins. For example, most of the shortcuts you see when you open the Administrative Tools program group on a computer running Windows Server 2008 are preconfigured MMC consoles that contain one or more snap-ins.

One of the primary advantages of the MMC environment is the ability to direct a snap-in to another computer on the network, enabling you to administer its properties from a remote location. Many MMC consoles that connect to the local system by default have a Connect To Another Computer menu item that, when clicked, displays a dialog box like the one shown in Figure 16-1, which you can use to browse to another system on the network.

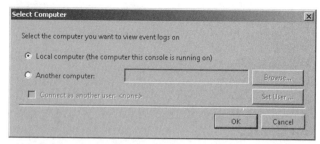

FIGURE 16-1 The Select Computer dialog box, which enables you to direct an MMC to another computer on the network

The ability to do this depends on the nature of the snap-in and the configuration of the console. For example, the snap-ins that you use to administer Active Directory Domain Services (AD DS), such as the Active Directory Users And Computers console, connect to the local domain by default. However, you can point the snap-in to another domain on a network that has one, or point it to a specific domain controller in the current domain, using the Change Directory Server dialog box, shown in Figure 16-2.

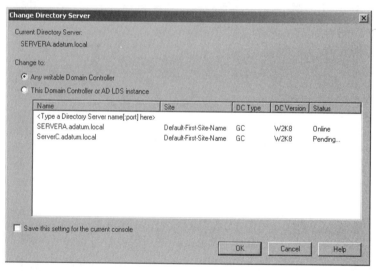

FIGURE 16-2 The Change Directory Server dialog box, which enables you to direct an AD DS console to a specific domain controller

TIP If you want to administer a role on a remote server from a computer that is not running that role, you can install the required snap-in using the Remote Server Administration Tools feature in the Server Manager console.

Another powerful feature in MMC is the ability to load multiple snap-ins and to create a console that performs a variety of functions. The Computer Management console, shown in Figure 16-3, is an example of a single console that contains many snap-ins, all pointed at the local computer.

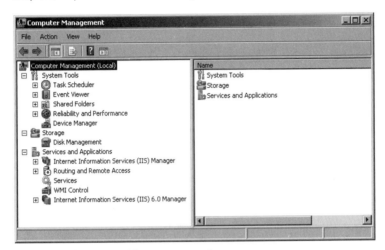

FIGURE 16-3 The Computer Management console

In addition to using the preconfigured consoles supplied with the operating system, you can create your own customized MMCs that contain any combination of snap-ins you want. Your custom consoles can contain a variety of snap-ins pointed at the same computer, or multiple instances of the same snap-in pointed at different computers. For example, you can create a console containing an instance of the Event Viewer snap-in for each computer on your network, so you can examine all the network's system logs using one tool, as shown in Figure 16-4.

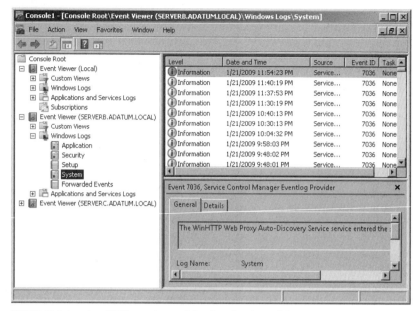

FIGURE 16-4 A custom MMC console containing three instances of the Event Viewer snap-in

IMPORTANT By default, Windows Firewall blocks the ports that most MMC snap-ins use to communicate with other computers on the network. You might have to open the Remote Service Management firewall exception before you can direct a snap-in to another computer.

To create a custom MMC on a computer running Windows SBS 2008 or Windows Server 2008, use the following procedure:

1. Log on to the server using a domain account with administrative privileges.

2. Click Start, and then click Run. The Run dialog box appears.

3. In the Open text box, type **mmc** and click OK. When the User Account Control dialog box appears, click Continue. A blank MMC appears, as shown here.

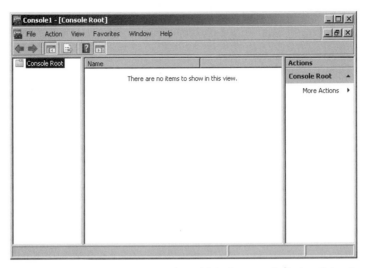

4. Click File, Add/Remove Snap-In. The Add Or Remove Snap-Ins dialog box appears, as shown here.

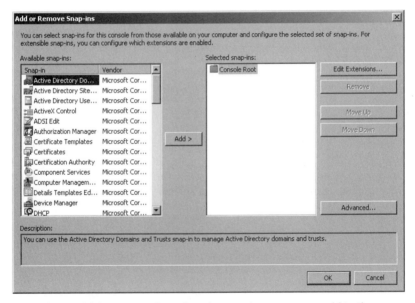

5. In the Available Snap-Ins list, select the snap-in you want to add to the console and click Add.

   Depending on the snap-In, a dialog box might appear, prompting you to select the computer or account you want to manage. The snap-in then appears in the Selected Snap-Ins list.

6. Repeat step 5 to select additional snap-ins for the console (if desired) and click OK. The snap-ins appear in the console, as shown here.

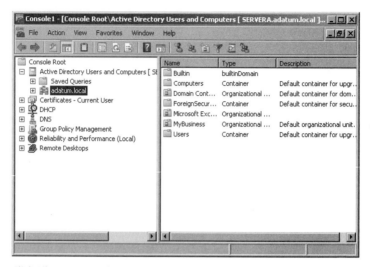

7. Click File, Save As. The Save As combo box appears.

8. Type a name for the console and click Save. MMC adds the new console to the Administrative Tools program group.

Using Server Manager

Windows SBS 2008 and Windows Server 2008 use elements called *roles* and *features* to implement their various applications and services. During the installation of a Windows SBS 2008 primary server, the setup program adds a number of roles and features by default. The default Windows Server 2008 installation includes no roles or features, however. The primary tool that Windows SBS 2008 and Windows Server 2008 administrators use to install, remove, and manage roles and features is called Server Manager, shown in Figure 16-5.

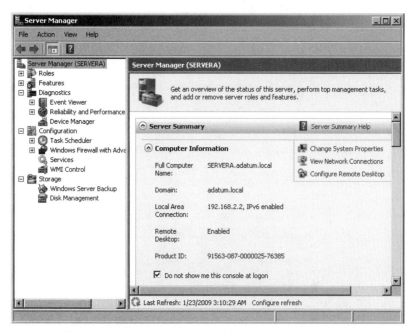

FIGURE 16-5 The Server Manager console

Server Manager is an MMC console that provides access to a variety of snap-ins, system configuration controls, and diagnostic tools. In addition, Server Manager includes wizards that enable you to install and remove roles and features. When you install a role that includes its own administration snap-ins, Server Manager, in most cases, provides access to those snap-ins.

Managing Roles

When you open the Server Manager console on your Windows SBS 2008 primary server and expand the Roles node, the scope (left) pane contains all the roles that the setup program added during the operating system installation, as shown in Figure 16-6. The detail (right) pane contains a section for each role that displays its status.

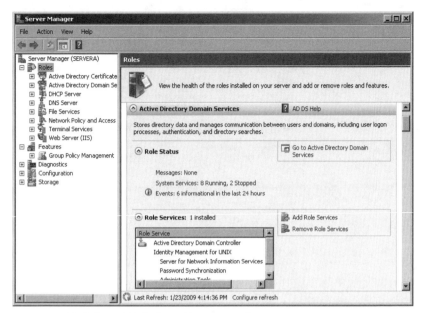

FIGURE 16-6 The Roles node in the Server Manager console

When you select one of the installed roles, the scope pane contains a more detailed status display that contains some or all of the following items:

- **Events**   Contains a list of the events pertaining to the role from the last 24 hours, as shown here, derived from the Windows logs and linking to the Event Viewer console.

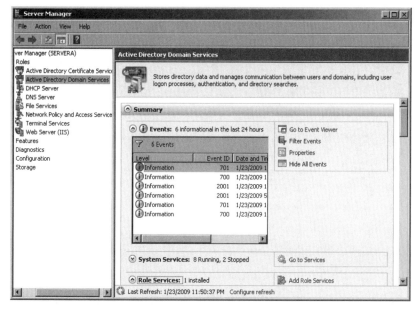

- **System Services** Contains a list of the services associated with the role, as shown here, and enables you to stop, start, and configure them, just as you can from the Services console.

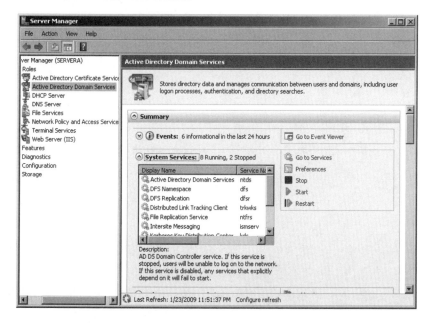

- **Role Services** Contains a list of the role's subcomponents, as shown here, and specifies which ones are currently installed. You can also add or remove role services using wizards.

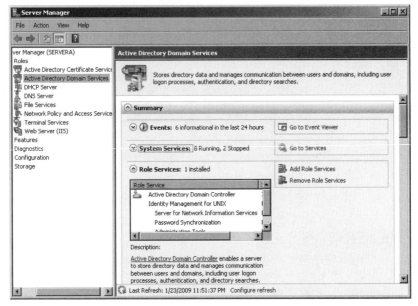

- **Advanced Tools** For roles with a large number of additional consoles or command prompt utilities, this section contains links to those tools and descriptions of their functions, as shown here.

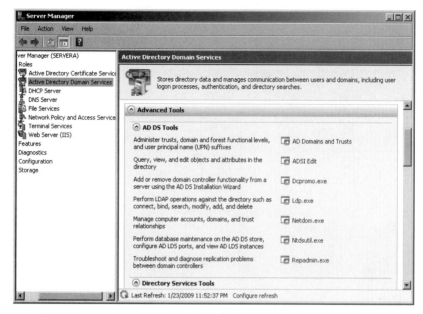

- **Resources And Support**   Contains links to help files, Web resources, best practices, and recommended procedures, as shown here.

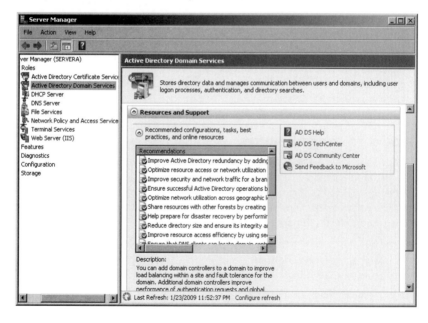

In addition to these resources, Server Manager incorporates many of the MMC snap-ins associated with a role into the console. When you expand a role in the scope pane, the snap-ins appear underneath, as shown in Figure 16-7.

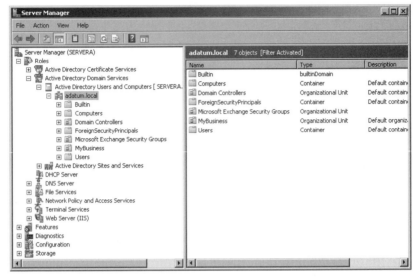

FIGURE 16-7 The Active Directory Users And Computers snap-in, incorporated into the Server Manager console

> **IMPORTANT** The Server Manager console does not necessarily provide access to all the snap-ins associated with a particular role. You might find additional consoles in the Administrative Tools program group, and others that are accessible only by adding them to a custom MMC.

Adding Roles and Features

Windows SBS 2008 primary servers run a large number of roles by default, and administrators should be cautious about installing additional ones. However, if you have additional computers running Windows Server 2008 on your network, you most likely have to install some roles on it yourself. To install a role with the Server Manager console, use the following procedure:

1. Log on to the server using a domain account with administrative privileges.

2. Click Start. Then click Administrative Tools, Server Manager. The Server Manager console appears.

3. Select the Roles node.

4. In the detail pane, click Add Roles. The Add Roles Wizard appears, displaying the Before You Begin page, as shown here.

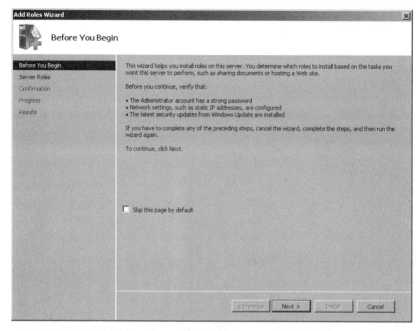

5. Click Next. The Select Server Roles page appears, as shown here.

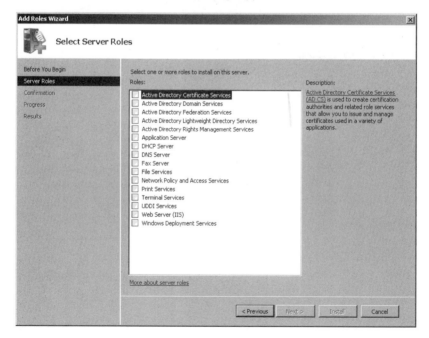

6. Select the check box for the role you want to install and click Next. An Introduction page appears, like the one shown here.

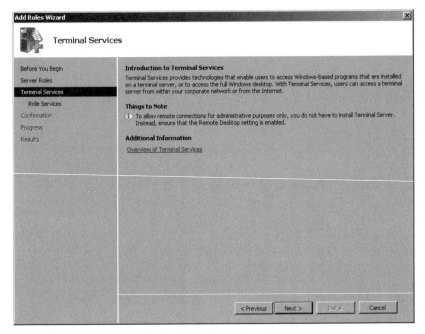

7. Click Next. For roles that include role services, the Select Role Services page appears, like the one shown here.

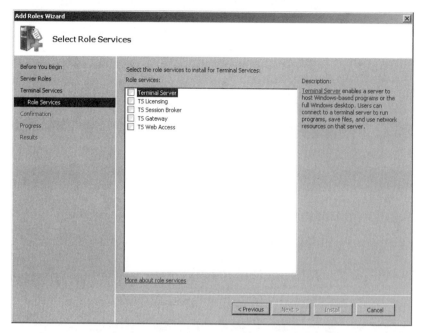

8. Select the check boxes for the role services you want to install.

Many roles and role services depend on other roles or features to function. For example, the TS Web Access role service in the Terminal Services role requires a Web server, so an Add Role Services And Features Required For TS Web Access dialog box appears, as shown here, listing the dependent modules and offering to install them for you. Click Add Required Role Services to select the dependent modules.

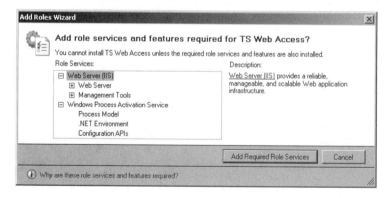

9. Click Next. The next role-specific page appears.

In most cases, the roles and role services you select for installation add pages to the wizard, like the one shown here, which you can use to configure role-specific parameters. Dependent roles and features can add their own configuration pages as well.

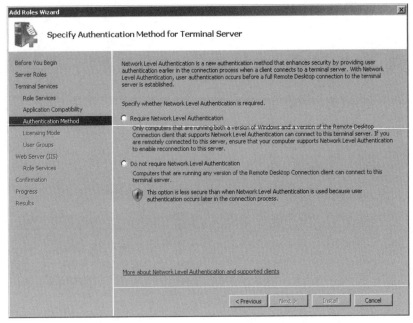

10. Complete all the role-specific pages in the wizard and click Next. The Confirm Installation Selections page appears, listing all the actions the wizard performs, as shown here.

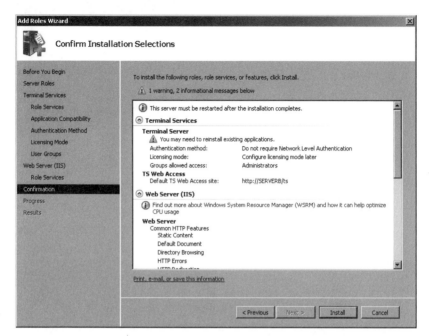

11. Click Install. The wizard displays an Installation Progress page as it installs and configures the selected modules. Then an Installation Results page appears, as shown here, which might inform you that you must restart the server.

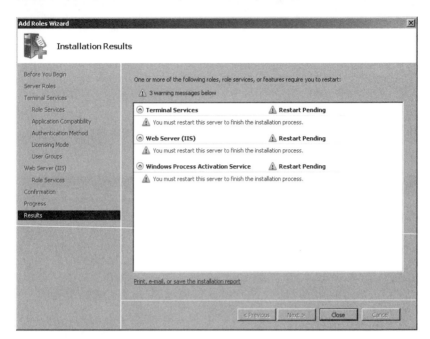

12. Click Close and restart the server, if necessary.

Using Windows Server 2008 Tools

Much of this book has been devoted to the administration and configuration tools specific to Windows SBS 2008, especially the Windows SBS Console. However, Windows SBS 2008 is a superset of Windows Server 2008 and includes all the tools that go with it. The following sections contain brief descriptions of the most commonly used Windows Server 2008 administration tools.

Using Active Directory Users And Computers

The Active Directory Users And Computers console is the primary administration tool for AD DS. The console provides access to all the objects in the AD DS hierarchy and most of the attributes in each object. If you want to work with objects or attributes that do not appear in the Windows SBS Console, Active Directory Users And Computers provides a more comprehensive view.

> **MORE INFO** For more information about AD DS objects and attributes, see the section entitled "An Active Directory Primer" in Chapter 5, "Working with Users, Computers, and Groups."

Windows Server 2008 installs the console on all domain controllers automatically; to run it on a computer that is not a domain controller, you can install the console using the Remote Server Administration Tools, Role Administration Tools feature in the Server Manager console.

The Active Directory Users And Computers console displays a hierarchical view of the AD DS domain to which you are currently attached, as shown in Figure 16-8. You can browse through the organizational units in the domain to find and manage existing objects, or create new ones. Double-clicking an object opens its Properties sheet, which, depending on the object type, can be simple or quite complex, and which provides access to the object's attributes.

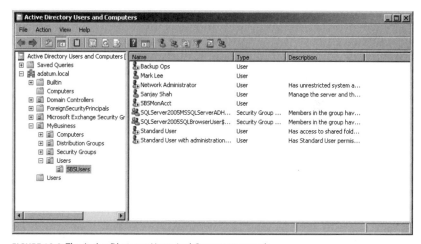

FIGURE 16-8 The Active Directory Users And Computers console

Using Group Policy Management

Group Policy is one of the most powerful and useful administrative tools provided with Windows SBS 2008 and Windows Server 2008. In Chapter 12, "Optimizing Network Security," you used Group Policy settings to control password and account lockout policies on your network, but they have many other applications as well. Group Policy is essentially a method for deploying Windows registry settings to large numbers of users or computers on a network. Windows SBS 2008 uses Group Policy settings to configure several critical functions on your network workstations, including folder redirection, Windows Firewall, and the Automatic Updates client.

The Group Policy Management console, shown in Figure 16-9, enables you to control the links between Group Policy objects (GPOs) and AD DS objects. GPOs contain the actual Group Policy settings, and linking them to AD DS domain, site, or organizational unit objects deploys those settings to all the users and computers contained by those objects.

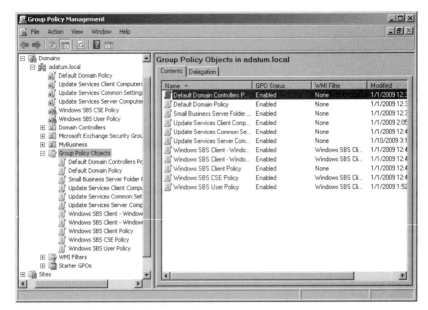

FIGURE 16-9 The Group Policy Management console

Windows SBS 2008 creates a number of GPOs for its own use, including the Default Domain Policy and Default Domain Controllers Policy objects. Although you can modify the settings in these GPOs for your own use, the best practice is to create your own GPOs and link them to your domain or organizational unit objects as needed. You can link multiple GPOs to a single AD DS object, and the users and computers receiving the settings apply them in the order you specify.

For example, by default Windows SBS 2008 links six different GPOs to your AD DS domain, which are numbered 1 to 6 in the Group Policy Management console, as shown in Figure 16-10. Each user and computer in the domain applies the settings in the number 6 GPO, Update Services Common Settings Policy, followed by the settings in GPO number 5, number 4, and so forth. If two GPOs contain different values for the same settings, the settings applied later overwrite the existing ones. This way, the settings in the number 1 GPO, which the users and computers apply last, always take precedence over those with higher numbers.

To modify the settings in a GPO, or to create settings in a new GPO, you use the Group Policy Management Editor console, as shown in Figure 16-11. Each GPO has separate settings for computers, which clients apply when the computer starts, and users, which apply when a user logs on to the domain. Each of the hundreds of settings has a Properties sheet that contains the controls you use to configure its value. In many cases, settings have three possible values: enabled, which explicitly activates the setting; disabled, which explicitly deactivates it; and undefined, which does not modify the setting's existing value, if any.

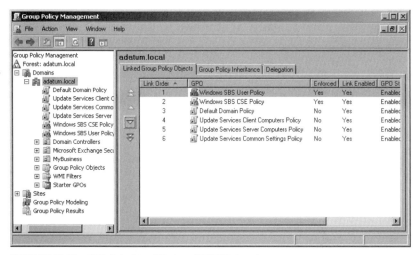

FIGURE 16-10 The GPOs linked to a Windows SBS 2008 domain

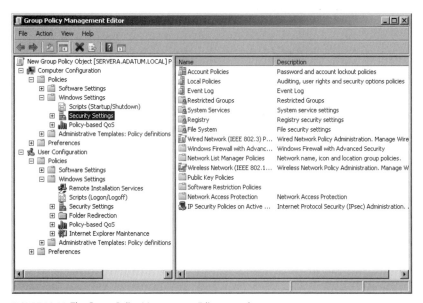

FIGURE 16-11 The Group Policy Management Editor console

Using DHCP

When you run the Connect To The Internet Wizard on your Windows SBS 2008 primary server, the wizard configures the Dynamic Host Configuration Protocol (DHCP) server to provide Internet Protocol (IP) addresses and other Transmission Control Protocol/Internet Protocol (TCP/IP) settings to the computers on your network. You should not have to modify DHCP server settings manually unless you expand your network by installing additional DHCP servers on other computers. If this is the case, however, you can configure the DHCP Server service using the DHCP console, as shown in Figure 16-12.

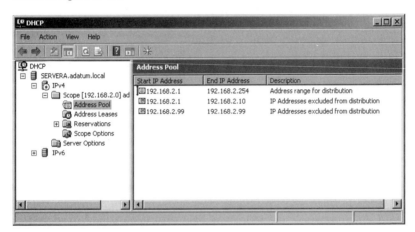

FIGURE 16-12 The DHCP console

> **MORE INFO** For more information on DHCP, see the section entitled "Connecting to the Internet" in Chapter 4, "Getting Started."

If your network includes remote sites with servers, you might want to configure them to function as additional DHCP servers. To do this, you must install the DHCP Server role using the Server Manager console and create a scope using a different IP subnet than the one on your primary server. You can create the scope using the Add Roles Wizard in Server Manager or the New Scope Wizard in the DHCP console. You must also add scope options to configure other TCP/IP settings, such as the Router and DNS Servers options, which provide your clients with their Default Gateway and Preferred DNS Server values.

Using DNS Manager

Windows SBS 2008 installs the Domain Name System (DNS) service on your primary server, as is required for AD DS, and automatically creates resource records for the computers on your network. To modify existing resource records or create new ones, you use the DNS Manager console, as shown in Figure 16-13.

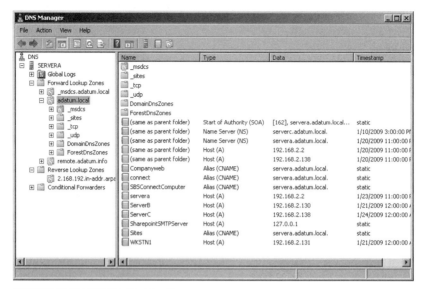

FIGURE 16-13 The DNS Manager console

A DNS server is essentially a database of resource records, most of which contain computer names and their equivalent IP addresses. In Windows SBS 2008, the DNS server stores the records as part of the AD DS database. Creating a new resource record is a matter of choosing a record type and supplying the information required for that type, using a dialog box like the one shown in Figure 16-14. For example, if you want to create a new Web site on your server, you can assign it a unique name by creating a new Host (A) resource record pointing to the server's IP address and then using the name from the resource record as the host header value when you create the site in Internet Information Services (IIS).

FIGURE 16-14 The New Host dialog box in the DNS Manager console

MORE INFO For more information on the Domain Name System, see the section entitled "Understanding Domains" in Chapter 2, "A Networking Primer."

Using Windows Firewall

During the operating system installation, the Windows SBS 2008 setup program configures Windows Firewall to open the ports that the system's various applications and services require. However, if you install or enable additional software on the server, you might have to open additional ports. For example, as noted earlier in this chapter, you might have to modify the firewall configuration to use an MMC to administer another computer.

You can use two tools to configure Windows Firewall. The first is the Windows Firewall control panel, which enables you to open the Windows Firewall Settings dialog box, as shown in Figure 16-15. By creating exceptions in this dialog box, you can open ports that enable specific types of traffic to pass through the firewall.

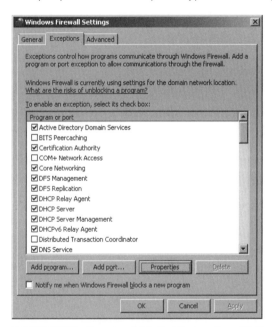

FIGURE 16-15 The Exceptions tab in the Windows Firewall Settings dialog box

For more detailed control over the firewall, you can use the Windows Firewall With Advanced Security console, as shown in Figure 16-16. This console presents firewall settings as rules, which you can apply to inbound or outbound traffic. The exceptions in the Windows Firewall Settings dialog box are actually collections of rules.

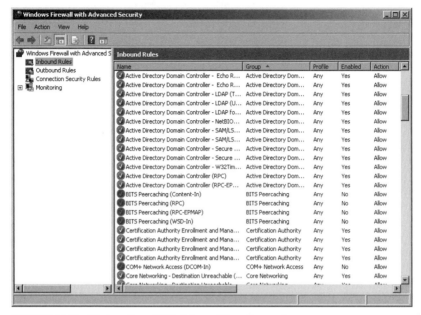

FIGURE 16-16 The Windows Firewall With Advanced Security console

Using the Windows Firewall With Advanced Security console, you can enable or disable the individual rules that compose the exception, rather than configure the entire exception as a whole. You can also create your own rules that filter traffic based on programs, services, IP addresses, and port numbers.

Using Routing and Remote Access

The Routing and Remote Access service (RRAS) in Windows Server 2008 enables you to configure a server's routing capabilities. You can conceivably use a server to connect two local area networks (LANs), but Windows SBS 2008 allows its primary server to have only one network interface adapter. The server accesses the Internet through a stand-alone router on the network.

However, you can use the RRAS service to configure a server on your network to function as a *virtual private network (VPN)* server. A VPN is a secure remote connection to your network that uses the Internet as a network medium. For example, a user at home or on the road can connect to a local Internet service provider (ISP) and establish a VPN connection to your server. To secure the connection, the computers use a technique called *tunneling*, which encapsulates their traffic in specially encrypted packets.

To configure RRAS on your primary server, you use the Routing And Remote Access console, shown in Figure 16-17. To enable VPN access to your network, you must configure your router to allow the traffic in from the Internet, and configure your server to respond to connection requests from remote clients, by running the Routing And Remote Access Server Setup Wizard. Once a VPN client is connected to the server, the user can access network resources just as though he or she were sitting at a workstation on the network.

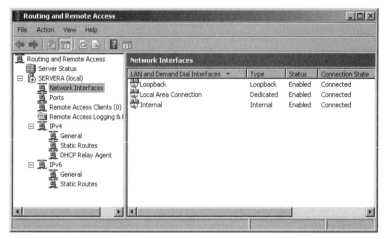

FIGURE 16-17 The Routing And Remote Access console

TIP You can configure another server running Windows Server 2008 to function as a VPN server, but first you must install the Network Policy And Access Services role using the Server Manager console, selecting the Routing And Remote Access role service in the process.

Using Event Viewer

Several Windows SBS 2008 tools, including the Windows SBS Console and the Server Manager console, display selected entries from the Windows event logs, but to view these logs in their entirety, you must use the Event Viewer console, shown in Figure 16-18.

In addition to providing access to the main Windows logs, the Event Viewer console displays logs for individual applications and services and enables you to create custom logs containing events of specific types, from specific sources, and from specific time periods, using the Create Custom View dialog box shown in Figure 16-19.

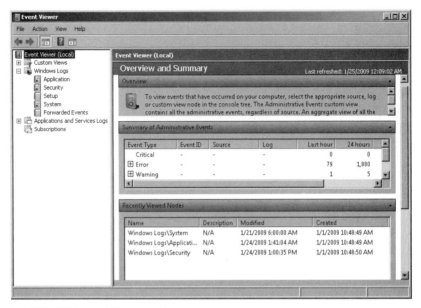

FIGURE 16-18 The Event Viewer console

Create Custom View

Filter | XML

Logged: | Any time

Event level:
☐ Critical ☐ Warning ☐ Verbose
☐ Error ☐ Information

⦿ By log | Event logs:
◯ By source | Event sources:

Includes/Excludes Event IDs: Enter ID numbers and/or ID ranges separated by commas. To exclude criteria, type a minus sign first. For example 1,3,5-99,-76

| <All Event IDs>

Task category:

Keywords:

User: | <All Users>
Computer(s): | <All Computers>

Clear

OK | Cancel

FIGURE 16-19 The Create Custom View dialog box, from the Event Viewer console

Another powerful feature of the Event Viewer console is the ability to audit the success or failure of specific system events, such as account logons and modifications to AD DS objects. For example, you can modify logon failures to determine if someone is making repeated attempts to guess a user's password. To use auditing, you must enable specific Group Policy settings, as shown in Figure 16-20. When the system detects one of the selected events, it creates an entry in the Security log, which you can evaluate later.

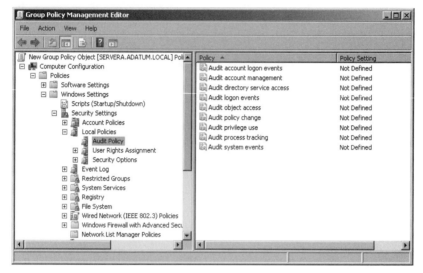

FIGURE 16-20 The Audit Policy settings in the Group Policy Management Editor console

BEST PRACTICES   Some audit policies, such as Audit System Events, can generate a large number of entries in a short period of time. This is one reason why auditing is not enabled by default. In most cases, the best practice is to turn auditing on for brief periods and then turn it off again, making sure that you have enough storage space for the Security log file.

Using the Reliability and Performance Monitor

The Reliability and Performance Monitor console contains a variety of snap-ins that you can use to monitor your server's performance and trigger specific actions. The snap-ins include the following functions:

- **Resource Overview**   Contains four line graphs that display the current CPU, Disk, Network, and Memory resource utilization in real time, as shown here.

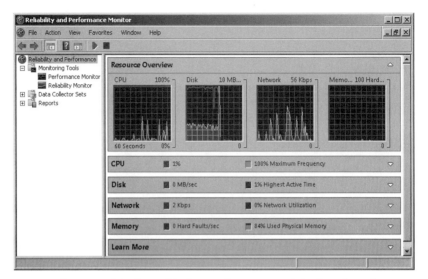

- **Performance Monitor** Displays performance statistics for selected counters representing specific properties of system hardware and software elements using a customizable graph format, as shown here.

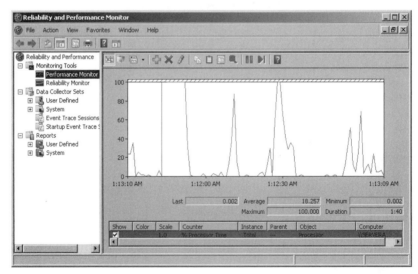

- **Reliability Monitor** Displays a System Stability Chart for a period covering several weeks, as shown here, containing failures and other events that can cause the computer's performance to degrade.

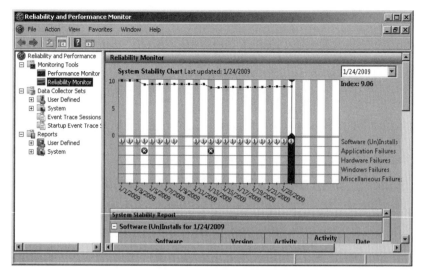

- **Data Collector Sets**   Enables you to collect and evaluate performance counter statistics over a period of time. You can also create *performance counter alerts* that trigger specific actions when the detected value of a counter reaches a specified threshold.

Index

About the Author

Craig Zacker is a writer, editor, and networker whose computing experience began in the days of teletypes and paper tape. After making the move from minicomputers to PCs, he worked as a network administrator and PC support technician while operating a freelance desktop publishing business. After earning a master's degree in English and American literature from New York University, Craig worked extensively on the integration of Windows operating systems into existing internetworks, supported fleets of Windows workstations, and was employed as a technical writer, content provider, and webmaster for the online services group of a large software company. Since devoting himself to writing and editing full-time, Craig has authored or contributed to dozens of books on operating systems, networking topics, and PC hardware. He has also developed educational texts for college courses and online training courses for the Web, and has published articles in top industry publications.